THE MORROW TRAVEL GUIDE TO THE PEOPLE'S REPUBLIC OF CHINA

The People's Republic of China
(old spelling)

ROMY PARIÑA

The Morrow Travel Guide to the People's Republic of China

Second Revised Edition

Ruth Lor Malloy

QUILL

New York _____ 1982

Library of Congress Cataloging in Publication Data

Malloy, Ruth Lor.
    The Morrow travel guide to the People's Republic of China.
    Rev. ed. of: Travel guide to the People's Republic of China. 1980.
    Includes index.
    1. China—Description and travel—1976-
Guide-books.   I. Title.
DS712.M34   1982   915.1'0458   82-3713
ISBN 0-688-01130-6 (pbk)   AACR2

Printed in the United States of America

First Revised Quill Edition

1 2 3 4 5 6 7 8 9 10

Book Design by Frank James Cangelosi

ACKNOWLEDGMENTS

It is impossible to mention by name the hundreds of people who helped with this guidebook, people I met on trains, in airports, and in hotels; business travelers, students, foreign residents, diplomats, travel agents, airline officials, and of course, tourists. Each contributed generously of their experiences traveling or living in China.

I am also indebted to the patient guides and officials of the China International Travel Service, some of whom spent sleepless nights worried about fulfilling my many exacting requests.

The C.I.T.S. is also responsible for the Chinese translations and most telephone numbers in the Directory and the names of cities in Chinese. Help also came from volunteers in Chinese embassies. China Consultants International (H.K.) did the Chinese for the Useful Phrases. Grafika Ricerra Manila is responsible for the maps.

For this edition I am especially indebted to Norris Smith, F. P. Lisowski, Ned and Katherine Chiu Lyle, Jim Drumright, John Dolfin, Jean Xiong, the U.S. and Canadian missions, and my children Linda, Martin, and Terry. And as with previous editions, this book would not have been completed without the cooperation of my long-suffering husband or a very patient, capable editor, Eunice Riedel.

RUTH LOR MALLOY

CONTENTS

THE MORROW TRAVEL GUIDE TO THE PEOPLE'S REPUBLIC OF CHINA

INTRODUCTION

WHY GO TO CHINA?

—Because it is available for the first time in recent history to tourists—and it may close to tourists again.

—Because it is historically and culturally one of the richest countries in the world and you can still see vestiges of this history in its monuments and lifestyle.

—Because you can experience a culture different from your own.

—Because what is happening now to the Chinese people is vital and exciting—a new openness to the outside world in which you, the foreign visitor, can play a part; a drama of immense importance to human history—will China, with its tremendous population of more than one-fifth of mankind, achieve goals of modernization by the year 2000? Can she do this with a minimum of social damage before the "Gang of Four" or any other movement takes power?

—Because the banquet food is rarely duplicated elsewhere in the world. Where else can you get dishes shaped like phoenixes or swans or rabbits? And today the art of the great master chefs is being passed on.

—Because China has some of the most spectacular natural scenery in the world.

—Because you can see for yourself its ancient handicrafts being made; for example, forty balls within balls within balls, each intricately carved and free-moving.

—Because if you are of Chinese ancestry, you can look for your roots and especially help in the development of your ancestral land.

RECENT HISTORY

Briefly and simply, China in the early 1980s was wrought with dramatic conflicts, frequently unnoticed by tourists unless they made a point to look.

The Pragmatists of the Communist Party had only a few years earlier taken power from the fanatic revolutionists. To emphasize their victory, they conducted the highly publicized trial of the "Gang of Four," sentencing the top leaders of that better-red-than-expert movement to long prison terms or suspended death sentences. Many of its other leaders were relieved of top positions. Some adapted to the new goals of unity, modernization, and improved living standards. Some continued in their old jobs, remaining in limbo, waiting.

The Pragmatists reiterated that Mao Tse-tung's contribution to China outweighed his mistakes. While the former Chairman of the Party had led the Communists to victory over the Nationalists, he did make serious errors later like the Great Leap Forward, the communes, and the Cultural Revolution.

Since most of China's citizens had been making sacrifices for the development of the country following Mao's line for many years, this admission by the ruling party that Mao had led them to the brink of bankruptcy was disheartening. Many had spent decades doing nothing but working, living austerely, and sitting through innumerable political meetings. Some had been jailed, their friends and relatives killed. All had been cajoled into producing more by frequent political campaigns.

Now they were tired. Now they also saw that some of their leaders had not been making sacrifices as claimed. Many citizens who could, especially the young, left China legally or illegally, feeling there was no future for them there.

The leaders tried to improve the situation. They embarked on a plan to catch up with the rest of the world by the year 2000—a very ambitious goal indeed. To encourage production, they gave even more bonuses to workers and enlarged the percentage of land set aside for private rather than communal plots, encouraging free markets so peasant families could sell their surpluses and make more money.

To improve services and cope with the unemployed, estimated between 20 and 26 million, they encouraged people to set up small businesses—street stalls, repair shops, restaurants—as long as labor was not exploited. Most workers had to be family members, a regulation that was later changed to allow more nonfamily members.

To encourage the free play of ideas which they hoped would also stimulate productivity and please human rights sentiments around the world, they permitted for a while free expressions of thought on Democracy Walls. In 1980, they conducted multicandidate county-level elections, an experiment in western-styled democracy, still being carefully studied. More foreign journalists were permitted to work and live in China; in 1981 there were 31 registered in Beijing, assigned there by British, U.S., and Canadian news media.

The State repaired churches, temples, and mosques not just for the tourists but for the people to worship in. So many did so that some churches had to have services on Saturdays as well as Sundays to accommodate the crowds.

To meet the desire for an easier life, a desire previously denounced as nonrevolutionist, China switched from heavy industry to light, producing more consumer goods. The State even allowed imports of color televisions until China could produce her own.

Abolished were the time-consuming political meetings which at the height of the Cultural Revolution took place all day, every day, instead of work. Stopped was the practice of sending educated city dwellers to learn about revolution from the peasants. The intellectuals were put back to their own work and ordered to concentrate more on projects related to economic development.

National self-reliance slogans gave way to an openness for help, even from capitalist foreigners. Laws were passed to encourage joint ventures with foreign companies, offering them cheap labor, materials, and space in return for expertise, foreign exchange, advanced foreign technology, and a share of the profits. The Chinese also borrowed from the World Bank, joined international organizations, and ignored national pride to accept foreign aid for drought and flood victims.

To encourage tourism, they built hotels and imported fancy tour buses and taxis. They sent students abroad to learn skills that should help modernize the country. They set up Special Economic Zones and trading zones. They gave freedom to some key enterprises to make their own business deals, plan their own production goals, set their own prices, and reinvest their own profits. Previously, all this was controlled centrally by the government.

They ordered many enterprises to generate profits, especially hotels and travel services. Many procedures they had opposed early in the revolution were now permitted, as in the firing of incompetent staff. In 1981 they modified the commune system, making the family the basic economic unit. They diminished the role of the Communist Party in just about every aspect of life.

All these, of course, did not proceed as hoped. Many bureaucrats, fearful of making decisions that might be reversed to their detriment the next day, stalled in taking any action. In other cases, because of inexperience, bureaucrats made unwise judgments; for example, they imported the latest and best technology available at high prices in the expectation that they could skip several stages of development. They did not know how to use the equipment efficiently or how to maintain it. There was much waste.

Some officials encouraged and accepted bribes like fancy cars and foreign television sets. Some even bought these luxury items with state funds. Many drove state cars for their own personal use.

Other crimes increased, especially the black marketing of foreign goods. More robberies took place to finance the new appetite for television sets and mopeds. Prostitution returned, though certainly nowhere near that of other countries. Young people started wearing "strange clothes" and acting in "decadent ways," aping foreigners. Political dissidents continued to talk to foreign journalists who in turn published embarrassing articles. Students demonstrated, dissatisfied with the lack of practical knowledge in their courses and with their shoddy, crowded living conditions. Previously, idealism and fear kept them quiet.

Bad planning fouled up many development projects. A shortage of high grade coal, electricity, construction materials, support facilities, the lack of market research, and little foreign exchange curtailed such ambitious projects as a steel mill. The Chinese had to compensate Japanese contractors no longer needed or apply for loans to continue. Much agricultural land was gobbled up by urban growth and better housing.

In many cases, especially in the countryside, income did increase and living standards did improve. But China also spent more foreign exchange than she made. She printed more money than she ever did before. Inflation resulted. And for the first time in the history of the People's Republic, China incurred a huge budget deficit.

Added to this were the natural disasters, drought and flood, the worst in decades. It is to China's credit that the damage wasn't greater.

A quickly growing population absorbed much of the progress. Entrepreneurs made as much in a day as state workers did in a month. Capitalism had its attractions.

The leaders tightened the reins or loosened them as the occasion demanded. They embarked on a period of retrenchment and reassessment, postponing projects including some hotels.

They attempted to walk a tightrope, making compromises with the revolutionists and their own Marxist-Leninist backgrounds and Chinese tradition. They continued their struggle against Soviet and Vietnamese "hegemonism." They stepped up their program of reunification with Taiwan, offering to open direct communications, trade and cooperation between the two segments of China. On the surface, their overtures were unrequited.

When you visit in the 1980s, such will be the background. Into this will come new factors, among them the success or failure of offshore oil explorations on which China is pinning a lot of hope. The possible sale of arms to Taiwan by the U.S. will probably adversely affect U.S. business relations with China, including tourism, if it comes about. (Just switch to a Canadian travel agency.) (See also MILESTONES IN CHINESE HISTORY.)

No matter what, the China of ancient temples and palaces should not be dull.

TRADE. Trade is most successful if based on long-standing relationships of mutual trust developed through frequent contact and hard but good-natured negotiations. The Chinese seem to prefer dealing directly with employees of foreign firms who are of Chinese origin and can understand their business traditions.

Because of the complications, the frequent policy changes, the hassle of China travel, and the problem of finding the right person to talk to, some foreign businesses prefer to deal through already established brokers. But these people are missing out on the adventure!

Newcomers should consult their government's trade representatives in China before signing any contracts because of complications unique to the Chinese. These representatives can also point out potential problems like shipping delays because of clogged ports or quality control.

Quotations and payment are usually given in foreign exchange.

The 1980–81 "readjustment" has meant that the Chinese were buying in some fields and not in others. In 1981 a continuation of the decentralization of trade was announced. The Special Economic Zones are in Guangdong (Shekou, Shenzhen, Zhuhai, and Shantou) and Fujian (Xiamen and maybe Fuzhou).

See also SPECIAL FOR BUSINESS PEOPLE.

TOURISM. Because tourism brings in much-needed foreign exchange and usually makes friends, its development in China has very high priority. Facilities and services have continued to improve since the beginnings of international tourism in 1978. Most tourist hotels are now air-conditioned. Most have televisions in each room, some with closed-circuit English-language programs. Most have shower curtains, a luxury which never existed before 1979.

The upgrading of the Dongfang and the opening of the Nanhu hotels in Guangzhou in 1981 heralded a new era in more luxurious hotels, soon to be followed by some others in Nanjing, Shanghai, and Beijing. Some government guest houses have been opened to tourists, notably the Diaoyutai in Beijing, which tourists have shared with visiting royalty. A new concept in hotels is the people-to-people Stone Flower Mountain Inn in Guangdong's Taishan where guests are encouraged to use bicycles to explore on their own or with a one-to-one guide. But the Stone Flower Mountain Inn should not be considered a trend.

Improvements have also come in the taxi service with stands at airports and train stations in Beijing, Shanghai, and Guangzhou—and others to follow. Air-conditioned cabs have appeared in some cities.

New destinations are opening to foreign tourists, important ones like Dazu, Leshan, Fuzhou, Xiamen, and Chengde. Within the already opened destinations, the drive to renovate old temples and excavate old tombs continues. There is more to see in and beyond Xi'an, Beijing, Wuhan, Shanghai, Guangzhou, Lanzhou, Turpan, Ningpo, Zibo—more than there was two years ago. There's skiing with chairlifts in Jilin and Harbin, luxury tourist boats on the Yangtze, cruises along the Grand Canal between Suzhou and Yangzhou, bicycle tours, trekking, direct flights from the U.S. to China, and from Hong Kong to several Chinese cities. Tours let you take part in exotic festivals, visit isolated mountains replete with old temples untouched by the Red Guards, or go to far-off places like Xiaguan and Dali in Yunnan and the Wolong Nature Preserve with its wild pandas—the latter available to small, special interest groups, and Hong Kong and Overseas Chinese tourists.

Most exciting of all, is the granting of visas to individual foreign tourists as well as Overseas Chinese (O.C.) and Compatriots. You can now plot your own trips at your own pace for much cheaper prices. Old China hands can now spend a couple of weeks in their "home towns" and visit with old friends for only the cost of the hotel, food, and getting there; budget travelers can spend months exploring while sleeping in cheap (¥4 a night) hostels; and families can relax at resorts, without paying US$80 a day, per person.

China International Travel Service (C.I.T.S.) is opening offices in Hong Kong, U.S., Britain, France, and Japan.

All this is not to say that China's tourism has reached Europe's stage of efficiency and ease. Some hotels are filthy and you may find roaches. Some toilets even on CAAC and especially on trains are still horrendous. One-year-old wall-to-wall carpeting can already be dingy and stained in some hotels and the lovely new wallpaper peeling off some walls.

Late in 1981 came a new ruling that only those O.C. and Compatriot travelers booking through China Travel Service (C.T.S.) would get lower hotel prices. It is still too early to see how this is working out.

Traveling individually is still not easy unless you have patience, flexibility, and someone along who can speak Chinese. A shortage of English-speaking guides still exists, and you still need travel permits for every city you visit (these are issued for two cities at a time). After obtaining the permit, *then* you can start to obtain your train ticket and hotel reservation for the next stop.

If you have a Guangzhou permit, however, you can now spend the night anywhere within 100 km. of the city without getting another permit, a rule which applies to many other cities as well. This is quite an improvement.

The prepaid group tour is still recommended for those who don't have the language and don't want to spend their time going to the Public Security Office for permits, but this has not been without problems either. In 1981 some Americans found they had to take a 30-hr. train trip instead of the planned Xi'an-Beijing flight; other groups have had to tag along with a guide from hotel to hotel, looking for rooms. This situation was caused by incompetence, the lack of computers, a big increase in the number of local Chinese tourists, and a free-for-all situation in which several different government agencies made their own deals with travel agents abroad, without telling anyone else.

The computer situation is currently being remedied and in October 1981, an embarrassed State Council, China's equivalent of a cabinet, ordered that all foreign tourism be centralized again under C.I.T.S. and C.T.S. It also ordered that the infrastructure be upgraded and more important ancient relics be put under state protection. Things should be better by the time you read this.

The standard of English has improved but it is still not enough. In 1981 China was going all out on training English-speaking guides, so more should be available in 1982–83. The authorities are also aware of rude, unhelpful staff in some hotels, restaurants, and stores (guides are still super) and training and incentive programs are going on. The tourism industry is now allowed to fire incorrigible help.

Booking plane tickets, reserving rooms at specific hotels, and avoiding upset stomachs still aren't easy. One small pay-as-you-go group had to postpone plans to visit a popular city like Guilin because transportation to Hong Kong from there was completely booked. They had been told earlier in their trip to wait until they arrived in Guilin to make the reservations. The same applied to their plans to take the Yangtze ferry. They were downgraded there to third class by the arrival of a larger tour group—such groups getting priority over individual travelers. If they had had the *guanxi*, the special relations with key people that are very important in getting things done in China, they would have fared better.

Visitors must remember that China is a developing country. That is part of its charm as well as its problem. Through effort, helpfulness, and kindness some people will try to make your trip a success, but you should still be prepared for the unpredictable. Only then will you be pleasantly surprised.

NOTE

PINYIN, A.K.A. DISCLAIMER

For decades China has been developing a new system of romanization based on the Beijing (Peking) pronunciation. This is no easy feat, since the language is monosyllabic and the word "ma," for example, can have at least four totally different meanings depending on the tone. However, in 1979, in spite of the limitations, China adopted the *pinyin* system as official and most foreign news media followed suit.

China International Travel Service (C.I.T.S.), which is responsible for foreign tourism, gradually changed to the pinyin spellings, but some hotels and even some new tourist attractions in English were not consistent, depending on the translator. Even now, many guides have trouble with the new spellings. So what was I to do? Putting both systems in would be cumbersome. Using only pinyin would mean people could not look up history books, or know what cities tour agents were offering. And what about the spellings I couldn't find in both? I couldn't find an English-Wade-Giles-pinyin dictionary.

So please bear with me. This is still a transition period in China. When in doubt, try to sound out the words phonetically. Just remember, in pinyin, X is like *sh* as in *she,* Q is like *ch* as in *cheek,* and Z is like *j* as in *jump.* See also "How to Pronounce Chinese Letters" in QUICK REFERENCE.

The prevailing system for place names is pinyin in this book. The prevailing system for historical names and the names of dynasties is the old system. To help you especially in directing taxis, there are also the Chinese characters in the directory of fourteen major cities.

Please don't be confused where pinyin and the old system are combined in one sentence. And don't ask when pinyin should be one word or more than one as in "pin yin" or "pinyin." There isn't a rule for that yet!

PRICES. Note also that prices given throughout this book are the most current as we went to press. These are mentioned only to give you an idea of costs.

NOTE ALSO: The information in this book is as accurate as could be compiled at press time. The situation in China is so fluid that changes will have taken place by the time you visit. When in doubt, ask.

The travel agencies and other organizations listed here *should* be able to help you. As far as I can see they are reliable; but a mention in this book is not necessarily a recommendation.

1

THE BASICS

WHERE? First of all, you must decide where in China you want to go. It's a big country, the third largest in area in the world. Make a list of your priorities and then see if you can find a tour that fits; otherwise plan one yourself. Here are some suggestions. For details, see DESTINATIONS.

1. Ancient capitals: Xi'an, Luoyang, Kaifeng, Datong, Nanjing, Beijing, Hangzhou, Shenyang, Chengdu, Suzhou. Imperial palaces still only in Beijing, Chengde, and Shenyang.

2. The Great Wall: best at Badaling (Beijing); also impressive at Shanhaiguan and Jiayuguan. See "Great Wall" in DESTINATIONS.

3. Interesting city walls: Nanjing, Kaifeng, and Xi'an.

4. Interesting excavated imperial tombs: Ming (Beijing), Qing (Zunhua and Shenyang), Qin Han, and Tang (Xi'an). The famous Qin Army Vault Museum (8,000 life-size soldiers) is visited from Xi'an.

5. For students of primitive man: Zhoukoudian—Peking Man (see "Beijing"); Qujiang County—Mapa Man (see "Guangzhou").

6. For neolithic site museums: Xi'an.

7. For Shang dynasty sites: Zhengzhou and Anyang.

8. For fans of foreign imperialist history: very little in museums, but much European architecture in Tianjin, Shanghai, Wuhan, Beijing, and Guangzhou (Canton). There were forty-six treaty ports, including Zhenjiang, Ningbo, Fuzhou, Xiamen (Amoy), Nanjing, Jiujiang, Shashi, and Chongqing (Chungking).

9. For well-preserved ancient cadavers plus their belongings: Changsha for a 2,100-year-old noblewoman; Zhenjiang (Chenjiang) for a male scholar (Song); Shanghai and Urumqi for large collections.

10. For the best ancient history museums: the National Palace Museum and the Museum of Chinese History in Beijing, the Shenyang Imperial Palace Museum, the Nanjing Museum, and the Provincial Museum in Xi'an.

11. For the most important revolutionary sites (with good museums): Beijing, Yan'an, Shaoshan, Nanchang, and Jinggang Shan.

12. For interesting old Chinese city architecture: Suzhou, Zhenjiang, Jiangmen, and Xinhui.

13. For interesting loess soil architecture: Yan'an and Xi'an.

14. For important Buddhist structures: Xi'an, Mt. Emei, Luoyang, Lanzhou, Dule—see "Tianjin"; for giant Buddhist cave sculptures—Datong, Luoyang, or Dunhuang; for beauty—Temple of the Azure Clouds just outside of Beijing and West Garden Temple in Suzhou; for martial arts fans—Shaolin Temple, reachable from Zhengzhou; Dazu; Chengde; Tibet.

15. For philosophers: Qufu, the birthplace of Confucius.

16. For memorable boat rides: the Yangtze gorges from Chongqing (Chungking); Li River, Guilin (Kweilin); Grand Canal (Suzhou to Yangzhou).

17. For interesting caves: Yixing, Guilin, Nanning and Conghua.

18. For the best gardens: Suzhou, Summer Palace—Beijing, Hangzhou, Yu Garden—Shanghai.

19. For plant lovers: any of the Academy of Science's botanical gardens— Mt. Lushan, Guangzhou, Nanjing, Hangzhou, etc.

20. For gorgeous mountain scenery: Guilin (tame); Mt. Lushan, Chengde and Jinggang Shan (a little rough); Mt. Tai (see "Tai'an")—a five-hour climb, but cable cars available; Huang Shan, Emei Shan, and Hua Shan (very rugged). Mountaineers have seven peaks including Qomolangma (Everest) and must contact the Chinese Mountaineering Association.

21. For seaside resorts: Beidaihe and Qingdao.

22. For interesting handicraft factories: See list under "Arts and Crafts" in SHOPPING.

23. For camel and pony rides and sleeping in yurts (tents): Hohhot, Inner Mongolia.

24. For ancestral villages and visits to relatives: See SPECIAL FOR OVERSEAS CHINESE.

25. For a steam locomotive factory: Datong.

26. For a performing panda: Wei Wei of the Shanghai Acrobats.

27. For pandas in a wildlife preserve: Wolong (see Chengdu).

28. For exotic hotels: the hostel at the Le Shan Buddhist Monastery in Sichuan, set in a temple; the People's Hotel in Chongqing, fashioned after Beijing's Temple of Heaven and Tien Anmen.

29. For golfers: the only course in China is planned near Guangzhou.

30. For the sites that the Chinese themselves consider the most important historically, see QUICK REFERENCE.

As a rule of thumb:

1. The cradle of Chinese civilization was the Yellow River.
2. The Silk Road went west from Xi'an and included Lanzhou, Wuwei, Dunhuang, Turpan, and Ruoqiang.
3. The foreign imperialists concentrated around the Yangtze River, but also Changsha. They were active in Tianjin, Guangzhou, and points in between. The Japanese controlled Northeast China, then known as Manchuria, and later, most of urban China. The Germans held ports in Shandong.

4. Most national minority groups live in the area north of the Great Wall, in south China in Guangxi and Yunnan, and of course, in Tibet. Turkish-related Moslem minorities live in Xinjiang, Jews in Kaifeng.

5. The earlier migrations of Chinese to America and Australia in the nineteenth and early twentieth centuries originated from Guangdong province; the migrations to S.E. Asia originated largely from Fujian, but also from Guangdong.

WHEN? If you care about the *weather,* the best time to visit is May-June or September-October. But do consult each region listed under DESTINATIONS, where you can find the hottest and coldest temperatures.

It is important to remember that the Chinese do not heat their buildings as warmly as foreigners do in winter. South of the Yangtze, there is no heat at all, except in tourist hotels, even though it can be very chilly. If cold bothers you, avoid northeast China, Inner Mongolia, Yan'an, Xinjiang, Tibet, and any mountains, especially around the lunar new year. Take thermal underwear, socks, and boots. The new year is around late January or early February. Even in Guangzhou at that time you need a topcoat and a sweater. Some tour agencies give discounts in wintertime. Industrial pollution is particularly bad in winter, too. Avoid the lunar new year in Guangzhou and Fujian as hotels are full and prices highest.

The hottest time of the year is July. Traditionally the "three furnaces" of China are Nanjing, Chongqing, and Wuhan. There's also Nanchang. Most hotels are now air-conditioned, but few other buildings are. Most tourist buses are air-conditioned but only a few taxis. This is the time to put mountain or seaside resorts at the end of a hot tour.

In late spring, April-May through the summer, there is rain and high humidity in south China (including Guangzhou and Guilin). Beijing and Inner Mongolia's problem is springtime sand storms.

As a rough gauge, China extends from the same latitude as James Bay in Canada to south of Cuba. Beijing is at almost the same latitude as Philadelphia, and Guangzhou as Havana. Take altitude into account. The higher, the colder. Winter (the cold weather) begins in early November. See lunar calendar in QUICK REFERENCE.

Other things to consider when planning dates:

1. If you are interested in schools, factories, and offices, avoid vacations and holidays. For dates see QUICK REFERENCE.

2. If you want to see a festival like the Third Moon Market or the dragon boats, consider those dates. See QUICK REFERENCE.

HOW? On a group tour organized by an agency; on a tour organized privately; individually; as an Overseas Chinese; as a Hong Kong, Macao, or Taiwan Compatriot; as a foreign student, expert, or lecturer; as a patient, a property-owner or convention-goer.

On a Group Tour Organized by an Agency. This is the easiest way to visit China. Just pick a good tour operator and most of your problems are solved. China prefers groups. They are easier to handle and are given preference.

Groups usually have 25 to 40 people, but they can be smaller or larger, the bigger ones broken up into more manageable units. Expenses are prepaid.

Basically all tours are treated the same in China. If the price of the same tour differs from one travel agency to another, it could be that (1) more restaurant meals are included (rather than hotel meals); (2) there is an orientation session on China and/or a guide (who has more than a superficial knowledge of Chinese history and culture) will be traveling with you from start to finish; (3) more than one agency is getting a commission; try to book from the source; (4) your agent is getting a bigger commission; or (5) the top hotels and luxury tourist boats are guaranteed.

Tour-group members or their leaders usually choose what they want to see in each city from a set list. You may have to pay for any "optional tours." Some tourists complain of the time spent in making group decisions; others are happy to have a choice. If you just want to see China, a general-interest tour is ideal. If you want to visit schools, several factories, or hospitals, better take a special-interest tour or ask if these are included.

Group tours are flexible insofar as you can choose to avoid most of the group activities. If you want to sleep in another hotel, you can in some cities. But of course, you pay extra. Just be sure to tell your leader so the group will not wait for you.

But you do have to travel from city to city with the group, there being an already acquired "group permit" to travel to each city. You are not allowed to buy plane or train tickets yourself in China without permission to visit that destination; foreigners sometimes are stopped by the police at airports and railway stations and asked for the permit upon arrival.

Some people have been able to leave their tours and stay over in China for a longer period, but you have to convince someone you have a very good reason and probably you have to have some clout. For example, some professors have stayed behind for more lectures, and of course, if you are sick, changes can be made. But C.I.T.S. is very reluctant to try to make changes once an itinerary is set up, except for business people.

Tour groups can be fun if you have the right people. But there is a tendency to look inward toward your own group and to regard the Chinese as "them" as opposed to "us." If you visited China to meet Chinese people, you do have to make an effort to break free of your groupiness. Do venture out into the streets alone. Lounge in parks. There are a lot of students waiting to practice their English on you. It is a good opening. You might even be invited to a home.

Group tours for tourists have no special arrangements for journalist interviews, for example. People of Chinese ancestry are not encouraged to take in gifts for relatives and expect them to be duty-free on a C.I.T.S. tour.

Luggage for C.I.T.S. foreign tour groups is usually not opened by Chinese customs, but that of Overseas Chinese might be. The weight of the luggage for the whole group is usually added together and averaged if it is to be flown.

If your group has a group visa, individual passports are not stamped. The group visa is usually held by the tour leader.

How to Pick a Good Group Tour. Consider seriously:

1. How experienced is the organizer with tours to China?

2. Do you care whether or not you pay several commissions? If you book directly from a wholesaler, it could be cheaper.

3. How many of the destinations you want to go to are offered? How many days will you have in each place?

4. Do the dates fit into your own schedule, weather preference, and Chinese holidays?

5. What is the price? Why is the price different from another organizer with the same cities and same number of days? What does the price include? Usually it includes visa fee, group transportation, hotel accommodation (double occupancy), meals and drinks, sightseeing, guide, transfers, transporting one piece of baggage, admission tickets to parks, tourist attractions, and theaters.

It does not include laundry, hairdressing, taxis, mails, long-distance calls, excess baggage, medical and other expenses of a personal nature. Nor does it include insurance or expenses for changes in the itinerary or prolonged tours "due to unforeseen circumstances." Frequently your tour organizer will pick up minor "extras," but you might be expected to pay on the spot or at the end of the tour for substantial changes.

6. What language will the guides speak? For example, a tour booked in Japan may only have Japanese-speaking guides, while some tours booked in Hong Kong are in English. Or a tour might be in Beijing dialect and you expected Cantonese.

7. What is the routing to and from China? Ask if you can make stopovers in Europe or in other parts of Asia or America. Will it cost more? How long can you stay there? Is it a direct flight? Do you care? If so, check with Pan Am and CAAC to see who organizes such tours.

8. Do you get a group visa or an individual visa? Some tours allow longer time in China to visit relatives or negotiate business, etc.

9. How many people are in the group? How old? Sexes?

10. How much in advance must you pay the deposit? In full? What refund do you get if the tour is cancelled? Can you get cancellation insurance? Are departures guaranteed?

11. Will you be able to see everything you want?

12. Do they offer the Yangtze River Boat Tour on a regular ferry or on an air-conditioned boat? (See YANGTZE GORGES).

13. If you are so inclined, will you visit schools, factories, and communes?

If you can't find a travel agent for China, here are some companies that might be able to help. Most agents can arrange group tours.

U.S.A.

1. *Arrow Tours USA*. Special and general interest.

2. *American Youth Hostels*. Bicycle tours.

3. *Club Universe*. Wholesaler. Guaranteed departures and no price changes. Trips on Yangtze use 1981-built MV *Goddess,* an air-conditioned cruise ship.

4. *China Connection*. Can book some hotels three weeks in advance. Helps individual travelers, small groups, and families.

5. *Inter Pacific Travel-in-China*. Offers direct flights; Tibet, Grand Canal. Individual and business travel arrangements.

6. *Kuo Feng*. One of the largest for both O.C. and F.F. Can arrange business contacts for tourists. Individual visas. Off-season discounts.

7. *Kuoni Travel*. Guaranteed departures.

8. *Lindblad Travel, Inc.* More comfortable than most tours since Lindblad has invested capital to improve services. General interest and off-beat tours like Inner Mongolia, the Grand Canal, and Tibet, the latter with optional tour to Xigaze and Gyaze. Wolong Nature Preserve for pandas. Exclusive use of M.S. *Kun Lun* luxury cruise ship on the Yangtze. Guarantees Diao Yu Tai (Angler's State Guest House) in Beijing, and Western Suburbs State Guest House in Shanghai.

9. *Mountain Travel*. General- and special-interest tours, wholesale/retail, some with Lindblad. Treks in Tibet, Sichuan, Qinghai, and Xinjiang. Including Wolong Nature Preserve and Everest. Mountaineering.

10. *Orient Paradise Tours*. China tours handled through China Youth Travel Service. Has a "Dine-Around" plan.

11. *Pacific Delights Tours*. Special and general interest.

12. *Pan Asian Travel Headquarters*. Wholesaler and retailer. Can help individual travelers too.

13. *Silkway (U.S.A.)*. Visas and packages for groups and individuals. See also *Silkway (Hong Kong)*.

14. *Society Expedition*. Wholesale and retail. Special-interest tours on art, history, and archaeology, with qualified lecturers.

15. *Special Tours for Special People, Inc.* One of the most experienced in special-interest tours. Has close relationship with Chinese educational, medical, scientific, and technological institutions. Can arrange individual travel but not for tourists.

16. *Travis Pacific*. Tied in with Travel Advisers (Hong Kong) with direct flight tours to Kunming, Beijing, or Shanghai. Wholesale.

17. *Voyages Jules Verne* (See HONG KONG). Train tours Hong Kong to Britain.

18. *Chinamerican Corporation*. Tours including the Stone Flower Mountain Inn in Taishan.

19. *U.S. People's Friendship Association.* At one time this was one of the few groups organizing tours to China.

Participants tend to be younger and more knowledgeable about China than the average tourist, visiting more factories and communes. The association tends to be leftist-oriented, but you do not have to be a member or socialist to join a tour. You may also be called on later to lecture about your trip.

The association was set up to encourage friendship and understanding between the U.S. and China and specifically to work for the resumption of diplomatic relations. It is now helping with China's Four Modernizations program, the sending of textbooks and teaching materials.

Write for the address of the chapter closest to you.

Canada

1. *Blyth & Co.* Bicycle tours.
2. *Canadian Friendship Tours.*
3. *Luna Travel Service.* Helps groups and individuals.

Hong Kong

See Chapter 4, GETTING THERE.

Australia

1. *Wim J. Bannink.* Has chartered the new cruise ship *Three Gorges* for the Yangtze.
2. *Marco Polo Travel.* Individuals and groups. Conventions.
3. *Travman Tours.* One of the largest tour operators.

China Friendship Associations all over the world can give information on travel to China as well as on their own study tours. Some of these can organize tours for individuals.

—Australia-China Society, 228 Gertrude Street, Fitzroy 3065, Victoria, Australia

—Canada-China Friendship Association, Box 373, Station Q, Toronto, Ontario, Canada

—China Studien- und Verlags-Gesellschaft, Paul-Lincke-Ufer 39/40, 1000 Berlin 36, Federal Republic of Germany

—Association des Amitiés Franco-Chinoises, 32, rue Maurice-Ripoche, 75014, Paris, France

—Associazione Italia-Cina, Via del Seminario 87, Roma, Italy

—Japan-China Friendship Association, 1–4 Nishiki-cho, Kanda, Chiyodaka, Tokyo, Japan

—New Zealand-China Friendship Society, 22 Swanson Street, Auckland, New Zealand

—Society for Anglo-Chinese Understanding, 152 Camden High Street, London, NW1, England. Organizes tours for trekking, bicycling, Tibet, courses in acupuncture and traditional medicine, and travel by the Trans-

Siberian Railway. It also organizes a Chinese language summer school in Beijing.

Cruises. *Minghua Friendship Cruises.* Chinese ship based in Australia; M.V. *Yao Hua.* 450 passengers. Twice a month to Xiamen, Nanjing, Shanghai, Tianjin (for Beijing). See Hang Wai Shipping Co., Hong Kong.

Individual Packages. For one, two to nine, over 10, or over 15 people who travel from Hong Kong to Shanghai, Hangzhou, Nanjing, and Wuxi (departures Mondays, Thursdays, and Sundays), priced according to numbers who sign up. Similar set-up for Guangzhou allows traveler to choose his hotels, transportation, and meals (included or not). Organized by C.T.S. (Hong Kong), these can be booked directly or through agents, but not during the Trade Fair or the busy tourist season.

On a Tour/Group Organized Privately. To meet your own dates and specific requirements. This can be done by a travel agent experienced in Special-Interest tours. If you would prefer to do your own thus giving yourself the free seat for groups on the plane, write to C.I.T.S. in Beijing, explaining the purpose of the trip and giving a rough itinerary, dates, the number of people, and what you want specifically to see and do. Replies will come faster if you write in Chinese. It would also be helpful to talk with officials at a Chinese mission.

Professional and athletic groups are advised to communicate directly with their counterparts in China, preferably through someone known to the Chinese. See IMPORTANT ADDRESSES. If a trip is possible, the Chinese will issue an invitation that will authorize a Chinese mission to grant visas.

Journalists apply to the Information Office of the Foreign Ministry, Beijing, or have the logistics arranged by the New China News Agency.

The best way to communicate after the first letter is by cable. If you telephone Beijing, be sure to have a Chinese-speaking person do the calling. You may not receive permission until the week you expected to leave!

The important thing to remember is that C.I.T.S. is set up primarily for tourists. It cannot be expected to understand the needs of people like American churchmen if they are primarily interested in meeting Chinese Christians. Incidentally, many Christian groups go through the U.S.-China Friendship Association.

Individually as a Business Person. The usual procedure here is to contact a Chinese trading corporation (see IMPORTANT ADDRESSES). If the Chinese are interested in what you want to buy or sell, they will send you an invitation that will give you a visa from a Chinese mission, C.T.S., or C.I.T.S. in Hong Kong. This may be to a fair or to the office of the corporation.

Business people and their spouses have increasingly been allowed to travel individually in China, not just for business but afterward as tourists. For the logistics of traveling inside China, you can discuss the matter with the people responsible for you in the trading corporation. You might also contact the local office of the China International Travel Service once you are inside China; they can arrange for permission to visit other cities, for transportation, and for hotels and sightseeing. See also Chapter 7, GETTING AROUND, and Chapter 13, SPECIAL FOR BUSINESS PEOPLE.

Individually or in Small Groups—paying as you go. Aside from business people, more foreigners are being allowed to travel individually. But it is not easy for non-Chinese speakers, the main problem being the shortage of guide interpreters and hotel spaces especially in Beijing, Shanghai, Guangzhou, Xi'an, and Guilin. See list of travel agencies in this chapter and in Chapter 4.

Currently it is possible for a foreign resident in China (not a foreign student) to invite a friend to visit China. On the basis of the invitation, the friend can get a visa from a Chinese mission. The resident should check with his embassy regarding the latest procedures. The friend can live with the resident or stay in a hotel arranged by the resident. C.I.T.S. can make travel arrangements around the country, usually on a pay-as-you-go basis, once you are inside.

It is also possible for a person to obtain a transit visa at a Chinese mission to spend about a week in China. Arrangements for sightseeing can be made after arrival. In the larger cities, C.I.T.S. does have some city bus tours that any foreigner can join.

As a Traveler of Chinese Ancestry. People of Chinese ancestry can choose to travel either under C.I.T.S., C.T.S, or through an authorized travel agent. The facilities with C.I.T.S. are not necessarily better but more expensive. Guides are English-speaking, if available.

Travelers with C.T.S. may not find anyone who speaks English but can get permission to places not usually open to C.I.T.S. travelers. C.I.T.S. guides do not usually know anything about places in Fujian or Guangdong, where you may have relatives.

C.T.S. also has group tours to other parts of China arranged in Hong Kong (more frequent) or in Guangzhou (whenever the occasion warrants it).

Chinese missions abroad now have a quota of individual visas for Overseas Chinese. It is possible to get a visa there or at C.T.S. in Hong Kong in four days. With a visa, it is then possible to travel *alone* or *with a group to China*. Individual visas can be extended.

An Overseas Chinese is officially anyone with a Chinese passport living abroad, who holds no other passport. However, the popular definition is anyone with a Chinese surname, face, the address of a relative or an ancestral village in China, and a foreign passport. It is this loose definition that is used in this book because it is recognized by the people who matter—hotel clerks, waiters, and officials with C.T.S. Overseas Chinese can argue for lower rates which could be 10 to 40% of those for other foreigners. Don't be shy about asking. The rule of thumb is: the cheaper rates are for those traveling under the care of C.T.S., or the most effective hagglers. It is possible to take a non-Overseas Chinese spouse, children, and a close friend to China with C.T.S. arrangements. It is possible to live with relatives in China or have relatives stay with you in your hotel. See SPECIAL FOR OVERSEAS CHINESE.

As a Hong Kong, Macao, or Taiwan Compatriot. Hong Kong and Macao Chinese who have reentry permits to Hong Kong or Macao can enter China the way Canadians enter the U.S. They can just buy a ticket and get on a train. Permission to visit places other than Guangzhou or the immediate border area can be obtained from the China Travel Service in Hong Kong, Macao, or in China. Luggage is carefully searched. Taiwan Compatriots are especially welcome to visit; arrangements are made at the C.T.S. in Hong Kong. See SPECIAL FOR OVERSEAS CHINESE.

As a Foreign Student, Scholar, or Foreign Expert.

1. Foreign students studying in China are usually there as the result of an agreement between governments. Information on student exchanges can be obtained from the China Desk, Department of State, or in Canada from the Association of Universities and Colleges of Canada.

Most exchange students are already university graduates and usually stay two years. The home government pays transportation to and from China and gives spending money. The Chinese government pays tuition, the cost of accommodations, and a small stipend. It is possible to save money. Students travel around China during vacations with lower prices.

Foreign students usually live in dormitories described by students at Beijing University as "cold and small" with little if any privacy. They may get hot water two hours a day. Food is usually better than that of the Chinese students but with less meat than at home.

Courses are "dull and uninteresting" and usually "poorly taught." Some students go to six hours of classes a week; some don't bother. But students get a good opportunity to learn about China and the Chinese language.

Some universities have bilateral exchanges, so inquire directly. Some Overseas Chinese make their own arrangements to study in China. There are schools for people of Chinese ancestry. Write to the nearest Chinese embassy, or directly to the university.

2. Scholarly visits are also arranged by government agreement, but much is being done privately now, bilaterally between institutions, or among scholars themselves. It is easier for physical than for social scientists.

In Canada, contact the Social Sciences and Humanities Research Council.

In the U.S., the Committee on Scholarly Communication with the People's Republic of China (CSCPRC) has developed programs with the Chinese Academy of Sciences, the Chinese Academy of Social Sciences, the Ministry of Education, and the Chinese Association for Science and Technology.

The CSCPRC's activities include a program for American graduate students, postdoctoral students, and research scholars to carry out long-term study or research in affiliation with Chinese universities and research institutes; a short-term reciprocal exchange of senior-level Chinese and American scholars; a bilateral conference; and an exchange of joint working groups in selected fields.

3. People who are going to China in other capacities can also give lectures to their Chinese counterparts, if invited to do so.

If you're thinking of getting much compensation, forget it. If you're thinking of helping China in exchange for a deeper insight and business or academic contacts, do offer to lecture—if you have anything worthwhile to say, that is. Don't expect anything more than a "thank you" and probably a tax writeoff for part of your expenses.

4. Foreign experts are hired by the Bureau of Foreign Experts. Currently China is trying to upgrade the qualifications of the experts she hires. Most are teachers of a foreign language whose contacts with the Friendship Associations or "friends of China" helped them get chosen. There is a long waiting list of people wanting to work in China.

China-hired experts should have a contract giving them their transportation paid from home and back and home leave after the first year and then every other year for a month or so. The stipend ranges from about ¥440 to ¥800 with a few getting as much as ¥1,200 a month. They also get free accommodations, free medical care, transportation to and from work, and a month's vacation in China.

Foreign teachers are usually locally hired and do not get the same benefits as Experts. Teacher-students teach part-time and study part-time.

Foreign companies also send experts to China in connection with their own projects. These make the most money, usually live in hotels, and after their work is finished, may travel as tourists.

Do read *China Bound: A Handbook for American Students, Researchers and Teachers,* published by the CSCPRC and the National Association for Foreign Student Affairs, Washington, D.C.

For Medical Treatment. Contact a Chinese mission.

As a Property Buyer. Foreigners and Overseas Chinese can now buy residential and business property, the Overseas Chinese in more places than the foreigners. The latter is usually restricted to 30-year leases. The buildings, sometimes joint ventures with Overseas Chinese builders, are in Guangdong, Fujian, Beijing, Shanghai, etc. Contact a Chinese mission or the municipal office in the city of your choice. Advertisements frequently appear in Hong Kong newspapers.

On a Convention. Guangzhou, Kunming, and Hangzhou should now be able to handle hundreds of convention visitors. Contact China International Convention Services (Hong Kong, New York, or Toronto) for information.

Should You Take Your Children?
I took my five-year-old for a five-week visit in 1973, my seven-year-old to

visit relatives in 1978, and my nine-year-old on a group tour in 1979. I was glad I did, but then, this depends on the child.

I did not use a babysitter because I took the children with me to evening movies and theatrical performances. Chinese dance dramas are easy for a child to understand, and acrobats and puppets are fun for all ages. My children did find the traditional operas boring, so unless you're sure of lots of action, skip them.

I would not take a child just to be left with a Chinese-speaking babysitter unless the child understood Chinese.

At communes and factories, there was always a willing hand around to amuse them while grown-ups talked. The children were interested in seeing how things were made. Guilin with its caves, mountains, and boat trip was ideal. My nine-year-old found the 2,100-year-old cadaver in Changsha fascinating.

The Chinese love children and are fascinated by those different from their own. You may have to protect children with blond hair and blue eyes, for instance, from being overly fondled. Tour-bus drivers bought mine popsicles; cheeks were pinched. In restaurants they disappeared with waiters to be shown off to the cooks.

Two of them became sick with bad colds, but doctors took care of them. They were well in a couple of days, missing only one day of the tour.

Two of them lived with relatives. the seven-year-old had a ball learning how to bring up water from an open well, washing his own clothes by hand, and tending a wood cooking fire. It took a while to adjust to the smelly outhouses but he managed.

The neighborhoods where we lived were full of other children, and in spite of initial shyness and the language barrier, they made friends. Strangers on the street and in buses would stop and try to talk to them. Barriers of formality melted right away, and I think on one occasion we even got a room in an overcrowded hotel because of my daughter.

Food was a problem. One lived only on scrambled eggs and char siu bow. They complained, but no one starved. Yes, there is ice cream, but hot dogs and hamburgers are hard to find. Try the International Club and Friendship Store in Beijing. No baby food in jars for infants, nor disposable diapers.

2

BEFORE YOU GO

PLAN YOUR WHOLE ITINERARY for before and after your China visit. It will be hard to make bookings while in China.

Airlines flying directly into China: Aeroflot (Moscow-Beijing); Air France (Paris, Karachi, Beijing); Braniff (still negotiating at press time); British Airways (London, Hong Kong, Beijing); CAAC (has reciprocal agreements and usually flies the same routes as other carriers. In addition, it flies Pyongyang-Beijing and Rangoon-Kunming-Beijing (see Chapter 7); Cathay Pacific (Hong Kong-Shanghai); Ethiopian Airlines (Addis Ababa, Aden, Bombay, Beijing); possibly Iran National Airlines (Tehran, Beijing, Tokyo); Japan Air Lines (Tokyo, Nagasaki, Shanghai, Osaka, Beijing); Yugoslav Airlines (Belgrade, Beijing); Lufthansa German Airlines (Frankfurt, New Delhi, Beijing); Pakistan International Airlines (Karachi, Rawalpindi, Beijing, Tokyo); Pan American (New York, San Francisco, Tokyo, Shanghai, Beijing); Philippine Airlines (Manila, Guangzhou, Beijing); Singapore Airlines (still negotiating at press time—Singapore-Guangzhou-Beijing a possibility); Swissair (Zurich, Athens, Bombay, Beijing); Tarom (Bucharest, Karachi, Beijing); Thai International (Bangkok, Guangzhou).

In addition, CAAC has direct scheduled flights from Hong Kong to each of Kunming, Hangzhou, Shanghai, Beijing, Guangzhou, Nanjing, and Tianjin. It may also fly direct to Xi'an and Chengdu.

Other means: regular **ferries** from Hong Kong to Shanghai, Fujian, and Guangzhou. **Trains** from Hong Kong to Guangzhou, from London via Moscow and Ulan Bator to Beijing, and from Pyongyang to Beijing. **Buses** are scheduled from Hong Kong and Macau. See also Chapter 4 on Hong Kong.

Note: Some of these are only once a week and not necessarily in the route order given.

Note: For taxis to meet you at the airport and for hotel reservations, ask your travel agent, airline, or your host organization in China. If they cannot do it, cable C.I.T.S. in the city you are going to. You can also ask for a C.I.T.S. guide to meet you at the airport.

See also Chapter 16 on advance hotel reservations.

FORMALITIES.

China Visa.

For F.F. with invitations and for overseas Chinese, this is obtained from a Chinese embassy, C.T.S. (Hong Kong), C.I.T.S. branches, or some travel agents. For F.F. without invitations, individual visas might be obtained from some U.S., Canadian, and Hong Kong agents. See Chapters 1 and 4. You can also write C.I.T.S. in Beijing or from Janaury to March C.I.T.S. branches abroad.

When writing for an individual visa, be sure to include full name, nationality, age, sex, occupation, purpose of journey, languages spoken, rough itinerary with exact dates and places of entry into and exit from China, and preferred means of transportation. Overseas Chinese booking with C.T.S. should add your name in Chinese and the name and address of relatives in China. Ask for a few more days in China than you think you need in case you cannot make a return reservation in time.

Note. When you get your visa, you will see it is entirely in Chinese. Ask what city you are permitted to go to. Except for short transit stops in other cities, you will only be permitted to stay in the city on your visa. To go anywhere else requires permission which may take several days to obtain.

Nationals of South Africa, Rhodesia, Israel, and South Korea are not allowed into China.

Passport. This will take you about three weeks to obtain from your own government, if you don't have one valid for your whole trip. Start working on this when you start on the China visa.

Other. If visas are required for other countries you will be visiting. Count on another two weeks for each visa if you have to do it by mail *after* you obtain your passport. It will take less time if you can get your visas in Washington (for U.S. citizens) or wherever there are the appropriate consulates.

Shots are not required for smallpox. However, if you will be in a cholera-prone area such as the Philippines or a yellow fever area just prior to visiting China, officials may ask to see your immunization certificate. Cholera shots may have to be given a month apart.

Immunization can usually be obtained from a county health department, a private physician, some Red Cross societies—just be sure that whoever gives you the shot is eligible to stamp your official certificate. Make sure you also have the required shots for all the countries you will be traveling through and for your own country. If you don't have the proper records, you might be given a shot upon arrival in another country—or put into quarantine.

While the above shots are the only ones required for entry to China, some cautious travelers have also gotten protection against typhoid, typhus, tetanus, diphtheria, malaria, and hepatitis—not necessarily for China, but for all the areas they would be traveling in.

PLAN YOUR BUDGET. How much money should you take to China? Be aware that (a) only a few credit cards were accepted in 1981, some of them with a 4% surcharge. See Chapter 16. Check to see if there are any new developments regarding credit cards; (b) personal checks were not generally accepted, but some were with a specific credit card; (c) checks of companies and embassies established in China are accepted if known to the person cashing the check; (d) it takes five banking days to cable money to you in China assuming everyone knows his job; (e) you might ask your embassy to cash a personal check, but I wouldn't count on it.

This all means, of course, that you should take enough cash, traveler's checks, or letters of credit. Cash brings a slightly lower foreign exchange rate than traveler's checks. (See Chapter 16 for acceptable traveler's checks.) Bank of China RMB traveler's checks might save you from the fluctuations in the exchange rate, but you do have to buy them with Hong Kong dollars in Hong Kong at the Bank of China at a rate lower than the direct US$ to RMB rate. Try New York or London branches. They are only good for six months.

In 1981, US $1.00 was worth ¥1.70, Canadian $1.00 was worth ¥1.44, and Australian $1.00 was worth ¥1.98. The British pound was worth ¥3.22. The Hong Kong $1.00 was worth ¥.28.

For equivalents, consult the table under QUICK REFERENCE.

Prepaid travelers are told to pay 15 days prior to their arrival in China. It should go to any branch or correspondent of the Bank of China for deposit into C.I.T.S.

A final accounting is tallied toward the end of the tour. If there are to be additional expenses, you are usually consulted on the trip. For example, flights delayed by weather might mean an option of paying for an additional day or cutting out another part of the tour. "Unforeseen circumstances" in my case mostly meant mistakes on the part of the C.I.T.S. tour planner which added ¥287 onto the original estimate.

Many travel agencies cover the additional costs themselves rather than antagonize their clients. On the other hand, you might get some money back.

So budget:

(a) an additional ¥70 per week for "unforeseen circumstances" which one hopes won't be needed;

(b) for "optional tours" that might mean you would otherwise be wandering around the city alone. The boat ride in Guangzhou cost ¥10 in 1981, the one in Shanghai ¥8. Add more for taxis at ¥.50/km.

(c) for whatever you want for shopping. It's painful to resist buying things you've watched being made;

(d) if you socialize a lot. If you enjoy buying a round of drinks in the evening, beer is ¥1.10 to 1.40 a liter, Coke is ¥1.10 a can, and a bottle of Scotch is about $US16.

(e) If you take people out to dinner. It could cost you from about ¥30 per person in a fancy restaurant.

(f) for laundry at about ¥3.00 a day per person:

(g) for a massage at a hotel barber shop at ¥12 or at a public bath at about ¥3.

After you total this up, add 15 percent to these 1981 prices for every year afterward.

Pay-as-you-go F.F.s should budget:

(a) ¥20–65 for a basic hotel room (one or two people)—the higher in Beijing's and Guangzhou's best, the lower in tiny isolated tourist hostels—but considerably more if you book a specific hotel from Hong Kong;

(b) ¥16 and up per day for food for the hotel's fixed menu, which is usually adequate;

(c) about ¥.50 to ¥.60 per kilometer for taxis. City buses and entrance fees to parks and museums are less than ¥1. However, bus tours arranged through C.I.T.S. can cost from ¥10 to ¥35 a day.

Note also (c) through (g) under "Prepaid Travelers" above and add 15% to these 1981 prices for every year afterward. O.C. should calculate 10% to 40% less on hotel rooms and meals, and about 10% less than F.F. prices on transportation from Hong Kong to China if they book through C.T.S. This should give you more than enough.

For Those Who Want to Save Money on a pay-as-you-go basis: save first before getting to China. Look for bargain airfares. In 1981 it was Laker and Pan Am across the Atlantic; or OC Tours to Hong Kong from Oakland for $279. CAAC discounts from December to March on some routes.

(a) In each city do not be afraid to ask if there are cheaper hotel rooms, and if they say no, keep trying every day. The Chinese might offer you the most expensive for your own comfort as well as the higher revenue. Argue; tell them you're a student or a foreign expert (even if you've just given *one* lecture). Some hotels have dorms with up to eight beds for about ¥6 a bed. Try railway hostels for about ¥4. Take a student card if you have one.

(b) Travel by train. It's usually but not always cheaper in soft class if you skimp on meals. Here is a sample comparison:

Beijing–Guangzhou	*air*	*train (33 hours)*
	¥244 (Y)	¥204.60 (soft-class berth)
	¥317 (F)	¥108.40 (hard-class berth)

(c) Book hard-class train or public bus if you're really budgeting, have a strong back, and want to meet Chinese people. Ask a local Chinese friend to book your ticket (at the cheaper prices).

(d) Travel by boat if you're allowed—on the Yangtze Gorge trip there are several classes. See also "Jiangmen" in DESTINATIONS.

(e) Avoid C.I.T.S. if you can. It's not easy. Its ¥10 Guangzhou boat trip is essentially the same as the ¥.50 trip I took in 1978. We booked directly at the wharf, though we had to wait a few days. Fellow tourists were friendly Chinese. Just remember, Shanghai C.I.T.S. charges ¥5.00 a person for meeting at the airport, ¥32.00 for a guide-interpreter by the day, ¥1.00 for arranging a travel permit, and ¥10.00 for a travel order to another city, e.g., asking that you be met with a taxi. Some branches charge about the same, smaller cities less.

(f) Eat in bun or noodle shops or in restaurants for the masses. In Beijing, they cost about a third the hotel restaurant price. Avoid tourist restaurants. Invite one of the young people trying to practice English to take you to a restaurant where ordinary people eat.

(g) If a car is assigned to you, remember it costs about ¥25 a day for the first 40 kilometers and then about ¥.50 a kilometer. If you're going less than 40 kilometers it's cheaper to take a taxi and have him wait (¥2 an hour). Ask about joining a tour group to the same place. Try to interest other individual travelers to share taxis. Take public buses.

(h) Overseas Chinese can save even more if you stay with relatives. Courtesy demands you bring a present, but this could be anything from a bag of fruit, candy, or cookies to an electric fan or TV set.

(i) Do not assume that the Chinese are giving you anything free. Always ask, "Will there be a charge?"

(j) I've heard of foreign hitchhikers traveling around China successfully, sleeping in hostels for Chinese locals, sometimes for less than ¥1 a night (take your own bedding). Some young people have ignored the rules and seem to get away with not having travel permits. Some speak no Chinese whatsoever so policemen in remote areas do not know what to do with them. Some have been jailed for short periods but then what? They were deported to the next town.

If the rule-breaking becomes common practice, I am sure the Chinese will do something to stop it, such as deportation right out of China.

WRITE AHEAD TO PEOPLE you want to meet, giving yourself at least thirty days for an answer. Do ask for their telephone numbers so you can call when you arrive. Officials and scholars could arrange their schedules to meet yours. Some will need to get permission.

Chinese friends and relatives will have time to arrange leave (with pay) from their jobs to visit you. If you receive no reply, it could mean they are not interested, or you have the wrong address, or they are terrible letter writers. Sorry, I can't decide for you.

China does go through occasional xenophobic periods. In 1979 you could visit Chinese friends (family is always okay) without suspicion. It was slightly more difficult in 1981. Who knows when the next period will come?

If you get replies welcoming you to China, then you can make plans to see them. If you have only a couple of days in their city and do not know your exact itinerary ahead of time, you could telegraph them after you arrive in China. See chapter 8 on looking up specific Chinese citizens.

Overseas Chinese in particular may want to write to ask what gifts their relatives would like. Don't be surprised if they ask for a watch, bicycle, sewing machine, television, or electric fan. Other relatives abroad could help pay for expensive gifts. If you cannot afford it, take a less expensive gift and they will (or should) be happy to see you anyway.

At this stage, Overseas Chinese should start collecting the names of relatives born in China, the names of ancestral villages, and particularly the names of ancestors born in China. This is so your relatives or the people in your village, who may not know you otherwise, will know just who you are in relation to someone they do know. These names, of course, should be in Chinese. See also chapter 12.

IN CASE OF EMERGENCY, tell people at home how you can be reached in China. Give copies of your itinerary to key people with your tour number. If you are with a C.I.T.S tour, they can telephone C.I.T.S. in Beijing, preferably in Beijing dialect, and ask that you be told to telephone home. The address is simply LUXINGSHE BEIJING. The tour number and itinerary are important to help locate you. Some foreign air lines have offices in Beijing and Shanghai. You could also be contacted through them if you are on one of their tours.

Also leave your passport number in case money has to be cabled to you through the Bank of China.

Since letters could take ten days to reach you, quicker if by "express," it is best to tell friends not to write. If they insist, find someone to write the address in Chinese for you. It should arrive faster. You also might use the address of your consulate (see Beijing, Shanghai, and Guangzhou directories) or a hotel. Some hotels have bulletin boards where letters and cables are posted, or you could ask at the reception desk. You don't have to be a guest to do this.

Overseas Chinese in particular should use both their Chinese and English names on correspondence. Chinese people remember Chinese more easily. If you don't know how to write your name in Chinese, then learn. If you don't have a Chinese name, get one. It doesn't have to be legal, but it will make things easier for you as you travel around China.

Note: In case of dire emergency, it may be impossible to get transportation out of China and especially small cities quickly. Although it is possible to charter a CAAC aircraft, it is difficult to get permission to fly one out of China. In case of emergencies, contact your embassy or consulate.

If you are wondering before you go to China if any particular place is unsafe to visit due to floods, earthquakes or civil disturbance, phone the State Department in Washington, (202) 632-6300, or the Citizen Emergency Center, (202) 632-5225. They have the latest information available. The State Department puts out a Travel Advisory which is distributed to travel agents and to its consulates abroad.

LEARN SOME CHINESE. If nothing else, learn to read numbers. Then at least you will know dates in museums and street numbers.

If you're going to live with relatives and they're Cantonese, Fukinese, or Shanghainese, they probably speak the dialect at home. If you're traveling around China, however, it would be more practical to learn the Beijing dialect, *pu tung hua,* which is understood all over China.

The same Chinese writing is also understood throughout the country. Chinese characters used in China today have been simplified since 1950, but Chinese people living outside China have a hard time understanding the revisions unless they have kept up with the changes. Just make sure that whoever teaches you the writing gives you the new script and the pinyin romanization. The new script is used in the USEFUL PHRASES. It might be a good idea to memorize some of these phrases so you can communicate.

As in any foreign country, the more of the local language you learn, the cheaper your expenses will be. In the meantime, use the USEFUL PHRASES. The standard of English is improving daily, but it is still pretty low.

I don't speak much Chinese but found it possible to get around and have a good time even without an interpreter. The Chinese try very hard to understand. I had a dictionary handy, drew pictures, and tried charades. I also had a set of useful phrases in Chinese and English that usually worked. At hotels, I looked for individual travelers especially in restaurants, many of whom are lonely and delighted to make friends. Some of these speak Chinese and were able to interpret for me.

Overseas Chinese who speak no Chinese should take C.I.T.S. tours if they are interested primarily in getting facts while sightseeing. If you are primarily interested in a China experience, in getting closer to the people, go the individual C.T.S. route.

LEARN ABOUT CHINA. To get the most out of your trip, learn something about China before you go. There is a dizzying list of good books on China, of which here are only a few suggestions. See BIBLIOGRAPHY for details.

If you know nothing about China, start out with a general history like Brian Catchpole's *A Map History of Modern China,* which is extremely easy to read (high-school level), half maps and diagrams, the rest text. Heavy but valuable with lots of pictures is the China section in *East Asia, the Great Tradition.*

The Chinese themselves have published *An Outline History of China,* compiled by Tung Chi-ming, which covers 500,000 years ago to 1949, and *China: A General Survey* by Qi Wen, which gives a broad picture of geography, history, politics, economy, and culture.

Then read historical background on the destinations you will visit. If you are going to any of the ancient capitals, then read dynastic history. Raymond Dawson's *Imperial China* is a book to carry to China—a good index and lots of juicy gossip about the likes of Tang Empress Wu and her boyfriends. If you are going to Hangzhou, there's the classic *Daily Life in China* by Jacques Gernet, with a map of the city in 1274—if you want to look for the changes. There's also *The Romance of the Three Kingdoms,* the classic historical novel whose characters you will hear mentioned in Luoyang, Zhenjiang, and Chengdu. Of course there's Marco Polo (Yuan dynasty).

For Shanghai, 1949, read *The Fall of Shanghai* by Noel Barber. For Beijing, read biographies of the Empress Dowager (and *her* boyfriend). For Shanghai, Tianjin, Wuhan, Zhenjiang, and Guangzhou, read George

Woodcock's *The British in the Far East,* about the bad old but interesting imperialists like Captain Charles "Chinese" Gordon. For U.S. involvements, there's John Fairbank's *The United States and China.*

If you're interested in missionaries, there's Pat Barr's *To China with Love.* Then read *China—A New Day* by Stanley Mooneyham, about prospects for Christianity in China now and what is happening politically.

The classical novels are still being read in China, and you might even see them as traditional operas, or their characters in porcelain. So if you like fiction and want to struggle through a great number of characters, do read *Dream of the Red Chamber* (a.k.a. *Dream of the Red Mansions*) and *Pilgrimage to the Western World.* The latter is based on the journey of a Chinese monk to India to obtain the Buddhist sutras during the Tang. The monk's remains are in Nanjing and Xi'an.

Of the modern novels, the Communists say that Pearl S. Buck romanticized China too much and did not make any political analyses. Do read anything of Lu Hsun's, China's foremost modern writer, for you will also see him in porcelain and hear of his grave in Shanghai.

Another novel is Richard McKenna's *The Sand Pebbles,* about an American gunboat engineer and a missionary woman set in Changsha and the Yangtze in 1925. (Remember Steve McQueen and Candice Bergen?)

Han Suyin's autobiographical trilogy *The Crippled Tree (1885–1928), A Mortal Flower (1928–38),* and *Birdless Summer (1938–48)* are good background for the period. She grew up in Chengdu. Among the books on revolutionary history are Schram's or Chen's biography of Mao Tse-tung. The classic novel *Man's Fate* by André Malraux is set in Shanghai during the 1927 massacre of the Communists. For an understanding of Chinese thinking, read contemporary Chinese fiction, too. Kai-yu Hsu's overview will help. Chen Yuan-Tsung's *The Dragon's Village* is a good picture of land reform in one village in the early 1950s.

For an understanding of Communist history, there's John Fairbank's *East Asia the Modern Transformation.* Another classic is Edgar Snow's *Red Star Over China,* which not only relates the history of the Long March but has the only autobiography dictated by Mao Tse-tung. Don't let the Chinese tell you that Yang Kai-hui was his first wife. According to Snow, Mao had four—his first was a village girl whom he ignored.

Then there are the personal accounts of people who lived in China, notably Jack Chen's *A Year in Upper Felicity* and Ken Ling's *The Revenge of Heaven,* both about the Cultural Revolution. Sidney Rittenberg's autobiography is about his life in China including fifteen years in prison.

You will be hearing a lot about the Cultural Revolution and the Gang of Four. Jean Daubier has *A History of the Chinese Cultural Revolution.* Roxanne Witke has *Comrade Chiang Ching.* The biography of Teng Hsiao-ping by Chi Hsin contains the text of Teng's self-criticisms, his Three World Theory, and some speeches.

And for background, there's my own Chinese-Canadian novel set during the Cultural Revolution, *Beyond the Heights,* and Orville Schell's *Watch Out for the Foreign Guest.*

Nagel's Encyclopedia-Guide China still can't be beat for background, but it is outdated and expensive, and weighs two pounds. I would recommend only an edition revised later than 1982 if you want to cart it to China.

If you're interested in Chinese arts and crafts, I would take along Margaret Medley's *A Handbook of Chinese Art,* Michael Sullivan's *The Arts of China,* or C. A. S. Williams's *Outlines of Chinese Symbolism and Art Motives.* These are all reference books, profusely illustrated, that will help you appreciate the architecture, symbols, mythology, and customs of China. But do keep in mind that Williams's was written before Liberation. Books on cultural background such as these are important to take with you since your guides will know very little about the subject.

Look up back issues of magazines like *China Reconstructs* and *China Pictorial,* both easy reading, which have articles about many of the places you will be visiting, descriptions of Chinese movies and plays, and Chinese history. *60 Scenic Wonders of China* and *15 Cities in China* are good touristy background.

China also has, in English, magazines specializing in literature, women, sports, foreign trade, movies, medicine, and the sciences. None are as political as they used to be. The *Ta Kung Pao Weekly Supplement* and the *China Daily* (Beijing) are both helpful for news. Tourism news is in the magazines *China—Sights and Insights* (C.I.T.S.), *China Tourism Pictorial,* *New Horizons* (CAAC), *Pearl,* and *Shanghai Hotels and Tourism. China Tourism Pictorial* is written for and by Hong Kong and Overseas Chinese.

The best Western news sources are *The New York Times,* the Toronto *Globe and Mail,* the *Asian Wall Street Journal,* the *South China Morning Post,* and the *Far Eastern Economic Review.* Updated travel information can be found in *Asia Travel Trade.* Your most comprehensive stores for books from China in the U.S. are China Books & Periodicals, Inc. Write for a catalog. In Hong Kong there's the Peace Book Co.

The National Committee on U.S.-China Relations has a briefing kit for US$13, tailored for doctors, lawyers, etc., and can provide lecturers. Talk also to old China hands, contacted through the friendship associations, Hong Kong's Edgar Snow Society, and the likes of the Yangtze River Patrol Assoc., which has 300 members in the U.S. with service in China prior to 1941. Free newsletter on education can be had from the U.S.-China's People's Friendship Association. The National Council of Churches has a China committee if you are interested in contacting Chinese Protestants.

LEARN ABOUT YOUR OWN COUNTRY. This is indispensable in your preparation for China if you want to see factories and schools. Visit a factory in your own country and learn so you can compare with China's such things as incentives to work, unions, employee benefits, maternity leave, child care for working mothers, job security, and so forth.

When was the last time you were in a school? Find out what subjects are taught at what level, how discipline is maintained, how many students there are to a class, and about "open" classrooms, teacher qualifications, incentives to learning, the slow learners, the exceptionally bright children, and the handicapped. Who makes the decisions as to what children should learn? Take your notes with you so you can ask how the Chinese deal with these things. And with good facts on hand, you can help to clear up Chinese misconceptions about your country.

If you are thinking of inviting relatives to join you as immigrants, it has been increasingly possible for Chinese citizens to join their families abroad. It has also been possible for Chinese students to study privately abroad as distinct from an official exchange.

Check the requirements with the China desk in your government's foreign office, with your embassy, or consulate.

But it is a long process and you should not expect all procedures to be completed in less than a year, if that.

CHECK YOUR OWN CUSTOMS REGULATIONS. Usually there is a booklet. Find out what you cannot take back into your own country. Dried mushrooms and dried beef have been confiscated. Some kinds of fruits and plants are forbidden; orchid plants grown without soil are allowed in some instances. Certain animal products are forbidden or restricted; for example, the U.S. will allow only "a couple of" pieces of ivory and no crocodile or alligator, leopard, or tiger (endangered species). China has mink, fox, and wolf fur coats and hats for sale, also.

In many countries, coin and stamp collections, antiques (over a hundred years old), and "works of art" (i.e., one of a kind—not factory-made copies) are duty-free. Be sure to get a certificate of proof at time of purchase. Canada allows sculptures duty-free if valued over $75.

Some items may be duty-free but liable to sales tax in Canada. Do keep your receipts, and in China mark in English what each is for. The red wax seal on an antique is China's proof that the item is over one hundred years old, but you have to convince a customs officer. As you leave your own country, register valuable items, such as cameras and expensive jewelry, especially if the items look new. This is to avoid a hassle with customs officials as you return. Honolulu customs is notorious for trying to charge duty on items you have owned for years, even clothes, if you are a "returning U.S. resident."

Incidentally, at Honolulu airport I found that the nonresident line was very easy to pass through. Of course, we had plane tickets after five days in the U.S. to Canada.

If you know the rate of duty, list the items with the highest rate first on your declaration form. The customs official might just dismiss the little souvenirs. Do report unaccompanied luggage so these will be exempted too. Since much depends on each individual customs official, you may not have trouble at all. On the other hand, undeclared dutiable items if found may be confiscated.

For the U.S., write for a booklet from the U.S. Customs Service, Public Information Division, Washington, DC 20229. In 1981, Americans were allowed an exemption of $300 every thirty days, plus an additional $600 worth of goods taxed at 10%. You could also mail parcels back duty-free if not valued at more than $25 each to friends and relatives in the U.S.

Canada has a duty-free personal exemption of $50 worth of goods every calendar quarter after seven days' absence or more and a duty-free exemption every calendar year of $150. These exemptions have to be claimed on separate trips. You may send duty-free gifts from abroad to friends or relatives in Canada, each gift valued at no more than (Canadian) $25. These must not be alcoholic beverages, tobacco, or advertising matter. The cost of shipping, however, may exceed the cost of the duty.

For more detailed information, please contact your local customs office, or write Customs Office, 1650 Carling Avenue, Ottawa, Ontario, K2A 3Y1, or a Canadian mission abroad. It is easier to get the information before leaving.

CHINESE CUSTOMS REGULATIONS. Check through the customs regulations in chapter 4 and see what you can and cannot take into China.

COMPARISON SHOPPING. If you are a serious shopper intent on bargains, I suggest doing some research and keeping notes.

First of all, many goods you can buy in China are available abroad, and one traveler sadly related how the painted eggs she bought there were the same price she found later in a Washington store. So look around at home, especially in local Chinatowns, where prices are usually cheaper than in curio stores.

On the whole, however, the choice for bargains is really between Hong Kong and China. The serious shopper should try to spend several days in Hong Kong going and returning. The Chinese government contracts with many stores to sell goods made on the mainland deliberately cheaper than in China to attract the foreign exchange. Prices are even cheaper than at the factories, sometimes.

There are basically two kinds of stores: Arts and Crafts and stores for the masses, which also include some arts and crafts but not the best quality. The selection is usually better in China, but you are taking a chance. Some items are available in China and not in Hong Kong, e.g., in 1979, three-color Tang reproductions and good dough figures. For these the selection was best at the factories.

Chinese Arts and Crafts stores are in the main Hong Kong tourist belts, one of the best being near the Star Ferry in Kowloon and another down the street from the Hilton. Still another is near the Holiday Inn and Hyatt on lower Nathan Road.

The Chinese Products Stores for the masses are important for people wanting to take gifts for relatives, such as clothes and foodstuffs. You can buy most anything, including a set of luggage wheels (necessary if you're traveling individually around China), towels, sweaters, and luggage (make sure the locks work), at the cheapest prices in the world. Look out for junk, though. See chapter 4 for duty-free "large gifts" for Overseas Chinese.

Buying in Hong Kong also facilitates shipping purchases abroad, since only a few Friendship Stores in China and even fewer factories were set up to do this in 1981.

In comparing prices, be sure to add the cost of shipping and customs duties if relevant.

3

WHAT TO TAKE

Besides the items mentioned in chapter 2 such as passport, ticket, money, gifts, reference books, cigarettes, and liquor, here are some more suggestions.

If you're going in a tour group, you're allowed one suitcase. You should have an extra carry-on bag for overnight train rides (your big bag may not be accessible) and for airplanes.

If you're not in a tour group, remember that CAAC, China's only domestic airline, is very lenient about hand-carried luggage but very strict about its 20-kilogram baggage limit, unless you have booked through to China on First Class and have a 30-kilogram allowance. The excess baggage rate for Guangzhou to Beijing is ¥2.44 per kilogram. If you don't want to pay it, put books and other heavy items in your carry-on luggage.

Also keep in mind the lack of porters. This is usually no problem with tour groups, but independent travelers should be prepared to cart their own luggage. Even if you are being met, you may be embarrassed if your pretty, little guide offers to carry your luggage. I wouldn't travel alone in China without luggage wheels unless I were able to cart all my bags up stairs and down for at least 100 yards.

CLOTHING. From early November to late March, north China, including Beijing, is bitterly cold, sometimes with snow. I even froze in Beijing in May; two sweaters and a topcoat were barely enough. Many of the buildings are not heated. Many foreigners complain of lack of heat in hotels. This even applied to Guilin in February.

The Chinese sometimes lend heavy padded jackets to visitors who didn't anticipate the cold, but you should take along your own coat plus long thermal underwear or heavy slacks. In some northern and western places, guides will warn you not to put your feet on the floor of the bus—it is *that* cold! So thermal socks and boots are in order, too.

I suggest you do as the natives do: Plan on layers of warm clothing and a loose-fitting outer layer like a warm but lightweight ski jacket. This is better than one thick heavy coat that would only be excess weight in the warmer south. Pants and safari suits are ideal for all but the coldest weather.

The rainy season is March to May in the south, with rain or drizzle almost every day. After it starts getting hot, a plastic raincoat might feel like a sauna. Take an umbrella, then. The Chinese sell plastic sandals which are great for rain, but they may be too small for big American feet.

All of lowland China is hot in July. Sundresses on foreign women in tour groups are common now in big cities. In smaller places, especially if you're alone, wear slacks and a conservative shirt, or a loose-fitting dress. The thing is, the more you deviate from what the Chinese wear, the more you will be stared at and surrounded by a crowd, a most oppressive experience on a hot day or when you're tired. You might also antagonize some very conservative people. Some Chinese once crowded around one sophisticated Chinese-Canadian asking each other, "Are her eyelashes real? Is her hair real?" They are very curious.

Most Chinese women wear trousers, blouses, sweaters, and jackets in winter, and increasingly, skirts and blouses, always with short sleeves, in summer. They tend to overdress for the weather. My aunt was always putting sweaters on my daughter even though the child was sweating. For men, shorts and loose-fitting shirts are ideal in the summer. See the hottest and coldest temperatures listed under some of the DESTINATIONS. This is to prepare you for the worst.

The natives are going to stare at you anyway, even if you are Overseas Chinese, so if you want to minimize the attention, wear conservative colors—dark blues and grays. Some Overseas Chinese men bought Mao jackets and blended in so well with the scenery they were not allowed back into their hotels without a lot of arguing. If you go native, carry your passport. The Mao jacket in China is known as the cadre or Zhong Shan jacket, named after Dr. Sun Yat-sen. A foreign friend in one still attracts attention. You really have to hide your hair and eyes.

It is sometimes advantageous to appear different from the local population, however. Special courtesies are extended to visitors; you may not have to wait so long in lines, and frequently people on public buses will give up their seats for you. On the other hand, looking different tends to isolate you from people and make you an object of curiosity. Such is the dilemma.

Laundry and dry cleaning are done in one day at hotels if in by 8 a.m. You can take drip-dry clothing if you want to do your own laundry, but also take a clothes line. I found that lightweight clothes took two days to dry in humid Guangzhou. In the humid south, too, I found anything but predominantly cotton mixtures stifling hot.

Dress for comfort, even at trade fairs. Do take good walking shoes, because you will be on your feet a lot and climbing stairs. You will frequently be on rough stone paths, treacherous for high heels. Chinese men do not wear ties and on hot days sometimes show up at formal banquets with just trousers and a white shirt open at the collar. You might feel more secure dressing up a bit more than that for formal occasions, but high heels and evening gowns for women are not used except for a very formal reception hosted by foreign diplomats. Lots of jewelry and makeup is out of place—though I must admit, there are signs, that the Chinese on the higher levels are becoming clothes-conscious.

Don't count on buying everyday clothes in China. You need to have coupons for cotton goods. In a pinch your guide or hotel service desk might get you some, but the selection in the Friendship Store, where you don't need coupons, is generally limited to luxury-quality things like hand-embroidered shirts and cashmere sweaters.

Most tour schedules are booked solid, but you may be able to squeeze in a summer *swim* after May. So take a bathing suit if you want—plus a *doctor's certificate* saying you're in good health and free of communicable diseases, etc. (In some places, the Chinese are strict about the certificate. You might argue your case if you have an official-looking document in hand—whether or not the lifeguard reads English. Tour groups usually do not have time to get a Chinese medical examination which involves a blood test.)

TOILETRIES. Take your favorite brands of shampoo, toothpaste, shaving cream, soap, sanitary napkins or tampons, and other necessities. China has its own equivalents, many but not all of which you can buy in your hotel's retail store. I found the toothpaste, for example, very sweet and perfumed. You will find very few foreign goods in China, and who wants to spend time looking? Few Chinese women wear cosmetics, but foreign lipsticks are beginning to appear in the Friendship stores. Finicky people might want to take a disinfectant for the bathtub and their own towel, but I've never had any trouble, even though some tubs look grubby.

SHORTWAVE TRANSISTOR RADIO. This is to get world news. You may otherwise get nothing. The Voice of America news broadcast is hourly from 6 a.m. to 9 a.m. Try 11760, 9770, 17740, and 15290. From 7 p.m. to 10 p.m. try 11715, 21615, 15160, 9760, and 15425, and from 7 p.m. to 2 a.m., 6110 and 9760.

The British Broadcasting Corporation has news at 6, 7, and 8 a.m. and 6, 7, and 8 p.m., best heard in south China on 31.35, 41.78, 48.43, 25.09 or 25.53 and in north and west China on 11.70, 13.92, 19.91, 24.80, and 31.88.

You can also get Radio Beijing news hourly in English, and in the largest cities, there's the *China Daily* (market reports, NFL football scores, some world news) and two days late the *Asian Wall St. Journal* and *International Herald Tribune.* Also available are *Time, Newsweek,* and the *Far Eastern Economic Review.*

CAMERA AND FILM. See "Customs Regulations" in chapter 4. I have taken in two cameras, registered them, and taken them out without any problem.

You can buy Kodak film in some hotels and Friendship Stores, but best take in your own supply.

More and more places are processing color film now, but the quality may or may not be good.

Be sure to take extra batteries and flash cubes if needed, since these are not readily available in China, and lots of Polaroid film if you want to be popular with your Polaroid camera.

MAPS AND BOOKS. See also "Learning about China" in the previous chapter for reference books to take on your trip. Do take a guidebook for the cities you will be visiting if you want more than the superficial description by guides. Some guides are top-rate; other guides can barely speak English.

You can usually buy a good tourist map in English in each city now. A Chinese-English dictionary is superfluous if you have a bilingual person with you most of the time. For wandering around on your own, I have tried to anticipate most needs in the USEFUL PHRASES in this book. Read through them, and if you think you're going to need more than that, have a Chinese-writing friend add what you think you will need.

MEDICINES AND VITAMINS. Take what you usually need since exact Chinese equivalents may be hard to find. The Chinese do have antibiotics and can give a test for possible allergic reactions. Take salt tablets and talcum powder for hot weather if you need them, and cold tablets and cough syrup for colds. But I have found Chinese traditional medicines very effective, so if you're adventurous, you might rely on those after you arrive.

GIFTS. This is one area that has changed most in the last few years and the change is not necessarily for the better. Government officials were accepting presents bigger than ballpoint pens. When I asked one hotel manager about presents for attendants, he suggested a television set for the enjoyment of the whole staff. In 1981, officially no large gifts were allowed, but the Chinese were saying privately that large gifts were for work units, only small gifts for individuals.

In 1981, service personnel were not allowed to accept tips, but some were accepting small presents like ballpoint pens, souvenirs, pins, tiny flashlights, and candies. I do not think these are necessary and believe they should be confined to a friend or to someone who has done you a very special favor.

The same principle should apply to trade officials whom you get to know well. You could give more elaborate gifts, of course, or something for their children. You have to be very careful in case you do insult them. If you want to continue having good relations, by no means let word get to the press if you give them something like a computer or a television set. There is no guarantee that an expensive gift will give you what you want, and the intent may be counterproductive. Usually a banquet to celebrate a deal is sufficient. (See "Courtesies" in the USEFUL PHRASES.)

On the other hand, from time to time, there are campaigns against corrupt officials who use their positions for personal gain.

It is not necessary to take gifts to schools, factories and communes that you visit, but if you insist, my suggestion is general gifts that everyone can enjoy. Giving to a few may antagonize the others. Let's not spoil these beautiful people.

Since people everywhere are studying English, textbooks and good supplementary reading books would be great. For primary schools take posters and educational picture books, novelty toys like Frisbees, and unusual (for China) sports equipment like a ball and bat. Don't forget to demonstrate their use. The Chinese already have basketball, Ping-Pong, and soccer.

Gifts are difficult to organize on general-interest tours where you meet your fellow travelers for the first time on a plane across the Pacific. So don't worry about gifts. But special-interest tours are different. Again it's up to you. China is so short of teaching materials, especially in science, technology, and languages, that they appreciate everything you can give them— educational movies (16 mm. is okay), taped English lessons and if possible tape recorders to match. The voltage is 220. Books on space and the history of the airplane come immediately to mind as excellent gifts. A geological delegation may want to give labeled rock specimens; a solar energy group may want to give a school a simple model.

You may want to write ahead to the universities you will be visiting to see what gifts they need and to arrange for duty-free Customs clearance. Give them your date and point of entry so the papers will be ready for you. Do not be surprised if you get a list of books worth $50,000. Never mind; take only what you can afford. The Chinese are used to spending very little money for books; they think books are cheap everywhere. (See Chinese Customs next chapter.)

Just don't be turned off by a request for expensive presents. In all fairness, the Chinese really do not know the value of money outside China. When you get there, just say something like, "I'm sorry I could only get these few books. They are only a token of what I wanted to bring." That should satisfy them.

For guides, surprisingly, the best gifts are reference books on *China*— guidebooks (many get their spiels from old copies of *Nagel's*), objective history books, books on traditional Chinese culture, and good novels (please, no sexy ones). Agatha Christie is fine and fun. A book on Dr. Norman Bethune or Chester Ronning's memoirs would be good from Canadians. Edgar Snow is popular. Yes, guidebooks and picture books from your own country are also important. C.I.T.S. is eager to improve its services and would like to see what other countries offer tourists.

Again, the rule is group, rather than individual presents, something everyone can learn from and enjoy, like cassettes of music. Again, gifts are not necessary. Guides will knock themselves out trying to help you anyway.

The next suggestion is entirely my own, so don't blame anyone else for it. So many things were stolen from China by looting foreigners in the old days that as a gesture of friendship and support for the current policy of openness to foreigners, some visitors may want to return relics on a trip to China if they have any. These, of course, must have historic value. The British once returned a sword belonging to one of the Taiping rulers. It is now in the Taiping museum in Nanjing. I think old photos of foreigners in China (against recognizable Chinese backgrounds), important old documents, and relics like military uniforms would be most welcome. I talked with a museum official in Zhenjiang who was eager to get anything like that.

There is a problem though—the Chinese bureaucracy. You really should write ahead of time to the Bureau of Historical Relics in Beijing and directly to the museum in the city relevant to the relics. Give details and ask if they would be interested in receiving the relics as a gift. Keep in mind that China has a problem of too many historical relics, but something unique would be appreciated. Just be aware that the captions on material from imperialist times may be in Marxist jargon. The Chinese are currently moving away from such bitterness, and your gift should help. I once asked a guide at the Beijing Museum of Chinese History about this idea, and she laughed in my face, saying, "No one would give up anything that valuable!" I hope someone will prove her wrong.

If visiting Foreign Residents in China, do write and ask what would be best to take them. Many are teaching English, so as many relevant books as you can possibly carry would be helpful. They also appreciate favorite snack foods: instant dried soups, cheeses, popping corn, candy bars, instant coffee and tea bags, and Mom's homemade cookies. Around the holidays, try cranberry sauce, spices, Sunkist oranges, the makings for minced meat and pumpkin pies. China has all kinds of fruit, vegetables and meats, but there's nothing like home.

Your next problem is getting gifts into China without paying duty. See "Customs Regulations" in chapter 4.

MISCELLANEOUS. If you're fussy about your coffee and tea, take in some of the instant variety, powdered cream, sugar, and a spoon. Chinese coffee tastes different from ours. Chinese hotels provide cups and a big thermos of hot water every day. Take prunes if traveling makes you constipated. I found a jackknife handy for cutting fruit for snacks, and a flashlight good for caves, dark houses, and late-night walks.

If you're fussy about your cigarettes or liquor, take some in with you. Visitors are usually pleased with the local beer and wine. In many hotels you now find ice (made from boiled water). Chinese brandy and vodka have been described as "outstanding," and of course there's *maotai*. But these are all a matter of taste.

Sometimes when you're on a train, you may not be able to eat without a lot of bother. Take instant soup or things to munch on. You may also get tired of Chinese food.

During the rainy season, you may be bothered by mosquitoes if there is no air conditioning (if you are in an isolated, tiny, rural guest house). I found the mosquito incense coils in China gave me a headache, so you might want to take in a foreign brand. If you're staying in Chinese homes mosquitoes will be a problem, so also take insect repellant.

Note that Chinese appliances are 220V and have either two- or, more commonly, three-pronged plugs. Some hotels have adapters and transformers, but not all.

Some Christians may want to take Bibles. One or two are no problem, but large quantities are. Officially religious literature is not allowed to be imported. The Chinese have published their own, but the demand has exceeded supply. More are being printed.

For people who want to do unusual things, yes, take your paints, or if you want to ice-skate in Beihai Park in Beijing, take your skates in winter. Take your skis, too, if you know that you will be in snow country. Jilin now has ski tows. There are no facilities yet for scuba diving. Keep in mind that the Chinese are very concerned about the safety of visitors, and C.I.T.S. will probably forbid any supposedly dangerous sports like hang-gliding and exploring nontouristy caves alone.

If you're big on bicycling, buy a bicycle in China (only one gear) or import from Hong Kong. You can sell it when you leave unless you want to take it out.

Think of everything you need before you go. If goods are sent in by mail, you may have to pay duty and go to much bother to pick them up at a hard-to-find government office.

4

GETTING THERE

The travel-agented traveler does not have to worry about logistics (read the section on Border Formalities, but just glance at the rest of the chapter for reference). The do-it-yourself traveler does. With a visa in hand, you can book your ticket by plane to the city in China listed on your China visa. Your airline can tell you if you are able to make stops en route in other Chinese cities. Bookings can be made with any of the airlines flying into China (they should be able to make domestic air bookings if your visa gives permission and if you give them lots of time).

Once in China, *then* you can make other travel arrangements. See chapter 7, GETTING AROUND.

VIA HONG KONG. While many travelers enter directly through Beijing, Guangzhou, and Shanghai, many more enter China via Hong Kong. This is because hundreds of thousands of Hong Kong Chinese and many foreign residents travel to China yearly. Competing Hong Kong travel agents have developed a high degree of expertise. They are usually the first to upgrade services. Many have direct connections with individual tourism officials in China. Hong Kong is also loaded with professional China watchers and experienced business people who can give advice.

While its prices have risen over the years, Hong Kong is still one of the bargain cities of the world with its duty-free cameras, watches, and radios, and its relatively cheap sandals and clothes. Bargains are also to be found in the Chinese government stores. See chapter 2, "Comparison Shopping." Some of these stores, like Yue Hwa, will have up-to-date lists on what Overseas Chinese can take into China duty-free, and will even pack and ship these to the railway station if you give them a couple of days' notice. Prices are fixed. They will give Overseas Chinese a 10% discount card. In the smaller owner-clerk stores, you can haggle. Prices will go up automatically because you are a foreigner, so if there's no one else around, try your hand at the fine art of bargaining.

Hong Kong was taken from China by the British during and after the Opium Wars. Parts are scheduled to revert to China in 1997. It is extremely crowded because of the refugees from China and Vietnam. You can get some of the flavor of old China there, especially in isolated island villages or in the New Territories—the temples, festivals, elaborate funeral customs, dirt, purse snatchers, and extremes of wealth. It is a good introduction to the contrast of new China next door, and it might be good for you to talk with refugees from China—why did they risk their lives to leave? Welfare agencies can help you contact them, or just ask around.

Another interesting place is the Sung Dynasty Village, an attempt to reproduce a Song village. You won't see anything like this in China itself.

FROM HONG KONG TO GUANGZHOU. Three **hovercrafts** daily (8:45, 9:45, and 10:30 a.m.) make the three-hour trip. They depart from Guangzhou at 12:45, 2:00, and 2:45 p.m. Recommended because maximum 68 passengers means shorter queues. Photos are not allowed in China.

Overnight ferries, the *Xing Hu* and *Tien Hu,* leave Hong Kong and Guangzhou nightly at 9:00 p.m. Comfortable in deluxe cabins (4 pass.). No announcements in English. Duty-free store. Early morning arrival means a full day in China. Ships and hovercrafts leave Hong Kong at Tai Kok Tsui near the Yaumati Typhoon Shelter in Kowloon, which is a convenient ferry ride from Blakes Pier in Central. Ferries dock at Zhoutouzui, on Guangzhou's south shore. It sometimes takes about an hour to clear formalities because of its 500 passengers.

Two through **trains** daily leave at 1:00 and 2:55 p.m. for a three-hour ride. Leave Guangzhou at 8:30 and 10:10 a.m. One train daily with change at Shenzhen leaves Kowloon at 8:35 a.m. and arrives 3:02 or 2:25 p.m. Not recommended unless you like waiting in railway stations, or standing. No toilets and many delays on the Hong Kong side due to construction to be completed in 1983. Leaves Hunghom railway station in Kowloon.

Planes leave for the 25-minute trip to Guangzhou at 9:15 and 11:45 a.m. and 7:55 p.m. Return flights leave Guangzhou at 7:45 and 10:15 a.m. and 6:25 p.m.

OTHER DESTINATIONS FROM HONG KONG. By air, see chapter 2. By ferry to **Shanghai,** about every eight days on the *Hai Xing* or *Shanghai,* a 2½-day voyage; to **Xiamen** on the M.S. *Gulangzu,* six times a month; and to Shekou and Jiangmen. Buses go regularly to **Shantou, Xingning, Xiamen** and **Fuzhou.** The terminal is on Peking Road, Tsim Sha Tsui. Schedules and programs listed here are subject to change.

Most **Hong Kong travel agents** listed here should be able to book some or all of these once you have your visa. A few will issue an individual visa and some can book the following tours from each other. Phone to check services before you come in case of changes. See Chapter 16 for advance hotel bookings.

China International Travel Service (H.K.) offers group tours, individual visas for people with invitations, general hotel bookings, and CAAC tickets.

Individual visas for two destinations from January to March only. (Visas HK$100 in 24 hrs., HK$70 in three days.)

China Travel Service (H.K.), the granddaddy of them all. Primarily for Overseas Chinese and Compatriots but can provide the same services for F.F. as C.I.T.S. does, although individual tourist visas are for Overseas Chinese only. Cheaper prices for Overseas Chinese too. Some packaged tours for one F.F. or more. Group tours for F.F. are also available through other agents. Bookings by mail accepted.

China Youth Travel can service groups at slightly cheaper prices.

Compass Travel is a general agent who can arrange an individual visa and other services. Ask for Enid Harper.

Crosspoint Tours has 15-day bicycle tours of the Pearl River Delta for US$895 from Hong Kong and an 18-day tour from Macao for US$1,150. Price includes most meals, transportation, escort truck, and motorcycle.

Hong Kong Student Travel Bureau makes arrangements at slightly cheaper prices.

International Tourism has tours to Zhongshan and Guangzhou via Macao.

Pacific World Ltd. can help F.I.T.s and groups.

Silkway Travel Ltd. seems to do everything for F.F. and Overseas Chinese groups and individuals. Visa service. They told me it was cheaper to take a Chinese-speaking friend than to pay the high per diem rate for an all-inclusive individual tour. I like that kind of agent. They can also help you find residential or office space in China, acupuncture courses, medical treatment, or a place to bury your grandfather (in Shenzhen, the only place that will accept human remains). Also plans self-driven car tours from Beijing.

Ministry of Foreign Affairs, Government of China, has an office here which will issue visas, similar to any other Chinese mission.

Travel Advisers has direct flight tours to Kunming, Beijing, or Shanghai.

Welcome Travel & Trading has Cantonese-speaking group tours for Overseas Chinese and Compatriots. My 14-day all-inclusive six-destination tour with it was US$55 a day from Hong Kong. Individual visas available.

United (Tai Shan) Travel has individual visas (within 24 hours) and info on getting to the Stone Flower Mountain Inn in Taishan.

Voyages Jules Verne has 41-day tours from London to Hong Kong by train with sightseeing stops in Beijing and six other cities. Shorter trips offered too. Claims competitive prices for groups to Tibet and other places out of Hong Kong.

Westminster Travel is a general agent who can arrange for an individual visa and for other services. Ask for Evelina Lindsay.

VIA MACAO. This Portuguese colony on the other side of the Pearl River Delta can be reached after a fifty-minute jetfoil ride from Hong Kong. It also is a free port, its prices lower than Hong Kong because rent and labor costs are lower. But its shopping selection is not as vast.

Noted for its gambling casinos and good Portuguese food, it might be closer for some Overseas Chinese to their ancestral villages.

Macao is the setting for the novel *City of Broken Promises* by Austin Coates, which has played as a musical in the U.S. The families of foreign traders used to live here in the eighteenth and nineteenth centuries while the men went seasonally to Guangzhou to trade.

Travel Agencies in Macao can arrange a taxi and air-conditioned bus ride from Macao to Guangzhou and points in between. They can also arrange day trips for foreigners to the birthplace of Dr. Sun Yat-sen. See Zhongshan County in DESTINATIONS for details.

BORDER FORMALITIES ANYWHERE IN CHINA. Have ready for inspection your passport, a completed Baggage Declaration Form, Health Declaration and Entry/Exit forms.

Immigration. In most cases, you will have to line up to have your passport stamped by immigration officials. If the whole group has one group visa, then that will be stamped and officials will take a quick look at each passport. In some cases, you may be taken into a comfortable waiting room where you can make your own tea while you wait for immigration authorities.

Customs Regulations. These were usually very leniently enforced for foreigners (bags rarely opened), lenient for Overseas Chinese (bags sometimes opened), and strict for Compatriots when we went to press. This is because many Hong Kong Chinese smuggle in goods for resale. It depends on the mood of the inspector. You have to register cameras, tape recorders, watches, and other similar items.

General Rules

1. On entering or leaving China, passengers (diplomatic personnel excepted) should fill out a "Baggage Declaration" and submit all their baggage and articles for Customs inspection. Mention any unaccompanied baggage.
2. Articles carried on behalf of others should be declared to the Customs.
3. *The importation of the following articles is prohibited:*
   Renminbi (Chinese currency) except for Foreign Exchange Certificates (F.E.C.s);
   Manuscripts, printed matter, films, photographs, gramophone records, cinematographic films, loaded recording tapes and videotapes, etc., detrimental to Chinese political, economic, cultural and moral interests;
   Radio transmitter-receivers and principal parts;
   Poisonous drugs, habit-forming drugs, opium, morphia, heroin, etc.;
   Unsanitary foodstuffs and germ-carrying foodstuffs from infected area;
   Animals, plants, and products thereof with disease germs and insects;
   Arms, ammunition, and explosives of all kinds.
4. *The exportation of the following articles is prohibited:*

Arms, ammunition, and explosives of all kinds;

Radio transmitter-receivers and principal parts;

Renminbi and securities, etc. in Renminbi except for F.E.C.s;

Foreign currencies, bill and securities in foreign currencies (with the exception of those allowed to be taken out);

Manuscripts, printed matter, films, photographs, gramophone records, cinematographic films, loaded recording tapes and videotapes, etc., which contain state secrets or otherwise prohibited export;

Valuable cultural relics and rare books relating to Chinese revolution, history, culture and art;

Rare animals, rare plants and their seeds;

Precious metals and articles made thereof, jewelry, diamonds and ornaments made thereof (with the exception of those within the quantity allowed to be taken out by outgoing passengers);

Other articles the exportation of which is prohibited by state regulations.

Passenger on a Short Stay

1. Baggage and articles carried by incoming or outgoing passengers, for a short stay in China or abroad not exceeding six months, shall be released duty free, provided they are required for personal use on the trip and during their sojourn and are in reasonable quantities.

However, wristwatches, cameras, radio sets and other articles for personal use carried by incoming or outgoing passengers shall be registered with the Customs as required, and must be taken out of or brought back to China by them at the time of exit or entry.

Movie cameras are limited to 8 mm ones. Movie film not exceeding 3,000 ft., ordinary film not exceeding 6 dozen rolls will be allowed.

2. The following articles carried by incoming passengers for a short stay shall be released duty free at the time of entry:

Foodstuff not exceeding 25 kilograms in weight per person,

Wine 4 bottles (not exceeding 750 grams in weight per bottle) per adult,

Cigarettes, 600 pieces per adult.

3. Cultural relics (ascertained by the authorities in charge of cultural relics as permissible for export), old work of handicraft art, jewelry, diamonds, ornaments made of gold and silver, jade articles and ivory carvings bought by incoming passengers on a short stay in China, in reasonable quantities for personal use with Renminbi, which they obtained by exchanging the foreign currencies they originally brought with them, may be taken out of China, if they do not exceed a total value of RMB¥ 10,000 and are verified by the Customs against the receipts for their sale issued by the Friendship Store or cultural relic shops and the Bank's foreign exchange certificates (or exchange memos).

4. Items purchased in China with F.E.C.s may be taken or mailed out of

the country after presenting receipts for Customs inspection. This can be arranged through the local Friendship Store or a Customs office.

Once a year, Overseas Chinese (with foreign passports) are able to take in as gifts to relatives *duty-free* one sewing machine (treadle is best), one bicycle (black preferred), an electric fan, thirty yards of cotton cloth, one watch, and one radio in addition to what everyone else can take in. Check with the Chinese stores in Hong Kong (Yue Hwa, China Products) for the latest regulations. The radio will be taxed if it has a built-in tape recorder. The duty-free privilege seems to be allowed only on the first trip to China of the calendar year, and includes three overcoats, twenty pieces of underwear, etc.

If anyone has to pay *duty,* it's 20 percent on a calculator, 200 percent on a watch, 50 percent on a tape recorder or recorder-radio combination, and 50 percent on a television set. The Chinese officials do the estimating based on the retail price in China. For example, the tax on a 12- to 15-inch color television is ¥450. You can also leave the item at the border to be picked up on the way out. Keep your Baggage Declaration Form and receipts for all later foreign exchange transactions. You will need both when you leave China; otherwise, you will not be able to change leftover Chinese currency. You are not allowed to take Chinese currency out of the country.

Payment of duty now is requested even on gifts of calculators, tape recorders, and other similar items for Chinese institutions, unless you make arrangements beforehand. This means asking the recipient institution several months in advance to do the necessary paperwork. The institution should be informed of the port of entry, date, and make and model number of the gift.

If the release form is not waiting for you at the border, a note can be made on your Baggage Declaration Form and you can take the gift in without paying tax. But you must take it out again or pay the duty, unless the paperwork is done while you are in China. The gift can also be left at the border to be picked up later by the institute or yourself as you leave.

Note: Although these regulations sound formidable, the enforcement is not. But like other places in the world, you do take a chance if you ignore them. The charge is smuggling.

Money-changing. There are usually facilities to change money into Chinese Foreign Exchange Certificates at border points. Change only what you think you need for three or four days at a time. It may be difficult to change *large* quantities of yuan back into foreign currency when you leave. Small quantities can be changed easily.

The F.E.C.s must be used in Friendship Stores, hotels, taxis, some restaurants—that are exclusive to foreign and Overseas Chinese visitors. They were introduced to control the black marketing of foreign exchange. Chinese citizens are not allowed to use them, but some street vendors and shopkeepers will accept anything, even Hong Kong dollars. However, there are periodic crackdowns. Some local Chinese value F.E.C.s so they can buy otherwise hard-to-get items like bicycles and TVs at Friendship Stores. Others are afraid to touch them. You may get change in local currency, which you can spend in places not exclusive to foreign and Overseas Chinese visitors.

Note: There are now duty-free stores on some boats to China and in the departure lounges of some international airports.

GETTING FROM YOUR ARRIVAL POINT TO YOUR HOTEL. Remember that there are no taxis waiting at airports and train stations except in cities like Shanghai (where drivers are incredibly aggressive), Guangzhou, and Beijing. There is usually an airport bus to the CAAC office in town.

If you neglected to make arrangements for transportation and you don't want to take the bus, telephone for a taxi. See "Arrivals" in the USEFUL PHRASES. A taxi might take forty minutes from the closest taxi station, and you will be charged from that point.

If you neglected to make hotel reservations, telephone a hotel (in Chinese), take the chance and go to one directly, or phone C.I.T.S. or C.T.S. and ask what you should do. See phone numbers in Chapters 16 or 18.

If you cannot find a telephone number, try to find the telephone number of anyone you can think of who speaks English, e.g., a foreign airline, a foreign bank, or an embassy, and ask them if they have the telephone number. Phone books in English are not readily available except in bookstores.

Chinese relatives can meet you outside the train station or at some downtown point if you are arriving by air. Do not expect them to meet you at the airport with a taxi. It could cost them a month's salary if you fail to show up.

ADJUST YOUR WATCH TO THE LOCAL TIME. All China is in the same time zone. You will not have to do this again until you leave.

LEAVING CHINA. Be prepared to pay the ¥10 airport tax on all international flights, including those to Hong Kong. Have your passport ready. Be sure your visa has not expired or you will be detained. You can change your money before or after Customs clearance if you have your foreign exchange receipts. Turn in your Baggage Declaration Form. If it is lost, you may be asked to fill out another even if you don't look like a smuggler. You may also be asked about jewelry, antiques, foreign currency, and the items on your form. I have even been asked about underground literature.

5

HOTELS

GENERALLY SPEAKING, in Beijing, Shanghai, Guangzhou, Xi'an, and Guilin you may have no choice of hotel room until 1983. Feel lucky if you have a bed. Some visitors in the past year were put in hotels 40 kilometers outside the city during the peak September to November and April to June seasons. Other cities usually have a surplus.

If you're unhappy with your room, consult your group leader or guide. Ask the receptionist for another. There might be one. It depends on the city.

Foreign visitors and Overseas Chinese on package tours with C.I.T.S. usually are accommodated in the best available rooms in the best tourist hotels particularly if the foreign travel agency and the foreign guide have a good relationship with influential local Chinese authorities. It also depends of course if and where rooms are available, and if the foreign travel agency is trying to skimp. Foreign Friends and Overseas Chinese from Europe and America seem to have priority.

Second choice for the best rooms seems to go to individual travelers who have booked and paid the higher rates in advance with a foreign agency (See chapter 16), or again, have good relationships with influential local authorities.

Individual Foreign Friends or Overseas Chinese travelers who have no connections get whatever is left, which still may be good.

In 1978, China started building at least one new hotel or hotel extension in every city. In some places, hotels were started with foreign help. The Chinese-built hotels are adequate; the foreign-assisted hotels are a little more luxurious, the closest to international luxury class at press time being the Nanhu and Dongfang hotels in Guangzhou, and the Beijing in Beijing. Some posh state guest houses may also be open to tour groups, but only Lindblad seems to be able to guarantee the Diao Yu Tai (Angler's Inn) in Beijing.

If you go to China in the next year or two on a general interest tour, your chances are: almost 95 percent that you will have a *hotel room* built or renovated within the last two years; almost 90 percent that you will have *air conditioning* if the weather warrants it in the summer (if it doesn't work, ask for another room); about 90 percent that your hotel will have a *coffee shop/ bar* open in the evening until about 11 or 12. It won't be fancy but you can relax there; about 95 percent that you will have *same-day laundry service* if it is left at the service desk on your floor before 8 a.m.; about 50 percent that the *food* in the hotel will be excellent, 35 percent good and 15 percent mediocre but edible—if you don't count the "Western" breakfast.

The hotels of China up to the end of 1978 were entirely run by municipal service bureaus to provide not much more than a bed and bath. Many were subsidized. The managers of what I consider the worst hotel in China told C.I.T.S. then that they preferred Chinese guests because foreigners were too fussy. "Americans should learn from the Japanese not to complain." Bookings could not be made very much in advance. The Gang of Four's attitude was roughly, "If people are comfortable, they will become revisionists. So don't let them be comfortable."

Since 1978, C.I.T.S. has been trying to overcome this attitude. Hampered by a bureaucratic mentality still much too frightened to be innovative and too inexperienced to be daring, China has been trying to improve facilities for foreign visitors. She has been making some mistakes, but the changes are showing. See INTRODUCTION.

In 1979, C.I.T.S. started taking over the management of a few hotels and will be taking control of some newer hotel rooms as they are completed. By 1982, one of the major hurdles in providing good service should thus be largely overcome. C.I.T.S. is a lot more sensitive to the needs of visiting foreigners. The next big step is the training of hotel staff. This has already started. At press time hotels for foreign tourists had at least one attendant on every hotel floor and a receptionist and telephone operator who could speak a little English.

FACILITIES AND SERVICES. Every hotel for foreign tourists in cities

—has at least one *dining room,* frequently more; some have a choice of Chinese or Western food;

—has facilities for *changing money.* If it does not, the service desk will accept your traveler's checks and several hours later have the currency ready for you. (Better do it here. The Bank of China is slower.)

—has *post office facilities.* Be sure you use the glue pot on your stamps. Many are not the licking variety. If there is no post office, the service desk can direct you to a nearby one or sell you stamps. It can also take cables;

—has a *retail store* always with souvenirs, but frequently with soap, toothpaste, fresh fruit, stationery, maps, books, toilet paper, postcards, and cigarettes;

—has a *service desk* in the lobby where you should be able to book tours, buy theater tickets, make restaurant reservations, and in some cases book plane and train tickets. It can book you a *taxi* and *long distance calls;*

—has attendants on every floor who clean your room and provide *hot water in thermoses* and *drinking water* in flasks daily. Upon request, they can usually provide cold beer, ice, soft drinks, and cigarettes. In some hotels, you can get adapters (for electric razors), radios, and portable electric heaters, and can have photographs developed and excess luggage stored. If attendants do not provide clean towels every day, ask them to do so. If the bathroom floor is grubby, ask them to clean it again. See USEFUL PHRASES. How else are they to learn? They have fixed my shoes for free;

—has at least one *television set,* usually in a meeting room, and in many hotels one in each bedroom, some of these with closed-circuit programming in English or with English subtitles either with an extra optional ¥4-a-day charge or an arbitrary addition to the room rate;

—has *hot water* from faucets but not all the time, usually in the evening. The plumbing has improved in the last years but toilets still make noises and sometimes showers do not work. See USEFUL PHRASES. Luxury hotels have hot water all day. Many now have shower curtains, previously unknown;

—has *telephones* in individual rooms or at the service desk on each floor. You can call any point in most cities by dialing "0" and then your number once you get the dial tone. If it is not a dial phone, tell the operator what number you want. You might be able to get an attendant to help. There is no charge for local calls. To get other rooms, in most hotels, just dial the room number.

The Chinese do not have private phones. There are telephones in every neighborhood, factory, and office where messages can be left with much assurance that they will be delivered to your friends. I suggest you leave a message to have your friend phone you. In a pinch, the operator might be able to find you a phone number if you give her an address. Needless to say, you'd better get some Chinese-speaking person to help you if you can't handle the language.

To ask for an outside line, say *wài xiàn* (why she-an).

To ask for the service desk where there just might be someone who speaks English, say *fú wù tái* (foo woo tie).

You can phone abroad from the main cities usually from your hotel and even from your room. You have to book the call at the service desk. If the attendant seems reluctant to help or says, "You'll have to wait," it might be because of his lack of English. He will give you a long-distance booking form. You can offer to speak to the overseas operator yourself. That operator should speak English. Sometimes an overseas call has taken ten minutes, sometimes an hour to complete. The reception is usually good. There is a service charge for overseas calls, completed or not. Long-distance credit cards are accepted if you check first with the operator when you book the call. There is no service charge for collect calls.

Don't forget the time difference. New York City is thirteen hours behind China, give or take an hour depending on standard and daylight savings time. Thus 8 p.m. China time is 7 a.m. New York or Toronto standard time, 12 noon Greenwich Mean Time, or 4 a.m. San Francisco time.

Some hotels have:

—a *barbershop, hairdresser,* and *masseur.* The massage that comes with a shampoo will have your scalp tingling for days. Chinese massages are vigorous, heavenly when stopped;

—*elevators* if they are over three stories; usually they are turned off around midnight;

—*great views* from their roofs. Guests can usually go up there. Hotels are frequently the highest buildings in a city;

—*sports facilities,* although swimming pools are rare. Badminton and billiards are common;

—*movies* from time to time;

—*attendants* who ignore guests, are reluctant to carry luggage, answer bells, and give any type of service. They may also barge into a room after a cursory knock. In some places there are trolleys you can borrow for luggage. But do complain about these attendants. The Chinese are trying to enter the world of international tourism. It would help if you complained to your guide and wrote in the comments and suggestions book. Managers do read this book;

—*clinics* with doctors who can fix you up with medicines for a cold or diarrhea for less than US$2.00. Some hotels will refer you to the closest hospital.

Some hotels are *fire traps,* with all but one stairway exit blocked or locked. As you should anywhere in the world, check the various exits;

—*charge* extra for air conditioning and heat;

—have *very dim reading lamps;*

—have *mosquito nets.* Shake out mosquitos before using and tuck under the mattress leaving no space for bugs to enter;

—have *nightclubs* and *discos* but don't expect the latest Western music;

—have *different room-key systems* and some rooms are not locked at all. While thefts in hotel rooms are rare, it is best to keep small valuables locked in your suitcase to avoid temptation. As yet, safe-deposit boxes are rare;

—have 2-inch *cockroaches* that look awful but do not bite people;

—have *special regional dishes* for about ¥20 for groups;

—have *rooms booked by foreign corporations* for months which are sublet when not in use;

—have rooms which can be booked in advance. See chapter 16;

—will deliver your mail to you, but some will have it in a pile at the reception desk. So look for it, if you're expecting.

For information on individual hotels, see each city under DESTINATIONS. For names of some hotels in Chinese, see DIRECTORY.

6

FOOD

See also USEFUL PHRASES and DESTINATIONS. For the names of some restaurants in Chinese and English, see DIRECTORY.

REGIONAL VARIATIONS. Chinese food has a lot of variety and there are wide regional variations. It is usually chopped up in bite-size pieces; knives are unnecessary. It is served in platters from which diners take what they want, and it is eaten with two sticks, manipulated as if they were an extension of fingers.

The Chinese food that visitors are served is usually very good. There are several basic *regional groupings:*

Southern (Cantonese): quickly cooked in a little oil, ideally peanut; crisp vegetables; somewhat sweet; starches in the sauces. Many dishes steamed to preserve natural flavors. Really exotic banquet dishes are dog, civet cat, monkey, and snake. Dim Sum.

Northern (Beijing): light; few sauces; roasts; lots of garlic, leeks, and scallions; flour-made buns, rolls, and meat dumplings, baked, steamed, fried, or boiled in soup. Salty. Most famous dish: Peking duck.

Western (Szechuan-Sichuan): some dishes highly spiced, peppery hot, and oily. Formal banquet cooking more bland.

Central (Shanghai, Yangzhou): longer cooking in sesame oil, neither sweet nor salty. Very ornamental.

East Coast (Fujian): lots of seafood and light soups, suckling pig, and nonfat spring rolls.

Mongolian: mostly mutton. Hot pot is cooked at the table in water. Also famous for barbecues.

THINGS TO REMEMBER ABOUT CHINESE FOOD

1. You can eat quite well for less than one yuan a meal if you're willing to try food stalls and restaurants for the masses. You can also pay about ¥6 for a good hotel meal and ¥10 for a good restaurant meal. Banquets can run from ¥20 to ¥200 per person.

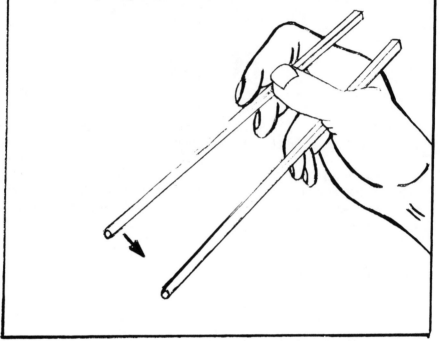

HOW TO USE CHOPSTICKS

The bottom stick is held firmly by the base of the thumb and the knuckle of the ring finger. The top stick is the ONLY one that is moved and is held by the thumb and the index and middle fingers. The tip of the top stick should be brought toward the tip of the bottom one. Keep the tips even.

2. If you want to eat cheaply, just don't expect the highest standards of cleanliness and service. **Bun and noodle shops** are great for speed (if the line-up isn't too long; they usually push foreigners to the head of the line). If you're finicky, just remember the soup usually sterilizes the utensils but you can also scald them with tea, the way the natives do. Usually there is a spittoon for discarding the tea. A knowledge of Chinese isn't necessary because you can point. See USEFUL PHRASES if you think they are asking you about grain ration coupons. As in many busy restaurants, it is customary to share tables with other customers even at the Dongfang Hotel.

At the **restaurants for the masses** it is best to take a Chinese friend who can help you order. You can also use the USEFUL PHRASES. If you want to keep the prices down, don't eat in a private dining room. Tell them you want to pay so much and no more. Payment is made when you order.

Some finicky eaters take their own chopsticks and spoons to places like this, but as far as I can see the dishes are scalded, and if the food is freshly cooked there should be no problems.

3. Every hotel has an à la carte menu and a **fixed menu.** You don't usually get to see the fixed menu. It is what they serve tour groups. Individuals can order this too. Say *fen fa,* and if they don't understand you, show them 份饭 .

In one hotel, lunch for one, *fen fa,* was (a) steamed meatballs, (b) curry chicken, (c) spicy hot beef, (d) greens and mushrooms, (e) two steamed buns with sweetened black bean filling, (f) egg custard cubes and tomatoes, (g) clear soup with bits of meat and vegetable, (h) white rice and (i) fresh watermelon. Of this I could only eat one third. Cost was ¥6.

While this was the most luxurious of the *fen fa* meals I had, most of the others were varied and excellent.

4. It is always best to **order meals ahead of time** by telephone in the more expensive restaurants. The cheaper ones won't take reservations. Ask the service desk at your hotel to do this for you, telling them how much you want to pay. Elaborate banquet dishes should be ordered at least twenty-four hours ahead of time—and there will probably be a hefty charge if you cancel. For banquets also, it is customary to let the chef decide the menu. If you have favorites, tell him, but he knows what is in season and usually does his best.

Even at relatively ordinary restaurants, it may take two hours before you get food after ordering. If you make a banquet reservation, do be punctual. The food is usually cooked and ready for you at the set time.

5. **If you order on the spot,** calculate one dish for each person, then add rice or buns, and one more dish. For two people, order three dishes plus rice. This will give you abundance. If you find you are getting too much, order less next time.

6. Every restaurant has its specialties—dishes the chefs are especially good at. So ask about these. They will probably be more expensive.

7. Aim for local dishes—fresh seafoods if you're near an ocean. Seafood reaches Beijing frozen. Among the best meals I've had in China were at a commune where the vegetables came right from plant to *wok.* Some hotels now advertise special regional dishes for groups for about ¥20 a head.

8. It is best to eat in a large group so there will be a greater variety of dishes. When ordering for many people choose one poultry, one pork, one beef, one fish, and one vegetable dish, and one soup. If you need more courses, start the rounds again. If you've already chosen chicken, then choose duck or goose. Vary the tastes and textures: sweet, pepper-hot, salty, steamed, deep-fried, stir-fried, poached or boiled, roasted, baked in mud—the choice is endless.

9. If you are not feeling well, order rice congee, which is rice cooked to a gruel consistency and served with a bit of flavoring (salted egg, fermented bean curd). Congee is easy on the stomach. Avoid fried dishes and spices. Order a boiled egg.

10. Don't feel that every meal should be a banquet. The danger in China is overeating.

11. Tour-group members should not expect special diets. Salt-free and diabetic diets are impossible. You might be able to swing it if you get to know the cooks. Vegetarians usually manage if they don't mind meat sauces on their vegetables. There are vegetarian restaurants. There are Moslem restaurants, but these are difficult in a non-Moslem tour group.

12. Don't look for chop suey or chow mein with crispy noodles, or fortune cookies—those are American dishes. There are fried noodles in China, but they are not the same as in the U.S.

13. For desserts, Foreign Friends will be offered Western-style sweet pastries and fresh or canned fruits. If you're in Guangdong in May or June, ask for fresh lichees—or buy them on the street. Look for pomelo, especially in Guilin in the fall. It's a sweet "grapefruit" with a thick rind. China also has ice cream, a form of ice cream with black beans, and deep-fried crystallized apples and bananas.

14. In August 1979 China stopped charging Foreign Friends extra for most drinks with prepaid meals. These include beer, Chinese soft drinks, and tea. Canned fruit juice is expensive and exempted. Coca-Cola is usually extra and paid for in foreign currency. Buy it at the hotel store, and ask attendant for ice and glass. Overseas Chinese pay extra for drinks.

15. Tea drinking is an art in China. Some springs are famous for their tea-making qualities. If you get to Hangzhou, try Lung Ching tea there.

A favorite tea in hot weather is *po li. Keemun* is good in the wintertime and when you've had greasy foods. *Lu an* should help you sleep. *Oolong* is the most common tea in south China, while most foreigners like *jasmine*, the sweet-scented tea with bits of jasmine flower petals in it. Jasmine is said to heat the blood and should be drunk with *po li* to balance it.

Everyone has his list of most famous green teas—*lung ching* (dragon well), *yun wu* (mist of the clouds), *mao hong* (red straw), and *bi lu chuen* (green spring).

If you have an upset stomach or cankers in the mouth try *hung pean* (chrysanthemum tea). It comes already sweetened with sugar in one-cup packages at the Friendship Store. In each city you will probably be served a locally grown tea.

16. The best **liquors** are: *Mao tai,* made from sorghum and wheat yeast and aged five or six years in Guizhou province, southwest China; very potent; usually served in tiny goblets; *Fenjiu,* mellow and delicate flavor from Shanxi province; *Wuliangye,* five-grain spirit from Yibin County, southern Sichuan; fragrant and invigorating flavor.

The best **wines** are: *Yantai red wine* from Shandong, *China red wine* from Beijing, *Shaoxing rice wine* from Zhejiang, and *Longyan rice wine* from Fujian.

Qingdao **beer** is the best. It is made from barley, spring water, and hops. *Laoshan* is the most famous **mineral water.**

17. The secret of eating a Chinese meal is finding out first how many courses you will be getting. If there are twelve courses, take no more than

one twelfth of what you would usually eat in a meal from each plate; otherwise, you will be too full to eat any of the later dishes. Also take your time. You can't rush through a big meal. Some famous banquets have taken days.

18. Do not worry about "Chinese restaurant syndrome"—its symptoms are an increased pulse and a tight feeling around the sinuses. This "syndrome" is a result of the large amount of monosodium glutamate put in Chinese food in America. Cooks in China use a little, but not so much.

19. Prepaid group tours do not need to order. They usually find their food already selected when they arrive.

20. Food is usually served family-style, each course in one dish from which each diner helps himself. The beautiful thing about a Chinese meal is the variety. If you don't like one thing, there is always something else you might like. If you do have special food preferences, let your responsible person know. You might even want to discuss with him or her the elaborateness of the food when meat and rice for the common man is rationed, if indeed this bothers you.

21. To start the eating, Chinese hosts will put food on the plates of the people around them. You can do this too if you want or declare a moratorium on such courtesies and have everybody dig in. Soup could come at the beginning or the end of the meal.

22. The variety of *dim sum* (little fried or steamed meat pastries) in China is limited except in some highly specialized restaurants. Hong Kong has more.

23. In ordering a restaurant meal, have a native do it. He might be able to get cheaper prices.

24. If you are invited by nonofficial Chinese friends, don't be surprised if they ask you to make the reservation. Most of the top restaurants are reserved for officials and foreigners. Sound unfair? Ask your responsible person about it. At one time it could be because gourmet food was bourgeois. Now it's probably because foreigners bring foreign exchange.

25. If you invite average Chinese people to dinner, be sensitive to the fact that a meal in an expensive restaurant is a real treat. Normally they cannot afford it. Since they get little meat, do order more for them. Do encourage them to take the leftovers home. They may be too polite to ask. I once invited a taxi driver to lunch. He ordered five dishes to my one plus three bowls of rice. The dishes were all meat. If the meal is paid in Foreign Exchange Certificates, Chinese guests do not have to pay grain ration coupons.

26. Restaurants in badly managed hotels expect their guests to get up and get their own drinks.

27. To eat:

—*mantou,* the plain steamed roll, either take bites off while holding with chopsticks or fingers, or break apart and stuff pieces with bits of meat. You can also dip it in the sauces. *Jiao zi* are the small ravioli-like pastries in soup; *bao zi* are steamed dumplings and may have beans, or meat and vegetables inside. The names get confusing;

—*white rice,* which is served in bowls, put the bowl up to your mouth and shove the rice in with chopsticks. More genteel people might want to pick up chunks with chopsticks;

—*hundred-year-old eggs,* you usually have to either acquire a taste or close your eyes and think of something else; they are best eaten with pickles;

—*tiny shrimps with shells left on,* take a bite of half, then with your teeth and chopsticks, squeeze out the meat. Cooking shrimps with their shells keeps most of the flavor in;

—*two- and three-foot-long noodles,* lean over your bowl and pick up a few with chopsticks. Put the noodles in your mouth and start slurping and chewing. You can bite off a piece or use your chopsticks to put more into your mouth. The Chinese like long noodles because they symbolize long life;

—*ice cream,* ask for a spoon.

28. To avoid an upset stomach and intestinal parasites, do not drink water out of a faucet, avoid watermelon and any other fruit with lots of ground water, and don't eat anything that isn't cooked. Animal and human manure are used as fertilizer.

29. To best enjoy a meal, never ask what a particular morsel is.

30. Coca-Cola is bottled in Beijing; cans from the U.S. Some Chinese think it tastes like medicine and don't like it. The Pepsi Cola plant in Shenzhen is for export only. Some foreign beers are increasingly available.

31. Among the eating guides is Harry Rolnick's *Eating Out in China,* which lists 97 major restaurants in Beijing, Shanghai, Guangzhou, Hangzhou, and Suzhou in English and Chinese. It lists off-the-tourist track eating places, and, for example, restaurants in Suzhou that use 1,500-year-old recipes. See BIBLIOGRAPHY.

32. Foreign tour groups are usually given Western breakfasts, which I personally cannot stomach because the fried eggs are so greasy. You also usually get toast, coffee, and fruit or canned juice.

Foreign tour groups can opt for Chinese breakfasts if enough people in the group want them. The Chinese breakfasts differ regionally: *dim sum* or rice congee with peanuts, pickles, salted or hundred-year-old eggs. In the north, you could get lots of different buns or "oil sticks" like foot-long doughnuts, deep-fried and delicious but hard to digest. You dip these in soy milk. In Shanghai you might get gelatinous rice balls with sugar inside, or baked buns with sweet bean paste inside.

33. Western.food is available, but I have never found it as good as the Chinese. Bread is cut thick and it is good. Sometimes "Western" food is Chinese food with bread instead of rice. Beijing has a Western-style bakery.

You can get an edible Western meal at the International Club in Beijing, and at the Red House Cafe or the De Da Restaurant near the Peace Hotel in Shanghai. Kissling in Tianjin and Beidaihe are good too.

There is a foreign-food restaurant in the Dongfang Hotel in Guangzhou where diners pay in foreign exchange.

Some restaurants have rooms reserved for foreigners that are not overly expensive. Do not be frightened by the crowds in the other sections. You really might get something to eat after all.

Please be aware that some wild animals used by the Chinese as food are or may soon be on the Endangered Species list. This includes pangolin.

✖7✖

GETTING AROUND

If you have someone taking care of all your travel needs, read this only for reference. The following is how things were at press time. Since then, the Chinese have probably made even more improvements.

Note: There is always a cancellation fee when you make changes in travel arranges. *Note also:* Always carry a wad of toilet tissue.

CHINA INTERNATIONAL TRAVEL SERVICE (C.I.T.S.), in Chinese Luxingshe (Loo-shing-sheh), is the main government organization making travel arrangements for foreigners in China. The other organization is the China Youth Travel Service of the China Youth Federation. It is not as large as C.I.T.S. and is supposed to handle travel for young people though this has not always been the case. It has the same basic services as C.I.T.S. Both can usually meet you at airports, arrange taxis, book trains and plane tickets, reserve hotel rooms, arrange sightseeing, and obtain travel permits. See chapter 2 for sample fees.

If it has available guides, it can also see you off. In Guangzhou during one trade fair, I found it very reluctant to book plane tickets. "You can do it faster yourself," the guides said.

C.I.T.S. was founded in 1954. In 1964 it came under the administration of the Travel and Tourism Agency, which is directly under the State Council. From 1967 to 1969, some branches were closed due to the Cultural Revolution. In 1978 the Travel and Tourism Agency became the General Administrative Bureau of Travel and Tourism in China. In 1981, the State Council appointed C.I.T.S. to also study, coordinate, and supervise the development of tourism in China. Its provincial branches are allowed to issue visas and organize tours also, but within the province. It has branches in Hong Kong, Paris, Tokyo, and the U.S., and almost every place where there is a tourist attraction in China. Inquirers are also referred to Chinese missions abroad, which are not always current on the travel situation in China. It is usually dependable and is essential for newcomers, especially those who do not speak Chinese. One does get the impression sometimes that the work of C.I.T.S. national office is sloppy. Two days after the deadline, I received a letter telling me to send money to the Bank of China. One travel agent told me she did not receive confirmation on a group tour until the day it was supposed to leave.

The two big mistakes in my own schedule were (1) a miscalculation of the time my plane would land and the time the connecting train would leave, thus adding the difference in taxi fare to prepaid charges; (2) the failure of someone to note that CAAC changed its schedule. This error meant an extra day's expenses. Some tourists had to cut short their stays in Beijing because of bad coordination on tickets or hotel rooms. These are not necessarily C.I.T.S.'s fault.

In all fairness, I must say that I am amazed that 95 percent of the China travelers I have met say their arrangements went very smoothly. This is probably due to the guides and the organizing tour agency. And I expect that by the time you read this, some of these hitches will be ironed out.

C.I.T.S. GUIDES. The people directly responsible for taking foreign visitors around are called interpreters in Chinese. Since they function also as guides, they are referred to here as such. Most are graduates of universities or foreign-language institutes, with three or four years of foreign-language training at this level. Some are university students gaining experience.

Ideally, guide training is on the job, usually learned by accompanying an experienced guide for several months. But I have had a guide who barely spoke English, had no training, and only one week's experience. The shortage is acute, but the situation should improve with time. Guides do spend one hour a day in language study if they can.

In Guangzhou the starting salary for a guide was about ¥30 a month but single guides could live in the C.I.T.S. hostel for 1 percent of that. There were reports late in 1979 that some C.I.T.S. branches were experimenting with bonuses for guides if foreign visitors spent money on extra banquets and on antiques and other shopping. Guides, of course, were steering their charges in these directions. Visitors intent more on seeing China rather than on shopping or eating should do some counter-steering.

Most guides I have met have been extremely conscientious. I have only met one who was not. One told me that if a guide failed to get a tour group to a plane on time, it was a very serious offense. Since CAAC gives no refunds for "no shows," the C.I.T.S. branch has to replace the tickets.

Please be patient when a guide is speaking English. If it is painful to listen to, keep saying to yourself, "This is better than nothing." One of the most common translation errors is a confusion over numbers. The Chinese think in terms of ten-thousands. Ask them to write down big figures for you. Speak slowly. Phrase what you want to be translated simply, one sentence at a time. Also remember that guides are not scholars. Their knowledge of traditional Chinese culture is frequently limited to the few books they read. Knowledge of the old culture was strongly discouraged during the Cultural Revolution, when many of these guides were students.

For most visitors, the guides who travel with you will be the only Chinese you will get to know. Guides are not usually allowed to eat with you; they do, after all, need to rest. When they are shepherding you around, many usually stay in your hotel. So in case of emergency, ask where they can be reached at mealtimes and at night.

For more information on C.I.T.S. see also chapters 1 and 2.

CHINA TRAVEL SERVICE (C.T.S.) is primarily for Chinese travelers, local and overseas. See also chapter 1, "As a Traveler of Chinese Ancestry." C.T.S. can arrange permission and transportation to travel to one's ancestral village. It can organize tours around the country and hotel reservations. It can help get medical treatment for Overseas Chinese in China and try to locate relatives. Just remember, it has few English-speaking guides, and Overseas Chinese hotels are usually cheaper and less classy than those for Foreign Friends. Groups under C.I.T.S. or C.T.S. can be mixed Overseas Chinese and Foreign Friends. Foreign Friends can stay in Overseas Chinese hotels and vice versa.

C.I.T.S. guides frequently do not know anything about travel for Overseas Chinese in China. So do not let them argue you out of any information here in this book. Go directly yourself to C.T.S. and tell them your needs. Ask C.T.S. your relevant questions, not C.I.T.S., and vice versa.

It might take C.T.S. several days to arrange permission for you to visit your relatives or ancestral village. So start making an application for permission as soon as you possibly can after arrival in China. The delay is because of the permission needed to stay overnight in any city not stamped on your passport unless it is within 100 km. of a major city. Some Overseas Chinese have needed permission for a day trip, but some have not. If you are short of time, inquire about going by taxi for a day if it is not too far.

C.T.S. tours from Guangzhou may only be once or twice a month. It depends on the demand. The tours go to places like Seven Star Crag (see "Conghua" in DESTINATIONS), Guilin, around Guangdong, or around the whole country. A list of tours is posted on the ground floor in the building to the right as you leave the Overseas Chinese Mansion in Guangzhou—the third door over. C.T.S. can also handle arrangements for Chinese citizens leaving China for abroad. Keep in mind that if C.T.S. is your host in China, if C.T.S. has arranged for you to take the train into China or whatever, then you can get the cheaper hotel prices (assuming you look Chinese). Keep the tag they give you throughout your trip and try to use it when arguing with room clerks.

Among agencies set up to help Overseas Chinese and Compatriot travel are the Guangdong Travel Service and the Fujian Travel Service.

TO GET PERMISSION TO TRAVEL IN CHINA to places not marked on your visa, check first with C.I.T.S. or C.T.S. The question here is who needs permission to travel where in China. Certainly business people invited to a trade fair in Guangzhou need permission to visit other cities. Overseas Chinese with Guangzhou on their visas may need permission to visit their ancestral villages. However, if an Overseas Chinese books an organized tour from Guangzhou, chances are the permit is included. And if you have Beijing on your visa and need to spend the night in Guangzhou on the way out to Hong Kong, you may not need a permit.

When in doubt, ask! Regulations change frequently. Sometimes C.I.T.S. doesn't have the staff to handle all the requests and will tell you to do it yourself. You will need time (two or three working days) and patience. Take your passport and go to the Foreign Affairs Section of the Public Security Bureau and make the application yourself. See USEFUL PHRASES if no one speaks English there at the time. Just in case, I would take along my invitation to the trade fair or whatever documents I had.

FLYING. All reservations, no matter what airline, must be reconfirmed or you risk being bumped off. You cannot reconfirm with CAAC by telephone. The ticket has to be stamped. Your host organization can help you for a small service fee. Even with reconfirmation, some passengers have had their reservations cancelled by CAAC, so get to the airport early—two hours ahead on an international flight.

CAAC, also known as the China National Aviation Corporation, the Civil Aviation Administration of China, or the General Administration of Civil Aviation of China, is the only airline operating domestically in the country. Chinese pilots are carefully trained. Before they can fly a 707 or 747, they must have 20 years experience. CAAC also flies other planes and hopes to expand its fleet, replacing its old planes. There is talk of regional airlines.

Domestic Flights

—Tickets can be booked directly at CAAC offices in many cities in China, Hong Kong, and New York, or through its agents around the world. There may be a service charge. While reservations should be made earlier, you are asked to pay for the tickets 24 hours before scheduled departure time. Seats are allocated for sale only in the city where the flight originates so cables have to be sent to book onward reservations. In China, some clerks don't seem to care about selling seats anywhere else. Some will tell you to book after you get there. If you are told the flight is fully booked, go back another day to try again. There may also be cancellations as well as reshuffling. If you're desperate, you can also go to the airport at flight time and try there. Give them your sob story. Offer to pay first class. Get on the waiting list. Let's hope there are computerized reservations by the time you get there.

—Most flights have only one class, economy. Very few routes have first.

—Open-dated domestic tickets are valid for ninety days; fixed-date tickets are good only for the date and flight on the ticket. If you cancel the ticket prior to two hours before scheduled departure time, you are charged ¥4 cancellation fee. If you apply within two hours of flight time, you are charged 20 percent of the fare. If you fail to cancel before flight time, *there is no refund.*

—The 20-kilogram free baggage allowance for full or half adult fare passengers is *strictly enforced* except for those flying into China with larger allowances.

—No babies under ten days of age and no pregnant women past the thirty-fifth week of pregnancy are allowed to fly.

—An infant under two not occupying a separate seat and accompanied by an adult costs 10 percent of the adult fare. Children between two and twelve are charged 50 percent of the adult fare.

—On some flights there are stops for refueling and meals at the passenger's expense. Do ask the flight attendant to have your meal ready for you when you land. Most flights serve no meals. Some have just dried-out snacks.

—There is strict grounding of planes in questionable weather. "Due to matters concerning the requirement by CAAC to make overnight stops en route, passengers will be provided with free accommodation," says CAAC's list of regulations. CAAC has a very good safety record.

—Since most airports are small and traffic is light, check-in usually starts about half an hour before flight time and boarding about five minutes before. Flights usually leave on time.

—Payment for tickets is usually in cash—no credit cards or traveler's checks, not even in Hong Kong. Foreign businesses and embassies established in China can sometimes pay by check. Since most Chinese passengers are flying at government expense, their fares are half what foreigners pay. The fares are the same on international routes.

—On some routes, small propeller-driven planes are still in use. Sometimes in the older Russian planes a lot of fog starts coming out of the walls during ascent and descent. It is condensation only—no problem. These tiny planes also have little head and leg room for big foreigners.

—In late 1979, flight attendants were beginning to show signs of the training they have been receiving from foreign airlines like JAL. Previously, they did only what was absolutely necessary, frequently without a smile.

International Flights

On international flights, CAAC follows the same rules as other airlines regarding security checks and safety, etc.

Reservations will be canceled unless reconfirmed on flights wholly within Europe. Full refund on international tickets will be made if you cancel before check-in time. A 25% cancellation fee is charged for "no shows." Free baggage allowance is 30 kg. for first class, 20 kg. for economy except on China-U.S flights which allow for two pieces, each not exceeding 32 kg.

Airport tax (¥10) is charged on all departing international flights, including Hong Kong. Exceptions are diplomats, transit passengers, and children under 12. Passengers holding international tickets with confirmed space on the first connecting flight should get free meals and hotel accommodations provided by CAAC within 24 hours after their arrival at the connecting points.

Booking in the city of origin is usually immediate but it takes several days if you are reserving a flight out of Shanghai from Changsha for example. Don't expect CAAC to be like other airlines!

Foreign Airlines are restricted in China. Some cannot sell tickets, but they can book their own flights on open-dated CAAC tickets. Unlike CAAC, they can book you on a return flight immediately if space is available. Some can book or change your onward reservations for your post-China journey if the first leg is on their airline. They can reconfirm your international tickets by telephone without the confusion frequently found in a CAAC office—again, if you are flying with them.

TRAINS. The fare is about the same as a plane for "soft" class, and considerably less for "hard" class. Going by train is a good way to see the countryside and if you are not in a tour group, a good way to meet Chinese people.

Soft class berths are the height of bourgeois comfort; we had clean pink slipcovers with lace doilies, lace curtains, a 16" × 24" table with a lamp and potted plant, an overhead fan, and sleeping spaces with bedding for four—two upper and two lower. There is overhead storage space for large suitcases, but you have to rely on a strong man to get them up there and down. Train conductors are usually very helpful and friendly.

It is best to take a small overnight bag if you are sleeping on the train unless you want to do acrobatics or limit your leg room. Most group luggage is stored at one end of the car and may not be accessible.

Compartment doors can be closed for privacy; do not worry if you cannot lock them from the inside. The conductor always locks the door when you go to the dining room. The plug for the fan and a switch for the loudspeaker are under the table. Usually no air conditioning. Very hot in summer.

The toilets are filthy, but on coaches put on especially for foreign tourists, you can be quite sure of toilet paper, soap (in a common soap dish), and light hand towels. There is also a washroom with several sinks which is almost as dirty. Many visitors wait until they get to their hotels before washing. However, sometimes on arrival early in the morning, hotel rooms have not been vacated yet, and tourists are frequently taken sightseeing instead.

Dining-car food is quite good. Passengers usually give their order to a steward beforehand and are notified when the food is ready.

Hard class has six people in the same space as soft, three tiers, but no privacy. The Chinese, however, are very civilized, and even single women should have no problems sleeping here. If you are worried about your money and passport, use your purse for a pillow.

If you have a choice of compartment, aim for the middle of the train. It's less bumpy and noisy.

Beijing is now connected by train to every provincial and regional capital except Lhasa. Booking is sometimes a problem along the way because of incompetence.

INTER-CITY BUSES. There are now more comfortable, air-conditioned buses, especially on the routes from Hong Kong and Macao, but in other parts of the country as well. Check first because other buses are small, hard-seated, and usually very crowded. Still, they are a great way to meet people—but you have to be young in spirit, strong, and adventurous. You usually book ahead of time if you go from a main station and you want a seat. Frequently Overseas Chinese and foreigners are given priority on them, and are let on ahead of everyone else. If the seats are full, you squat or stand in the aisles. Not for big people.

INTER-CITY BOATS. Boats between Hong Kong and Chinese ports usually have comfortable but not luxurious cabins in deluxe classes (private baths). On the overnight, air-conditioned Hong Kong-Guangzhou ship, no announcements were in English and we had to fight for a table to eat.

On the Yangtze, the ferries do not have cabins with private baths, nor much privacy. Bathrooms are crude. The meal servings are better organized than the Hong Kong-Guangzhou ship. But do not avoid these; you have time on them to meet Chinese people, especially on the Yangtze.

Other ferries, however, are less comfortable, but very cheap. Each passenger has a sleeping space on a platform. The newer boats are less noisy and more spacious. Day boats are more crowded. On some you sit on a platform, and if you are lucky, you can lean up against a wall or post. On others you have seats. Boat rides are highly recommended only in hot weather when you can enjoy the scenery and the breezes (see Jiangonen).

LOCAL TRANSPORTATION.

Bicycle and Scooter Rickshaws. Some cities, especially smaller ones, have these. The big cities seem to be phasing out the bicycle rickshaws, and foreigners are not encouraged to ride them since they could be dangerous. Prices are fixed and paid in advance at the rickshaw stand. Bicycle rickshaws cost very little, but you can only go short distances.

Taxis. These can usually be obtained by telephoning a taxi stand or going to a hotel. If the hotel doesn't have a stand, the service desk should telephone for you. Taxi fares are usually calculated according to the odometer. There are no taxi meters except in some big cities, so make a note if you care. Pay after the trip. In some cities, you get receipts. One can usually get a taxi quickly but sometimes at meal hours it is impossible. I am told this has something to do with the fixed meal hour for drivers. It might be better to have your driver wait for you or to hire him by the day if you are going to use the car a lot. There are no self-drive car rentals. See chapter 2 under "For Those Who Want to Save Money." Ask about waiting times; it varies. See USEFUL

PHRASES. Usually the driver has an allowance for meals. You need not pay if you are near his home base but he might appreciate it (instead of a tip, but don't tell him that). At some restaurants, there may be no need to keep a taxi waiting. Ask when you arrive at the restaurant.

In Shanghai there are taxi stands in various neighborhoods, and some air-conditioned taxis. In most cities you should be able to rent a taxi for out-of-town trips.

Public Buses. These are usually very crowded, especially during the early-morning and late-afternoon rush hours, and all day Sunday. But they are cheap and may be your only means of transportation if you can't get a taxi. Try them if you are athletic or adventurous, or during an off-hour. Hotel personnel can tell you which bus to take, or you can take a map with you and point. Fellow passengers are usually friendly and helpful, but you have to ask.

The ticket taker is usually near the rear door. If it's too crowded to get near her, you can pass your fare to the person next to you and point in her direction. Do not be surprised if the bus person asks a native to get up and offer you his seat. It is Chinese courtesy, but do consider that many people have been working long hours. On the other hand, if you refuse, they may feel uncomfortable having an honored guest standing. Take your pick. Beware of pickpockets.

Subway. In Beijing the subway is now open for foreigners. Just do as you would in any city. Walk down the stairs, pay your money (cheap), and choose your platform. At press time there was only one line, so you only needed to decide which direction you wanted.

Bicycles. It is hard to rent a bicycle. Better borrow, or if you stay long enough, then buy, and sell when you leave. Bicycle tours are now being organized from Hong Kong and America.

Note: It is always best, no matter where and how you go, to have your destination written in Chinese. If it is not listed in DESTINATIONS, have someone do it. Don't forget your hotel so you can return.

8

LOCAL CUSTOMS

DOES "YES" MEAN "YES"? Well, usually. Cultural differences do create misunderstanding. For example, a memorandum of understanding in trade means there is reason to believe that negotiations can begin in earnest. It does not mean, as many foreigners have sadly discovered, that a contract has been signed. Also, if a Chinese nods and says "yes, yes," he could be just trying to please you. He may not understand a word you are saying. So be wary. Ask a question that needs a full sentence in reply. For the same reason, a Chinese might give you dates and spellings and swear they are right. But what he means is that it is the best information he has and if you press him, he will check—but if you don't, he won't bother.

Chinese people are very polite, the result of centuries of crowded living. They try not to hurt feelings. If you make a mistake the very polite ones will not point it out to you. If you do something they do not like, they might ask one of your friends to talk to you. My aunt was asked to criticize me when my nieces thought my clothes were a little too risqué.

But Chinese people may not seem polite at times. Once I caught my knee in the door of a crowded bus and got a bruise that lasted for weeks. At the time, my cousins laughed while I felt like crying. It is just their way of reacting—probably embarrassment, probably an attempt to cheer me up, probably because they didn't know how else to react. Just don't feel offended.

DOES "NO" MEAN "NO"? Well, sometimes. You will have to judge for yourself when a negative decision can be challenged. If the wording is "it is not convenient" then it's a definite "no." If it's "it is too difficult" or "it is not allowed" then maybe there is a chance of a "yes."

One scholar was told he couldn't swim but insisted on it anyway, and his escorts didn't mind. The reason was concern for his safety, and when he survived, everything was hunky-dory. Can you imagine how embarrassed the Chinese would be if an honored guest drowned!

By protesting to a hotel clerk who said there was no room, I did get a bed in a dorm. This does not mean you should try to argue every time you are told "it is not possible," or that "your safety cannot be guaranteed." It could mean (1) language is a problem and they do not understand your request; (2) they don't want to be bothered trying; (3) they don't want too many people going there but if you insist, they'll let you go; (4) there is genuine concern for your safety; (5) you really aren't allowed to go.

Arguing is an art too. Do not lose your temper or you've lost the battle. You should argue as much as possible in their terms. For example, one single traveler was put, as is the custom, in a small banquet room in one hotel for meals. There were no other foreign guests and the room was dingy and depressing. With a waitress standing by watching, it was more like a prison. Two requests to move into the main dining room with the Chinese guests were refused. Single Traveler decided to go to a Chinese restaurant instead, pointing out to her guide that it was her problem. She said she was willing to pay for the hotel meals too, but she just couldn't bear eating alone under the circumstances. She was allowed to eat with the others.

Note: Sometimes no answer is a "no."

ASK QUESTIONS. An official of the Overseas Chinese Travel Service once told me the only advice he had for visitors was, "Ask questions." It is good advice. For some reason, the Chinese do not volunteer much information. It might have something to do with their own lines of communication. So when in doubt, ask!

HAND CLAPPING. You will frequently be greeted by applause as a sign of welcome or appreciation at institutions and cultural performances. It might even happen on the streets. The usual response is to applaud back.

CRITICISMS AND SUGGESTIONS. You may be asked for these and see many booklets in hotels, train dining cars, and restaurants with this title. I feel if you have any criticisms and suggestions, do give them. I wrote twenty-three pages myself on one trip. But don't go on about how things are done in North America. Much doesn't apply to China. Criticisms should be helpful in the context of a developing country. Criticisms and suggestions are considered seriously, especially now that China is trying to improve her tourist facilities. Yes, mention that the bathroom floor is filthy. Go further than that and ask the attendant to clean it. If an attendant has been particularly helpful, write it down. She may get a bonus because of it.

TIPPING. I have mixed feelings about this. I find it such a joy not to have to face tipping. On the other hand, hotel attendants can be very lethargic. At the moment, giving money to attendants and guides is not allowed. Officially it is considered insulting. The attendants themselves may have other feelings, but they are now only allowed very minor gifts. See "Gifts" in chapter 3.

GOOD MANNERS. Good manners at home are good manners anywhere.

Don't litter. Don't take "souvenirs," especially from historical places, such as a rock from the Great Wall. Don't pick flowers in parks.

In most other Asian countries it is fashionable to be late. Not so in China, where groups of children may be outside in the rain waiting for your car so they can applaud as you arrive.

Traditionally, Chinese conversations, even business conversations, start out with something innocuous: a discussion of the weather, of the calligraphy or a painting on the wall, or whatever. A mood of friendliness is set first. Then comes the business.

It is true that Chinese people themselves may not be polite in crowds. They may surround your bus and stare at you, crowd around when it's hot and ignore your pleas for help. But it is their country and just because you paid a lot of money to visit, it doesn't mean you can be rude.

And please don't spoil them. Guilin is already notorious. If strangers ask you for lighters or other "gifts," do not give them to them. If they beg you to send them a particular English textbook, use your own judgment. They may be selling them.

JOKING ABOUT POLITICS AND SEX. Many visitors are warned not to joke about sex or politics, particularly Chinese politics. To joke about sex is considered crude, and you condemn yourself when you do it. To joke about politics or even to argue about it is to show lack of sensitivity. Politics is taken very seriously in China. People are put into jail because of it, lose their jobs, waste years of schooling, spend long hours in meetings discussing political implications.

BEGGARS. Yes, there are a few. I have been approached a couple of times myself. Use your own discretion. As I would in New York City, I would ask them why they have to beg, and then decide whether or not to give. Or I might take them to the closest restaurant and give them a meal. Or ignore.

Occasionally there are crop failures due to "incorrect commune policies," and in the past few years, many people have been "waiting to be assigned jobs." (The word is not "unemployed," I'm told.) There are many people who go to the capitals to have grievances redressed. If it is warm and they have little money, they may sleep in the streets, and make a living selling handicrafts made while they wait.

GIVING A BANQUET. This is the accepted and most important way to return hospitality or to show gratitude for a favor. If your guide persists in refusing your invitation to eat with you, he may relent and join you the day before you leave as a farewell gesture.

You may want to throw a banquet for some of your Chinese colleagues and people who have been particularly helpful. Discuss your guest list with one of the Chinese you know so you won't offend anybody important by leaving him or her out. If your guide is invited, be sure he knows. Discuss spouses and times. See chapter 6 for information on food.

Your guide should be able to help with invitations and transportation for guests if needed. He can help you with place cards. Your guest of honor usually faces the door and sits to the left of the head of your group. Chinese banquet tables usually seat ten. At rectangular tables, the place of honor is the center of the long side of the table—again facing the door.

Unless you are with an official delegation, don't worry too much about protocol, though people do appreciate your efforts to be polite. Consider language problems also when you make the seating plan. You can spread copies of this book open at USEFUL PHRASES around the table so no one needs to be tongue-tied.

Enjoy your banquet. It could go on for three or four hours. The guests usually make the first move to leave.

TOASTING. Chinese do not like to drink alone. Toasting at banquets is a complicated art, but you are not expected to know the finer points. Just do what you do at home. Stand, clink glasses, drink. *Gan pei* means "empty your glasses!" Glasses are small and usually filled with *mao tai,* which is very potent.

The first toaster is usually the host, who gets the ball rolling. A frequent toast is to the friendship of the people of your country and China, and the health of friends and comrades present. The next toaster can talk about your sadness about leaving China perhaps, and the new friends you have made, and wishes that you will all meet again in your country. Tell funny stories.

Toasts might continue all evening—and so might the meal. If the banquet is extremely large, the host may circulate to all the tables, drinking toasts at each one. On smaller, less formal occasions, the Chinese may want to drink you under the table. Be alert; they may be putting tea in their own glasses. You may want to try that one yourself after a while.

I have been to banquets where I haven't touched a drop of liquor (I can't get *mao tai* past my nose—it's so strong). I don't think I offended anyone. Maybe I get away with it because I'm a woman, but if you don't want to drink so much, try to divert them. Try exchanging songs. Ask them to teach you their songs. It may be the only occasion where you'll hear the national anthem of China.

FLIRTING. You may be tempted to flirt with a Chinese citizen of the opposite sex. Friendliness is appreciated, but anything beyond that used to mean an interview by the Security Police, where you were asked why you insulted a Chinese citizen. It could also mean that you might be on the next plane out of the country. You will notice that even hand holding is not common. Chinese are more likely to socialize with members of their own sex than to pair off in public. But things are changing. You will probably be considered uncivilized if you indulge in too much display of affection in public, even with your own spouse. The Chinese will be embarrassed. Marriages between Chinese and foreigners are difficult to arrange.

WILL YOU BE FOLLOWED? Most probably not. There are just too many foreigners now visiting China. But a foreigner is conspicuous. If you do anything wrong, your movements could be traced.

You will notice that telephone reception is usually very good in China. There are exceptions, notably at embassies. Foreign residents suspect that the fading is the bugging equipment.

PHOTOGRAPHY. China is now like most other countries regarding photographs. At one time I couldn't even take a photo of my five-year-old on a public boat. There are still restrictions: You are not allowed to photograph police stations, for example. In 1978 I once allowed my bored child to take a photo of friendly policemen only to be told officiously by the officer in charge who suddenly appeared that "taking photographs in police stations is forbidden, but since he is only seven years old, we will not prosecute." We had been waiting to be registered.

Today you can take pictures out of airplanes, on and off boats—everywhere except military installations and certain museums which, like ours, find they cannot sell their own photos if cameras are allowed. The Chinese also feel that flash photography damages relics. They charge a fee or confiscate your film.

Please don't take flash photos at cultural performances. It disturbs the audience. This is my personal request. The Chinese may let you. Stage lighting is usually sufficient for black and white and fast color film. Do, however, ask if you can get right up next to the stage and squat down, shooting with available light as professional photographers do. Flash shots from the middle of a theater rarely work anyway.

Out of courtesy, please do ask people for permission to photograph them close up. Would you like someone to stick a camera in your face without permission?

DEMOCRACY WALLS. These are not new. Writing criticisms and complaints in public places has occurred from time to time in China for centuries. These walls were especially popular during the Cultural Revolution, when they were used for political debates and attacks on "capitalist roaders." The institution was protected by the constitution.

Late in 1978 the writing of big character posters on Democracy Walls flourished unhindered. Four months later, the right to "speak out freely, air views fully, hold great debates, and write big-character posters" was restricted. Taboo were criticisms of socialism, the dictatorship of the proletariat, party leadership, and the ideas of Marx, Lenin, and Mao.

In 1979 foreigners could visit Democracy Walls, talk with anyone who wanted to talk to them, and accept any leaflets anyone wanted to give them. But some of the Chinese were arrested and charged with passing state secrets to foreigners. In December 1979, however, wall posters were curtailed. In September 1980, these rights were deleted from the constitution because they were "easily abused by careerists and schemers like the Gang of Four."

If you're thinking of encouraging dissident movements, just because you believe in democracy, please ask yourself a few questions first. Can China afford an American-style opposition? Would political unrest upset China's program of feeding her tremendous population and furthering her goals of modernization? Do the dissidents represent a sizable majority? Has China ever had a Western-style democratic government?

If you want more information on this subject, Amnesty International does have a report on China, and the Western press does watch this carefully; sometimes too carefully. Readers get the impression that the Wall is much more important in Chinese life than it really is.

RELIGION. The constitution says, "Citizens enjoy freedom to believe in religion and freedom not to believe in religion and to propagate atheism." This is probably a reaction against the foreign missionary movement that was forced on China by the unequal treaties in the nineteenth century. At Liberation, the Christian churches were encouraged to become independent of their foreign roots. As a result, the Chinese Catholic Church still celebrates mass in Latin, and the Vatican has no control.

During the Cultural Revolution, churches and temples were destroyed or closed as part of the movement against the "Four Olds" by the Red Guards, who ignored the constitution. In 1978–79 the government started rebuilding many of the temples and churches, opening them for worship and tourists. Over 180 churches across China were flourishing at press time, some having to open Saturdays as well as Sundays. People worshipped in homes because they didn't have enough buildings. Foreigners made judgments about the validity of the state-supported and the "house Christians." If there is a difference, only God should judge.

Foreigners wanting to contact Protestants should ask for the Three-Self Patriotic Movement. Catholics should ask for the Chinese Patriotic Catholic Association. You should also consult with the national headquarters of your own churches or national church organizations. Some of these have full-time China watchers who can give you addresses.

I would suggest you restrain yourself from giving money to Chinese Christian groups. The problem years ago was that Chinese Christians became an elite group, frequently appealing successfully to their foreign protectors even if they got in trouble in Chinese courts, for example. To reintroduce Western materialistic values into a spiritual movement will contaminate its spiritual strength. They want to be self-reliant. Better visit with the attitude that the Western churches have something to learn from China. Do read Mooneyham's *China: A New Day*. Do join them for *worship* but do not disturb their service with a camera, or by being late, or leaving early. Church services are not tourist attractions.

PEOPLE'S FEELINGS. If you read Chinese history, particularly the history of imperialist times from 1840 to 1949, you should be struck by the lack of sensitivity foreigners had for the Chinese people. As a result, the Chinese started hitting back in whatever way they could. They demonstrated; they stoned churches; they murdered individual foreigners. Of course, they were desperate people then, pushed to extremes, but let's not provoke incidents.

Please dress modestly and save your jokes for the privacy of your own rooms. Someone who speaks English may hear you and be offended. Be aware if your driver is blocking a road, causing people pulling heavy loads to go around your bus. Your driver is trying to please *you*. Tell your driver to move somewhere else.

In 1981 a British student was deported for writing "Long Live the Gang of Four" as a joke.

FORMS OF ADDRESS. "Attendant" is the best translation for all service personnel like waiters, room boys, and chambermaids. If you have to get their attention, you can call them what sounds like *tung ger*—"comrade." It's nicer.

You can call your guide "mister" or "miss," and if you feel comfortable with it, you can call him/her what the Chinese call each other: *lau* (as in "loud") plus surname, or *xiao* (like "show" as in "shower") plus surname, no matter the sex. *Lau* means "old" and "*xiao*" means "small." *Lau* is not derogatory in China and refers to anyone forty and older.

Relatives are referred to and called by their relationship to you, like "Second Aunt Older Than My Father," or "Fifth Maternal Uncle of My Grandfather's Generation" (two Chinese words for each of these). Your relatives will tell you what to call them.

Chinese names have surnames first. Chou En-lai would by Premier Chou. You rarely address a person by his given name, except children or relatives.

POLITICS. Here are some things to remember about the new China:

1. Guides and officials usually give foreign visitors the accepted current political line, but a few are frank with their own ideas.

2. Chairman Mao is the Lenin of the Chinese revolution; he will always be considered the father of the revolution.

3. At press time China gave the impression it was shelving Mao's revolutionary struggle (from socialism to communism and the classless society) in favor of modernization. This does not mean the revolution has stopped. So much in China happens out of the public eye.

Much will depend on what happens in the 1980s: the success of the modernization program, relations with bordering countries like Vietnam and the Soviet Union, the struggle between factions within the Communist Party of China, the succession, the reaction of the army, etc.

GOVERNMENT. During most of 1981 China's constitution was being rewritten, a common practice. Up to mid-1980 it read ". . . China is a socialist state of the dictatorship of the proletariat led by the working class and based on the alliance of workers and peasants . . . The Communist Party of China is the core of leadership of the whole Chinese people." When you get to China look for a copy of the new constitution to see the changes.

About 38,000,000 citizens of China are members of the Communist Party. The total population is estimated now as one billion. June 30, 1982, marked the first census in decades. In recent years the Party has gotten less involved in running everything. The Party is going through a transition period (see INTRODUCTION) but some things have remained constant.

The highest organ of state power is the National People's Congress. The State Council is the executive organ accountable to the National People's Congress and is similar in makeup to a cabinet.

The Fifth National People's Congress was made up of workers (26.7 percent), peasants (20.6 percent), soldiers (14.4 percent), revolutionary cadres (13.4 percent), intellectuals (15 percent), patriotic personages (8.9 percent), and returned Overseas Chinese (1 percent). There are eight political parties besides the Communist Party.

LOOKING UP SPECIFIC CHINESE CITIZENS. As a courtesy to your hosts, do inform them if you want to take time off from your schedule to visit with friends or relatives. You might ask when the best time would be for you to meet with friends. Local Chinese may go to your hotel to see you, but they have to ask permission before entering, giving your name and showing their I.D. cards, with many questions asked. In some hotels, they have to present their permission slip to the service desk on your floor for stamping. Procedures differ. If they are uneasy about seeing you in a hotel, you could arrange to meet in a restaurant, a park, or their home. I have taken local Chinese with me on trips to communes and schools, and you could ask to do the same if there's room in your taxi.

Your chances for going to a specific Chinese home will depend on the political climate at the time. In 1979 it was possible without complications, but on many occasions before and since it was not. Your friend could have been grilled as to who you are, what you wanted, and what you talked about. In 1981 a Chinese Catholic priest was jailed. So do not insist if he seems reluctant.

Making contact may be a problem. There is no intracity telegraph service. Letters may take three days, more if not addressed in Chinese.

Telling him to contact you at your hotel room may be difficult since he may be shy, and telephone operators and front-office clerks are frequently discouraging. If he hasn't contacted you (see page 40), you may have to send a messenger, preferably some dark-haired, dark-eyed, and short member of your group who speaks Chinese. You could also ask your guide to contact him but your Chinese friend may have reason to fear officials. Having an unknown Chinese around might dampen the enthusiasm of your friend.

One Chinese with foreign connections was only allowed three foreign visitors at a time in 1981 and none could stay overnight. He entertained two whole tour groups in 1980. During the Cultural Revolution, if foreigners did turn up uninvited, his life might have been endangered. This is not the case now but one foreign expert told me in 1981 that only three Chinese in her work unit had permission to be friendly with her. China is not like other countries!

Do not persist in asking questions that a Chinese seems reluctant to answer. Do not expect any spontaneous rap sessions, though you may get some now. I once asked a friend what happened to his family during the Cultural Revolution and was bluntly but politely told it was none of my business. Be sensitive and play along if they whisper to you or pass you a note. They are afraid someone is listening.

I do feel Overseas Chinese have a freer time fraternizing with Chinese citizens. I have visited many Chinese homes accompanied only by my relatives and occasionally alone. No complications that I know of.

CHINESE HOSPITALITY. This can be very lavish and people may go into debt to show how happy they are to see you. It is always appropriate to take a gift when you go to a Chinese home. Especially welcome are cigarettes (State Express 555 are a current favorite) and imported booze unless the family is religious. On the other hand, they may be asked where they got such foreign things, which might cause trouble. So ask if it is all right. Just remember, it is customary for Chinese to refuse at first so persist unless they point out that accepting is illegal.

But don't insult them by being overly generous. It is all right, however, to give their children money (about ¥5) if you are a relative or a close friend. Otherwise, it is insulting. If you have time for a return banquet, that would be the easy way out.

If you are accompanied by a Chinese friend or relative, avoid buying anything in a store because he may want to pay for it. The salary range for most people is quite low. Of course, rent is low. A Chinese doesn't have to pay exorbitant medical bills if he is sick, and most pay no income tax. But he has to save a long time to buy what you wouldn't think twice about paying for. Hospitality may demand that you be given a gift. Be gracious and suggest something inexpensive like a poster if you are asked.

I have visited many homes—of peasants, officials, workers, and professional people. By Western standards, they are crowded. One professional couple with two children might have one or two tiny bedrooms—period. They would share a kitchen and bathroom with several other families. In only rare cases will there be room for overnight guests, especially in the cities. Toilets may be the squatting kind. In smaller communities you may find a container of earth or a bucket of water for covering or flushing. Sometimes the family even sells the urine for fertilizer.

In rural areas, you might have to sightsee on foot or on the hard back ends of bicycles, since there may not be any other means of transportation. It is a real adventure!

FIRECRACKERS are allowed in China, but usually at a place designated by the hotel. Many Hong Kong Chinese, forbidden to set them off at home, go berserk when they celebrate in China. It is not machine-gun fire!

IF YOU GET INTO TROUBLE. Chances are these things won't happen, but just in case . . .

If You Run Out of Money. Ask your embassy to cable home for some. It takes five banking days. Or borrow from fellow travelers.

Hostile Crowds. This is highly unlikely but you might *think* you're surrounded by a hostile crowd. Try smiling. Chances are they're just curious. In Shanghai, I have had my car surrounded by people five deep. Pointing a camera at them will make them fall back only for a moment—so don't bother trying that. Besides, a camera might antagonize them. Either ignore the crowd, do nothing and hope it will lose interest, or try making friends. Speak to individuals quietly, in English if you don't know Chinese. Someone may understand. Above all, smile and act friendly.

If you are convinced it is a hostile crowd, try to find out why it is hostile. The Chinese do not get angry at foreigners because they are foreigners, not even at Japanese, the hated enemy for so many years. It is probably something you have done that has upset people. It used to be taking pictures of the wrong places, but this is rare now. It could be you have insulted a Chinese by flirting. Try not to lose your temper; keep cool, polite, friendly. Keep apologizing. Talk about the friendship of the Chinese people and the people of your country. If someone is drunk, just leave.

Demonstrations. Don't be afraid of them. They are usually orderly. The blond wife of one foreign correspondent used to wave at marching demonstrators with a big friendly grin on her face during times less friendly to foreigners. Participants used to be so surprised by this, they'd break step, stare, and grin back. Recent demonstrations were mainly for more freedom and constitutional rights, the redressing of injustices committed many years previously, better living conditions, jobs, and against government interference in student elections.

Car Accidents. If your car accidentally injures anyone, do what you should in your own country. Give first aid, and then arrange to get the victim to a doctor or a hospital quickly. Otherwise, stay where you are. Do not get involved in arguments. Wait until the police arrive (they usually come very quickly). The police will take statements, and if you are found to be in any way responsible as the driver or even as a passenger (were you distracting the driver?), you may be liable to a fine or payment for damages. The fine would be to remunerate the family of the injured or deceased for the rest of his productive years. There is a standard formula. If the accident is serious, contact your embassy. There have been cases where a Chinese was found at fault and his work unit paid for a broken windshield. There have also been cases of drunken diplomats causing traffic accidents. Many were asked to leave China. But since most tourists will not be driving, car accidents are not really a problem.

Breaking the Law. If you are accused of breaking a Chinese law, try immediately to contact your embassy. Do not expect the kind of justice known in the West. China has only recently rewritten its civil law, put into effect in January 1980. Just don't do anything illegal!

What If You Get Sick? China has been among the healthiest and cleanest countries of Asia. But standards are getting sloppy. There are reports of cholera, malaria, and rabies in isolated rural areas far off the tourist routes. Venereal diseases are back, but certainly rare compared to other Asian cities. I have heard of two cases of encephalitis among foreigners, and cases of intestinal parasites in Beijing recently. The streets are swept several times a day and the hotels are mopped several times also. You will note in some hotels that there are no screens on the windows. If you are bothered by mosquitoes, use the net above your bed. You can also burn incense coils that keep mosquitoes away. To keep visitors happy, a lot of insecticide is used in rural areas.

Medical facilities are good. The Chinese designate only their best hospitals for foreigners. Many Overseas Chinese go to China for acupuncture treatment, but I don't recommend the "abortion tours" from Hong Kong. I once met a lady from Indonesia in Shanghai for heart surgery. Some foreigners have had infected appendixes successfully removed.

If visitors are sick, it is usually the common cold or an upset stomach. See chapter 6. Your host can arrange for you to see a doctor. Many hotels have them in residence. If you are traveling individually, you can ask the service desk. If you become ill at night, try the attendant on your floor. Some of them sleep in a room close to the service desk. If you have a language problem, point to the phrase you need in the USEFUL PHRASES.

You will probably be given a choice of Western or traditional Chinese medicine or both. The usual antibiotic is Tetracycline. Chinese herbal medicines are effective and have no side effects, but one of my kids had to be bribed with a lot of candy to drink his herbal tea, it tasted so awful.

For most ailments, Chinese hospitals are up to Western standards, except that they might be grubbier and Blue Cross won't believe it if you bother to make a claim. In Xi'an, an office visit at the hotel clinic plus medicines cost less than ¥2 for an upset stomach.

The Chinese are usually very concerned about the health of their guests. They frequently check whether you have enough clothing on. If you are a chronic complainer about your health, you might get a doctor even if you don't request one.

It must be pointed out that most tour organizers state emphatically that tours to China are rugged. They are not for invalids or people on special diets. The organizers are also complaining that some travelers are cheating, insisting they are in the best condition and health when actually they are not. It is true that the Chinese are especially nice to older people, and many people want to see China before they die. And some people of Chinese ancestry want to be buried in China and the only way they can do this is to die there, since the Chinese will only allow human remains to be imported to Shenzhen. But for the rest of you, here are some things to be considered:

1. When I talked to the American consulate in Beijing at press time, they were handling a couple of tourist deaths a month—usually heart attack with pneumonia complications.

2. So do take it easy. You can cut out excursions and rest instead. You don't have to climb mountains. You can wait at the foot with the bus driver, who is usually very nice. You can teach him English or walk around on level ground and enjoy the view. Have someone carry you up the Great Wall. You don't have to go out to the theater in the evening. You can stay and try to fathom Chinese television in the hotel.

3. Facilities for treating heart attack victims are not as sophisticated as in America or Europe. I once watched a medical team work on a victim in the dining room of the Dongfang Hotel in Guangzhou. They used mouth-to-mouth resuscitation and manual heart massage. I did not see any oxygen.

4. So what happens if there is a death? The Chinese contact the relevant embassy, which in turn tries to get in touch with next of kin. If no word is received within three days, then the Chinese will cremate the remains. (They have also been known to cremate clothes and wallet!) The embassy can make arrangements for the remains to be repatriated. No embalming available.

5. The Chinese do not store O-negative blood in their blood banks because Chinese people do not have it.

6. Take any essential medicines with you. Do not expect a prescription made out to a pharmacist in the U.S. to be filled in China, especially if it uses brand names.

7. In life-or-death situations, contact your embassy.

IF A CHINESE FRIEND asks for help to visit or study in or emigrate to your country, use your own judgment. It is possible but not easy. If you're willing to go to a lot of trouble for him, so be it. But don't make empty promises.

If he asks for help in buying goods, like a bicycle, from the Friendship Store, it has been done with no trouble and he should pay you for it. If he asks for foreign exchange, that is illegal and occasionally foreigners get caught. It may mean deportation for the foreigner. Do not break a law just because you have been given a lavish meal.

People enjoy complaining anywhere in the world, but only in China do their complaints make headlines. The Chinese people have been isolated for years. They are not aware of the problems of people outside.

9

SHOPPING

ARTS AND CRAFTS. China is famous for its arts and crafts, though as I said before, your best prices for China-made products are in Hong Kong. But you may find something you like in China that you won't find in Hong Kong. And besides you may not be going to Hong Kong. (See chapters 2 and 4.)

Usually your *best prices* in China are at the factories, your next best at the Friendship or Arts and Crafts Stores in the same city as the factory. Sometimes demand has something to do with prices. Rubbings bought at temples where they were made cost more than the same thing at Friendship Stores. There is a red souvenir seal on the temple-bought rubbing, but is it worth an extra ¥2.50? Sometimes store managers do not know how much to charge for an item, and so the same thing will have different prices in different stores.

All arts and crafts are sold in government-controlled retail stores except for the occasional handicraft sold directly by the maker at a "free market" or by a peddler on the street or at the top of a tourist-track mountain. In these three instances, you might be able to haggle (if your conscience will let you). You cannot haggle in a government retail store—unless you can spot a flaw and convince the clerk the item can't be sold to anyone else. The thing to remember is that there is a lot of junk being made in China but also a lot of very good art. The Chinese are constantly experimenting with items that would interest foreigners. If you buy the junk, they'll just make more of it.

Price is not always the deciding factor. You have to know quality to get the good buys. Learn it by studying a lot of good art, and try your own hand at carving and painting before you go to China. Read books, talk with dealers like Hanart in Hong Kong, and even take university courses.

Go to several factories first. Plan your trip so you can see how they make a craft of which you are especially fond. Write to the export corporation (see list in IMPORTANT ADDRESSES) for a list of the factories that make the best quality of whatever crafts you are interested in. When you visit the factory, study how the pieces are made, ask about the most difficult techniques, the criteria of a good piece, how to tell a phony from a genuine piece. Ask about the best way to clean a piece and where the best materials are from. Frequently you will be allowed to handle some of the pieces. Feel the weight, the surface texture.

The factory will have examples of the very best they have produced. Look at these carefully. Compare these with the ordinary quality. Take notes if you can't remember details. For reproductions, study the originals in the museums. Remember also that handmade articles are each different—of course. So before you buy, check each piece carefully, not just for flaws, but for the rendering that you like best.

Usually *a piece should be judged* by (1) the amount of work involved in making it—the finer, the more intricate it is, the better; (2) good proportions, lines, balance, and color; (3) how closely it represents what it is supposed to represent, and (4) whether it will be a joy forever, or whether you will get tired of it after a month.

Remember too, that the Chinese in China have a reputation for honesty. If they know something is better, usually they will tell you. Just ask.

If you are looking for an *investment,* I think your best bet today is revolutionary art—art depicting peasants, workers, revolutionary heroes. Like art labeled "Made in Occupied Japan" now, someday good revolutionary art will be valuable, for it represents a period in China's history. As far as I can see, very little of it is being made today, while the traditional themes are being made by the containerload. But of course, it has to be artistically good in its own right. And think, twenty years from now collectors will be collecting art showing the different stages of the Long March!

Another investment is good rubbings—not the cheap ¥2.50–¥12 kind made from wooden reproductions of the original stone, but the expensive kind, like the Wing of the Cicada, thin and transparent, or the shiny Black Gold. Some day, the original stones will be too worn to make any more rubbings. Then, if you have picked a famous stone you will have something very valuable. Of course, all this is speculation. China may goof up my predictions by producing a lot more revolutionary art. But you can't buy busts of Chairman Mao today.

Most general tours include at least one handicraft factory and always one Friendship or Arts and Crafts store. Most factories have a retail outlet. Many cities also have handicraft *institutes* where new crafts are developed and craftspeople are trained. In these, you may not be able to buy; however, these are very important for the education of the serious buyer.

If you are more interested in handicrafts than temples, it is best if you take an individual or special-interest tour. On a regular tour, the average tourist will be back at the bus waiting for you while you're still talking about texture or the iron content in glazes.

The *destinations* with the largest number of various handicrafts are **Beijing, Tianjin, Shanghai,** and **Guangzhou.**

Here is a list of some crafts and where they are made.

Bamboo: Guangdong (especially Huaiji County), Guangxi, Hunan and Hubei provinces

Carpets: Tianjin, Shanghai, Qingdao, Beijing, Changchun, Urumqi, Inner Mongolia

Clay sculptures, painted: Tianjin, Wuxi

Cloisonné (metal base, wire designs filled in with enamel and baked): Beijing, Tianjin, Xi'an

Dough figurines: Beijing, Guilin, Shanghai. Peddlers used to make these for fascinated children who then promptly ate them. Today these can still be found in some restaurants—I found one in Zhenjiang—but for permanency, a chemical that makes the dough very hard is now added. For fine sculpture, this is your cheapest buy.

Furs: Shijiazhuang, Dalian, Tianjin, Beijing

Glass, artistic: Chongqing, Dalian, Shanghai, Tianjin, Zibo in Shandong, Beijing

Glass snuff bottles: Beijing

Ivory: Guangzhou, Shanghai, and Beijing

Lacquer: Yangjiang in Guangdong, Shanghai, Beijing, Xi'an

Metal handicrafts: Jiangdu County in Jiangsu, Hangzhou, Shanghai, Chengdu, Zhangzhu in Jiangsu

Metal—swords and knives: Husaba in Longchuan County, Yunnan, Longquan in Zhejiang

Paintings and calligraphy: everywhere

Paper—wood-block printing: Beijing (Rong Bao Zhai), Tianjin

Paper-cuts: everywhere. Transient peddlers used to make these on the spot and then sell them. Now you can get postcard-type paper-cuts and every theme imaginable. For those mounted on colored paper: Hailun County in Heilongjiang; for multicolored ones: Yuxian County in Hubei

Paper New Year's pictures: Formerly of the kitchen god and the doorway gods, etc., these are now of cherubs and mythological characters. They are for posting around the house at New Year. Brighter more cheerful colors than traditional art: Weifang in Shandong, Tianjin

Porcelain: most famous—Jingdezhen (blue and white, eggshell); Yixing (for purple, unglazed); Foshan (for Shiwan); Shantou (for multicolored and chrysanthemums in high relief); Liling in Hunan south of Changsha; Pengcheng County in Hebei (for the Cizhou kiln's "iron embroidery" ware); Longquan in Zhejiang, Hangzhou, and Jingdezhen (for celadon, that porcelain attempt to imitate green jade). The finest porcelain is said to be white as jade, shiny as a mirror, thin as paper and resonant as a bell.

Reproductions: of ancient porcelains: Jingdezhen; of bronzes: Hangzhou, Luoyang; of three-color Tang: Luoyang and Xi'an

Rubbings: Xi'an (best), Luoyang, Suzhou

Shell art: Qingdao in Shandong, Xi'an

Silk: Guangzhou, Shanghai, Suzhou, Hangzhou, Nanjing, Changzhou in

Jiangsu; **brocade:** Shanghai; **double-faced silk paintings:** Zhangzhu in Jiangsu; **embroidery:** most famous schools—*Suzhou, Xiang* (Hunan—Changsha), *Yue* (Guangdong—Shantou), and *Shu* (Sichuan). Also of note: Shanghai, for **embroidered silk blouses; festival lanterns** (also glass—each city has different shapes, sizes, materials and colors): Beijing, Zhejiang, Shanghai, Foshan, and Jiangsu, Fujian and Anhui provinces; **flowers:** Shanghai

Stone carvings: Fuzhou in Fujian, Qingtian in Zhejiang, and Liuyang chrysanthemum stone carving in Hunan; **jade:** Shanghai, Beijing, Guilin, Xi'an. Jade can be nephrite (hard as glass, greasy look known as mutton fat, best pure white) or jadeite (wide range of colors, including emerald green; used more in jewelry, the more translucent the better). Since jade is very hard and thus difficult to carve, the most expensive is the most intricately carved and multicolored. The colors are cleverly worked into the design. Serpentine is not true jade but frequently passes as jade. It is softer. The Chinese use the word jade to mean a wide range of hard stones.

Straw: Fujian, Sichuan, Guangdong, and Shandong (Yantai) provinces

Tribal weaving: the Miao in Guizhou province

Wood carvings: Quanzhou and Putian in Fujian, Changchun, Dongyang in Zhejiang (gingko wood), Fuzhou (longan wood), Wenzhou, Shanghai, Beijing. For **gilt camphor wood:** Chaozhou and Shantou. For **sandalwood fans** (smell before buying): Suzhou and Hangzhou

Wool needlepoint: Shanghai Arts and Crafts Studio; Yantai in Shangdong.

The shopping fanatic should also check the "China Trade Directory" in IMPORTANT ADDRESSES. Look under China National Arts & Crafts Import & Export Corporation, for the handicrafts available under each city branch.

Favorite mythological and/or historical subjects of arts and crafts:

Poet Shi Yung—late Spring and Autumn Period. Knot on top of head. Sword on back.

Wei Tou—guardian of Buddhism and of the Goddess of Mercy.

Kuan Yin—originally a god, but in recent sculpture, always the Goddess of Mercy. Depicted with children, or carrying a cloud duster (like a horsetail whip), or with many heads, or with a vase.

Princess Wen Chen—the Chinese princess who married a Tibetan king and took Buddhism to Tibet.

Scholar Dong Kuo—who was kind even to wolves. He once saved a wolf from a hunter and was admonished by the hunter that a wolf can't change its habits.

Li Shi-zen—Ming dynasty author of the classic book on medicinal herbs. Depicted carrying herbs in a basket, and a hoe.

God of Longevity—old man with peach.

God of Wealth—well-dressed man with scepter.

God of Happiness—man with scroll.

Laughing Buddha—sometimes with five children or standing alone with raised hands.

Eight Taoist Genii—see "Learn How to Identify Details of Chinese Designs" in chapter 10.

Fa-Mu-lan—famous woman general who inspired Maxine Hong Kingston's *The Woman Warrior*.

Characters from classical Chinese novels—Water Margin, Dream of the Red Chamber, Pilgrimage to the Western World.

Favorite revolutionary subjects of arts and crafts:

Soldier O Yang Hai—usually shown on railway track pushing a horse. He was killed but the horse was saved.

Dr. Norman Bethune—usually the only foreigner depicted. Canadian doctor who worked with the Eighth Route Army until his death from blood poisoning.

Yang Kai-hui—first or second wife of Mao Tse-tung. Killed by Nationalists in 1930. Usually in black skirt, high-necked white jacket, and short hair. Sometimes has book in her hand.

Lu Hsun—famous modern Chinese writer.

Soldier Lei Feng—PLA truck driver based in Shenyang who was always helping people selflessly and like the Lone Ranger, anonymously. Killed in accident about 1964.

ANTIQUES. If you're after antiques, each city has stores, but be sure you get a signed receipt of purchase and a red wax seal attached to the antique. Otherwise you may not be able to get it out of China or duty-free into your own country.

As with antique stores everywhere, you have to know your goods if you want a bargain. If it is a non-Chinese antique, the Chinese pricers may not know the value and you may get a whopping good buy. But Chinese pricers know Chinese antiques. They are not cheap. Actually your best buy in Chinese antiques is in America or Europe, if you know your stuff better than the person you're buying it from.

Remember, the Chinese will not allow much out of the country that is older than a hundred years; and to be duty-free in your own country, antiques have to be older than a hundred years. Not much latitude there. You might have to try the "work of art" category.

Overseas Chinese might be entertaining ideas of taking out of China an antique that has been in the family for centuries. Think again. When my cousin investigated, he found he would have to pay a lot of money for it *if* the government consented to let it out. But do try.

SECONDHAND STORES. Even if you're not shopping, some of these can be very interesting. You might even be able to pick up a European antique. Many of these stores have musical instruments and old theatrical costumes—

new ones, too. But frequently it might just be old watches and electric fans. Each city should have several.

NOVELTIES. If your speed, like mine, is not in the $3,000 carpet class, China does have a good variety of novelties, things distinctively Chinese to take back to your nieces and nephews and bridge buddies. Most of the following are obtainable from Friendship Stores but some only from big department stores:

Acupuncture dolls: These are about ten inches high with genuine acupuncture needles and an instruction booklet (in Chinese) for do-it-yourselfers. If these are too expensive, try **acupuncture posters,** found in bookstores—cheap.

Posters, postcards, and comic books are fun and cheap, and so is a **map** of the world showing China in the center, or of Canada and the U.S. in Chinese characters.

Books. There are some children's books showing Chinese characters with equivalent pictures, like our ABCs. If you're in a foreign-language bookstore, you'll find a great many books in English (cheap), all printed in China. They also make great souvenirs.

Museum reproductions. Some of these are quite good and not too expensive. Check out the retail store in any museum you visit.

T-shirts. So far I've seen them marked "Xi'an," "Shanghai," and "Shaoshan." Laundry bags marked "Beijing Hotel" are popular. China is just beginning to realize the commercial value of printing a city's name on something, and images of tourist attractions in soapstone are appearing. Lots of cheap souvenir pins with the name of a touristy site (¥.08 to ¥.12). Then there are Chinese **kites,** traditional **baby bonnets** of silk or rayon trimmed with fur ears to make baby look like a tiger kitten, **Mao caps, plastic eggs** with chicks inside, **folding scissors.**

There are fancy gold-trimmed **chopsticks** from Fuzhou, lovely metal-tipped chopsticks from Hangzhou and stone **seals** where you can have a rubber stamp made of your name in Chinese (get a friend to translate) with a fancy, carved stone handle. Hong Kong visitors say these are cheaper in China than Hong Kong.

Some visitors take back Chinese **wines** and **vodka** or Chinese **teas.** Or any of the **arts and crafts.** I found a tiny three-color Tang camel for ¥6 in Luoyang, complete with the scary face on the saddle bag that symbolizes the Silk Road. In Beijing are **fur caps** for ¥8.70, **carved bone spoons** for ¥.43; in Kunming **woven cotton bags** for ¥4 and reasonable **silver filigree.** ¥.08 for a good-sized calendar.

FRIENDSHIP STORES are set up so that foreigners won't have to buck curious crowds in ordinary stores. There is at least one in every city, and taxi drivers will know where they are. Prices are about the same as in other Chinese stores, but you can buy things there you cannot find elsewhere. Higher-quality, luxury-class items are only for export or the Friendship Stores. Some stores allow local Chinese to enter without restriction, but most will only sometimes allow those accompanied by a pushy foreigner or Overseas Chinese. You will need a foreign face or a passport to get in yourself.

The Friendship Store in Beijing is the largest, but for quality, I prefer shopping in Shanghai. In addition to arts and crafts, you can buy textiles, television sets, radios, watches, bicycles, sewing machines, cosmetics, herbal medicines, notebooks, cheap playing cards, canned or powdered milk, jewelry, thermos bottles, electric fans, cashmere sweaters, and silk blouses and shirts in most well-stocked Friendship Stores. You do not have to use ration coupons in Friendship Stores for cotton.

OVERSEAS CHINESE STORES are for relatives of Overseas Chinese who receive foreign exchange and can buy certain rationed items there.

SHOPPING TIPS.

1. Wood-block prints of works by famous painters like Chi Pai-shih (Tianjin) are your best buys in China for scrolls you can hang on the wall. But Chi Pai-shih reproductions are cheaper in another part of Asia, best left unnamed.

2. In some antique stores, the reproductions are on the same shelves as the genuine articles, so do ask which is which.

3. Silk Chinese rugs are good buys, especially if Iran isn't producing any.

4. Beware of wood or lacquer. If these are not properly dried, they will crack in overheated North American buildings. One precaution is to put them in a room with a lot of humidity for the winter after you get home.

5. You can ship purchases internationally from Tianjin, Shanghai, Beijing, and Guangzhou Friendship Stores. The Chinese are trying to make it possible to ship from other cities as well. In most cities, however, the store can crate your purchases. In Beijing, crating and shipping a ¥70 porcelain horse to the U.S. (about 12 inches high) cost about ¥120. Shipping a 9′ × 12′ carpet costs ¥350 and takes three and a half months to the U.S.

6. You may ship parcels by mail from China. These will be opened and inspected by the postal clerk when you buy your stamps. Just be sure you have a red seal on any antique you are exporting.

7. China does not mass market the way America does. There are no "national brands" in handicrafts. The things you see available in Guangzhou may not be found in Beijing. So buy what you like when you see it. You may not see it again.

8. When comparing prices with those in North America, don't forget to

include the rate of duty and the shipping costs if these apply. See "Check Your Own Customs Regulations" in chapter 2.

9. Save your sales slips so you can argue with customs in your own country. They will be in Chinese with English numbers, so make a note on them of what each slip is for.

10. Antiques sold privately are beginning to appear in at least one street market in Guangzhou. These are not government authorized, and officially foreigners are not allowed to take them out of the country.

11. Clothing imported from Hong Kong was prominently displayed for sale recently. It is cheaper of course in Hong Kong.

🏵10🏵

WHAT IS THERE TO SEE AND DO?

HOW OBSERVANT ARE YOU? By the time you've been in China a week, you should have some idea: (1) if the Chinese people are happy; (2) if the modernization campaign is succeeding; (3) who the premier is; (4) what the population is; (5) what kind of a government China has and how it functions.

You should also know: (6) the name of the capital; (7) the names of two provinces; (8) the names of two rivers; (9) the names of the four foreign men whose portraits hang in some schools, factories, and communes.

And, one hopes, you would have looked at the inside of a Chinese home and chatted with some Chinese people besides your guide.

If you haven't done 80 percent of these, then think about why you came to China in the first place. Visiting China is a great opportunity to learn about another culture, another history, another way of life. It is a chance to speculate if China is going to affect your future: Will there be a war that would involve your country? Will its cheaper labor affect your economy? Will China's solutions to its problems help solve your country's problems? How did it eliminate prostitution? Drug addiction? Crime in the streets? What is it doing about controlling the growth of its population? The energy shortage? Its ethnic minorities? Is there anything China can teach you about arts? Patience? Alienation? Living for other people besides yourself?

Note: Visitors to China in previous years have gotten the impression that everything was going well in China. Yet in 1979, the Chinese themselves were saying that things were very wrong in several of the previous periods. So do evaluate what you hear critically. The person who briefs you is telling you the truth as he sees it. Do cross-examine pleasantly if he gives you information that just doesn't quite ring true to you. It may also be something you've misunderstood.

THINGS TO DO

Checklist. To help you observe, especially when you have nothing to do on a train or bus, use this list. Make a check if you see any of these things:

1. a foot-operated water pump ( )
2. an electric water pump ( )
3. an earthen cone-shaped tomb ( )
4. a funeral ( )
5. a pregnant woman ( )
6. a cat ( )
7. a village watchtower (mainly in south) ( )
8. a pony or mule cart (mainly in north) ( )
9. a village without electrical wiring ( )
10. a television antenna on a private home ( )
11. a mud sled with runners ( )
12. an old woman with tiny bound feet
13. *aqi pao/cheong sam,* the narrow, women's dress with a side-slit
14. coal-dust bricks drying ( )
15. a brick kiln ( )
16. three kinds of wild birds, ( ), ( ), and ( )
17. a boy carrying a baby ( )
18. a statue of Chairman Mao
19. a small tractor ( )
20. a road not lined with trees ( )
21. criminals marching to be executed ( )

Walk. Go for a walk by yourself or with ONE friend and a copy of this book. Go early in the morning before breakfast when you are fresh (if you are fresh in the morning). Walk slowly without a camera, for cameras tend to separate people; they keep you from feeling, from savoring the waking of a world that is unlike any other on earth. Walk away from the main streets; explore the alleys.

Life swims around you; a woman brushes her teeth on the street. People line up doing the ethereal *taijquan* exercises in slow motion. Most are following one leader. Join them and try it yourself. Usually they won't mind.

Look at the tiny houses, the charming paper windows, the carvings on the door hinges, the store fronts open to the street; wait—maybe they're tiny factories or homes with workshops in front. Go to a park; you might even hear some beautiful but very shy singers practicing. You might be asked to help a student practice his English. If the park is a historic monument, savor it slowly. There is no tour guide rushing you from place to place. Imagine how it looked three hundred years ago when the common people and you were not allowed here. Think of the centuries of bustling human activity that took place here.

Go back to the street and watch the people riding to work on bicycles, buses, or trucks. Do they look harried, content, blank? Imagine yourself riding with them. Imagine yourself living in one of their apartments. Do you know enough about them to know how they feel?

Look for signs of Westernization. Any Coca-Cola ads yet? Any Western movies? Permanent waves? High heels? Is that bright-red billboard a Four Modernizations slogan? Or is it a poem by Chairman Mao? What are the sounds you hear? Traffic noises? The strains of "The East Is Red" on the loudspeaker or something from *The Sound of Music?* Listen to the language. It is tonal, like singing almost.

Look for old churches (Gothic-type windows) and temples. Was that bicycle cart an ambulance? Is that a woman pulling a heavy cart? Smile back at people who stare at you. Give them a cheery "Ni hao?" You might get a smile back. If you get lost, don't worry. See the DIRECTORY or USEFUL PHRASES.

Visit a factory, any factory, just as long as it's not a handicraft factory where you'll get involved in discussions of artistic techniques and buying. C.I.T.S. or the service desk in your hotel can arrange the trip and a guide. Tell them you want to visit a worker's home and talk to some workers. You won't need the Chinese in the USEFUL PHRASES if you have an interpreter, but these might give you some idea of what questions to ask first.

What is interesting about Chinese workers is mobility (or lack of it), job security, what happens if they don't like their jobs, housing, time off and vacations, medical benefits, travel, work incentives before 1978 and now, what they think of as they bicycle to work, and how did they meet their spouses. How are young people today different from the previous generation? What are the incentives for a planned family? What if someone in the work unit absents himself too often? Workers' schools? Taxes?

Who decides on what products to manufacture? Is the factory collectively or state owned? What is the difference? Do they have political meetings? How often? What about criticism-self-criticism sessions? Don't tourists disrupt production? What is the extent of recently introduced capitalistic practices? Will workers follow the Polish example?

Learn about the manufacturing process and how different things are in China from your home country.

Visit a commune. The ones around Guangzhou are more fun than others, for sometimes they have shooting galleries, ox-cart rides, lion dances, free markets, and bicycle rentals.

On communes, there are many techniques you can ask about. Depending on the location, you can learn how to preserve fruit the Chinese way and sample some. You can find out how to grow jasmine for jasmine tea and worms for silk. Around Beijing, you can see how Beijing (Peking) ducks are grown (and force-fed). Gardeners will have a field day learning about the strange vegetables. Have you ever seen rice growing before? Water chestnuts? Ask about bamboo shoots and fungi, all those yummy ingredients you find in Chinese restaurants.

Communes are not just farms. They are self-contained rural economic units with small-scale factories. Some have around 17,000 people, build transformers and boats, and make their own tools. Ask about health and birth control. Peek in on a school. Some commune visits include a great lunch.

Most of China's population is rural, so how peasants live is important in any evaluation you make of China. See "Yan'an" in DESTINATIONS for the statistics on one commune to give you some reference point on the one you visit. Again see USEFUL PHRASES, "Conversations—Especially for Communes" to stimulate some questions for you to ask. You will probably be given a briefing with the basic statistics. You could also ask: How do you keep your young people from wanting to live in the cities? How do people feel about the limit on the number of children they can have? What about old-age pensions for peasants? What security is there if not children? How are the Four Modernizations affecting this commune? Do peasants ever get vacations? Is it a problem when tourists come to visit? Have any commune-born youth ever gone to university? What happened to them? What about the shirker? What happens to the physically disabled? Who supports him? Is the standard of living in the countryside ever going to catch up with that in the cities? Is the gap widening? Why are some communes richer than others? Is China abandoning the commune system? Who decides on the quota of produce the government should get? What percentage is it? Are government officials still spending time doing manual labor in the countryside and learning from the peasants? Is the percentage of land allocated for private plots increasing? What percentage of time is spent on private plots and what on communal work? How many television sets? Are there still barefoot doctors?

Visit a school. Nursery schools are always entertaining. You have to be very hard-hearted if you aren't charmed by them. Count on half a day. In some nursery schools, visitors are involved in some of the children's games. In all nursery schools you will tour the classrooms, have a performance of songs and dances, and get a briefing with an opportunity to ask questions. Nursery-school songs are a good indicator of the current political atmosphere. At one time the children were singing songs about shooting down American planes. In more advanced schools, you may be expected to read an English lesson. Suggest that your reading be recorded so the children can hear it again and memorize your accent and inflections.

Chinese schools were closed during the Cultural Revolution, so that the students could "make revolution." After they were opened again, the curriculum placed more emphasis on politics than academics, even as a criterion for university entrance. How was this allowed to happen? What has happened to this generation of academically unprepared students? Is education going too much the other way now? Are students losing touch with peasants and workers? Do they still spend time working in factories? What is happening with the new examination system? Why are only a few people going to university when China needs highly trained people? What kind of teaching aids do they have? How many students in each class? What about the slow learners? The exceptionally bright child? What scientific apparatus do they have? What prospects for graduates? Why have there been student demonstrations?

See also chapter 3, "Gifts."

Offer to help, but only if the Chinese seem interested. (See also section on visiting as a scholar in chapter 1). This is not just for China's sake but also to give you a deeper experience in China. You may make some good professional contacts.

Two hours in a Chinese school will not tell you much about the education system, but struggling with an English class will tell you a lot more. If you are at a university and Chinese scholars start asking probing questions, then grab your chance. If you are in a tour group, make a date to meet them again. If you have brought along slides or pictures, tell them. If you are talking with a museum director and Chinese history is your field, offer to write the English titles on the exhibits or catalog their English-language library.

If you are already successfully helping hotel attendants with their English, and you're not on a tightly scheduled tour, offer to stay a few more days to make tape recordings or give more lessons. Hint that you don't have much money and can't stay too long. If the hotel management is sharp, they should grab the opportunity for a teacher in return for a room and maybe foreign experts' rates on food. This way they don't have to go through the red tape of getting a teacher. Student groups might offer to help plant trees with Chinese student groups if they're in China on tree-planting day in April.

Get off the well-beaten tourist track—it's safe. Just don't go anywhere there's a sign that says foreigners are forbidden. If anyone asks what you are doing, tell him. Just don't take photographs in police stations.

Actually, **police stations** are interesting. If you're lost, you might look for one to ask directions back. I once saw three teenagers locked in a cage under the stairs.

Public baths are interesting. Tour guides will probably try to discourage you, since they may not be as clean as your hotel bathroom, but you will get another perspective on Chinese life. And the massages are much cheaper than at the hotel. For about ¥3, you get a private bathtub and towel, or you can use the communal showers. The sexes are segregated, and I am told men have a very hot, communal-type bath similar to those in Japan.

Visit a **public market.** The free market is where commune members sell the surplus from their private vegetable plots. You will see some women with three eggs or a couple of pounds of cabbage.

Look for an old map of the city you are in. The museum may have one you can copy. Follow the **old wall** or look for remains of gates. Follow rivers and canals. Figure out how the city was defended.

Explore **old cemeteries.** Try to figure out the principles of geomancy, the *feng-shui,* the wind and the rain—do they all face south? How about the contours of the hill? Look for tombs carved in English.

Learn Chinese. No, it's not all that hard to understand. Listen carefully as it is spoken. Some words reoccur frequently. Ask what these mean. You probably know some Chinese already. *Shanghai* means "above the sea." *Shang* is "above." When you get to Beijing, you will hear about Beihai Park, "North Sea Park." *Hai* again is "sea." As for *Bei,* also found in *Beijing,* it means "north." *Beijing* is "Northern Capital." *Jing* is the same *jing* as in *Nanjing,* "Southern Capital."

Learn your numbers and make the elevator operator grin. *Lou* as in "loud" means "floor." Reading numbers will help in museums. You only have to learn ten. The rest are combinations. See USEFUL PHRASES. Learn the polite things first: "good morning," "please," "thank you," and "good-bye." When someone asks you to help with English, ask him or her to help you with your Chinese.

Visit museums. These can be deadly dull if you don't do it right. I have seen people hurrying past pieces that set my heart pounding, without batting an eyelash. You will get much more out of a Chinese museum (1) if you read something about Chinese history first; for a quick course, see chapter 15, MILESTONES IN CHINESE HISTORY; (2) if you take a knowledgeable guide; and (3) if you are eager to learn things like the date of the earliest pottery, blue and white porcelain, weaving, writing, money, sewer pipes, paper, gun powder, metal implements, etc. It might excite you even more to compare these with the earliest in your civilization. Try to figure out how and why things were made. Trace their development. How did neolithic man get his fire? When did the Chinese first use fertilizer?

China is so rich in archaeology that most cities have good collections. These are lessons in history. The problem for foreigners is that most museums do not have titles in English. If you don't have a guide and have learned your Chinese numbers, at least you could look up the dates in MILESTONES and get a general idea of the period and what the relic might be. There is also a list of dynasties in the QUICK REFERENCE section with the names in Chinese and English. Each gallery is usually labeled with a dynasty name and/or a date. You could try to figure from this too.

Chinese museums are usually set up chronologically from primitive to revolutionary times. City and provincial museums usually have relics found in the area. Some have exhibits of how things like bronzes were made. Most have excavations from ancient tombs, pottery figures of humans and animals, some of the most lifelike statues in China. Some of the most important pieces may not be original, but will be good reproductions. The originals are too valuable to expose to light and to the possibility of deterioration. You might notice that the lights are dim. It is deliberate.

Some museums have booklets in English. Some museums have been built over archaeological sites, a most exciting idea. You stand where you know people stood six thousand years ago and look at the remains of their houses, and where they stored their farm tools and buried their children. The skeletons are still there, excavated and protected by glass so you can see them. If you are at all psychic, you might feel some ancient vibes in a situation like this. Take your time. Meditate. I have a friend who gets visions sometimes if she holds a relic. She believes she sees the culture the relic came from as if it were a movie.

Some guides are steering tourists away from the revolutionary sections of museums, thinking they may not be interested. Do tell them if you are. It is good to see China's version of historic events. It may differ from what you have always heard. For this reason, Chinese history from 1840 on should be of tremendous interest. Did British soldiers really sack and rape in every city they captured? Was the British ship *Amethyst* acting cowardly or heroically? Did the missionaries deserve to be thrown out of China? Why do the Communists glorify the Christian-inspired Taipings and the fanatical Boxers? Was the Long March a cowardly or heroic act? Was the Great Leap Forward a mistake? Was the Cultural Revolution a mistake?

Ask political questions. Don't be afraid to do this. If it is done in the right spirit, both the Chinese and you can learn a lot. Political discussions can get heated. Please keep the conversation friendly and relaxed. If you succeed in convincing them of your opinions or vice versa, it won't be because of shouting and red faces.

Do ask them why they think Richard Nixon is a hero, what is meant by "democratic centralism," what they think will happen if the Four Modernizations fail, and whether it was right to imprison novelist Ding Ling (Ting Ling) and poet Ai Qing (Ai Ching) after the Hundred Flower Movement. If they look like they're uncomfortable with the question, don't pursue it. They may be under a lot of pressure to give the correct political answer and they may not know it. The better you know a person, the franker an answer you will get. And no answer will also give you an indication of the answer, if you know what I mean.

Go to cultural events. During and after the Cultural Revolution, at the instigation of Jiang Qing, wife of Chairman Mao, only eight operas were allowed to be performed, all with strong revolutionary messages. Since the end of 1976, many of the restrictions on entertainment have been lifted. It no longer has to "serve the revolution." Some of it can be and is frivolous.

Recently the Shanghai **Ballet** presented excerpts from *Swan Lake* and *Coppelia*, beautifully performed. The Beijing **Puppet** Theater presented

Hans Christian Andersen's *The Wild Swans.* In past years the few U.S. movies shown were not very recent.

But one doesn't go to China to see American or European movies. Some theaters are equipped with simultaneous interpretation, but these are only good if the interpreter is good. So bring your own if you can. Most movies are in Chinese. Of the **Chinese movies,** some are still blatantly full of propaganda, depicting pure and good Communists and evil Nationalists. Look for movie versions of operas, set in China, comedies about life in the factories, and cartoons. The *China Daily* has announcements about cultural events in Beijing and on national television.

Chinese **television**—what I've seen of it—consists primarily of documentaries and tear jerkers. Occasionally it will have something good like a visiting British ballet company or live coverage of special historical events. Your hotel television may have closed-circuit programming with more of what you're used to.

Chinese traditional opera should be experienced at least once. It is very popular with older people but not so much with younger ones, since it is sung in its own classical language. Your guide might not understand it except for the subtitles for the songs. The jabbering in the audience is not a result of boredom; it is those who understand it explaining to those who don't. To the uninitiated, traditional Chinese opera can be dull, with its many long monologues, its high-pitched singing, and its sluggish action. The villain is always known at the beginning. The chairs in the theater are frequently hard, and there may not be heat or air conditioning. The performance usually takes three hours (it used to be all day), and it is impolite to walk out in the middle.

The stories are usually ancient, so a knowledge of history helps. Or they could be something out of classic literature, *The Dream of the Red Chamber* or *Pilgrimage to the Western World*. Some are based on modern history. Two books, published in Beijing, should be helpful: Latsch's *Peking Opera as a European Sees It* and Wu's *Peking Opera and Mei Lanfang*.

Usually the staging, the costumes, and the acting are outstanding. There is one opera company, the Shaosing, that has only female players. The male roles are extraordinarily well done. The makeup might throw you, but the fighting scenes, if any, are breathtaking and graceful, like ballet. Cymbals and hollow wooden knockers punctuate the action, and somewhere in the orchestra is an instrument that sounds like a bagpipe.

It is the symbols that must be learned, and opera fans know them all,

every gesture, every move of the eyebrow. A particularly well-executed swing of the hair (anguish) or prolonged trembling (fear) will elicit gasps of appreciation and applause. Among the symbols: Two bamboo poles with some cloth attached are a city wall or gate; an old man and a girl with an oar are a boat; a chariot is two yellow flags with a wheel drawn on each; a riding crop means a horse; a couple of poles on either side of an actor is a sedan chair. A face painted black indicates an honest but uncouth character; a white face shows a treacherous, cunning but dignified person; a white patch on the nose is a villain; a hat with two long dangling pheasant or peacock feathers is worn by a high military officer, usually a marshal; a hat with wobbling wings out to the side just above the ears belongs to a government official; generals have flags matching their costumes like wings on their backs. An actor lifting up his foot as he exits is stepping over a high threshold of a door; crossed eyes mean anger; walking with hands extended in front means it's dark.

After the performance, you may want to go backstage to see the costumes and the musical instruments and to meet the actors. See USEFUL PHRASES.

The best **acrobats** are from Shenyang, Shanghai, and Wuhan, and foreigners usually find acrobats very entertaining. Also offered are **song and dance troupes** and **sports competitions.** I highly recommend exhibitions of **wushu,** the traditional martial arts.

Most tour groups will be taken to one or two cultural presentations. If you want to go to more, you can on your own. They are very cheap—usually less than one yuan. Tickets are frequently hard to get at the box office and must be booked in advance. See USEFUL PHRASES.

In Beijing, foreigners can go to good movies at the International Club (very comfortable seats). In almost every city, batches of seats for various kinds of performances are reserved for foreigners. You might be able to get some of these at your hotel service desk or through C.I.T.S.

In Beijing also, foreigners can go to **dance parties** at ¥10 a head. These have been held at the Minzu Nationalities Cultural Palace, the Friendship Hotel, and the International Club, up to three times a week from nine in the evening until two. You are supposed to bring your own partner, but many men, particularly Japanese, show up without them hoping for a chance with the few women available. Local Chinese, unless they can pass for Overseas Chinese, were forbidden to attend as of press time. Music is international. Some dancers bring their own cassettes. Sometimes a Chinese orchestra plays old songs. Other cities, too, can organize dance parties.

Learn how to identify details of Chinese designs. You will see these everywhere in China: in palaces, temples, pagodas, museums, fancy restaurants, gardens, parks, on dishes, windows, and screens. Knowing what they are will help you recognize bits of Chinese culture abroad too, especially on rugs, in textiles, in Chinese antiques, and in Chinese restaurants.

Illustrated are some of the more common designs. While their origins might be Taoist or Buddhist, Chinese symbols are primarily Chinese, taken over as part of the national culture, and not confined to any particular religion.

The pearl-border

"T" pattern

Key pattern

These are favorites for the rims of cups and bowls.

The swastika, symbol of luck

Swastika border design

The swastika was a Buddhist good luck symbol of Indian origin long before the Nazis existed. You will find it on the bellies of some Buddhist statues and latticed on screens and windows in complicated variations.

The Dragon of Heaven

The Chinese Dragon is said to have the head of a camel, the horns of a deer, the eyes of a rabbit, the ears of a cow, the neck of a snake, the belly of a frog, the scales of a carp, the claws of a hawk, and the palm of a tiger. It has whiskers and a beard, and is deaf. It is generally regarded as benevolent but is also the source of thunder and lightning. The five-clawed variation was once reserved exclusively for the emperor. The flaming ball is said by some to represent thunder and lightning, by others, to be either the sun, the moon, or the pearl of potentiality. It is frequently surrounded by clouds.

The cloud design is now most frequently seen in blue as the lower border of a rich man's gown either in a traditional opera or on a painted antique portrait.

The thunder-line
    Hieroglyphic form for thunder
    Later development of hieroglyphic form for thunder
    Decorative compositions of the hieroglyphic form
    The thunder-line

The cloud design

Cloud border

Still water

Sea waves; the little clouds over the angles represent the sea spray.

Lightning and fire design

Mountains and crags

In the center the dual Yin-Yang, the principles of being, surrounded by the eight trigrams of divination.

The Yin-Yang symbolizes the dual nature of universal life. Everything exists because of the interaction between the Yang and the Yin, i.e., between heaven and earth, sun and moon, light and darkness, male and female, penetration and absorption, etc.

The Eight Trigrams represent eight animals and eight directions. At eleven o'clock are the three unbroken lines of heaven; then clockwise, clouds, thunder, mountains, water, fire, earth, and wind. These are used in fortune telling. You may have heard of the I Ching.

The scepter of the supreme heavenly deity

This scepter is frequently about half a meter long and made of metal, stone, bone, or wood. It is like a magic wand and is frequently given as a gift, a symbol of good wishes for the prosperity and longevity of the recipient. The larger ones are found now in museums.

1.

2.

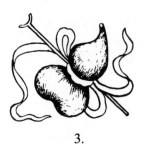

3.

4.

5.

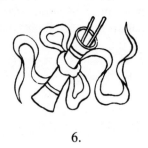

6.

7.   8.

The attributes of the eight Taoistic genii
1. The fan
2. The sword
3. The pilgrim's staff and gourd
4. The castanets
5. The flower basket
6. The tube and rods
7. The flute
8. The lotus flower

The Eight Taoist Genii or Immortals or Fairies were originally eight humans who discovered the secrets of nature. They lived alone in remote mountains (one of them in a cave at Lushan), had magic powers and could revive the dead. They are usually found together on a vase or in one painting, or as a set of eight porcelain pieces. Chung Li-chuan carries the fan to revive the spirits of the dead, Lu Tung-pin the supernatural sword, Li Tieh-kuai the staff, Tsao Kuo-chiu the castanets, Lan Tsai-ho the flower basket, Chang Kuo the bamboo tube, Han Hsiang-tzu the flute, and Ho Hsien-ku the lotus flower. Two are women.

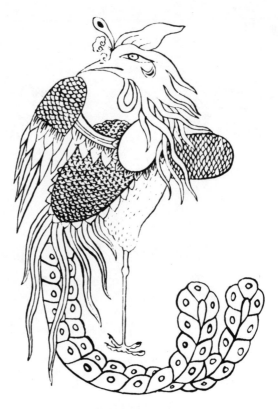

The phoenix

The phoenix is said to resemble a swan in front, a unicorn behind, with "the throat of a swallow, the bill of a fowl, the neck of a snake, the tail of a peacock, the forehead of a crane, the crown of a Mandarin duck, the stripes of a dragon, and the back of a tortoise." Its appearance is said to mean an era of peace and prosperity. It was the symbol used by the empresses of China and is often combined in designs with the dragon.

The lion

The lion is not native to China. The design is unique to China because the craftsmen never saw a real one. Lions are frequently seen in front of buildings as protectors either playing with a ball (male) or a kitten (female). They are considered benevolent. The ball is said by some to represent the imperial treasury or peace. Others say it is the sun, a precious stone, or the Yin-Yang. Seen also on festive occasions as a costume for dancers, the lion is sometimes confused with the Fo dog, which is usually blue with longer ears.

The eight Buddhist emblems of happy augury
   a. The wheel of the law
   b. The conch shell
   c. The state umbrella
   d. The canopy
   e. The lotus flower
   f. The covered vase
   g. The pair of fishes
   h. The endless knot

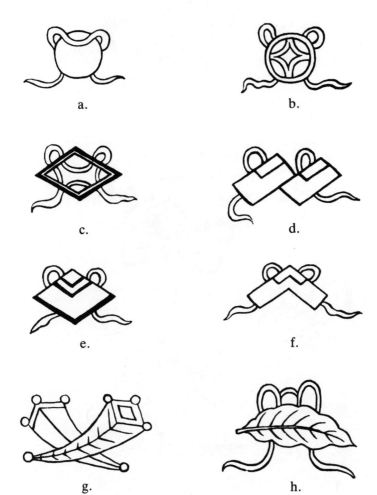

The eight precious things
  a. The pearl
  b. The coin
  c. The rhombus (victory)
  d. The books
  e. The painting
  f. The musical stone of jade (blessing)
  g. The rhinoceros-horn cups
  h. The artemisia leaf (dignity)

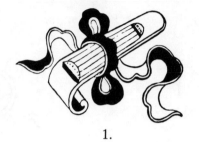

1.

2.

3.

4.

The four symbols of literature and science
1. The harp
2. The chessboard
3. The books
4. The paintings

The intellectual elite was associated with these four symbols in ancient times.

1.

2.

Character sign symbols
1. The round *Shou*
2. The long *Shou,* both meaning "long life"

These are only two of the many variations frequently seen. There is even a teapot in the *shou* design.

The *Fu,* meaning "happiness"

This is but one of the many variations of the character for happiness. Sometimes it is circular and doubled, especially prominent at weddings.

The bat

Bat and peach

The word for bat in Chinese is *fu.* So is the word for happiness. A bat is thus a symbol of happiness. These are everywhere: on the walls and ceilings of the Forbidden City, on the ceiling of the restaurant of the Peace Hotel in Shanghai. The peach is a symbol of longevity.

Five bats, surrounding the character *Shou*

When five bats are combined with the longevity character, they mean the five great blessings: happiness, wealth, peace, virtue, and longevity.

Scepter, writing brush, and uncoined silver, symbol of success

Together, these are a symbol of success.

The three fruits

These are fragrant fingers of Buddha, peach, and pomegranate. Together they mean happiness, longevity, and male children.

Peach blossom　　　　　　　　　Lotus flower

Chrysanthemum　　　　　　　　　Narcissus

These are featured singly or combined in a set of four, since the peach blossom represents spring, the lotus flower is summer, chrysanthemum is autumn, and narcissus is winter. Frequently there are only one of each of these on a four-panel screen.

Prunus

Orchid

Bamboo

Peony

The prunus or plum blossom symbolizes beauty; the orchid, fragrance; bamboo is an emblem of longevity, and the peony means wealth and respectability.

Among **other common symbols** are the *crane* (longevity), the *stag* (longevity and prosperity), and the *lotus* (purity and perfection). The Buddha is usually seated on a lotus.

Among the many **strange beings** are the two at the top two corners of many temple roofs, tails pointing to the sky. This is a *carp turning into a dragon.* There is also the *unicorn,* known as *qi-lin,* with the "body of the musk deer, the tail of an ox, the forehead of a wolf, and the hoofs of a horse." The male has a horn, but the female does not. It is a good, gentle, and benevolent creature.

The wooden *"fish,"* a red object found in most Buddhist temples, is a clapper, used for beating time while the monks chant the sutras. Some say that the monks dropped the sutras in water as the holy scriptures were being brought from India. A fish ate the sutras, so it was beaten to force it to regurgitate. Others say, if you don't beat the fish, there will be an earthquake.

The *tortoise,* usually seen with a giant stele on its back, is one of the four supernatural animals, the others being the phoenix, the dragon, and the unicorn. Real ones are frequently kept at Buddhist temples, for they are sacred, an emblem of longevity, strength, and endurance.

In Buddhist temples you will find statues of: (1) *Sakyamuni,* the Buddha, Prince Siddhartha. He is central; (2) *Bodhisattvas,* known in Chinese as *pusas—Kuan Yin,* the goddess of mercy, who may have several heads and arms and may be carrying a vase or a child. She is usually behind Sakyamuni facing north; *Maitreya,* Mi Lo Fu, the Laughing or Smiling Buddha who is first to greet all visitors. He is the Buddha to come. Beside Sakyamuni could be either *Amitabha,* who is the Bodhisattva in charge of the souls of the dead, *Manjusri,* the Bodhisattva of wisdom, usually with a sword in his right hand and a lotus in his left, or the Bodhisattvas of pharmacy, universal benevolence, or of earth; (3) *Arhats,* known in Chinese as *lohan,* lesser saintly souls in groupings of sixteen, eighteen, or five hundred.

Buddhist statues are usually based on Indian saints, though they most frequently look Chinese. Except for Kuan Yin, they are all male, although at one time, Kuan Yin was depicted as male. Said one guide, "Men believe he is male and women believe she is female."

Temples also usually have four giant guardians and a Wei Tou, a warrior, the Guardian of Buddhism. You may also notice that the features of many Buddhist statues are round and feminine. Said one Buddhist guide, "Both men and women like to look at women, and we want people to look at the face of the Buddha."

Another interesting study is the clothing of the Buddhas, some with the plain-draped robes of Indian holy men, others the fancy, feminine Chinese court dress with jewelry. Buddhism arrived in China from India, but Buddhist art quickly became distinctly Chinese. You will probably see many more Buddhist temples than Taoist and Confucian. These are the three traditional religions of China.

Relax in a Chinese garden. This is different from rushing through on a guided tour. Go back to one you especially like, and just sit and absorb. A Chinese garden is not just something attached to a house. It is an art form. It must have mountains, water, plants, and buildings. The most famous gardens are in Suzhou and Hangzhou, and at the Summer Palace in Beijing. But there are others. The gardens were built for a leisurely lifestyle in which poetry, philosophical contemplation, and the beauty of nature were of utmost importance in life. The ugly world of poverty and injustice was kept outside by high walls. "Above Heaven; below Suzhou and Hangzhou" referred probably more to the gardens than anything else.

Take your time to explore the gardens. Look at the integration of the buildings with nature, the pinpointing of places of particular beauty by window frames and moon gates. Absorb the tranquillity of the water. Look at the reflections. Think of poetry. The meaning of life. A garden takes time.

Do a study—of tile faces *(Wa dang)* or eave tiles, for instance, the circular pieces of tile at the lower edge of a roof. Some have animal faces on them, some flowers, some Chinese characters. The designs were chosen in some cases as good-luck symbols. Study the animals on the roofs too. Are they always the same? Do all pagodas have an odd number of stories? Do all tombs face south? Why do the Chinese get so excited about calligraphy? If you figure that one out, let me know. I haven't been able to fathom the criteria of what is good and what isn't.

Find out details. Why do you have to step so high to get through some doorways? What is the difference between a Chinese temple and a Tibetan-style temple? What are the bumps on the head of some of the Buddhas? What do the different positions of Buddhist statues mean? What is the Chinese word for temple? What is the difference between a *guan, si, ang, ci tang, ta,* and *miao*? Why are pagodas so tall and thin? Do a survey here too. You will get a lot of different answers.

Who was China's most prolific graffiti artist? My vote would go to Qing Emperor Chien-lung. Who are the children of the dragon? Why is "son of a tortoise" one of the worst insults you can give? When did Kuan Yin become a woman? Was Mao's theory of the Unity of Opposites influenced by Yin-Yang?

DESTINATIONS OPEN TO FOREIGN VISITORS

(Note: Some cities in Fujian and Guangdong may only be open to Overseas Chinese. Some cities, like Lhasa, allow only a limited number of visitors.)

1. Haikou, Guangdong
2. Conghua, Guangdong
3. Foshan, Guangdong
4. Zhaoqing, Guangdong
5. Wuming, Guangxi
6. Bingyang, Guangxi
7. Guiping, Guangxi
8. Liuzhou, Guangxi
9. Guilin, Guangxi
10. Yangshuo, Guangxi
11. Lunan, Yunnan
12. Jinghong (Xishuangbanna), Yunnan
13. Hengyang, Hunan
14. Xiangtan, Hunan
15. Shaoshan, Hunan
16. Yueyang, Hunan
17. Chongqing, Sichuan
18. Leshan, Sichuan
19. Emei Shan, Sichuan
20. Wan Xian, Sichuan
21. Shashi, Hebei
22. Xianning, Hubei
23. Xiangfan, Hubei
24. Danjiang, Hubei
25. Jinggang Shan, Jianxi
26. Lushan, Jianxi
27. Jiujiang, Jianxi
28. Jingdezhen, Jianxi
29. Wenzhou, Zhejiang
30. Bei Yandang Shan, Zhejiang
31. Shaoxing, Zhejiang
32. Ningbo, Zhejiang
33. Mogan Shan, Zhejiang
34. Huang Shan, Anhui
35. Jiuhua Shan, Anhui
36. Wuhu, Anhui
37. Ma'anshan, Anhui
38. Yixing, Jiangsu
39. Zhenjiang, Jiangsu
40. Changzhou, Jiangsu
41. Wuxi, Jiangsu
42. Suzhou, Jiangsu
43. Yangzhou, Jiangsu
44. Xuzhou, Jiangsu
45. Lianyungang, Jiangsu
46. Zijin Shan, Jiangsu
47. Yuxian, Henan
48. Kaifeng, Henan
49. Gongxian, Henan
50. Luoyang, Henan
51. Sanmenxia, Henan
52. Xinxiang, Henan
53. Hui Xian, Henan
54. Anyang, Henan
55. Linxian, Henan
56. Yan'an, Shaanxi
57. Qufu, Shandong
58. Tai'an (Mt. Tai), Shandong
59. Zibo, Shandong
60. Weifang, Shandong
61. Qingdao, Shandong
62. Yantai, Shandong
63. Shengli Oil Field, Shandong
64. Xibaipo, Hebei
65. Dagang Oil Field, Tianjin
66. Tangshan, Hebei
67. Shashiyu, Hebei
68. Zunhua, Hebei
69. Chengde, Hebei
70. Qinhuangdao, Hebei
71. Dazhai, Shanxi
72. Yangquan, Shanxi
73. Datong, Shanxi
74. Baotou, Nei Monggol
75. Xilinhot, Nei Monggol
76. Dalian, Liaoning
77. Anshan, Liaoning
78. Fushun, Liaoning
79. Jilin, Jilin
80. Daqing Oil Field, Heilongjiang
81. Jiuquan, Gansu
82. Jiayuguan, Gansu
83. Dunhuang, Gansu
84. Turpan, Xinjiang
85. Handan, Hebei
86. Beidaihe, Hebei
87. Xiamen, Fujian
88. Zhangzhou, Fujian
89. Fuzhou, Fujian
90. Shantou, Guangdong
91. Xin Hui, Guangdong
92. Jiangmen, Guangdong
93. Tai Shan, Guangdong
94. Lhasa, Xizang

129

11

DESTINATIONS

Over one hundred destinations are now open to foreign tourists in China, and I have attempted to mention most of these. The most important I have described in depth, hoping that the flavor will rub off. The list here is alphabetical by pinyin. Look in the QUICK REFERENCE section and CONTENTS for alphabetical lists by the old spelling. Shoppers and handicraft fans should also look in SHOPPING and IMPORTANT ADDRESSES for lists of cities where handicrafts are made. Hours are approximate, those in summer about an hour later than those in winter. Schools, communes and factories are usually common in the whole of China, and these are not mentioned unless there is something unique about them. See also DIRECTORY.

For those trying to learn Chinese: *guan* = pass; *jiang* = river; *hu* = lake; *jing* = capital; *sha* = sand; *shan* = mountain; *xian* = county; *zhou* = city. You will note some redundancy in names such as Lu Shan Mountain, but that's for people who don't know Chinese.

ANSHAN in Liaoning, 90 km. southwest of Shenyang, has China's biggest iron and steel works. It is also known for Mt. Qianshan, with temples as old as Tang, and Tanggangzi Hot Spring, with a hospital and guest house.

ANYANG in Henan province north of the Yellow River near the Hebei border is one of the oldest cities in China. It was here that the oracle bones, the ancient means of divination by means of tortoise shells and shoulder blades of oxen, were found. It was founded in the Shang dynasty. Today it is also the place from which you can visit the famous Red Flag Canal.

BAOTOU (Paotow), an industrial center, is 14 hours by train from Beijing in the western part of Inner Mongolia, a 1½-hr. flight twice a week. A trip here is not for the weak. (See HOHHOT.) A two-hour jeep ride along a riverbed takes you to a Tibetan monastery. Take a scarf for the sand storms, and your own food. A lakeside restaurant serves fish from this lake.

BEIDAIHE (Pehtaiho, Peitaihe; North Dai River) is a lovely little seaside resort five hours by train via Tianjin due east of Beijing. It is about 10 kilometers south of Qinhuangdao on the Bohai Sea in Hebei. An airport is at Shanhaiguan, 35 kilometers north for the 50-minute charter flights from the capital.

Beidaihe was built as a Qing resort after the completion of the Beijing-Shanhaiguan railway in 1893. By 1949, 706 villas and hotel buildings had been completed, many of them for foreign diplomats and missionaries as well as wealthy Chinese. After Liberation, the Chinese government rebuilt some of the old buildings and added thirty-three new ones, allocating them to various government agencies as rest and recreation centers. In July 1979 the resort was opened to foreign tourists under the Beidaihe Travel Service Company, Beidaihe Branch Office of the China International Travel Service. Beidaihe stretches along 12 kilometers of hard, golden sand sloping gently out into the Bohai Sea. The beaches are divided by rock promontories. At the **Pigeon's Nest** in the east, you can see Qinhuangdao across the bay and the best sunrise. At the **Tiger Stone** in the center, crab fishermen bring their catch for sale in the summer.

There are several swimming areas attached to each of the three hotels, manned by lifeguards and protected from sharks by nets. One lifeguard hasn't heard of a shark there since 1962, he said. Each hotel has changing rooms on the beach with hot and cold fresh-water showers, open 8 a.m. to 10 p.m. The swimming season goes from May to September, depending on how cold you like your water. The hottest days are in August (maximum 36°C for a few days), but the high is usually 31°C or 32°C, sometimes dropping to 24° or 25° at night.

The city itself has a population of 10,000. In addition to the Pigeon's Nest and the Tiger Stone, there is a **Kuan Yin Temple** (1911) on the grounds of the West Hill Hotel. The buildings are beautifully renovated, but the statues destroyed by the Red Guards were not yet replaced in 1979. The temple is about 1½ kilometers behind the hotel's service bureau, a nice morning's hike.

The **Xiao Bao He Zhai Production Brigade** is also good to visit because it was one of the first in China to have pensions for its older citizens and one of the first with a birth-control program. (In 1979, only three babies were allowed; total population, a little over 1,000.) It grows apples, peaches, and pears for the Hong Kong market so an ideal time to visit is late August–September.

Excursions

The Great Wall at Shanhaiguan—see GREAT WALL.

Qinhuangdao—see separate listing.

Yansai Lake, a.k.a. Shihe Reservoir, at the foot of Yanshan Mountain, about an hour's drive northeast of Qinhuangdao. Built in 1974, 36 kilometers long, 6.6 kilometers wide and 30 meters deep, the lake is held by a dam (367 meters × 60.6 meters) controlling the Shihe River. From the reservoir run 75 kilometers of irrigation ditches, a most impressive network along the side of the mountain. There is a one-and-a-half-hour boat ride on the lake which is breezy, restful, and beautiful (take a hat if it is sunny). A lakeside restaurant serves fish from this lake.

Meng Jiang Nu Temple, 6 kilometers north of Shanhaiguan and 46 kilometers from Beidaihe, was built in memory of another of China's chaste, supernatural heroines. This one's husband was killed as a sacrifice to keep the Great Wall from falling down. She committed suicide in the sea rather than submit to the advances of the Qhin emperor. The temple was built in the Song dynasty, but the statues were destroyed in the Cultural Revolution. They were restored in the late 1970s in a gaudy, crude, painted clay style. But the view is interesting.

Future Plans: Since this resort was opened to foreign tourists only in mid-1979, it hasn't had time to develop its facilities. They are basically good, but leave much to be desired for visitors who spend more than two days here (unless you want to swim all day). Planned are bicycle rentals, boat rentals, and repairs to nearby caves.

Hotels: In 1979 the Central Committee of the Communist Party gave C.I.T.S. four areas totalling 170,000 square meters along the beaches. The former R&R center of the State Council, with 86 buildings spread along 4 kilometers of seashore in the central sector, is now the **Zhonghai Tan (Chunghai Tan) Hotel;** 148 buildings owned by the Party Central Committee and the Military Committee of the central government are now the 3-kilometer-long beachfront **West Hill Hotel** in the western sector.

Because of its high-level former owners, the buildings were in excellent repair when taken over for foreign tourists. However, few of them had private baths, having been originally designed for large families. This situation is now remedied.

The best swimming is said to be at the West Hill Hotel, which also appears to have the best services. You can tell it still has high-level clientele by the armed but friendly PLA guards on the premises. These villas are mostly yellow stucco. On the premises are the Kuan Yin Temple and the **Beidaihe Beach Club,** which has a comfortable theater seating about 850, table tennis, billiards, art exhibitions, and a restaurant. Open 3-11 p.m. Bring your own cassettes if you want to dance. The **Zhonghai Tan Hotel** is also very pleasant. Its service bureau is on the main street of the town, which runs behind the hotel.

The resort is ideal for walking, there being few cars and bicycles; the beach area is extremely beautiful. There are several arts and crafts shops on the main street and a good European restaurant, the **Kissling,** a branch of the one in Tianjin. The railway station is 15 kilometers away. There are hopes of charter flights here from Hong Kong.

BEIJING (Peking; Northern Capital)

Location: Surrounded by Hebei province on the northern fringe of the north China plain, the capital of the People's Republic of China is at almost the same latitude as Philadelphia. It is 183 kilometers from the seacoast, 43.71 meters above sea level, and has mountains to the north, west, and east. It can be reached by air from Tokyo in about four hours and from Guangzhou or Hong Kong in three. It can also be reached by train from Ulan Bator, and beyond that from Moscow. The train from Guangzhou takes 36 hours.

Weather: The best time to visit is in the autumn. The hottest days are in July and August—36°C–38°C; the coldest are in January and February—about minus 20°C. Dust storms blow from December to late March, and sometimes into May. It rains June to August off and on.

Population: 8.49 million (4.67 million urban).

Area: 16,800 square kilometers (including rural areas).

Background: Beijing has a history of three thousand years dating from the Western Chou, when it was known as Ji (Chi). Its name was later changed to Yen. The Liao built a new city here and called it Nanjing (Nan Ching; Southern Capital) as distinct from its old capital in Manchuria. The name was changed again to Yanjing (Yen Ching) in 1013.

In 1125, the Jin, a Tartar dynasty, overthrew the Liao and enlarged the city, calling it Zhongdu (Chung Tu; Central Capital). The Mongols (Yuan), under Kublai Khan, overthrew the Jin and built a new capital called Dadu (Ta Tu). In 1368 the Ming drove out the Yuan and established its capital at Nanjing with Beijing, then called Peiping Fu, as an auxiliary capital in 1409. It became the main capital again in 1421 and continued as the Qing capital into the early 1900s. In 1860 it was invaded by foreign, mainly English and French, troops and in 1900 was entered by the Boxers. In 1928 the Nationalist government moved the capital to Nanjing, and Beijing became Peiping (Northern Peace). The Japanese held it from 1937 to 1945. When the Communists took over in 1949, it regained its old name and former position as capital of China.

Fortunately, Beijing was relatively untouched by bombs during the Second World War. In 1959 ten massive buildings were completed for the tenth anniversary of the founding of the People's Republic. These included the Great Hall of the People, the Museums of History and the Revolution, the Agricultural Exhibition Hall, and the Palace of the Minorities—in the plain Soviet style.

In 1966 Beijing's Tian Anmen Square was the setting for mass Red Guard rallies of over a million people, all waving the little red book of quotations from Chairman Mao. In 1976 this was also the site of a clash between supporters of the Gang of Four and supporters of Premier Chou En-lai. Beijing is centered around the Forbidden City and Tian Anmen Square. The

133

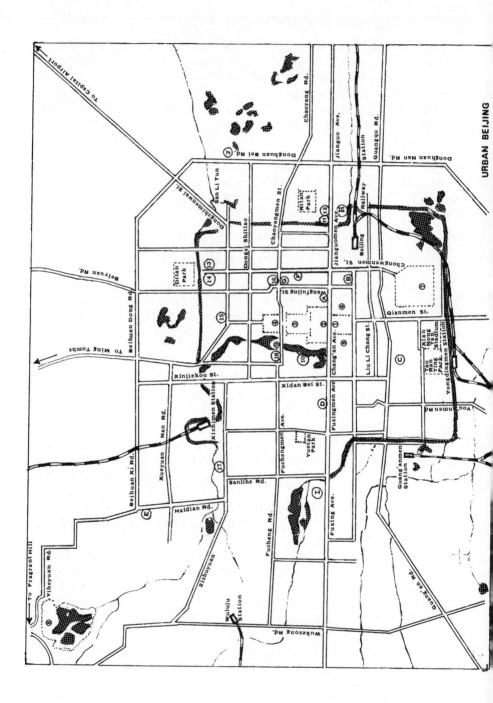

URBAN BEIJING

old foreign legation area was around the Xin Qiao Hotel. The Chinese city was south of the Qianmen (Chien Men) gate on the southern edge of Tian Anmen Square.

Beijing consists of ten districts and nine counties. The area's 265 communes are interesting because many raise the famous force-fed Beijing duck. Its industries include iron and steel, coal mining, machine building, basic chemicals and petroleum, electronics, electric power, textiles, and light industries. It has over 1,900 factories. Tourists would probably be interested in the Beijing Arts and Crafts Factory, which produces cloisonné, jade carving, ivory carving, lacquerware, traditional Chinese painting, snuff bottles, filigree, and dough figurines. Traditional wood-block printing can also be seen on Liu Li Chang Street. Carpets are also made in Beijing.

The people of Beijing speak *pu tung hua,* the official national language. They are predominantly Han, but you can see many flat, wide Mongolian faces. There are many Chinese visitors to the capital, many of them here to have problems solved and grievances redressed by the central government. Some of these people you may see sitting in subway entrances, trying to sell handicrafts while waiting.

Beijing people tend to be reserved compared to other Chinese. Don't be put off by this, for they are warm and friendly once they get to know you.

If you have only two or three days, the most important sights to see are those around the Tian Anmen, the Temple of Heaven, the Summer Palace, the Great Wall, and the Ming Tombs. If possible, you should avoid driving to the Summer Palace and the Great Wall on Sundays because of the traffic jams.

Of Interest to Visitors

Tian Anmen (Tien An Men) Square, 98 acres. Bounded on the north by the Tian Anmen gate, on the west by the Great Hall of the People, on the east

Tourist Hotels
A. Beijing (Peking)
B. Xin Qiao (Hsin Chiao)
C. Qianmen (Chien Men)
D. Minzu (Min Tzu, Min Dzu) [Nationalities]
E. Youyi [Friendship]
F. Heping [Peace]
G. Huaqiao (Huachiao) [Overseas Chinese]
H. Jianguo Hotel
I. Yenjing Hotel
J. Chang Cheng (Great Wall) Hotel

Of Interest to Visitors
1. Tian Anmen [Gate of Heavenly Peace] Square
2. Tian Anmen Gate
3. Forbidden City and Palace Museum
4. Coal Hill Park
5. Great Hall of the People
6. Museums of the Chinese Revolution and Chinese History
7. Temple of Heaven
8. Summer Palace
9. Beihai Park
10. Zhongnanhai (Chung Nan Hai)
11. International Club
12. Friendship Store
13. Lama Temple
14. Temple of Confucius
15. Drum Tower
16. CAAC
17. Beijing Zoo
18. Beijing Library

by the Museum of the Chinese Revolution and the Museum of Chinese History, and on the south by the Qian Men (Chien Men) gate. In the center from the north to south, there are the Monument to the People's Heroes and then the Chairman Mao Memorial Hall. The big portraits are, left to right, Marx, Engels, Lenin, and Stalin, put up only on special occasions.

Tian Anmen (Tien An Men; Gate of Heavenly Peace) is the most famous structure in China except for the Great Wall. From its high balcony the imperial edicts were read, and on October 1, 1949, Chairman Mao Tse-tung proclaimed the People's Republic of China. It is therefore the symbol of old and new China. China's leaders frequently appear here on national days to review the parades and festivities. It was built in 1651 and stands 33.7 meters high.

Through the gate once under Chairman Mao's portrait, to the left is Zhongshan Park, the memorial park to Dr. Sun Yat-sen. To the right is People's Cultural Park. These two parks are great for 6 a.m. walks because of the magnificent walls, towers, gates, moats, and pavilions and also because of the people limbering up for the day. They are exercising not just their muscles but their vocal chords. Some very beautiful voices resound off the walls and gate from very shy singers hiding behind bushes and screens.

In the square between the two parks is a tiny white marble pavilion looking like a Japanese lantern. In imperial times, if an official made a serious error, his black gauze cap was placed inside, and he was taken out to be executed at the marketplace 7 kilometers southwest of here near the Qianmen Hotel.

Gu Gong (Imperial Palace), a.k.a. Palace Museum or Forbidden City. 8 a.m.–4 p.m. or 8:30 a.m.–4:30 p.m. (summer). Visitors usually enter by the Wumen (Meridian Gate) inside the Tian Anmen. This was the home and audience halls of the Ming and the Qing. Many buildings here are as the Qing left them, minus relics now in the National Palace Museum in Taiwan. Many are used as exhibition halls for historical treasures from all over China. To walk at a leisurely pace from one end of the Forbidden City to the other takes about twenty minutes. But to explore it thoroughly takes at least a full day—some would say a week.

The Forbidden City was originally built from 1406 to 1420 as the palace of the Ming emperors. It covers more than 720,000 square meters (178 acres). There are over 9,000 rooms with a total floor space of about 150,000 square meters. The surrounding wall is over 10 meters high. It was built by a hundred thousand artisans and one million laborers.

Toward the end of the Qing, 280,000 taels of silver were needed annually to maintain it, the money collected in taxes and rents from the 658,000 acres of royal estates. During the Ming, there were nine thousand ladies-in-waiting and a hundred thousand eunuchs serving here. Some eunuchs (castrated males) gained a great deal of wealth and power from their position in the palace, which was sacked by foreign powers in 1900. The Forbidden City was restored and now maintains a permanent staff so that every twenty years, the whole place is renewed.

The city is divided into two major sections: the outer palace (for business) and the inner residential courts. **Outer Palace:** Directly beyond the Meridian Gate are the five marble bridges "like arrows reporting on the emperor to Heaven," the River of Gold below shaped like a bow. Note the gates; red was used only for important places like this. Each has 81 studs—nine is the number of heaven and also the emperor, hence nine times nine. There are seven layers of brick in the courtyard so no one could tunnel from underneath. Note the white squares, on each of which a royal guard stood whenever the emperor went out.

Throughout the palace there are huge caldrons for fire prevention. On the north side underneath the caldrons are air vents to fan the fires set to keep the water inside from freezing in the winter.

The first building is the **Taihedian (Tai Ho Tien; Hall of Supreme Harmony),** surrounded by incense burners, eighteen bronze ones representing the eighteen provinces, and others in the forms of a stork (longevity) and a dragon-headed tortoise (strength and endurance). There is also a copy of an ancient sundial. Note the small openings on the side of the pavilion to allow air to circulate inside. The building was used for major ceremonies like the emperor's birthday and for state affairs. Here ministers and officials knelt in rows out in front of the hall while smoke poured from the incense burners and musicians played on the balcony. The 18-meter-high cedar pillars are each one piece of wood. The floors are made of tile, each taking 136 days to bake, after which they were immersed in oil for a permanent polish. Each brick is solid, about 5 inches thick, about 18 inches square. The base and throne are carved sandalwood.

Zonghedian (Chung Ho Tien; The Hall of Complete Harmony) was used by the emperor to receive his ministers, to rest, and to dress. The two Qing sedan chairs here were for traveling within the palace. The braziers were for heat, the four cylindrical burners for sandalwood incense. Note the dragons on the ceiling.

Baohedian (Pao Ho Tien; The Hall of Preserving Harmony) was for imperial banquets and, during the Qing, the retesting of the top scorers in the national examinations. Behind this hall is a giant carving of one piece of marble from Fanshan county 16.57 meters × 3.07 meters × 1.7 meters and weighing about 250 tons. It was brought here in winter by sliding it over ice made from the water of wells especially sunk for the occasion.

Beyond this third hall are the **Inner Courts,** the three main buildings similar to the three in the outer palace: **Qianqingmen (Chien Chien Kung; The Hall of Heavenly Purity),** where the emperors used to live and where Cixi (Tzu Hsi), the Empress Dowager, received foreign envoys; **Jiaotaidian (Chiao Tai Tien; Hall of Union),** where ceremonies involving empresses took place (women were not allowed in the outer palace); and the **Kunninggong**

(Kun Nin Kung; Palace of Earthly Tranquillity), used as a residence in the Ming and as a shrine in the Qing. Its eastern room was used as a bridal chamber by the Qing emperors. In the back of the inner court is the **Imperial Garden,** where there is also a snack bar for hungry tourists. Then there is the back gate where tour groups usually meet their buses.

Retracing your steps to the entrance of the inner court, turn east past the washrooms and the Nine Dragon Screen, and then turn left again. Here are several pavilions with exhibitions well worth seeing. One has a stunning collection of gold artifacts—bells, incense burners, table service (with jade handles), and scepters. There are also precious Buddhist relics and the biggest jade sculpture in China, a five-ton Ming statue depicting one of the earliest attempts in the Xia to control the Yellow River. Also notable north of this area is the 12-inch-diameter well in which the Pearl Concubine was drowned by a eunuch after she incurred the wrath of the Empress Dowager in 1900.

Coal Hill, outside the north gate of the palace, was originally the site of a Ming coal pile. It is 43 meters high and is now a park with a good view of the Forbidden City; it was built with earth excavated from the moats.

Great Hall of the People, a.k.a. People's Congress Hall: built in 1959. 171,800 square meters. Three main sections include a 5,000-seat banquet hall, a three-story, 10,000-seat auditorium, and lounges in the style of each of the thirty provinces. Tour groups can arrange a visit through C.I.T.S. Banquets can be booked starting at ¥50 a person.

Museum of the Chinese Revolution: The exhibits here keep changing with each different political emphasis. On October 1, 1979, an exhibit opened celebrating the thirtieth anniversary of the founding of the People's Republic of China.

Museum of Chinese History is China's best. You need at least eight hours to do it justice, more if you are a real museum freak. Please take it in short spells; there is so much here! (See "Visit Museums" in chapter 10 and MILESTONES IN CHINESE HISTORY.) Both the historical and revolutionary museums are entered opposite the Great Hall of the People. The history museum is to the right. Open 9 a.m.–12:30 p.m.; 2–5:30 p.m. Guidebook in English available but mainly on the historical background with a few helpful photos.

Relics here start from 1.7-million-year-old human teeth and continue to items from 1911. They include a model of the cave where the Peking Man was found, a 14th-century B.C. ivory cup inlaid with jade, a Shang bronze wine vessel with four protruding rams' heads, a Western Zhou sewer pipe with the head of a tiger, a model of a Warring States irrigation system, tomb figures galore, a model of a first-century B.C. wheel used to operate a bellows to melt iron, and the Flying Horse of Kansu, which people around the world waited many hours to see in their own museums. No queues here!

There are also a model of a 1,700-year-old drum chariot with a figure of a child on top always pointing south, and another miniature drum chariot with a figure that beats a drum every 500 meters, a Yuan water clock, and some Yuan rockets attached to spears. I can only whet your appetite. It is best to take an English-speaking guide unless signs in English have been added by now.

Monument to the Peoples' Heroes: If you had taken my advice and learned your numbers in Chinese, you would know the dates under each sculpture. Then if you looked up MILESTONES IN CHINESE HISTORY you would know that the sculptures here represent the burning of the opium and the Opium War, 1840–42; the Taiping Heavenly Kingdom, 1851–64; the Revolution of 1911; the May 4, 1919 demonstration against the Versailles Treaty; the May 30, 1925 Incident in Shanghai, a demonstration after a worker was killed by a Japanese foreman; the August 1, 1927 Uprising in Nanchang; and the Anti-Japanese War, 1937–1945. In April 1976, during the Ching Ming festival where the dead are honored, attempts to remove wreaths in memory of Premier Chou En-lai were resisted by pro-Chou supporters at this monument. This is now referred to as the April Fifth Movement against the Gang of Four.

Chairman Mao Memorial Hall was built in 1977. In 1979 it was open Tuesdays, Thursdays, and Saturdays from 8:30 to 11:00 a.m. It is a mausoleum where the remains of China's great leader can be viewed. The building, a simple white building with 44 granite columns and glazed yellow trim, is 33.6 meters high and 105 meters square and was completed in nine months. The sculptures on the north side are symbolic of the achievements of the Chinese people in the preceding half century under Mao's leadership; those on the south express the people's determination to "act on his behests and carry the cause of our proletarian revolution through to the end."

Foreign and Overseas Chinese visitors are lined up separately from Chinese citizens, and the visit takes less than twenty minutes. As a token of respect, visitors are advised not to wear bright colors, especially red, but no one who did was stopped when I was there. No cameras or purses are allowed and children are told beforehand not to speak inside. One enters first the North Hall where there is a seated 3-meter-high marble statue of the leader, in front of a 7-by-24-meter wool needlepoint tapestry of the mountains and rivers of China. Then, two by two, you enter the Central Hall where Chairman Mao (1893–1976) lies in state, guarded by four members of the PLA. In the South Hall there is a poem by Chairman Mao in his own calligraphy, "Reply to Comrade Kuo Mo-jo to the tune of Man Chiang Hung."

Whether this will remain open is in doubt.

Tiantan (Tien Tan; Temple of Heaven) is set in the middle of a 667-acre park with many pine and cypress trees, some over five hundred years old. It is about 5 kilometers south of the Forbidden City. Give yourself at least twenty minutes for a quick look, an hour for a more thorough tour. The Temple of Heaven was built in the same period as the Forbidden City (1406–1420). It was used a couple of times a year when the emperor, bearing all the sins of the Chinese people, humbled himself before Heaven and performed the rituals calculated to bring good harvests. The temple has two concentric walls, both round at the north and straight at the south, Heaven being round and earth square. The raised 360-meter passage between the main buildings is the Red Stairway Bridge. To the north is the Hall of Prayer for Good Harvests with triple eaves, 38 meters high and 30 meters in diameter. The four central columns represent the four seasons. Around these four are two rings of twelve columns each, the inner symbolizing the twelve months and the outer the twelve divisions of day and night. Here, rituals were performed on the fifteenth day of the first moon of the lunar calendar.

South of this is the Imperial Vault of Heaven in which were stored the tablets of the God of Heaven, the Wind God, the Rain God, etc. Sacrifices were made on the circular Sacrificial Altar behind, on the winter solstice. The surrounding wall has a strange echo effect. Count the number of stone slabs on the floor, staircases, and balustrades. They are in multiples of nine.

The Yiheyuan—Summer Palace, open 6 a.m.–5:30 p.m., is a 717-acre garden about 20 kilometers northwest of the Tian Anmen. It is three-fourths water. In 1750 Qing Emperor Chien Lung built the Garden of Clear Ripples here. In 1860 this garden was destroyed by Anglo-French forces. Twenty years later, Empress Dowager Tzu Hsi built the Garden of Cultivating Peace, now known as the Summer Palace, on the site with funds meant for the Chinese navy. This was badly damaged by the eight imperialist powers in 1900. The existing buildings were restored in 1903.

The imperial court lived here every year when possible from April 15 to October 15, receiving diplomats and conducting business in the **Hall of Longevity and Benevolence.** Empress Dowager Tzu Hsi, who was the power behind and on the throne from 1861 to 1908, lived in this hall near the **Grand Stage** where she could indulge in her passion for theatricals. The stage floor is hollow so that "ghosts" could emerge from it. The Empress Dowager's personal servants included twenty-eight ladies-in-waiting, twenty eunuchs, and eight female officials. For lunch, she was offered 128 courses daily.

In the **Hall of Jade Ripples** to the south of the main entrance, she kept Emperor Guangxu (Kuang Hsu) imprisoned every summer here from 1898 to 1908 after he tried to institute reforms to modernize China and tried to take his rightful power back. Note the walls around the compound. The rooms here and elsewhere are furnished as they were then.

The **Long Corridor** extends 728 meters along the lake to the famous Marble Boat. There are about 1,400 paintings here, repainted in 1957 and in 1979, a most spectacular display. To the right (north) up the hill are the **Hall of Dispelling Clouds,** the **Tower of Buddhist Incense,** and the **Temple of the Seat of Wisdom,** where the empress used to hold her birthday celebrations and religious services. The **Garden of Harmonious Interests** was designed like the Chichang Garden in Wuxi. In Kunming Lake there is the seventeen-arch bridge, and the Dragon King Temple on an island. A good restaurant is in the **Pavilion for Listening to Orioles,** where you can also have your picture taken in elegant Chinese dress for ¥10.

To prepare for visiting the Summer Palace and the Forbidden City, read a biography of the Empress Dowager. Her life reads like an incredible novel. See also "Zunhua" (Qing Tombs) and MILESTONES IN CHINESE HISTORY.

Great Wall—see separate listing.

The Ming Tombs, open daily 8 a.m.–4 p.m., are sometimes combined with a trip to the Great Wall at Badaling or the Summer Palace in a one-day excursion. It is a 50-kilometer (1¾-hour) drive northwest of the Tian Anmen. Avoid the Sunday traffic jams.

These thirteen imperial tombs were built from the 14th to the 17th centuries and are spread over 40 square kilometers. Each tomb consists of a Soul Tower, a Sacrificial Hall, and an Underground Palace, surrounded by a wall. Approaching from the south, one sees a big white carved marble archway erected in 1590, beyond which are the Great Red Gate, ornamental pillars, and the Tablet Pavilion. The Sacred Way has 24 stone animals (lions, Hsia Cheis, camels, elephants, Chi-lins, and horses—four each) and twelve bigger-than-life-sized humans (military officers and government officials). At least two of the tombs are open to visitors: Chang Ding, the biggest and earliest, and Ting Ding, which has been excavated and can be entered. Ting Ding is the tomb of the thirteenth Ming emperor, the Wan Li, who ruled for forty-eight years starting at age ten. The tomb was begun when he was twenty-two years old. It took six years and cost eight million taels of silver to build. Look for the new restaurant near the Chang Ding.

The underground palace has three halls, the central one with passages to annex chambers. The marble doors each weigh four tons. In the central hall are three marble altars, two for the empresses, one for the emperor. Note the "Five Altar Pieces" and the porcelain lamp. The rear hall has the three coffins and plaster replicas of twenty-six chests. The museum has on display some of the objects found in the tomb such as the gold crown, headdresses, a jade belt, and a gold bowl.

If you have more time, then also see:

Beihai (Peihai; North Sea) Park, open 7:30 a.m.–4 p.m.; 168 acres. This is only a few blocks northwest of the Forbidden City. (Take bus 103 along Wang Fu Jing Street from the Beijing Hotel.) This is a historic park that needs much time to explore, particularly now that many of the old buildings are being restored and opened to the public. There are rowboats for hire and in the winter, ice skating on the lake, but bring your own skates. There is also the fabulous Fang San Restaurant, where you can get the same fancy dishes once served to the Empress Dowager (well, almost!)

In the tenth century (Liao), an imperial residence was built on the site and called Precious Islet Imperial Lodging. In the twelfth century (Jin) auxiliary palaces were built here and a lake excavated, the earth used to build the Round City at the southern edge and the artificial hills. Rocks from Kaifeng in Henan province were also used. During the Yuan, the Qionghua Islet was expanded and the palace of Kublai Khan was made the center of the city. It is no longer standing. Also on the islet, in 1271 the large white bell-shaped structure, the White Dagoba, was built in the Tibetan style. Successive dynasties added buildings, and the park was looted by foreign powers in 1900. Most famous are the White Dagoba and the Nine Dragon Screen (1756), made of glazed brick. It is 5 meters by 27 meters by 1.2 meters. Also noteworthy is Kublai Khan's 3,000-liter jade liquor container (1265) and the jade Buddha in Chengguang Hall.

Zhongnanhai (Chungnanhai) is not open to the public because they are the residences and offices of China's leaders, but they are also historical. The Kuang Hsu emperor was imprisoned there during the winters, and for a while, probably Chiang Ching, widow of Chairman Mao and one of the Gang of Four. If you linger too long on the bridge south of Beihai Park, an armed guard will ask you to move. The south gate, brilliant red and fancy, is on Changan Road west of the Tian Anmen.

Western Hills: Another day's excursion that could be combined with the Summer Palace is the Temple of the Azure Clouds, the Temple of the Sleeping Buddha and Fragrant Hill—all within 10 kilometers of each other about 30 kilometers from the Tian Anmen. Eight more temples in the area are expected to be opened soon. Because of traffic jams, avoid Sundays here too.

The **Temple of the Azure Clouds** is the most important of these, with its stunning collection of religious statues. It was first built in the Yuan as a nunnery. During the Ming, it was a burial ground for powerful eunuchs. In 1748 the Chien Lung emperor had built the Hall of Five Hundred Arhats and the Diamond Throne Pagoda. The 508 arhats are life-sized, strikingly beautiful, each different. In 1925 the body of Dr. Sun Yat-sen lay in state here, where there is now a small museum. The Diamond Throne Pagoda on the highest of the six terraces is in Tibetan style and has some excellent carvings showing a great deal of Indian influence.

The **Temple of the Sleeping Buddha** was built in the Tang and reconstructed and renamed in the Yuan, Ming, and Qing. The lacquered bronze Sakyamuni, which was cast in 1321 (Yuan) is 5.33 meters long and weighs 54 tons. On either side are the twelve bodhisattvas, the disciples of Sakyamuni. A long hiking trail extends to the left behind the fish pond up the mountain.

Xiang Shan (Hsiang Shan; Fragrant Hill) Park, open 7:30 a.m.–5:30 p.m., was a 384-acre hunting ground for many emperors and is most beautiful in the autumn. It contains an excellent restaurant and a hotel. The posh Xiang Shan Hotel is expected to open here in 1983. On the grounds are a small Glazed Pagoda, a Western-style house that was presumably the hunting lodge, and a Tibetan-style temple. The Xiang Shan temple is not there any more.

Lugouqiao (Lukouchiao; Reed Valley Bridge), a.k.a. Marco Polo Bridge, is primarily for modern history fans. Built in the twelfth century, it is 250 meters long with eleven stone arches, with 485 lions spaced along its railings, each one different. It is named for Marco Polo because the Venetian explorer described it at length in his book. It is about 20 kilometers southwest of the city, and is the site of the incident that touched off the Japanese war on July 7, 1937.

Qing Tombs—see listing under "Zunhua."

Chengde, a.k.a. Jehol—see separate listing.

Zhoukoudian (Choukoutien) is where the Peking Man, who lived 400,000 to 500,000 years ago, was found in a cave 48 kilometers south of Beijing. Since 1927, forty-four skulls have been discovered. There is a small museum. A model of the area is in the Museum of Chinese History in Beijing.

Of the newly opened attractions, the most worthwhile visiting is the **Lama Temple,** the Yong He Gong, the Temple of Harmony and Peace. First built in 1694, this Mongolian/Tibetan yellow-sect temple is within walking distance of the No. 2 Overseas Chinese Hostel (not the one on Wangfujing). It is beautifully renovated, pavilion after pavilion of increasingly startling figures—the largest in the back hall 18 m. high—and surrounded by intriguing balconies. The statue was carved from one piece of sandalwood from Tibet.

The steles are Han, Manchurian, Mongolian, and Tibetan. The statues in the main halls resemble those in most red-sect Buddhist temples, but some statues do wear the white Tibetan scarf, a traditional gift, and some wear the pointed Himalayan caps. On either side of the symmetrical structure, however, the more typically Mongolian/Tibetan demons, human skulls, and tankas appear.

Of great historic and artistic interest is a picture made of pieces of silk by the mother of the Chien Lung Emperor of the Qing. In one of the courtyards stands a 1.5 m. bronze rendering of the Buddhist Mountain Xumi.

Originally built as a palace by Qing Emperor Kang Hsi for his son Yung Cheng, it was turned into a temple by Chien Lung in 1744. Prayer wheels for sale. Young monks abound.

The **White Dagoba Monastery,** that imposing, white, inverted cone in Beihai Park, now has a museum. The Dagoba itself is 50.9 m., built in 1271 by Kublai Khan. The present one stands from 1731. During repairs made in 1978 after the Tangshan earthquake, archaeologists found over 20 relics inside dated 1753, from the Chien Lung Emperor. These include a pure gold 5.4-cm. gem-studded Buddha and a glazed Goddess of Mercy.

The **Confucius Temple** dating from the Yan now houses the Capital Museum, an exhibition of Beijing history from the Peking Man to the 1911 Revolution. Worth seeing. Also worth seeing is the **Big Bell Temple and museum** which has China's biggest bell.

The **Tan Zhe Si** and **Hui Zhi Si** temples are only 6 km. apart, so can be seen in one day's tour. Southwest of Beijing, they make a pleasant excursion into the mountains. During the Yuan Dynasty, the daughter of Kublai Khan is said to have resided at the Tan Zhe Si to try to atone for her father's sins. The Tan Zhi Si has its roots in the Tang dynasty. In 1888 a Qing prince retired here. After the 1911 Revolution many foreigners used it as a summer resort, and after Liberation it was a workers' health spa. The Ming temple bell here is over 400 years old.

Another exciting development is the opening of some historic monuments for **banquets and receptions:** in addition to the Great Hall of the People, there's also the Marble Boat and any other boat at the Summer Palace.

Near the Summer Palace are the ruins of the **Yuan Ming Yuan,** the Old Summer Palace. Originally 160 hectares, it is now only one-tenth its original parcel. Sacked by French and British forces in 1860, it was partially repaired only to be destroyed again in 1900 by an international army opposed to the Boxers and the Qing court. Most famous are the remains of the Xiyang Lou, a rococo palace built between 1747 and 1760, following a design by F. Giuseppe Castiglione, an Italian Jesuit, and his colleagues. The first European-type building in China, it welcomes visitors.

Also worth seeing is the **Niu Jiu Mosque.** The Chinese have, in addition, been busy repairing the following relics and they should be opened in the near future: The **Pavilion of Purple Light** and the **Fairy Tower** in Zhongnanhai, the ancient astronomical observatory on Jianguomen Ave., and the **Deshengmen** (Victory Gate) through which emperors and generals returned from battle.

Also being repaired are the **Temple of Five Pagodas,** the **Pagoda in memory of the Sixth Panchen Lama,** the **Temple of White Clouds** which is the largest Taoist temple in China, and the 1,300-yr.-old **Buddhist Fayuansi Temple.**

Shopping: Beijing is the best shopping area in China after Shanghai. Most stores are open 8:30 or 9 a.m.–7 or 8:30 p.m. The main shopping street is Wang Fu Jing east of the Beijing Hotel. Another area less frequented by tourists is Xi Dan, two blocks east of the Minzu Hotel. The best area for antiques, arts, and crafts is Liu Li Chang on both sides of Nan Xin Hua, the main street where the buses stop. There are about thirty stores here, open 9 a.m.–5:30 p.m. (winter) or 6 p.m. (summer). An interesting store is the **Arts and Crafts Peking Trust Company,** open 8:30 a.m.–7:30 p.m., one block east of the Beijing Hotel and ¼ block south. Known also as the **Theater Shop** because of its theatrical costumes on sale (¥600–¥800), it also sells traditional-style furniture, old clocks, and secondhand goods. Some U.S name-brand, factory-overrun clothing has been found in the area south of the Qian Men.

The **Friendship Store** open 9–9, is probably the largest in China because it caters also to the foreign diplomatic and business communities. Next to the factories, this is a good place to buy cloisonné, jade carving, ivory carving, lacquerware, traditional Chinese painting, snuff bottles, filigree, dough figurines, carpets, and wood-block prints.

The **Free Market** is where peasants can sell their surplus produce and their handicrafts. A big one is at Bei Tai Ting Zhan.

International Club, open 9 a.m.–9:30 p.m., is on a street east of the Beijing Hotel near the old east city wall and is open to all foreigners. Usually there is no need to show a passport. It has a coffee shop and dining room (12–2:30 p.m. and 6–8:30 p.m.) with Western food. Movies are shown most evenings.

Chinese guests have to have special permission to dine there but can patronize the theater. The swimming pool is open only in summer and requires a health certificate that may take a week to obtain. Tennis is available. There is a small retail store with Kodak film, foreign cigarettes, liquor, and Coca-Cola. There is also dancing.

Bicycle Rentals: Foreigners are discouraged from riding bicycles in Beijing, but are not forbidden to do so. There are a couple of rental shops. You leave your passport and a deposit.

Walks: Around the Xin Qiao Hotel for the old European architecture. This foreign legation area was under seige during the Boxer invasion of Beijing on June 13, 1900. On June 20, most foreign diplomats and missionaries and two thousand Chinese Christian refugees took shelter in the British legation until the International Relief Force arrived on August 13.

Around the Minzu Hotel toward the Forbidden City. This area is full of old houses, antique doors, carvings, grinding stones used as steps, and fancy carved stone door hinges, and contains the Xi Dan market.

Everywhere in the old city you can see many of these things. Look for signs of symbols hidden during the Cultural Revolution, and for the back lanes with interesting old houses. Look for remains of small neighborhood temples and shrines. Early morning is the best time, especially in the parks, for tai chi chuan practitioners and shy singers.

Public Baths: This is an informal way to meet the masses, but you have to take part too. You still may not break through the reserve but you can get a brutal massage (feels great when it stops) for about a tenth of the cost in the hotel. You can also take a hot tub bath or a communal shower. Men can usually get a hot soak similar to a Japanese *ofuro,* while women cannot. Lockers, keys, and towels provided. Go by yourself. Your guide will probably try to discourage you. There is the **Qing Hua Bath House** at 223 Wang Fu Jing (open 8–8). Or head south from the Qian Men and turn left after a couple of blocks at a sign "Xian Yu Kou Yu Chi." Walk half a block and it's no. 74 with a green elevated roof on the left; phone 750087 or 750007.

Beijing Buses: A new tourist bus service run by the Beijing Motor Bus Co. is quite inexpensive. Air-conditioned buses to the Great Wall and the Ming Tombs, and a one-day tour to Fragrant Hills and Summer Palace. Other trips to the Yun-shui Caves (about 20 km. west of Beijing—"just nice caves") and Tan Zhe Temple. Also to Beidaihe.

Foreigners have not been encouraged to use these buses as the commentary is in Chinese, but anyone armed with a detailed guide can try to take advantage of the cheap ride. The office is east of the Qian Men with stops at the Overseas Chinese Hotel and Xin-jie Kou Hotel.

Beijing Subway (first stage) was built from 1965 to 1969. It is 24 kilometers long; each station is in different color marble. Trains go every eight minutes from 6:30 a.m. to 10 p.m. west from the railway station. Note the station at the south end of Tian Anmen Square. Up until early 1979 foreigners were forbidden to use the subway without prior permission, but now it is open to everyone. The second stage, a 16-km. loop completing the rectangle around Tian Anmen Square and the Forbidden City opened in 1982. It reaches near the Friendship Hotel.

Beijing International Airport: New, with 54,500 sq.m. of floor space, several lounges, observation deck, shops, duty-free store, restaurants with Chinese and European food, and bars, and a C.I.T.S. suboffice. Other buildings include a six-story hotel for transit passengers, shops, cinema, recreation hall, and power station.

Cultural Presentations: Traditional opera, acrobatics, puppets, songs and dances, ballet, gymnastics, concerts, sports competitions, movies, dancing. Ballroom dancing is held sometimes three times a week at the Friendship Hotel, the Nationalities Palace near the Minzu Hotel, and at the Friendship Club. The Minzu (Nationalities) Palace has a disco on Wednesdays, Fridays, and Sundays; games, dancing, shooting, and billiards on Tuesdays, Thursdays, and Saturdays. Sometimes it goes from 8:30 p.m. to 2 a.m., ¥10 a head; bring your own cassettes and partner (but this latter rule is not always enforced). Sometimes there is a live band; usually there is a shortage of women.

    Beijing Opera (see also "Go to Cultural Events" in chapter 10): Traditional opera in Beijing should be the best in the country.

Beijing Food: (See also "Food" under USEFUL PHRASES and chapter 6, FOOD.) This is usually salty (as opposed to sweet) and is not highly spiced. There are fewer sauces than in Cantonese cooking. Everyone must try Beijing duck. The best part is the crispy skin, which is dipped in dark brown hoisin sauce, seasoned with a green onion, and then wrapped in a thin pancake and eaten by hand. Also worth trying, especially on those early-morning walks, are the rolls, or the Chinese equivalent of doughnuts—the long, deep-fried "oil sticks"—dipped in sweetened hot soy milk (¥.025) in a neighborhood restaurant. Also famous are the *baozhe,* meat dumplings either steamed or boiled in soup.

    Beijing is a gourmet's delight, with food from all over the country. Unique is the **Fang San Restaurant** in Beihai Park along the lake in an old pavilion. Its cooks were taught by the cooks of the Empress Dowager herself. Fancy. Some popular restaurants, particularly the **Wang Fu Jing Beijing Duck Restaurant,** may need reservations a week in advance. Other recommended restaurants: those in the *Xin Qiao Hotel, Feng Huang (Phoenix) Restaurant* (near U.S. Embassy), and the *Honan Restaurant* behind the Minzu Hotel— "good food, friendly concerned manager, Mrs. Hong." Also, the *Zhi Mei Lou* (Shantong), *Sichuan Fan Dian* (Sichuan), *Donglaishun* (Shanghai), and of course the three Peking Duck restaurants. New U.S. joint venture bake shop.

Hotels: For addresses and phone numbers see chapter 18. For advance reservations see chapter 16.

Beijing (Peking) Hotel, East Chang An Road. Built 1915 and 1954—300 rooms; 1974—600 rooms. This hotel is in a class by itself, particularly the new wing. It is one and a half blocks from the Tian Anmen and I consider it second best in China to the Dong Fang in Guangzhou. It has all the basic services and more so—bells that work, longer foreign exchange hours, a larger retail shop, bookstore, outgoing telex, a higher standard of English. If you can't change your money at another hotel because of the limited hours, come to this one. However, in 1981, the service was considered terrible in the main restaurant and the food mediocre. Try the buffet breakfast if you are in a hurry.

There are fifteen dining rooms, but also room service for meals. Its largest banquet room seats one thousand people. Before the Great Hall of the People was completed, it was used for state functions. Ten of its dining rooms can accommodate over one hundred; the East Wing dining room seats five hundred. Its three hundred cooks prepare four kinds of Chinese food, plus British, French, and Russian dishes. The total staff is almost 1,500.

Its suites have dimmers, electrically controlled drapes, double glass windows (for quiet), bidets, two toilets, refrigerators with free drinks, pastel telephones, air-conditioning, and televisions. Every floor in the new wing has a set of scales and an ironing board. It is not without problems, but its standards are very high.

With many foreign business firms using this hotel for offices and hanging on to rooms even when they are not used, it has been difficult to book a room here. Seasoned travelers sometimes contact the corporations directly and ask if they have any rooms to spare. Payment is to the corporation, not the hotel. This procedure is not without problems, however. The hotel has no directory of guests by corporation name. The inquiry desk has a copy of each registration form grouped by nationality, so you should know the name of an executive—unless you have access to a China Phone Book (published in Hong Kong) or help from a local foreign resident. This tight situation will probably continue until 1983.

Xin Qiao (Hsin Chiao) Hotel, Chung Wen Men. Built 1954. Over 300 rooms. This is in the old legation section, surrounded by interesting old European architecture. It is within walking distance of the Tian Anmen and the Beijing Hotel. It has the reputation for the best food of any hotel in town.

Qianmen (Chien Men) Hotel, Yung An Lu. Built 1956. 382 rooms. This is the hotel closest to the Liu Li Chang antique stores and the new seven-story Beijing duck restaurant. It has two dining rooms for Chinese food, one for Western. Another dining room is being constructed in the back.

Minzu (Min Tzu, Min Dzu; Nationalities) Hotel, West Changan Road. Built 1959. 500 rooms. About 3 kilometers west and on the same street as the Tian Anmen. One block from the Nationalities Palace dances. Close to the subway.

Youyi (Yoyi; Friendship) Hotel; Baichiquiao Road. Built 1952. 1,500 rooms but only a few hundred for foreign tourists. Located in the northwestern suburbs beyond the zoo 12 kilometers from the Tian Anmen. It is surrounded by apartment buildings and wide tree-lined boulevards, and is the only hotel with a traditional Chinese roof (the others have a heavy, Soviet-style look). The Friendship is currently the hotel closest to Beijing and Qinghua (Tsinghua) Universities and the Summer Palace.

Heping (Hoping; Peace) Hotel, Chinyu Hutung. Over 300 rooms. Completely renovated. Located in a back alley, it does have the advantage of being within walking distance of the Forbidden City and Wang Fu Jing. Good food.

Huaqiao (Huachiao; Overseas Chinese) Hotel; Wang Fu Jing. Built 1958. About 300 rooms. It is across the street from the CAAC booking office. It is also diagonally across from the Fine Arts Museum and within walking distance of the back gate of the Forbidden City and Coal Hill.

New Hotels: Diaoyutai (Angler's Inn) in western Beijing, the most expensive hotel in China. Set on 42 acres of old Imperial Gardens. Fifteen separate villas, the largest a 17-room mansion for about US$3,000 a night; the smallest, 10 rooms for US$2,800 a day or so. ¥10 for breakfast and ¥65 per person for a banquet. Service good. Food not exceptional. The Diaoyutai is still a state guest house but is available to some tours and to business travelers. Only Lindblad, however, seems to guarantee it. Decorated with antiques, it was originally a hunting and fishing resort for the Jin rulers 800 years ago and improved on since.

Yenjing Hotel (Yanjing). Briefly named Fuxing Hotel. Chang An Rd. at Fuxing Rd., slightly farther west from the Forbidden City than the Minzu Hotel. 508 rooms, 21 stories. Built 1981. Outgoing telex. Small rooms. One of the few hotels with smoke alarms in each room and drawers with keys in rooms for locking valuables. Tubs above seventh floor; showers only on lower floors. Standard double ¥55 for lower floors, ¥60 for uppers. Decor pleasant but not luxurious.

Jianguo Hotel. 530 rooms. Built 1982. Owned by C.I.T.S. and Chinese-American interests. Managed by Peninsula Group, Hong Kong. Copied after the Buffalo, N.Y., Hilton. Across from Friendship Store. Indoor/outdoor swimming pool, cocktail lounge, disco, fitness center, business center, executive offices for rent, telex (2-way), 24-hr. laundry service, 24-hr. room service, imported ingredients for Western foods, safe deposit boxes, complimentary morning newspaper, messenger and babysitting services, ballroom/theater. Should rival Beijing Hotel as best in town.

Xiyuan Hotel near zoo. Due 1983. Over 700 rooms. Tel. 890721; **Changcheng (Great Wall) Hotel.** Due 1983. 1,007 rooms, main wing 22 stories. Glass elevators, tea garden, 7 restaurants, health club, cinema, nightclub. Near Agricultural Exhibition Hall.

Xiangshan (Fragrant Hills) Hotel. 353 rooms. Due 1983. West of Summer Palace in park. I.M. Pei, architect. Inspired by traditional Chinese architecture. Tel. 819225.

Hotels Recently Opened to Foreign Friends: Wannian Ching (Evergreen) Hotel, Yenshan Hotel, both fairly near Friendship Hotel. **Yanxiang/Yang Xiang Hotel,** 144 rooms. Joint venture with U.S. company. **Beijing Exhibition Hotel,** near Beijing Exhibition Hall. **Xiang Yang No. 2 Guest House,** near Xin Qiao Hotel. No restaurant. Several floors have offices.

Zhouxian Hotel, Zhuo County, Hebei province, about two hours (80 km.) from the Forbidden City by bus. Tourists are put here during peak season when nothing else is available. Qing tombs about 50 km. away. Tourists also bedded in Tianjin.

CHANGCHUN, a 1½-hour flight northeast of Beijing, is the capital of Jilin province, formerly part of Manchuria. It is noted mostly as an industrial city manufacturing automobiles (China's first plant), trucks, railway carriages, tractors, machine tools, and textiles. Tourists might be interested in visiting its film studio, one of China's largest.

Changchun is very cold in winter (lowest minus 30°C), with lots of snow. It has ice carvings in the parks then. The summers are cool. The population is 1,200,000. The city was founded 170 years ago, the walls built in 1865. Invaded by Tsarist Russia in the 1890s, it became a Japanese concession in 1905 and the capital of Japanese-controlled "Manchukuo" in 1931.

The Baishan Guest House (530 beds) should be completed by 1982. The Nanhu Guest House (250 beds) was built in 1960.

CHANGSHA (Long Sand)

Location: Capital of Hunan province south of the Yangtze River. 85 minutes' flight southwest of Shanghai, one hour northwest of Guilin, and 3 hours 20 minutes south of Beijing (by small plane). On the main Beijing-Guangzhou railway line, it is 726 kilometers north of Guangzhou.

Population: 1 million.

Area: 200 square kilometers.

Background: Changsha, in one of China's main rice-growing areas, was a small town two thousand years ago. It is famous because Chairman Mao was born nearby and studied for about five years at the Hunan Provincial First Normal School (1912–1918). According to Jonathan Spence's *To Change China,* Mao was briefly editor of the *Yale-in-China Review.* The Christian-motivated mission from the American university also rented him three rooms for his bookstore. Yale started its mission in Changsha about 1904 and eventually established a medical school, hospital, and middle school; the

Americans left shortly after Liberation. You can visit Mao's homes here.

Changsha is also known as the site of an important Han excavation. Its embroidery is one of the four most famous in China. A visit to the Hunan Provincial Embroidery Factory is worthwhile. The novel *The Sand Pebbles* was set largely in Changsha during the Northern Expedition. Most of the city was destroyed during the Japanese war.

Of Interest to Visitors

Shaoshan, birthplace of Chairman Mao. A very pretty village about 2½ hours' drive southwest of Changsha. See separate listing.

Hunan Provincial Museum: The 1972–74 excavations of three 2,100-year-old tombs have overshadowed the revolutionary and ancient collections in this museum. You will probably see the new finds, important because of their excellent state of preservation and vast numbers. You may want to return and see the rest later. The Han remains are in the white middle building on the right after you enter the gate. The tombs were of Li Tsang, Chancellor to the Prince of Changsha and Marquis of Tai, his wife, and his son. The son died in 168 B.C. The body of the woman, 1.52 meters long and 34.3 kilograms, is incredibly well preserved with flesh, sixteen teeth, and internal organs. The lungs, intestines, and stomach were removed after disinterment and preserved in formaldehyde as well. They are all on display in the basement. An autopsy revealed arteriosclerosis, gallstones, tuberculosis, and parasites. Death came suddenly at age fifty; there were undigested melon seeds in her stomach. The remarkable state of preservation is attributed to the body's being wrapped in hemp and nine silk ribbons and sealed from oxygen and water in three coffins surrounded by 5,000 kilograms of charcoal and sticky white clay. She was buried 20 meters deep. She died later than her husband; her tomb is the largest, and she is the best preserved of all.

The five thousand relics include 1,800 pieces of lacquerware, many of which needed only cleaning to look new, ear cups for wine and soup, and a toilet box with comb, mirror, powder, and lipstick. She had food—chicken, dog, deer, crane, dove, beef, pork, goat, and rabbit; incense burners, clothes, silk fabrics, medicinal herbs, nine musical instruments. An inventory of the relics was written on bamboo strips, paper then still being rare. In the building to the left as you leave the lady are the three coffins and a model of the tomb site. To the right is an antique, arts, and crafts store.

The **tomb site,** only 4 kilometers away, is now just a large hole in the ground under a roof. One can see the pyramid-shaped hill, the neat, earthen walls, and staircase inside. Geomancy fans can figure out the *feng shui.* Was it practiced then? Did the tomb face south?

Tianxin Park is the highest part of the city. This park still has a small section of the 600-plus-year-old city wall. Note Qing inscriptions on brick.

Exhibition Hall has more than three thousand pieces of ceramics on display, including a 7-foot vase, most made recently in Changsha. Exhibit hall of traditional styled painting and shop upstairs.

Juzi (Orange) Island, 5 kilometers long, is probably the "long sand" after which Changsha is named. In the middle of the Xiang River at Changsha, it is 300 meters at its widest. Buses can drive almost to the southern tip, a park. The island is inhabited, cultivated with orange groves, and stacked with reeds for making paper. It has a small sand beach for swimming and a place to change soon. Good for relaxing evening walks and bicycling, if you can talk someone into lending you a bicycle. Bicycle tours and boat rides depending on the weather.

Hunan Normal School: Small museum. Mao studied and taught here.

Hotels

Xiang River Hotel. Built 1977. More than 500 rooms. Close to shopping, post and cable office. On Zhongshan Road, near the former site of Teach-Yourself College. Dance parties about twice a month on request.

Hunan Hotel. Older. Mainly for state guests. Near museum and Memorial Park to Martyrs.

Fu Rong (Hibiscus) Hotel. More than 500 rooms. Probably 1982.

Recommended Restaurants:

Fire Palace and Another Village.

Excursions:

To Miluo, Yueyang, Taoyuan, and Nanyue (Mt. Heng).

CHENGDE (Chengteh, Chengte, and Jehol) is about 250 km. northeast of Beijing in Hebei, the imperial summer resort/hunting park built for Qing Emperor Kang-hsi in 1703. Here he could not only relax but curry favor with the Mongolian nobles in the area. To also help win them over, he built the Outer Eight Lama Temples.

The summer weather here is good because of the altitude, and the monuments are spectacular. You can fly here in 30 minutes or travel by train for 4 hours. In 1860 the trip took the Manchus three days by horseback, palanquin, and chariot.

The resort oozes with history. It was here in 1793 that Lord Macartney of Britain refused to kowtow to Qing Emperor Chien Lung and where he was dismissed as a "bearer of tribute" from "vassal king" George III, his requests refused. The Emperor would not receive him in Beijing, but since he had come so far, did consent to receive him at the resort.

In 1860 the Manchu court fled here as Anglo-French forces approached Beijing. Emperor Hsien Feng died here, which led to the rise in power of Tzu Hsi, the Empress Dowager, as regent. Think of the palace intrigue that went on as he lay on his deathbed. Tzu Hsi visited here again in 1900 by train.

The imperial garden, the largest surviving one in China, is 5,600,000 sq. m. and is surrounded by a 10-km. wall. Inside stands the Palace with its living quarters and the emperor's bed with its secret escape passage, said to have been used by Tzu Hsi in her bid to gain power. She lived in the Pine and Crane Pavilion. Among the buildings along the lake are the **Jinshan Pavilion,** the **Yuese Jiangsheng Pavilion** and the **Misty-Rain Tower,** the latter built by Chien Lung, a copy of one on the Yangtze.

Of the Eight Outer Temples (actually 11), important to see are the **Pule,** the **Xume Fushou** (inspired by the Zhashenlunbu Temple in Shigatse, Tibet), and the **Puning** (with its 22-m. "Thousand-armed-thousand-eyed" Goddess of Mercy). There is also the **Putuo Zongcheng** Temple patterned after the Potala Palace in Lhasa, Tibet, with its Great Red Terrace.

CHENGDU (Chengtu), slightly over two hours by air southwest of Beijing, is the capital of Sichuan. It can also be reached by a 21-hour train ride from Kunming with about 250 kilometers of tunnels and a view of Mount Emei. The city has a history of over two thousand years. In the fourth century B.C., the king of Shu moved his capital here and named it Chengdu (Becoming a Capital). In the Han, after brocade-weaving became successfully established, it was called "the Brocade City." During the Three Kingdoms, it was the capital of the Shu. It was also a capital during the Five Dynasties. Many American, Canadian, and British missionaries and teachers lived here before Liberation.

Today it is an educational and industrial center with a population of 3.7 million. Its industries include machine building, coal mining, metallurgy, aluminum, and electronics. Its buses run on natural gas, of which it has abundance. The Five Cassia Production Brigade, less than an hour from the city, rates a visit because it uses manure as fuel as well as fertilizer. The brigade also produces honey. The area grows rice, wheat, and sweet potatoes. It also grows medicinal plants and herbs that are sold all over the country. With an altitude of 500 meters, its hottest temperature is 33°C in July and the coldest 3°C in January. Tourist season is June to October.

Chengdu's attractions include **Tu Fu's Thatched Roof Cottage,** a replica of the residence of the famous Tang poet who lived here and wrote 240 poems during four years from 759. There are statues, books and art exhibitions.

The **Wuhou Temple** in the southern part of the city was built in memory of Zhuge Liang (Chuke Liang), a famous strategist and statesman, prime minister of Shu during the Three Kingdoms. There are tablets written during the Tang, larger than life-size statues, and the tomb of Liu Bei, the king of Shu, one of the heroes of *The Romance of the Three Kingdoms,* still unexcavated.

Wanjianglou Park in the eastern part of Chengdu on the Jinjiang River has over one hundred varieties of bamboo and many pavilions such as "Pavilion for Poem Reciting" and "Chamber to Relieve Your Resentment." See if they inspire you. Sit in them quietly for half an hour, undisturbed, and breathe deeply.

The **Bao Guang (Divine Light Monastery)**, 18 kilometers from the city, is famous. Originally started during the Eastern Han about 1,900 years ago, it was the site of a palace ordered built by Tang Emperor Li Huan. During the Ming, the monastery was destroyed by war, but it was reconstructed on its original foundation during the Qing in 1671. There are now pagodas, five halls, and sixteen courtyards. The Tang pagoda is thirty meters high, thirteen stories with a glazed, gold top. The 500 arhats are from the Qing in 1851, each about two meters high and each vivid and different. The Stone Carved Stupa is also Ching, 5.5 meters high in granite. The Thousand Buddha Tablet was made in 450 A.D. Look also for the Buddhist scriptures written on palm leaves from India.

The **Dujiangyan Irrigation System,** two hours' drive away, was originally built in 256 B.C. Impressive because of its age and scope, it diverted half of the Minjiang river to irrigation. This area also has old temples, murals, sculptures, and a swinging bridge. The Fu Long Kuan Temple has an 1,800-year-old stone statue. The Er Wang Miao Temple is a memorial to Li Bing and his son for harnessing the river. Near Dujiangyan is a deer farm where you can buy Pilose Antler Juice "for aching back . . . impotence and premature ejaculation." New hotel.

There is also **Lidi Park** (batik for sale), a Kodak film store in the middle of the free market in Guan County City, the Institute for Nationalities, zoo, and the War Lords' Temple in Chengdu.

Mt. Emei and **Leshan** are both about 170 km. away. **Qingcheng Shan** (Green City Mountain), one of the birthplaces of Taoism, is 50 km. away and rises to 1,600 m. Of 70 Taoist temples, only 38 survive. There are guest houses midway up and on top. **Wolong Nature Preserve,** 180 km. from Chengdu, has about 1,000 pandas in the wild but tourists can usually only see eight. (The Chengdu zoo has ten.) Very rough road. No hotel. Tourists stay in Forestry Bureau hostel. Not generally open to tourists. Check with World Wildlife Fund or Lindblad if you want to go. See separate listings for EMEI MOUNTAIN and LESHAN.

Chengdu is a good place to buy silver, brocade, embroidery, lacquer, and woven bamboo. Its food is spicy hot, but it is toned down for tourists. Flower petals and herbs are used in such specialties as "fried lotus flower," "governor's chicken," and "smoked duck with tea fragrance." Try also the dumplings, wonton, and Dan Dan noodles.

Chengdu has two hotels—the main one is the **Jin Jiang** (1958), with over 800 rooms, which was a Red Guard headquarters during the Cultural Revolution. The other hotel (for V.V.I.P.s) is the **Jing Liu.** The **Ming Jiang** near the Jin Jiang is in the construction stage.

CHONGQING (Chungking), in the southeastern part of Sichuan, is an old city on mountainsides between the Yangtze and Jialing Rivers. Two hours' flight southwest of Beijing, it can also be an overnight train ride from Chengdu. The city was badly destroyed by Japanese bombs during the war when it was the Chinese capital. It is smoky and drab, now primarily of interest to students of modern history. It is the point where you can get a two-day trip to the Dazu sculptures and through the Yangtze Gorges.

Chongqing has a history of three thousand years. It was capital of the Kingdom of Ba in the twelfth century B.C. During the Sung, it was named Chongqing, which means "double celebration." During the Japanese war, Chou En-lai lived here as he tried to work with the Nationalists against the foreign invader. You can now visit Red Crag Village, which was headquarters of the Communist Eighth Route Army during the negotiations, and Zhengjiayen no. 50. The Nationalist headquarters was in the building across from the People's Hotel. The Americans sent many missions here to try to reconcile the two. Read Theodore H. White's *In Search of History* for that period.

Today the city has a population of about six million in its urban and rural areas. Its 2,300 industrial enterprises include mining, iron and steel, coal, electricity, machinery, light industry, building materials, electronics, and measurement instruments.

Among the tourist attractions are **Loquat Hill Park,** the highest point in the city. **Eling (Goose Hill) Park** is between the Yangtze and Jialing Rivers, with pavilions, ponds, and gardens. **Huangshan Hill** on the south bank of the Yangtze has over a thousand varieties of flowers such as peony, magnolia, camellia, azalea, and oriental cherry. At nearby **Tu Hill** is the site of the residence of King Yu of the Xia, the first ruler to control the rivers, and **Lao Jun Cave,** where Lao Tze, founder of Taoism, lived.

North of the city are historic hot-spring and summer resorts and the 1,500-year-old **Jinyun Monastery.** Twenty-four kilometers south of the city is **Nanwenquan,** another hot-spring resort. But the only worthwhile attractions are Dazu and the Yangtze Gorges.

For shoppers—glassware, inlaid bamboo and wood, and lacquerware.

Lucky tourists are put in the **People's Hotel,** a replica of the Temple of Heaven. Some tourists found no heat in November, however, but lots of blankets. 300 beds. Another 200-bed hotel, the Huixianlou is planned for the city center.

CONGHUA (Tsunghua, Chunghua) is a hot-spring resort about 90 kilometers northeast of Guangzhou in Guangdong province. The sulphurous spring water is said to bring relief for "high blood pressure, rheumatism, enteropathy, stomach and duodenal ulcers, neuralgia, and skin affections." The temperature of the water varies between 30°C and 70°C. The area is also noted for its hot sands, its yellow quartz caves, and a 16-meter waterfall. The Conghua Hotel bath has been described as "divine," the food "mediocre."

DALIAN (Talien, a.k.a. Luda), near the tip of the Liaoning Peninsula in northeast China, is an ice-free port and an important industrial center— shipyards, locomotive works, oil refinery. Its naval base was originally built by the Russians. Urban population is 1,200,000. Tourists might be interested in its ornamental glass factory. There is also a natural sciences museum and Tiger Beach Park.

DATONG (Tatung) in Shanxi province bordering on Inner Mongolia was a garrison town built between two sections of the Great Wall. It is famous for the **Yungang Grottoes,** said to be the best preserved in China, 53 caves containing over 51,000 stone carvings of Buddha, bodhisattvas, apsaras (angels), birds, and animals. These statues range from 17 meters to a few centimeters high, and some of them still retain their original color. Restoration was completed in 1976. The grottoes are at the southern foot of Wuzhou Hills, 16 kilometers west of the city. They were built between 460 A.D. and 494 A.D. in the Northern Wei before that dynasty moved its capital to Luoyang and built another set of grottoes there. They extend east-west for a kilometer.

Founded in the Warring States about 2,200 years ago, the city also has a 600-year-old nine-dragon screen, and the **Huayan Monastery.** The main hall of this Buddhist temple was built in 1062 and rebuilt in 1140. It is 53.75 meters long and 29 meters wide. The library hall was built over 940 years ago, and still has 38 wooden chests from the Liao for storing books. The **Shanhua Monastery** was built in 713. There is also a steam locomotive factory and a brass products factory (hot pots, plates, tea pots).

The population of Datong is 770,000, including the rural suburbs. The highest temperature (in summer) is 37.7°C, the lowest minus 29.9°C. Rainfall is 400 millimeters a year. The best time to visit is May through October.

DAZHAI (Tachai) in Shanxi southeast of Taiyuan is a commune famous as a model because of its spirit of hard work and self-sacrifice. Up until 1978, you could frequently hear the slogan "In agriculture, follow Dazhai." In 1979, however, officials pointed out that while this spirit to struggle hard was correct, the copying was not. Because every commune had different conditions, every commune had to improve its production in its own way. Production figures said to be falsified.

DAZU. The **Dazu Stone Buddhist Sculptures** are considered by some to be better preserved and of finer quality than Luoyang, Datong, or Dunhuang. About 50,000 of them are located in over 40 places in Dazu County, about 120 km. from Chongqing, usually a two-day trip. The best are at Beishan and Baodingshan, the largest being a 31-m.-long Sleeping Buddha and the most famous a 1,000-armed Goddess of Mercy. Built during the Tang and Song.

En route, visitors can also visit the **North Hot-Spring Park** with its huge swimming pool, 1,300-year-old Buddhist Temple, and Sichuan dinosaurs.

DUNHUANG (Tunhuang, Tunhwang) in western Gansu has one of the biggest art treasures of the world. Between the fourth and fourteenth centuries, more than a thousand caves were cut out of the cliffs 20 kilometers southeast of the city and filled with Buddhist carvings, gilt and colored frescoes, and murals. Known as the **Mokao Grottoes** or the **Thousand-Buddha Caves,** 480 of these remain today in three or four rows on a 1½-kilometer-long wall. The sculptures are reached by plane or train (27 hours) from Lanzhou and then a 25-kilometer stretch of improved road. Payment has to be made for taking photos, and the lights are dim. Dunhuang town has a guest house.

Dunhuang was an important cultural exchange center and oasis on the Silk Road from the Han. It was a military outpost under the Tang. In a library here early in 1900 was found the Diamond Sutra of 868, said to be the oldest existing dated printed book.

EMEI (Omei) Mountain in Sichuan, 170 kilometers southwest of Chengdu in Sichuan, is one of China's sacred Buddhist mountains. The whole climb can be done in three days. Along the stone path are monasteries, magnificent views, monkeys, and birds. Hotels at the base of and on the 3,100-meter-high mountain. Reached by train from Chengdu. Bao Guo Temple at the base has a scale-model map with lights. Land-Rovers can drive to 15 kilometers of the peak. Guides ¥32 a day, none English-speaking at press time.

FOSHAN (Fushan; Cantonese Fashan), Guangdong province. Named Hill of Buddhas because of a mound of Buddhist statues excavated here, 20 kilometers southeast of Guangzhou, this is one of the Four Ancient Towns of China. Population is 280,000. The city is over 1,300 years old, and is famous for its handicrafts. It currently has 147 factories making machines, electronics, chemicals, textiles, plastics, pharmaceuticals, cement, etc. Tourists are taken to see the **Foshan Folk Art Institute** (palace lanterns, T-shirts, and paper cutouts), the **Shiwan Artistic Ceramic Factory,** and a silk factory.

Ancestral Temple: Now the **Foshan Municipal Museum,** this building was erected in the Song (960–1279) and contains sculptures, ancient relics, and a 2,500-kilogram bronze Buddhist figure. Note the differently decorated bases of the arches and the stone, wood, and brick carvings. Four of the statues are said to be made of paper, the others of wood or clay. The roof, decorated with Shiwan pottery figures, is one of the most elaborate in the country. The double dragon screen near the gate is a recent replacement for one destroyed earlier.

Xiqiao Mountain, located 55 km. southeast of Guangzhou via Foshan is a good place for a leisurely family vacation. With two resort areas, one at the base and the other on top, hikers have a 400-m.-high mountain with a 10-km. circumference to explore. The mountaintop has three lakes (one in an extinct volcanic crater) with new (1981–82) bicycle paddle boats, 36 caves and grottoes, 72 peaks, 8 villages with a total population of 600 people, 207 springs, and a very pretty 26-room (70 bed) air-conditioned hotel (¥32 for a double) with hot water but no heat.

More crowded and noisy are the hotels at the base (one in Spanish architecture), because the area makes firecrackers, which are frequently set off by firecracker-deprived Hong Kong tourists. Guangzhou swingers come to learn dancing, and schoolchildren on excursions visit the three-story Ming tower and the Qing Taoist temple. Also, a one-km.-long artificial lake, horses, shooting gallery (machine guns!), waterfalls, basketball court, badminton, roller skating, a C.I.T.S. and taxi office.

Can be reached by taxi, bus, and boat from Guangzhou. You need only a Guangzhou visa, even to stay overnight.

FUSHUN in Liaoning province is frequently combined with Shenyang and Anyang because they are close together in the industrial northeast. It is China's biggest coal center.

FUZHOU (Foochow, Fuchou) is the capital of Fujian, and in 1979 was open only to Overseas Chinese. It was open to foreign trade in 1842 and had British and American dockyards and factories for making tea-bricks.

GEZHOUBA. Gezhouba is the new town (1970s) where tour boats pass through the locks on the Yangtze river, 3-km. downstream of the Three Gorges and about one-km. upstream of Yichang. The biggest multipurpose water conservancy project on the river, it includes a 2,500-m.-long and 70-m.-high dam, two power stations (2.715 million kw. capacity), a silt-discharge gate, a reservoir, a flood-discharge gate, and a channel for migrating fish. The water level differs by 20 m., making the gorges safer for shipping. The locks were first used in 1981 and continue to be a source of great interest both for local people and tourists.

GREAT WALL, known in Chinese as the **Wanlichangcheng** (Ten-Thousand-Li-Long-Wall), is officially 12,700 Chinese li, or 6,350 kilometers or 3,946.55 miles long. The length depends on what you measure, there being many offshoots and parallel walls. It is in various states of repair.

It was first built in shorter pieces starting in the fifth century B.C. as a defensive and boundary wall around the smaller states of Yen, Chao, and Wei. The first Chin emperor (221–206 B.C.), who unified China for the first time, linked up and extended the walls from Liaoning in the east to Gansu in the northwest as protection from the Huns and other nomadic tribes to the north. The Wall was subsequently repaired and extended by succeeding dynasties, especially the Ming.

Originally built by slave labor, it has been called the world's longest graveyard because many of its builders were buried where they fell in constructing it. It was designed to allow five horsemen or ten foot soldiers to march abreast along the top. It was almost a superhighway, considering the rough mountain terrain. A system of bonfires communicated military information to the emperor at a speed rapid for that period.

The Great Wall is most frequently visited at **Badaling (Padaling),** about 75 kilometers (two hours) by road northwest of Beijing. Please avoid the Sunday traffic jams. Usually the trip can be done by taxi in four hours if you don't linger. Most tourists now go from Beijing by soft-class train to Badaling, leaving at 8:05 a.m. daily except Wednesdays and arriving at 10:09. Leaving Badaling at 12:38 p.m., some passengers then get off at Nankow for a bus to the Ming Tombs. The train journey means a walk of about a mile except for the old, weak, and disabled, who can use a minibus shuttle. A new 500-seat restaurant and flush toilets!

Badaling is about 1,000 meters above sea level and is at Juyongguan (Chuyungkuan) Pass. Here the wall averages 7.8 meters high, 6.5 meters wide at the base, and 5.8 meters wide at the top. Watchtowers are located every few hundred meters. Note the giant rocks and bricks of uniform size, the gutters, and the waterspouts. You can walk several hundred feet in either direction until you meet a sign that says no farther. Skateboarding on the wall has been allowed, but is not recommended when it is thick with people, which is most of the time. Try first thing in the morning, probably at 8 a.m.

Also of note is the gate in the center of Juyongguan Pass, about 10 kilometers south of Badaling, built of finely carved marble and called Cloud Terrace. Originally the base of a tower built in 1245 A.D., the walls are decorated with carvings of Buddhas, four celestial guardians, and the text of a Buddhist sutra in Sanskrit, Tibetan, and four other languages. Tours do not stop here except by request.

Because of the congestion, another section of the Great Wall is being opened at Jinshanling Hill with a hotel.

Another section of the Great Wall is opened at three-thousand-year-old Shanhaiguan, over 40 kilometers north from Beidaihe and about 30 kilometers from Qinhuangdao. It is not as spectacular as at Badaling, nor is the section that is open as long. It is very interesting, though, because the wall has been only partially restored and you can see more of its innards. There is also a museum in the tower with a 215-pound sword "for practicing," a Ming cannon, and military uniforms from the Chin, so well preserved it is hard to believe they're two thousand years old. Note the sign "The First Pass Under Heaven." The gate was built in 1381.

The Great Wall can also be visited in Datong in Shanxi and the Jiayuguan (Chiayukuan) Pass in Gansu, its western terminal. Jiayuguan is in between the Qilian (Chilien) Mountains and the Mazong Mountains in Gansu. The city was built in 1372 when the first Ming emperor had the wall repaired and strengthened to keep out the defeated Mongols. Relics excavated from Wei and Jin tombs in the area are among those in the Jiayuguan Exhibition Hall. These include bricks with paintings depicting life in those eras.

GUANGZHOU (Kwangchow), a.k.a. Canton

Location: 125 kilometers northwest of Hong Kong in Guangdong province on the Zhu (Pearl) River. It can be reached by a nonstop 3-hour train ride, a 3-hour hovercraft plus a bus journey, or a ½-hour flight from Hong Kong. It is also a 2½ hour flight or 36-hour train ride south of Beijing.

Weather: Subtropical. Coldest: about zero°C January-February; hottest: about 38°C July-August; average rainfall: 1730 millimeters. Extremely humid summers.

Population: Urban—about 3 million.

Area: 54 square kilometers.

Background: Guangzhou is also known as the City of the Five Goats because five fairies came here supposedly in 1256 B.C. riding five goats from whose mouths the fairies drew the first rice seeds. It was founded over two thousand years ago and is best known abroad as a trading city, a role it has played at least since the Qin dynasty. It was the site of the Canton Trade Fair, for twenty-three years China's main foreign trade institution.

It is also known as the capital of Guangdong province, home of many Chinese immigrants to Australia, the United States, Canada, and many parts of Southeast Asia. Being a long way from the center of China and with so many native sons going abroad, the people here developed a rebellious, independent spirit which resulted in Guangzhou's becoming the starting point or site or many important historical events including:

—the movement against the importation of opium, when 20,000 chests were burned (1839), and the movement against foreign imperialism, for example, at Sanyuanli during the Opium War in 1841;
—the movement against the Manchus by the Taiping Heavenly Kingdom, whose leader Hong Xiuquan (Hung Hsiu-ch'uan) was born about 66 kilometers north of the city and was given the Christian tract that changed his life and China's history in Guangzhou;
—the movement against the Manchus in 1911 led by Dr. Sun Yat-sen, who was born south of the city near the Macao border;
—the general strike against the unequal foreign treaties starting in June 1925. It lasted for sixteen months and almost closed Hong Kong;
—the Communist Revolution. Mao Tse-tung trained peasant leaders here in 1926 at the National Peasant Movement Institute;
—the Northern Expedition whose officers were trained at the Whampoa Military Academy (Chiang Kai-shek was director; Chou En-lai was in charge of political indoctrination). In June 1926 this expedition to unify China started off from Guangzhou;
—the movement against the Nationalists who tried to exterminate the Communists here in December 1927.

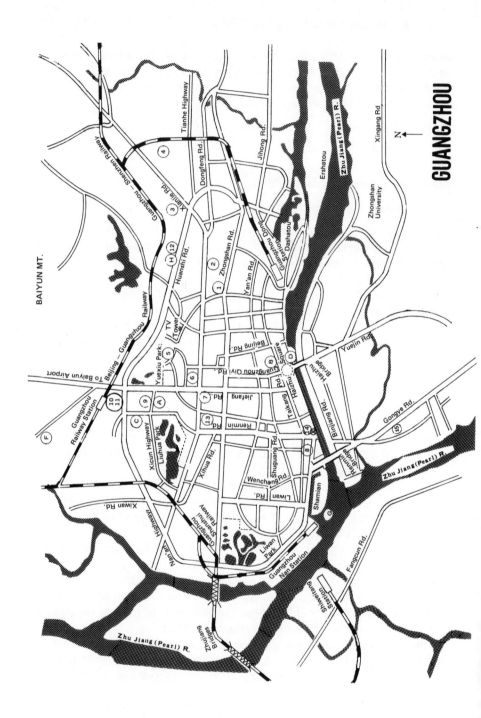

GUANGZHOU

BAIYUN MT.

Many foreign missionaries established schools and churches here after the city was opened to foreign trade and residence by the Treaty of Nanking in 1842. From 1938 to 1945, Guangzhou was occupied by the Japanese. The Communists took over from the Nationalists on October 14, 1949.

In recent years, Guangzhou has been one of the main suppliers of food, water, and electricity for neighboring Hong Kong. It has eleven institutions of higher learning, including Zhong Shan University on the site of the missionary-founded Ling Nam University. It has 3,200 factories producing fertilizer, heavy machinery, machine tools, insecticides, textiles (silk and ramie), petrochemicals, paper, sewing machines, ships, electronics, etc. Tourists would probably be interested in its ivory-carving factory, where about thirty concentric balls within balls are made from one piece of ivory.

The city is divided by the Pearl River, which is crossed by three bridges and innumerable ferries. Most of the places of interest to tourists are located on the north side of the river.

Dialect: while *pu tung hua* (Beijing dialect) is understood by almost everyone, the language spoken in most homes is Cantonese.

Of Interest to Visitors: If you have only a few hours, see Shamian Island (for architecture and history), take the boat trip (if you like boats), see the Temple of the Six Banyan Trees (for old Chinese architecture), the Botanical and Orchid Gardens (if you like plants), or the Ivory Factory if you like arts and crafts. Be sure to try one of the garden restaurants also.

National Peasant Movement Institute on Zhongshan Road was a school for 327 peasant leaders from twenty provinces and regions, open only from May to September 1926. Mao Tse-tung was director and Chou En-lai a teacher. The building was an old temple. Subjects included rural education, problems of peasants and class analysis. The institute was restored after Liberation, including the straw sandals and old rifles used by the students. Mao's office is on the right as you enter, with rattan trunks and straw mat on his wooden bed.

---

1. National Peasant Movement Institute
2. Memorial Gardens to the Martyrs of the 1927 Guangzhou Uprising
3. Mausoleum of the Seventy-two Martyrs at Huanghuagang
4. Guangzhou Zoo
5. Zhenhai Tower
6. Dr. Sun Yat-sen Memorial Hall
7. Temple of the Six Banyan Trees and Liurong Temple
8. Guangzhou Cultural Park
9. Guangzhou Trade Center
10. C.I.T.S.
11. CAAC
12. Friendship Store
13. Huai Sheng Mosque a.k.a. Guang Ta Monastery
14. Nanfang Department Store
15. Zhoutouzui (Ship Quay)

Hotels
A. Dongang (Tung-fang) and China Guangzhou
B. Guangzhou
C. Liu Hua
D. Huaqiao [Overseas Chinese] Mansion
E. Renmin [People's]
F. Kuang Chuan [Spa Villa] Hotel
G. Bai Tian E (White Swan)
H. Baiyun and Garden Hotels

Memorial Gardens to the Martyrs of the 1927 Guangzhou Uprising: Built in 1957, this park contains pavilions to Soviet and Korean friendship and the graves of those slaughtered by the Nationalists.

Mausoleum of the Seventy-two Martyrs at Huanghuagang (Huanghuakang; Yellow Flower Hill) commemorates an attempt in 1911 led by Dr. Sun Yat-sen's Chinese Revolutionary League to overthrow the Qing. This park on the road near the zoo is of interest to visitors of Chinese ancestry. It was built with donations from Chinese Nationalists' leagues around the world. The stones in the main monument are inscribed in English with the names of the donors: the Chinese Nationalist League of Chicago, Illinois; Moose Jaw, Saskatchewan; Lima, Peru. If you look closely, you may find your own hometown.

Guangzhou Zoo is in the northeastern suburbs. Opened in 1958, it has 200 species including pandas. We were allowed to feed bamboo to the elephants. With 350,000 square meters, second largest zoo in China.

Zhenhai (Chenhai; Sea-dominating) Tower, known also as the Guangzhou Museum, was built in 1380 to assert the power of the Ming dynasty. It has been rebuilt several times since then. Located at one of the highest points in the city, it has been used as a pleasure palace for high-ranking imperial officials, as a Nationalist hospital, and now as the city museum. Starting with prehistory on the second floor to revolutionary history on the fifth, the exhibits include some interesting old clocks, ceramics, and a picture of the burning of the 20,000 chests of opium.

Sun Yat-sen Memorial Hall, a theater seating 4,500, was built in 1931 and expanded and renovated in 1975. It is distinguished by its bright blue circus-tent-shaped ceramic roof.

Temple of the Six Banyan Trees has a 57.6-meter nine-story Flower Pagoda. Founded in the sixth century, it is prominent in the Guangzhou skyline. It can be climbed. Also known Liu Rong Temple.

Guangzhou Cultural Park, near the Nanfang Department Store, is best seen after 7 p.m., when its several exhibit halls are open. There are also theaters and children's playgrounds.

Foreign Trade Center: The Guangzhou Export Commodities Fair (Canton Trade Fair) was started in 1956 in a large building on the northwest side of Hai Zhu (Hai Chu) Park near the Guangzhou Hotel. It was moved in 1974 to a site across from the Dongfang Hotel near the railway station. Until late 1979 it convened from April 15 to May 15, and October 15 to November 15, a showcase of almost everything China had available for export, a venue for making purchases from abroad. At the autumn fair in 1979, a change of format was announced. The trade fair building would be expanded into a permanent trade center with two general fairs a year, smaller in scope than the fairs to date, with a series of specialized minifairs. Foreign traders would have space to exhibit also. Tourists can visit the Trade Center. Best buys are samples sold near the end of the fair.

China International Travel Service (C.I.T.S.) is to the left as you leave the front door of the railway station in a building facing the station.

CAAC is beside C.I.T.S., closer to the main street, out the door and to the left of the railway station.

China Travel Service (C.T.S.) office is to the right as you leave the front door of the Overseas Chinese Mansion. It is primarily for Chinese-speaking people of Chinese ancestry. It can arrange travel for individuals to visit relatives or for groups around Guangdong or China, or back to Hong Kong. Bus to Shantou.

Orchid Garden has more than a hundred species and almost ten thousand plants. It is behind the Foreign Trade Center.

South China Botanical Garden, a.k.a. Guangdong Botanical Garden, opened in the late 1950s and covers about 240 acres. There are more than two thousand species of tropical and subtropical plants.

Shamian (Shamien, also Shameen) Island in the Pearl River in central Guangzhou became a British and French concession in 1859–60. It was then an 80-acre sandbank, later built into a European ghetto, much resented by the Chinese. The architecture reflects its European owners. The island is joined to the mainland by two bridges. If you continue walking in the same direction as the bridge nearest the Renmin Bridge, you will find a small church on the right, which was a printing house, where visitors were welcomed. It is believed to have been originally French. There is a small hotel, the Shengli, and a good but seedy-looking restaurant, the Economical. The other buildings are now offices and apartments. Shamian is a breezy place to go for an evening stroll in the summer. At the far end, the western tip, is a 31-story, 992-room, luxury hotel, the **Bai Tian E** (White Swan), built 1982, with all the services of a first-class hotel, including automatic sprinklers, swimming pool, computerized room records, and advanced bookings.

Zhen (Chen) Family Hall is currently being repaired and may be opened by now as a crafts museum. It contains famous brick and ceramic carvings.

Huai Sheng Mosque, considered the oldest in China, was built 1,300 years ago by Arab traders. It is now open on Fridays for worshippers and tourists. For other days, see C.I.T.S. Tourists can climb its minaret, which has also been used as a lighthouse. The minaret is said to be original. The tomb of the founding Moslem missionary is in the Orchid Garden. Mosque also known as Guang Ta.

Yuexiu Park, the largest in the city, is 92,000 square meters. It contains a small lake where rowboats can be rented, an Olympic-size swimming pool, stadium, botanical exhibit, and the city museum in Zhenhai Tower.

The Pearl River boat ride (a ¥10 optional tour) usually takes 1½ hours on a new 250-passenger tour boat. It first cruises eastward downstream past the Renmin Hotel. At the Pearl River Bridge is the old Trade Fair building, the Guangzhou Hotel, and the Overseas Chinese Mansion. The bridge was destroyed by the retreating Nationalists, but rebuilt after Liberation. After the bridge is a row of apartments for resettled former boat dwellers. And just where the boat turns around, on the opposite shore, is Zhongshan University. After passing the starting point, the boat turns left at Shamian Island (look behind you quickly) and then goes past the shipyards before heading back. During the trip, you can see an interesting assortment of tiny sampans operated by oars, junks, ferries, ocean freighters, and passenger ships—ancient and modern. Individual foreign travelers should book tickets just before the 3:30 departure at N. 1 Quay, Yanjiang Rd. There is a similar but much cheaper ride for natives and budget travelers at another quay on the same street.

Baiyun (White Cloud) Mountain, northeast of the city, has thirty peaks ranging over 28 square kilometers. The highest peak is 382 meters high. On its slopes are old temples dating back to the Northern Sung. It is currently being developed as a recreation area with an amusement park and possibly cable cars and horseback riding.

Guangzhou's garden restaurants are among the prettiest in China. The **Nan Yuan** and **Bei Yuan** are like traditional old China, tables surrounded by fish ponds, latticed windows, living bamboos, and flowers. They rate a visit for the atmosphere as well as for the food. At the Nan Yuan in 1979, a very satisfactory meal could be had for ¥10 a head. The **Pan Xi** and **Datong** are also recommended for atmosphere and food.

The communes of Guangzhou have been making an effort to make visits there more interesting for visitors and more profitable for themselves. At some, you can rent bicycles to go wherever you want, get your picture taken on a water buffalo, try your hand at target practice with an air rifle, or watch a lion dance or martial arts demonstration. Meals are sometimes served, and these I found to be among the best in China. Many of the area communes grow and preserve fruit and olives for export, an interesting as well as delicious process to watch, as visitors are frequently given samples.

Shopping: One of the free markets here also sells unauthorized antiques which have not been checked out by the authorities. You may or may not get a good buy. You are not supposed to take any antique without a red seal out of the country. So if you shop at Qing Ping Ziyou Shi Chang, you risk having your purchases seized as you leave the country.

Hotels: Even as new hotels start opening in 1981, the hotel situation in Guangzhou will continue to be grim, especially during a trade fair. The worst was the opening of the spring 1979 fair, which coincided with Easter vacation in Hong Kong. Many foreign businessmen had to sleep on cots in meeting rooms or lobby couches. With the new trading format, however, that situation will not be repeated.

Foreign traders are usually billeted at the Dongfang or Baiyun. Since the Dongfang is more convenient and better, some guests who were taken to the Baiyun, which is 4 kilometers from the Trade Center, have taken taxis to the Dongfang and successfully waited in the lobby for a vacated room.

The **Dongfang Hotel,** built in 1963 and renovated in 1981, has over 1,100 rooms. This is the best hotel, conveniently located across the street from the Trade Center, and within walking distance of the railway station, CAAC office, and the C.I.T.S. There are also two jogging parks nearby. It is 6 km. from the airport. In addition to the usual services, the hotel has room smoke alarms, wall-to-wall carpeting, push-button IDD telephones with bathroom extensions, closed-circuit TVs, and room refrigerators. It also has computerized billing and wake-up systems, a Guest Location Information desk, a 24-hr. coffee shop, saunas, and the offices of several foreign bank representatives and the U.S. consulate. Lovely big garden (frogs and fish).

In 1981 its restaurants were world standard in decor, price, and service. Its good food (Melitta coffee for ¥1.50) included some imported ingredients. To walk into its new restaurant was to walk out of the drabness of most of China, a weird sensation. It is a good place for business people, not just because of its location, but because of this closer-to-home atmosphere. L'Oréal de Paris has a hairdressing salon on the premises (¥54 for shampoo and set).

The games room has 104 machines which are not to be called gambling machines since successful players receive gifts, not money. Its hotel-guests-and-members-only International Club has a disco with a proper light-and-sound system. The ¥1,500 rooftop suite also ranks as world class (gold bathroom fixtures, carpeted bathroom floors, mirrored master bedroom, prayer room!, and garden). Some suites (¥140) have padded walls. Standard rooms are ¥65.

Baiyun (White Cloud) Hotel—Cantonese "Bok Yuen"—is 33 stories high, on Huan Shi Road East, tel. 67700. (Buses no. 6, 10, or 30). Built 1975. 722 rooms including 14 suites. Located in the northeastern suburbs, with a lovely view of forested hills behind. Renovations in 1982, 1983. Some rooms to be furnished ancient Chinese style, and more restaurants added. Yes, they are doing something about the rats!

Guangzhou Guest House, Hai Zhu Square, tel. 61556. 1968. 510 rooms. During a trade fair, it is primarily used for Japanese traders and Chinese trade fair officials, a practice started years ago when the fair was held almost next door. The office of the Japan International Trade Promotion Association is in the hotel during a fair. At others times, it houses Overseas Chinese, etc. and a few foreign tour groups.

Lin Hua Guest House, Renmin Road, tel. 68800. Built 1972. 656 rooms. Mainly for Overseas Chinese. Located across the square from the railway station, it tends to reserve its south wing for Overseas Chinese trade fair visitors. Five dining rooms and a coffee shop have total seating capacity of 1,300.

Hua Qiao (Hua Chiao; Overseas Chinese) Mansion, Hai Zhu Park, tel. 61112. Built 1958. 312 rooms. It has all the basic services including a clinic. Convenient to office of China Travel Service next door. Situated near the Pearl River Bridge, it is within walking distance of the Nanfang Department Store and downtown shopping. It is 4 kilometers from the Trade Center. No money changing.

Renmin (People's) Mansion, 207 Chang Ti, tel. 61445. 413 rooms. Built

1966. This downtown hotel is on the riverfront near the Bank of China and the Nanfang Department Store.

Kuang Chuan (Spa Villa) Hotel, in the northern suburbs on San Yuan Li, tel. 32540, 61334. 124 rooms. Built 1964, 1974, and 1979. On several acres of land, this is more like a resort than a hotel. It has an Olympic-sized swimming pool usually filled with warm (31°C) mineral water. Its charming fish pond, moon gates, and garden make this one of the prettiest hotels in town.

Nanhu Hotel, completed in 1982, is 20 minutes by car northeast of the railway station on a lake at the foot of White Cloud Mountain. Guangzhou's new **Nanhu Hotel,** partially opened in 1981, is actually an extension to a "Reception House" for China's leaders built originally by the notorious Lin Piao in the early 70s. The older buildings are available to tourists when not needed by China's top people. With 9-m. high ceilings, cavernous rooms, and bathrooms bigger than the average hotel room, the old section should provide a fantastic experience. One of the 6 older buildings has 26 beds, just right for a tour group.

The hotel has 4 sq. km. of land and lake and is surrounded by pine trees, bamboo and orange groves, fan palms, and lots of green and blue. The closest village is about 2 km. away. There is lots of space for hiking, swimming, fishing, badminton, tennis, billiards, Ping-Pong, Mah-Jong, water bicycles, motor boats, and for setting off firecrackers and for the shooting gallery which will have machine guns, as well as other arms.

The management advertises the Nanhu (South Lake) as a resort hotel, and I would dearly love to take my family there except for the stupid rule that swimming be confined to the swimming pool. The one sq. km. lake will have a coffee shop barge in the center, but it is off limits to swimmers because the lake is "too deep."

The hotel should not be considered exclusively a resort, however. It is only a 25-min. drive (14 km.) from the Trade Fair. The services on hand: China's only safe-deposit boxes (so far), taxis on the premises, free transfers, a bus every hour to the Dongfang and the railway station for ¥2, a bar, dance floor, and five restaurants. With the relaxing sylvan setting, it is ideal for a businessman who wants to get away after a hard day at the Fair. The food has a good reputation too.

The two new buildings have 300 rooms, wall-to-wall carpets, bedside controls, music, and TV. No smoke alarms but a manually controlled "water pipe" system in case of fire. Standard twins start at ¥50 in the new buildings; ¥30–35 in the older. No suites except in the older section.

An Ancient Chinese Cultural Center, patterned after Hong Kong's Song Dynasty Village, only bigger, is being talked about for this location. It would take in the Han, Tang, and Qing as well as Song.

For **Bai Tian E,** see Shamian Island on page 163.

Hua Yuan (Garden Hotel), across from the Baiyun, completion date unknown. **China Guangzhou Hotel,** 1,200 rooms, next door to the Dongfang.

Luxury class. Chinese interior. Tennis court. Pool. Partial opening late 1982, full in early 1983.

Other points of interest in Guangdong province. Please see separate listings: Foshan, Zhaoqing, Taishan, Xinhui, Jiangmen, Conghua, Shantou, Hainan Island, and Xiqiao.

Quijang (Chu Jiang) County, about 180 kilometers north of Guangzhou, is where the 100,000- to 200,000-year-old relics of Ma Ba (Ma Pa) Man were found. A museum at the site.

Macao: It has been possible to take a taxi or air-conditioned bus to this Portuguese colony on the south bank of the Pearl River.

GUILIN (Kweilin; City of Cassia Trees)

Location: In northern Guangxi, the first "province" west of Guangdong. 75-minute flight northwest of Guangzhou and 80-minute flight southwest of Changsha. Direct charter flights from Hong Kong. See chapter 4 on transportation between Guangzhou and Hong Kong. A 6-lane superhighway is expected to open by the end of 1985.

Weather: Hottest: 34°C, in August; coldest: minus 3°C. Rainy season: February–July. The best time to visit is late spring, when it is warm enough not to let the rain bother you. The scenery is best seen in the mist, the way it inspired centuries of landscape painters. The sun and clouds conspire to give you a constantly changing picture. From November to February, the water in the river may be too low for the boat trip all the way to Yangshuo.

Area: 525 square kilometers.

Population: 620,000 including surrounding area.

Background: Founded in 214 B.C., the city is famous for its vertical limestone mountain formations rising above tree-lined streets, surrounding rice fields and the meandering Li and Peach Blossom Rivers. It was the provincial capital until 1014. During the Japanese war, 99 percent of the city was destroyed, the Seven Star Cave alone sheltering 5,000 refugees.

Because about one-third of the 10,000,000 people in the province are of Chuang nationality, Guangxi is an "autonomous region" rather than a "province." Your national guide may not understand the local dialect.

The city itself, a favorite of honeymooners, is small, full of parks and ideal for walking. The ground is level except for the mountains, each of which has a bright-red pavilion complementing nature, an invitation to visit.

In the autumn you can buy very sweet oranges and yellow, grapefruitlike pomelo. The arts and crafts factory makes boxwood, jade, and soapstone carvings and bamboo chopsticks. Its dough sculptures are some of the best I've seen in China and at ¥6 for a lovely three-inch fairy encased in plastic, excellent buys.

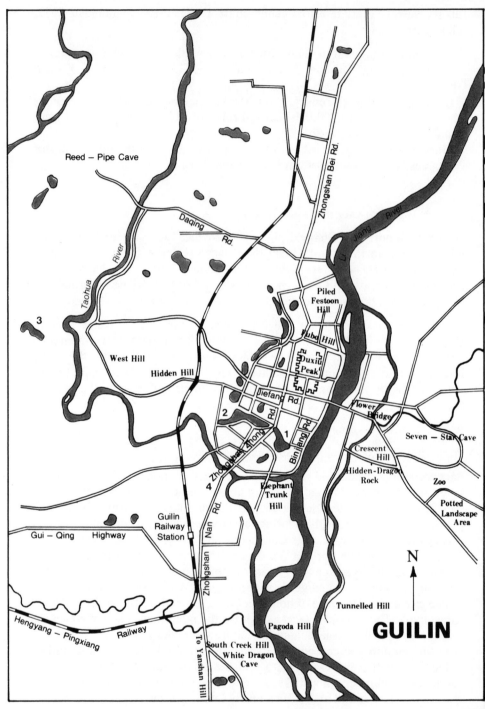

ROMY PARIÑA

1. Li Jiang (Li River) Hotel   3. Jiashan Hotel
2. Ronghu Hotel   4. Osmanthus Hotel

Of Interest to Visitors: Reed Flute Cave, the second largest of the city's caves (1 km. long), takes about 40 minutes to see; the temperature inside is a cool 20°C. The lighting is cleverly placed so that with a bit of imagination, the limestone formations resemble a giant goldfish, a Buddha, a wall of assorted vegetables, etc. It is named after the reeds that grow at the entrance.

Die Cai (Tiehtsai; Piled Festoon) Hill is the tallest in town at 73 meters. The four peaks are Bright Moon Peak, Yue Peak, Crane Peak, and Seeing Around the Hill Peak. Part way up past the ornamental arch is the Wind Cave with Ming and Tang poems and memorials on its walls. Watercolor sketches on sale here and at other touristy spots are good buys if you know how to pick them and are satisfied with the quality of the paper. Do not hesitate to haggle. Prices were ¥2–¥10 for one about 13 inches by 20 inches. Paintings in stores may be of better quality.

Fo Bo Mountain, named after famous Han marshal Ma Fu Po, is 60 meters high. At the base is a three-ton iron Qing bell belonging to the temple originally here. To the right is the Cave of the Returned Pearl where guides will tell you a dragon left a gift of a pearl for a poor family who returned it, thus showing the honesty of the working people. There is also a rock where Fu Po tested his sword, and a cliff with Tang Buddhas. Part way up on the right is a pavilion with a view of the river. Guilin is full of such mountains to climb, many with caves to explore. You might also try Guilin-style canoeing in warm weather. The canoes here tip easily, though.

Du Xiu (Tuhsiu) Park was the site of a fourteenth-century Ming palace. During the Qing, it was the civil service examination hall and later the headquarters for the local government and the Nationalists. Destroyed during the Japanese war, it is now the site of the teacher's college. Today only the original wall, its gates, and the steps over which only the emperor was carried remain. The steps are white marble, carved with the scales of the imperial dragon. The old houses in the neighborhood deserve an early morning visit, they are so interesting.

Seven Star Park, about 10 square kilometers, contains a zoo, Camel Hill, and Seven Star Hill, its seven peaks placed like the Big Dipper. Seven Star Cave has three levels and is bigger than Reed Flute Cave. The pavilions are each constructed of different materials, e.g., concrete, bamboo, etc. There are many cassia trees and a 700-year-old stone replica of the Flower Bridge (Song), originally built of wood and destroyed in a flood. The bridge was designed so that the water below reflects its arches to form a complete circle. There is also a "Cave for Hiding a Dragon" where you can easily imagine a snugly fitting dinosaur-size dragon. The most famous of the stone Song steles nearby has a list of people meant for execution. The emperor sent copies around China and when the verdict was reversed, all but the stele in Guilin were destroyed. Newly opened is the 517-meter-long **Chuanshan Grotto** in southeast Guilin.

Li River boat trip: The 5-hour, 83-kilometer boat trip south to Yangshuo (return by land) is the compulsory attraction. The Li River, 30 to 60 meters wide, winds its way between some incredible rock formations, the highest about 80 meters. The boat, pulled by a tug, moves silently without vibrations. A substantial lunch is served on board. The middle section of the trip after the first 2½ hours is the most beautiful, so do not use up all your film before you get to it. As you leave Guilin, with a little imagination, you will see in succession on the right Elephant Hill, Fighting Cocks Hill (one on each side), and Reclining Flower Vase Hill on the right. The vase appears as if it were cut in half lengthwise. Later you pass the state farm for Compatriots from Indonesia and Vietnam, and Ta Shi, one of the largest towns in the area. Book at C.I.TS. or at the Quay in Guilin.

At 1½ hours out: Sword-Cut Cliff (as if neatly severed by a giant sword). At 2¼ hours out: Left side, Crown Cave (shaped like the British imperial crown). At 2¾ hours: Cock with tail up bending down to pick up rice, followed shortly by the U-shaped Ram's Hoof Mountain on the right. Look for large cormorant birds, usually sitting in rows on fishing boats. If you're lucky you might even see them at work fishing on behalf of people. At 4 hours out, on the right is Conch Shell Hill, then a temple on a cliff.

Yangshuo, the tiny town at the end of the boat ride, has two handicraft stores near the landing and seems to specialize in copies of three-color Tang porcelain camels and horses at the cheapest prices I've seen in China—half the Guilin Friendship Store prices—but I won't vouch for the quality. If time allows you might be able to walk through the main street, which is to the right of the boat landing and then left. Note an old temple, now an office building, on the left. Yangshuo Hotel, 1959, enlarged 1982.

Chuan Yen (Pierced Hill) Village is 7 kilometers from Yangshuo. Buses usually stop for the scenery—a giant thousand-year-old banyan tree and the hill, apparently "pierced" by a very big arrow. In the cave are several dwellings reached by a tiny ferry. Villagers here try to sell simple soapstone carvings for four times the price in the department store in Guilin. Look for artists. You can also hire boats here to go farther upstream.

Ling Canal, dug over two thousand years ago (Qin), may be of interest to engineers and history fans. It had eighteen locks and there are still sections to be seen starting about 66 kilometers north of Guilin. The canal made it possible to go by boat to Guangzhou.

Hotels

Ronghu (Yunghu, Banyan) Hotel. 200 rooms. Built 1950s. Primarily for official delegations and state guests. Best because of two-story villas. **Li Jiang (Li River) Hotel.** Almost 300 rooms. 12 stories. Built 1976. Great view from the roof. Bring your own paints. Three kilometers from railway station, 15 from airport. Three kilometers from Seven Star Park and one to the old Palace. Close to shopping. **Dangui (Osmanthus) Hotel,** 157 rooms, grubby wall-to-wall carpeting, across from railway station. Built 1981. **Jiashan Hotel,** Australian joint venture. Built 1980.

HAINAN ISLAND. This large tropical island 20 miles off the southern coast of China is best reached by a 1½-hr. flight from Guangzhou to Haikou, or a ½-hr. flight from Zhanjiang in Guangdong. The island is about as big as Taiwan. Foreign oil experts have been visiting it for years, but it is not yet developed for tourists, though some have been there. The few tourists have raved about unspoiled beaches, and the experience of going to a place where time has stopped—until now.

During the 30s and 40s, a Communist army detachment had refuge there, and after Liberation part of the island became an autonomous region because of the large percentage of its tribal minorities. Mainly Li and Miao, many of these still wear beautiful distinctive dress.

The island produces tea, coffee, rubber, fish, sugar, coconut, cashews, and rice. Other industries are being developed. Population runs around 5.2 million.

Haikou has an Overseas Chinese Hotel. Visitors have also slept in the Overseas Chinese Commune in Xinglong where there is a hot spring. At Luhuitou, 300 km. from Haikou, are several hostels from which visitors can swim in the ocean.

HANGZHOU (Hangchow), capital of Zhejiang province, is on the Qiantang River at the southern end of the Grand Canal on the east coast of China. It is 189 kilometers south of Shanghai and a 2-hour flight southeast of Beijing. Direct flight from Hong Kong. The population is 980,000.

Hangzhou is one of the most famous beauty spots of China with its Xihu (Sai Woo; West Lake). It is also of historical importance. Founded over 2,100 years ago, it began to prosper as a trading center after the completion of the Grand Canal in 610. It was the capital of the tiny state of Wuyueh (893–978), at which time the first dikes were built. It was also capital of the Southern Song after 1127. The best source for a detailed picture of the city from 1250 to 1276 is Jacques Gernet's *Daily Life in China on the Eve of the Mongol Invasion,* essential for visitors who want to know a lot of history, to compare life then with today, and to look for old ruins. The city was seized by the Mongols under Kublai Khan in 1279 and visited by Marco Polo near the end of the century when it was known as Kinsai. The Venetian explorer raved about the city, then the largest and richest in the world.

Hangzhou has been a famous resort for centuries, attracting retired officials as well as tourists. It is also an industrial city now, with iron and steel, machine making, basic chemicals, an oil refinery, and electronics. It also produces power generators, machine tools, light trucks, and small tractors. Tourists would probably be interested in its factories making silk textiles, satin, brocades, sandalwood fans, silk parasols, and woven silk "photographs." The communes here grow the famous Lungching tea and silk worms, which make a visit especially interesting.

The city is on the east side of **West Lake,** the hotels on the west side. The lake was originally part of the Qiantang River until its outlet became silted up. It is now 15 kilometers in circumference with an average depth of 1.8 meters. Boats are for rent. The best time to see the lake is in the mist or just before sunrise, before the sun makes strong shadows. One of the best spots for viewing it, especially during the harvest moon, is Ping Hu Qiu Yue at the southeastern end of **Gu Shan (Solitary Hill)**. The **Yu Shu Lou (Pavilion for Storing Imperial Books)** was built in 1699.

The **giant golden carp** can be seen at Huagang. The **Nine-Bend Bridge** joins the mainland to the famous islet **Three Pools Mirroring the Moon.** Everywhere there are exquisite gardens. (See "Relax in a Chinese Garden" in chapter 10.) The large mansions around the lakes, once owned by the rich, are now resorts for workers.

Liuho Ta (Pagoda of Six Harmonies) is on Yuelun Hill on the north bank of the Qiantang River. Built in 970 A.D. (Song), it is 59.89 meters tall, 13 stories, and is made of brick and wood.

Other important sites are the **Lingyin Temple** and the **Yellow Dragon Cave.** The Lingyin Temple has a gilded, camphorwood Buddha 82 feet high. At the **Hu Pao temple** you will find a spring whose water will not overflow from a full cup even though many coins are added to it. There is also a 750-acre botanical garden.

Cable cars now run to Northern Peak and Lingyin Temple with a view of the lake. Visitors can go to **Yu Wang (Jade Emperor) Mountain,** overlooking the river at a spot where a Song emperor pretended to do manual labor. Vegetarian restaurant and small temple. Travel also to **Wu Shan Hill,** the highest spot in the city which has a 800-yr.-old camphor tree and a cave made for the Song emperor. The **Yue Fei Temple** is a tribute to the Song general who defied his emperor, was executed, and then proved to be right about the Jin invaders from the north. Kneeling figures, spat on even now, depict the four people who caused his death.

Excursions now to **Ningbo, Shaoxing, Tiantai,** and **Xikou,** the latter the grave of the mother of Chiang Kai-shek. **Shaoxing** is over 2,000 years old, capital of the Yue kingdom during the Warring States. It has historical temples, tombs, and calligraphy. Was Lu Hsun's home town. The Shaoxing Hotel (1930s) is in old Chinese style, although it is air conditioned. See separate listing for Ningbo. The Guoqing Temple in **Tiantai** is the home of the Tiantai Buddhist sect. Tiantai also has the Wise Man's Tower Courtyard and a Sui pagoda. Excursions also to **Yao Ling Cave,** 10,000 sq. m. large and 121 km. southwest.

HARBIN (Haerhpin) is the capital of China's northernmost province of Heilongjiang, formerly part of Manchuria, an hour and a half's flight northeast of Beijing. It has a population of 2 million and is an industrial city close to the Taching Oil Fields. Its highest summer temperature is 36°C; its lowest in winter is minus 38° with lots of snow. The winter is six months long so take your long johns. Wintertime, however, is brightened by the **Ice Lantern Show,** which has ice sculptures of pagodas, bridges, lanterns, human figures, animals and flowers. Ice sailing and bobsledding. Also, bring skates and skis.

The area was first settled by people of the Nuzhen nationality in 1097. In the Yuan the city was renamed Harbin. In 1898 it was opened as a port and became a Russian concession with a Russian ghetto and Tsarist troops and police patrolling. From 1932 the Japanese occupied it until the end of the war.

Its tourist attractions include a 10-kilometer-long **dike** along the Songhua River, the **Stalin Park,** and the **sports club** where you can rent sailboats and sampans to ride on the river. At the **zoo** is a Manchurian tiger, a red-crested crane, and a moose. The **Heilongjiang Provincial Museum** has one of the best skeletons of a mammoth found in China.

Recommended restaurants are the **Jiangnanqun** and the **Jiangbin Restaurants** for Chinese food, and the **Huamei** for Western. Muslim food is at the **Beilaishun Restaurant.** Local delicacies include bear paw and moose nose.

HEFEI (Hofei) is the capital of Anhui province in east China. With an urban population of 550,000, it covers an area of 45 square kilometers. Because of its strategic location, numerous battles were fought here, including *Xiaoyaojin,* when General Zhang Liao of the State of Wei fought hard against General Sun Chuan of the State of Wu. The site is now a park with three islets, on one of which is the tomb of General Zhang Liao. Near the park is a zoo.

The **Temple to Lord Bao** was built in honor of Baocheng, an honest and outstanding official of the Northern Song. It has a stone statue of the magistrate/prefectural head/Vice Minister of Rites carved in the Ching.

The **Mingjiao Monastery** south of Xiaoyaojin was originally built in the Tang. Destroyed in the nineteenth century during the Taiping War, it was rebuilt by General Yuan Hongmo of the Taiping Heavenly Kingdom.

Mt. Dashu, 10 kilometers outside of the city, has a spring where the water is said to taste as sweet as that of the Yangtze Gorges. North of it is one of China's biggest man-made lakes, Lake Shushan.

Huangshan is reached from Hefei by train across the Yangtze. See separate listing. **Jiuhuashan,** one of the Four Sacred Mountains (alt. 1,341 m.) is a day's trip by road. It has 50 Ming and Qing temples and 6,000 Buddhas which were untouched by the Red Guards. Cars can drive up to 600 meters.

Favorite local dishes include dumplings sandwiched with mushrooms and chicken, and chicken blood soup.

HOHHOT (Huhehot), capital of Nei Monggol (Inner Mongolia), with an urban population of 500,000, is accessible by train northwest of Beijing. But it is ONLY for the strong adventurous traveler who likes to rough it and doesn't mind a mutton diet. The area is of historical and religious importance. The ancestors of the Mongols, one of the nationalities living here, conquered parts of Europe in the thirteenth and fourteenth centuries. The traditional religion, as reflected now in the monasteries and temples, is a distinctive branch of Buddhism known as Lamaism, and is related to that of Tibet.

The best time to visit is June and July. The highest temperature then is 28°C, but the nights are cool. The winters are very cold, with a minus 32°C low, and you need long johns even in early May. The spring and summer have sand storms. The altitude is 1,000 meters above sea level.

In summer, visitors can, if they wish, sleep in a *yurt* on a commune. You can also drink tea laced with milk, butter, and grain, said to be very filling and great for cold winter days. It is "too greasy for hot weather." If you are an excellent rider you will be allowed to try the famous Mongolian ponies and camels. Camel riding is uncomfortable but at least you can get your picture taken on a two-humped shaggy Bactrian if it's not summer, the season when they shed. Visitors go to one of three communes located 90 to 180 kilometers away, usually by jeep. The yurt is made of compressed sheep's wool with paper windows, is shaped like an igloo, and can be folded up and carried by camel. Eight people can put up a large one in 40 minutes. Visitors staying in yurts sleep on padded mattresses described as "hard but comfortable." Everything smells of sheep. Unless things have changed, there is no running water, but there are outdoor toilets. The people are charming and colorful. They will even sing for you in your yurt. Of course, there's a hotel in Hohhot for the weak.

The art in Lamaist monasteries is full of gory scenes of hell and torture. Reincarnation is central but much superstition has crept into the theology. Huhhot used to have many temples but they were destroyed "by the imperialists and Nationalists." Among the survivors is the **Sheli Temple and Pagoda,** built of glazed tile and brick with an Indian-style Buddha. In the **Five Pagoda Temple** is the only Mongolian astronomical map found up to now. Carved in the Ming. The **White Pagoda** on the eastern outskirts of the city is from the tenth century. Forty meters high, seven stories high, it is octagonal. Also a **Lama Temple.**

Hohhot dates from the Ming, four centuries ago. It was called Guisui under the Nationalists. After Liberation, it was renamed Hohhot (Green City), the name preferred by the natives. Today it produces woolen textiles, carpets, and tapestries. It also manufactures Mongolian-style riding boots, sabers, saddles, stirrups, and felt stockings. Long-haired goatskin rugs are about ¥20 (3' × 4') and up. Also on sale are objects made of camel bone, silver bowls (about ¥70), and typical Mongolian silk jackets (¥70–100), fancy enough to wear to dinner parties. Also antique bottles of jade or agate.

THE HUANGSHAN MOUNTAINS in southern Anhui are among China's most spectacular. A climb has been described by one writer as "walking into an unending Chinese landscape painting." My request for a visit there was turned down because C.I.T.S. didn't think I could do it. The highest of the 72 peaks, Lotus Flower, is 1,873 meters above sea level. To reach the valley before the final ascent to the top means climbing eight hundred stone steps cut into an eighty-degree cliff, nose almost to rock. C.I.T.S. is probably right.

One section on the second-highest Heavenly Capital Peak (1,810 meters) is a ridge less than a meter wide called "Carp's Backbone." Although iron chain railings exist to assure the unsure, some people resort to crawling to get across. This is just to say that Huangshan is for the very strong who will be rewarded by giant vertical peaks, pines (at least one over four thousand years old), hot springs, lots of streams, mist, magnificent views, and a great feeling of achievement, if you make it.

Huangshan has three guest houses accommodating a total of two hundred people. It is reached by train from Hefei.

JIANGMEN (Kiangmen; Cantonese Kongmoon) is a tiny, old, waterfront city, 4 hours by tourist bus but over 6 hours by public bus, about 100 kilometers southwest of Guangzhou in Guangdong province. It was one of the foreign treaty ports.

It can also be reached by overnight passenger boat, an interesting experience to say the least. While I have made the trip three times both ways, I have yet to meet a Foreign Friend who has been allowed. Several ferryboats leave the docks daily about a kilometer east of the Overseas Chinese Mansion in Guangzhou. The price is so cheap it is not worth mentioning. Tickets and permission are obtained from the China Travel Service office. The boat leaves before sunset, so you have a chance to see the never-ending river traffic, the maze of tributaries and canals, many lined with breakwaters, irrigation gates, and factories. If you're lucky, you have a full moon—and it's beautiful! You are in another world.

You sleep (if you can—it's somewhat noisy) twelve abreast on wooden platforms, softened only by straw mats and separated from fellow passengers by four-inch high dividers. There are upper and lower platforms lining three sides of the room. You could have over sixty roommates, some of them curious, some friendly, but all discreet. There are few women, but I've never felt threatened. There is no privacy here, not even for bathing, which is from a very public sink (with brown river water). The toilets, however, are in tiny, private cubicles, a hole in the floor through which you can see river water rushing by (and also your pants, if you don't hang on tight!). You can rent pillows and sheets and buy proletarian food. Boiled hot drinking water is available, but you should have had the foresight to carry your own enamel mug and towel like all the other guests.

At dawn, or sometimes before, you find the boat entering a canal. You wait for the lock behind you (built in 1978) to be closed and the water raised before you can go on to disembark at Jiangmen. In Jiangmen there is an Overseas Chinese village and a "comprehensive factory," the Jiangmen Sugarcane Chemical Plant where they make medicinal alcohol, paper, and sugar. There will probably also be a demonstration of gymnastics and traditional martial arts.

Foreign tourists and Overseas Chinese stay in a four-story, 1974-built hotel.

JILIN (Kirin), in the center of Jilin province a few kilometers east of Changchun, has a population of nearly one million. Like the rest of the area formerly known as Manchuria, this also is extremely cold with lots of snow in winter. By Chinese standards Jilin is young, only about three hundred years old. Tourist attractions include **Beishan Park** with a good view of the city, the **Deer Farm at Lungtan Hill, Jilin Exhibition Hall,** and **Jiangnan Park. Songhua Lake,** a large artifical lake, is in the outskirts. The city produces ginseng, deer antlers, and ermine. A 1,600-m.-long ski-chair lift for its 3.5 sq. km. "professional" ski area, 16 km. from the city, designed for international competitions. Best snow December through February. Small beginners should be able to rent skis; pros should bring their own. Another tow is planned for Songhua Lake.

JINAN (Tsinan) is the capital of Shandong province, a 1-hour-and-40-minute-flight northwest of Nanjing. It is due south of Beijing almost on the south shore of the Yellow River, on the Beijing-Shanghai railway. It has an urban population of 1.25 million; its industries include metallurgy, textiles, chemicals, paper, and instruments.

The city dates from the Spring and Autumn Period in the sixth century B.C. It is known for its hundred springs, forced to the earth's surface by a subterranean wall of volcanic rock. The most famous springs (also translated as "pools," "wells" and "fountains") are in parks with tea houses, gardens, and pavilions.

The **Daming Pool** (a.k.a. Lake) is 197 acres and is surrounded by the **Xia Garden** (1909—with calligraphy of Song general Yue Fei), the **Lixia Pavilion** (Northern Wei—386–534), the Beiji Palace (Yuan—1271–1368), and the **Xiaochanglang** (1792), a pavilion with corridors along the lake.

The **Baotu Fountain Park** is said to have the best and greatest amount of water, one of its sixteen fountains sometimes gushing up six inches above the surface of the pool. In the center of the city, this park covers over seven acres. The water in **Heihu Fountain Park,** just east of Baotu, flows from the mouths of three stone tigers. The other important springs are the **Five Dragon** and the **Pearl.**

Other places of interest almost as old as the city are the **Hill of a Thousand Buddhas** (285 meters high, the Buddhas carved in the Sui), and Liufu, 34 kilometers southeast of the city with sixth- to eighth-century houses and the one-story **Four Door Pagoda** built in 544, the oldest existing pagoda in China. There are also the **Dragon and Tiger Pagoda** and the **Nine-Tip Pagoda.** Fifty kilometers south is **Tai Mountain,** one of the sacred Buddhist mountains; see "Tai'an."

JINGDEZHEN (Chingtechen) in northeast Jiangxi province northeast of Nanchang is a must for porcelain lovers. It was from here that some of the best pottery went to Europe centuries ago, including the Ming blue and white. Today it is still producing some of the best porcelain in China. The city was founded in the Han and is considered one of China's Three Ancient Cities.

Jingdeshen is accessible by small plane from Nanchang or by car or tour bus that leaves Nanchang after breakfast and arrives about 4 p.m. with a stop for lunch. There are hotels, one of them built in 1979. Visitors are usually taken to their choice of five different factories, each with its own specialty. In 1979 it was only possible to have porcelain crated here and shipped within China. One may be able to ship directly overseas some time in the 1980s.

JINGGANG SHAN (Chingkang Mountains) are the rugged mountains near the Hunan border in southern Jiangxi province where Mao Tse-tung led his forces after the Autumn Harvest Uprising in 1927. There the Communists established a base until October 1934, carrying out land reform among the peasants. Mao's former residence, the **Jinggang Shan Revolutionary Museum** and other revolutionary sites are open to the public. These are centered around the town of Ciping (Tseping).

Larger than Lushan (also in Jiangxi province) in area, Jinggang Shan has guest houses, hotels and reception houses, the latter for Chinese workers and operated by their work units. There are also a cinema, restaurants, and library. Up until recently, foreign tourists have not been encouraged to go to Jinggang Shan because of its isolation, although it is very beautiful. In 1979 it could be reached by a 2-day drive (300 kilometers) from Nanchang in the north (overnight stop in Ji An) or by road from the south.

The Jinggang Shan has a circumference of 275 kilometers. Huangyangjie, one of the five main outposts, is 1,800 meters above sea level. There is now a modern paper mill and bamboo handicraft factory located there.

JIUJIANG (Kiukiang, Chiuchiang, a.k.a. Xunyang) is in northern Jiangxi province on the south bank of the Yangtze River where it bends south between Wuhan and Nanjing. It is bounded on the east by Boyang Lake and Mt. Lushan on the south. Accessible by train from Nanchang or passenger boat along the Yangtze, this two-thousand-year-old city has been used as a port for the porcelain city of Jingdezhen since ancient times. It was also a treaty port. The population is 200,000.

Of interest to visitors are (1) the **Yanshui Pavilion** in the middle of Lake Gantang, an 1,840-square-meter island covered with gardens, hall and pavilions; (2) the **causeway** between Lake Gantang and Lake Nanmen built in 821 A.D.; (3) the **Dasheng Pagoda** in Nengren Temple; and (4) **Suojiang Tower.** In the summer look for a flight once a week from Guangzhou and Shanghai.

KAIFENG in northern Henan on the Shanghai-Xi'an railway line, with a history of 2,600 years, was the capital of several dynasties including the Wei, the Liang, the Later Tsin, the Han, the Later Chou, the Kin, and the Northern Song. During the Song it was an important commercial and communications center producing textiles, metalwork, porcelain, and printing. It was sacked by Jurched tribesmen in 1126 and never recovered its previous glory. In 1642, during a peasant uprising led by Li Tzu-cheng, the Yellow River dike was destroyed by the Ming so that the city was completely inundated and several hundred thousand people were killed. Even today, the riverbed, raised by centuries of silt deposits, is 10 meters higher than ground level near Kaifeng.

The "**Iron Tower,**" 13 stories, 54.6 meters high, was built over nine hundred years ago. The **Xiangguo Temple,** built in 555 A.D., was rebuilt in 1766 after the flood. It has a famous many-armed, many-eyed Buddha of gingko wood. The **Lungting (Dragon Pavilion)** is at the site of the Northern Song palace. The existing buildings are from the Qing, the stone lions in front from the Song. Kaifeng is also famous for its embroidery and its Jewish community, the remnants of which are still apparent today. A famous

painting of the ancient city "Qing Ming Festival at the Riverside," inspired the design of the Song Dynasty Village in Hong Kong.

The bottom of the Pota Palace was built in 977, the top in the Qing, after the original was destroyed for superstitious reasons.

KUNMING in south China, the capital of Yunnan province, which borders on Vietnam, is at an altitude of 1,894 meters and is known for its year-round spring weather and flowers. The hottest temperature is usually in July (29°C) and the coldest (minus 1°C) in January. It is beautifully situated on the 330-square-kilometer Dianchi Lake, China's sixth largest. A 2-hour cruise can be arranged, but go only for the rest as not much can be seen. The city is completely surrounded by mountains. Sightseeing here is rugged; for example, the Dragon Gate necessitates a climb of two hundred stairs, but the effort is well worth it.

With a population of 1,800,000 today, the city has many industries, including steel, machine tools, textiles, chemicals, plastics, marble, and soft coal. It is at the southern end of the Chengdu-Kunming railway. And with a history of 2,400 years, the city has a good museum and an Institute for Nationalities, minorities being one-third of the population. Batik and feather products here, too. Rain from May to October. The best season is a chilly February when the camellias are in bloom.

Kunming is one of the areas singled out for tourist promotion with a direct flight from Hong Kong. It is one of the cities being used for international conferences. The attractions include the weather, the mountain scenery, the colorfulness of its national minorities, and the artistry and history of its temples and architecture. Food specialities include "Rice Noodles Crossing the Bridge" and goat's cheese, although the adventurous could try snake, elephant trunk, bear paw, and deer tendon.

Adding to the more established attractions, the Chinese are now promoting the **Anning (Emerald) Spa,** 47 km. southwest of Kunming. With comfortable accommodations and hot springs, their two villas are the best accommodations in the province. Two km. north is the **Caoxi Temple,** built in the Song with Song relics inside. Every 60 years, the midautumn moon is reflected in a mirror on the Buddha's forehead. The plum trees date from the Yuan.

The best hotel in Kunming, the 360-room **Cui Hu (Green Lake) Hotel** (1956, with renovations in 1981), is better than most small town hotels (¥30 for F.F., ¥24 for O.C.). It stands across the street from the roller skating and exotic architecture of the **Haixin Pavilion** (Qing) of **Green Lake Park** and about a mile from the **Yuan Tong Ji,** the only Tang temple in the city. Also recently opened is the **Xi Yuan (West Garden) Hotel** (1940s, rebuilt 1981), formerly the house of the governor, built in old European style. The mansion can sleep people (¥300 a day for all) and should have a swimming pool by 1984. Peacefully located by Dianchi Lake. The **Kunming Hotel** is downtown with 750 beds, 500 more to be added soon.

Consider the whole Yunnan province. It extends from year-round snow-capped mountains to tropical jungles where elephants and monkeys roam. One-third of its 10 million people belong to national minorities; many of the women still wear their distinctive clothes, even while working in the fields. The terrain is hilly and very lovely.

A limited number of visitors are being encouraged to see such places as **Xiaguan** and **Xishuang Banna,** the latter a tropical autonomous prefecture 700 km. southwest (1-hr. flight) of the capital. In Xishuang Banna (main city **Jinghong**), the Dai people have customs similar to S.E. Asia such as the **Water-Splashing Festival** (about April, their new year). A tropical plant research institute and pagodas more related to Burma than to traditional China are also here.

Another region to visit, around **Li Jiang** in northeast Yunnan, lies about 700 km. from Kunming where the **Yu Lung (Jade Dragon) Mountain** rises spectacularly 6,000 m. above sea level.

Festivals worth seeing include the **Yi Torch Festival** about late July in the Stone Forest, the **Third Moon Market** in Dali (see Xiaguan) and the **Horse and Mule Market Meeting** around early April in Li Jiang. Dates vary each year because of their lunar calendar.

Along the west shore of the lake is Sleeping Beauty Hill and a series of swordlike hills. The villas there, formerly of the wealthy, are now sanitoria for workers. On the southern tip of the lake is **Jinning** county town, the birthplace of the famous Ming navigator Zheng He, who sailed to East Africa half a century before Vasco da Gama. A memorial hall to the explorer is on a hill above the town. **Xishan (West Hill)** has the fourteenth-century **Hua Ting Temple,** the largest in Kunming. South of here is the **Taihua Temple** (Yuan) with the best view of the sunrise over the lake. The copper-cast **Golden Temple** northeast of the city is 300 years old.

The **San Qing Pavilion,** 2 kilometers farther south, was the summer resort of Emperor Liang of the Yuan. It has nine tiers, each about 30 meters above the other. On the top is the **Long Men (Dragon Gate)** with another great view of the lake. The Dragon Gate had its stone corridors, chambers, paths, and intricate carvings cut from 1609 to 1681.

The **Qiong Zhu (Bamboo) Temple,** 12 kilometers northwest of Kunming, has five hundred arhats in addition to the usual impressive Buddhist statues. Carved in the Qing, these are very expressive. Here also, you might find an artist to make paper cuts of your profile for 8 *mao.* Built in 1280.

The **Da Guan Lou Pavilion** across the lake from Xishan Hill has a 180-character couplet at its entrance, the longest ever found in China. Composed by a Qing scholar, the first half praises the landscape while the second deals with Yunnan history. Also important is the **Black Dragon Pool** with its Ming temple and tomb. Other temples are also being renovated and opened. The city has three tiny Friendship stores. Batik is a good buy.

The **Stone Forest of Lunan,** one of the highlights of a Kunming visit, is 126 kilometers southeast of the city, and tourists usually stay in the adjacent Stone Forest Hotel. About 200 million years ago, the area was covered with water. The limestone pushed its way out of the receding sea and rain continued to corrode the stone into these incredible formations. One-fifth of the 64,000 acres is open to visitors. Here too are many steps and safety fences. There are two routes (the shortest, 2½ hrs. long), and it is easy to get lost, so stick with your guide.

Near the hotel is a tribal village and minority handicrafts for sale. You can buy direct from the weavers some evenings by the lake. Prices here are better than elsewhere. A 92-meter waterfall is planned.

LANZHOU (Lanchow), the capital of Gansu province, almost in the center of China on the Yellow River, is an industrial city with over 2 million people, most working in petrochemicals, machine building, and smelting. It is near the oldest oilfields in China. Founded in the Qin, about 2,200 years ago, it was called the Gold City after gold was found there. Lanzhou later was an important stop on the Silk Road.

At an altitude of 1,510 meters, the city is very cold in winter. With dust storms adding to the already heavily polluted air, tourists are encouraged to wear masks to protect their lungs and throats. The coldest winter temperature is minus 23°C. The hottest, 39.1°C. Both some time ago.

Tourists usually visit the university, factories, a smog-colored formerly white pagoda, and a temple. The **White Pagoda (Baita) Hill** is on the north bank of the Yellow River near the Gold City. The old buildings here are **Sanxing (Three-Star) Hall, Yingxu (Greet the Sunrise) Pavilion, Yunyue (Cloudy Moon) Temple,** and the **White Pagoda Temple.** The **White Pagoda**

Temple was built in the Yuan, rebuilt and expanded in the Ming and Qing. It has seven stories and eight sides and is about seventy meters high.

The **Wuquan (Five-Fountain) Hill** is south of the old city. Legend credits General Huo Qubing (Huo Chu-ping) in 120 B.C. with stabbing the ground with his sword after finding no water for his horses. Five streams of water appeared. Most of the old buildings were destroyed in war. Existing still are the **Jingang (Buddha's Warrior Attendants) Shrine** (Ming), the **Qianfo (Thousand Buddhas) Hall,** the **Mani Temple,** the **Dizang Temple,** and the **Sanjiao Cave.** The two most important relics to see are the Taihe Iron Bell, three meters high, five tons and cast in 1202; and the Tongjieyinfo Buddha, cast in copper in 1370 and weighing nearly five tons.

The only really important relic for indefatigable, strong-hearted and strong-backed tourists is the **Maiji Grottoes.** So be sure these are guaranteed before you sign up for Lanzhou. The Maiji Grottoes are 45 kilometers southeast of the city of Tianshui, 350 kilometers from Lanzhou, and are spectacular. There are 194 caves full of thousands of stone and clay Buddhist statues, and a thousand square meters of murals dating from the end of the fourth century to the nineteenth, a period of 1,500 years. These are on a mountain, which rises almost vertically, and are reached by wooden staircases and protected by doors and windows. Some of the statues are out of doors. One 15.28 meters high is from the Sui. The work on the mountain was done by craftsmen who piled blocks of wood up to the top and started carving while standing on them. As they worked their way down, they gradually removed the blocks.

The elaborate 5th-century **Pingling Temple** is 120 km. southwest of the city. Part of the trip is by boat. There are 183 caves and shrines with 694 stone Buddhist statues and 82 clay statues, the biggest 27 m. high, the smallest only 25 cm.

LESHAN. Leshan is an overnight trip from Chengdu that can also include lunch at **Meishan** (Three Scholars Temple) and the base of **Emei Shan.** The long trip is even more worthwhile because of the Sichuan countryside.

About 170 km. from Chengdu, Leshan is the home of the 71-m. Great Buddha, built in 713 A.D. over a period of ninety years. At the confluence of three rivers the former monastery stands at Buddha's eye level. Visitors can climb down to his feet, or take a ferry from the opposite bank for a full-length view. A public bus goes to the front gate.

The 30-bed guest house (1981) itself is exotic, the rooms with Chinese beds, set around a pool. Part of the **Tai Fu (Great Buddha) Temple,** it offers a lovely situation for photographers who can shoot to their hearts' content at dusk and sunrise (when the mist rises on the river). The other statues, all recent reproductions, look better at twilight.

Note: When I went the hotel was very damp and I kept my eye out for mildew.

The **Wu You (Black) Temple** can be reached 15 minutes by footpath from the Tai Fu Temple, or by 336 steps from where the tour buses stop. It has a good museum for its size. Rains April through June.

LHASA, the fabled capital of Xizang (Tibet), has been visited recently by only a few select tourists and journalists, the area being politically sensitive. Han Chinese are being replaced by ethnic Tibetans. The altitude is over 5,000 meters. Usually it takes about two weeks to get acclimatized. Oxygen is available in the hotel rooms. All food and energy have to be imported by truck or plane.

The area is important because of the uniqueness of the culture, and the changes made in the last thirty years. It would be good to read books written by travelers in the past as well as the recent *Lhasa: The Open City* by Han Suyin and *The Tibet Guidebook.* There are also accounts by journalists in *The New York Times* and the *Wall Street Journal* of trips in the summer of 1979, and the *National Geographic,* February 1980.

Open to visitors are the palaces of the Dalai Lama and some very important temples. The **Potala,** built in the seventh century, is the most famous place, rising above the city at the top of a cliff. Few foreign tourists before or after Liberation have been inside. If you get there, consider yourself privileged.

There is a 300-meter climb *before* you arrive at the front door. In spite of its thirteen stories, there are no elevators and in places no stairs, only ladders, so it is not for the weak. It was the residence of various incarnations of the Dalai Lama, the head of the religion, a branch of Buddhism. The current Dalai Lama has been residing in India since he left Lhasa in 1955.

The Potala has 1,000 rooms, 10,000 chapels, and the tombs of six Dalai Lamas, some of the tombs about 70 feet high. The building was destroyed and rebuilt several times, the latest structure dating from 1642. There are about 200,000 statues.

The **Norbulingka** was the summer palace of the Dalai Lama, 4 kilometers from the Potala. It is set in a 100-acre garden. The building was originally erected in 1755 but was rebuilt in 1956. It is also full of statues and murals. The bedroom is as the Dalai Lama left it.

The **Jokka Kang Temple** was built in 652 to commemorate the arrival of Buddhism from China with a Tang princess. Among the other temples and monasteries open to tourists are the **Jokhan,** the **Daipung,** the **Ta Chiu,** the **Chi Pong,** and the **Sik La.**

The Tibetan religion is a distinct branch of Buddhism. It believes strongly in reincarnation and a vicious, torturous hell for nonbelievers, which is reflected in its art. At one time, a quarter of the male population of Tibet were monks and the theocracy was such that no matter how cold it was, on whatever day spring was proclaimed, everybody had to change into their summer clothes.

LUOYANG (Loyang; North Bank of the Luo River)

Location: 2 hours by train west of the Henan provincial capital and closest airport, Zhengzhou, and an 8-hour train ride from Xi'an. About 25 kilometers south of the Yellow River. Central China.

Weather: Hottest: July–August—39°C; coldest: January–February—minus 12°C. Generally mild. Altitude: 136 meters above sea level.

Area: 1,110 square kilometers, of which 79 square kilometers are urban.

Population: 1,114,000, of whom 500,000 are urban.

Background: First built in the eleventh century B.C., from 770 B.C. it was the capital at one time or another of the Eastern Chou, Eastern Han, Wei, Western Jin, Northern Wei, Sui, Tang, Later Liang, and Later Tang dynasties. Moves were frequently made here because of drought in Xi'an, a city which was preferred. Because there are hills on three sides it was relatively easy to defend, and whoever wanted to control western Henan had to take Luoyang. Consequently, many battles took place in this area and many treasures were buried to save them from the soldiers. Luoyang was one of the earliest centers of Buddhism, from the first century. During the Tang, it was the biggest city in China. It declined later because the capital and therefore the whole court moved away.

The Old City is in the eastern part of Luoyang and is architecturally more interesting than the more substantial newer buildings from 1954 on. Today there are over four hundred factories manufacturing tractors, ball bearings, gloves, glass, mining equipment, road rollers, truck cranes, and farm machinery. Tourists might be interested in the arts and crafts factory, which makes three-color Tang reproductions, reproductions of Shang bronzes, and palace lanterns.

Luoyang people will tell you that the Silk Road actually started from Luoyang and not from Xi'an as is commonly supposed. "Knowledgeable merchants always came here for silks," they say. "It was cheaper."

Area communes grow cotton, corn, winter wheat, a little rice, sesame, sorghum, sweet potatoes, apples, pears, and grapes. They also raise yellow oxen, sheep, and mules.

Of Interest to Visitors:

Baima (White Horse) Temple, 13 kilometers east of the Old City and 25 kilometers from the Friendship Hotel, was founded in 68 A.D. after second Han Emperor Ming dreamt that a spirit with a halo entered his palace. His ministers convinced him that he had dreamt of the Buddha, so he sent scholars to India to bring back the Buddhist sutras—or so the story goes. After three years, forty-two Buddhist articles and two famous Indian monks, Shemeteng and Zhufalan, arrived here on white horses. After the monks arrived, the emperor put them in his resort, the Cold Terrace, at the back of what is now the temple. There they translated the sutras into Chinese, and the temple, the first Buddhist temple in China, was completed and named after the white horses. Both Indian monks died in China and were buried in east and west corners of the grounds beyond the moon gates.

None of the buildings here is original, though the red brick foundation of the Cold Terrace is Han; none of the others are earlier than Ming. Tang Empress Wu made one of her favorites the abbot here. **The Celestial Guardians' Hall** has a Maitreya (Laughing) Buddha made of hemp and lacquer with a beautifully carved frame. Here the four guardians are in charge of rain (with parasol), the wind (holding a pagoda), the amount of rain and wind (with musical instrument), and good harvest (with spider).

In the main hall at the right of Sakyamuni is Manjusri, the bodhisattva of wisdom, carrying the sutras, and at Sakyamuni's left, Samantabhara, Bodhisattva of Universal Benevolence. In the next hall are eighteen clay *arhats,* each with a magic weapon, the oldest statues here (Yuan). One is Ceylonese, one Chinese (the Tang monk Hsuan-tsang who went also to India), and the rest Indian. Inside the back halls are statues of the two Indian monks, the Pilu Buddha (Sakyamuni), and drawers where the sutras were kept. A stele with characters written horizontally here is most unusual.

The **Cloud Touching Pagoda** nearby is in the Tang style but was originally built in the tenth century (Five Dynasties). Only the base with the darker brick is original. It was repaired in the Northern Song and Jin dynasties and has fourteen stories. The stele on the tortoise is about the repair work. There is an echo effect if you stand either north or south of the pagoda and clap your hands.

The Luoyang Municipal Museum has two thousand pieces on display and roughly fifty thousand in its collection. The building was completed in 1974. Relics include (1) historical maps of the city. The first imperial city is where Laboring People's Park is now; the Han and Wei city was east of the White Horse Temple; the Sui and Tang cities were on both sides of the Luo River; (2) two mammoth tusks found right in town in 1960; (3) double boilers used 3,700 years before the British used them; (4) cowry shell money; (5) a sword made from an elephant tooth; (6) a crossbow with a trigger (476–221 B.C.); (7) iron farming tools (Han); (8) figures from the tomb of a grandson of a Northern Wei emperor including a band with one musician falling asleep; (9) the *original* three-color Tang horses and camels from which the copies are made. Study these carefully for comparison.

Longmen (a.k.a. Lungmen) Grottoes: Large statues carved on cliffs or in caves are symbols of permanence. There are three such collections of Buddhist statues in China; here, at Datong in Shanxi, and Dunhuang in Gansu. Although predating the Longmen caves and built also by the Wei, those at Datong are said to be better preserved, more elaborately colored and bigger. The stone at Longmen, however, is better. The grottoes are 20 kilometers south of the city from the Friendship Hotel and extend north-south along the Yi River for about 1,000 meters. They were not touched by the Red Guards. The buses stop by a 303-meter copy of a famous Sui bridge built of only stone and cement in 1962.

Work on the caves began about 494 A.D. when Emperor Hsaio Wen of the Northern Wei moved his capital from Datong to Luoyang. Work continued at a great pace through the Eastern Wei, Western Wei, Northern Qi, Northern Zhou, Sui, and Tang. A few statues were added during the Five Dynasties and Northern Song. There are 1,352 grottoes, 750 niches, and about forty pagodas of various sizes. They contain more than a hundred thousand Buddhist images ranging in size from two centimeters to 17.14 meters. It is interesting to compare the dress of the statues. Some are clothed in the plain robes of Indian holy men; others wear female Chinese court dress, sometimes with jewelry. The narrow, regular pleats are characteristic of the Northern Wei. The Tang statues tend to have rounder faces. While it is said that the gods could change their sex at will, the feminine faces are because, as one adherent said, "We want people to look at the face of Buddha. Since women's faces are more attractive than men's, the statues are made to look more feminine."

Wan Fo (10,000 Buddhas) Cave has actually 15,000 Buddhas on the north and south walls. It was completed in 680 A.D. (Tang). Note the musicians and dancers at the base. The back wall has fifty-four bodhisattvas, each sitting on a lotus flower. Outside the cave is a Kuan Yin with a water vessel in her left hand and a whisk in her right. There used to be two lions here, but they are now said to be in the Boston Museum of Fine Arts.

The **Gu Yang Cave** was the earliest, built around 494 A.D. (Northern Wei). The cornlike design is actually a string of pearls. The ceiling is covered with Buddhas, lions and tablets.

Feng Xian Temple, the largest and most spectacular, was completed in 675 (Tang). The main statue (17.14 meters) is the Vairocana Buddha (i.e., Sakyamuni). If you look carefully you will see on the left side of the face traces of a five-centimeter crack extending from the hairline to the chin, which was repaired recently at a cost of ¥20,000. The square holes around the statues were used to hold the roof structure that was taken down when it was found that sunlight was good for limestone. Behind the smaller disciple to Sakyamuni's right is an imperceptible cave large enough to hold four hundred people and from which climbers used to negotiate the top of the head. Fortunately, this is now blocked. On Sakyamuni's far left is Dvarapala, whose ankles are worn black and smooth by individuals trying to embrace it (for happiness).

Some of the Buddhas in Longmen were built by wealthy people wanting special favors, or generals wanting to defeat their enemies. Some caves are mixtures of dynastic styles. During imperial times, the common people had to look at them from afar, and in later periods, peasants broke pieces off the statues to make lime fertilizer.

In 1979, there were plans to widen the road beside the caves and to divert the ox and mule carts across the river by a new bridge. Later a dam will be built to control the water level here so that the area can be used for boats and other recreation.

Other Attractions include the **Tomb of Kuan Yu (Guan Yu)** (or at least that of his head). Kuan Yu was one of the heroes of *The Romance of the Three Kingdoms* and is also known as the Chinese god of war. The tomb between the grottoes and the city was built in the Ming.

Two **Han Tombs** are in Wang Cheng Park. The **Tomb of Liu Xiu** (first emperor of the Eastern Han) is 1,900 years old and a visit could be combined with a trip to see the longest new bridge across the Yellow River. **Mang Shan Hill** north of the city is full of old ruins, palaces, tombs, and ancient summer resorts.

If you have more time, ask about the school for traditional Chinese opera.

Shopping: There is a **Secondhand Store** in the Old City with used theatrical costumes for ¥80 to ¥300, cheaper than in Beijing, but less choice; they also have new theatrical caps for ¥9.

In 1979, the **Arts and Crafts Store** was selling reproductions of the Flying Horse of Gansu for ¥50 to ¥255, depending on size. The largest camel, 1½ feet high, was ¥60 to ¥70. With five people on top, it was ¥90. Tang ladies ranged from ¥28 to ¥56. You can see these being made upstairs, along with palace lanterns and reproductions of Shang bronzes.

These reproductions are also available at the **Friendship Store,** along with brushes, chopsticks, artificial flowers, and inkstones, which are made in the city too. The cheapest "tang" camel was ¥6 here. The store also sells porcelains, cloisonné, and ivory, boxwood, and red lacquer carvings. The store can crate your purchases but cannot ship them, though this problem may be solved by the time you get there.

Store hours: 7:30 a.m.–7 p.m.; some 9 a.m.–7:30 p.m.

Food: Local specialties include sweet and sour carp from the Yellow River, and Monkey Head, which is actually a mound of mushrooms. Du Kang wine is said to be the strongest in China. Three cups will put you to bed for three years. Ask a guide to tell you the story.

Restaurant: Guangzhou Market Restaurant.

Hotels: Youyi (Friendship) Hotel. Western part of Luoyang on Wei No. 4, tel. 2157. 64 rooms in east and west wings. 1956. 3 stories. 7 kilometers from railway station, 10 from Old City, 3 from museum. In residential district. Park in front. Guangzhou (free) Market two blocks behind. Swimming pool.

A new hotel, unnamed in 1979, located next door to the Friendship Hotel. 160 rooms. 12 stories. Due 1981.

LUSHAN (Mountain of the Straw Huts)

Location: 180 kilometers northwest of Nanchang in Jiangxi, overlooking Poyang Lake and the Yangtze River. 32 kilometers south of Jiujiang. As yet no airport or railway, but an airport big enough for 707s 40 kilometers away is expected to be opened before 1985. Hong Kong will thus be two hours away. Bus service from Jiujiang.

Weather: Hottest: 30°C (rare); coldest: minus 16°C. Snow—end of November–February. Best time to visit is June–October. Lots of mist and rain, especially April and May. Altitude: 1,094–1,400 meters.

Population: About 9,000 in Gulin. Record of 10,000 summer tourists in one day.

Area: The mountaintop tourist belt is about 8 by 4 kilometers.

Background: Legend says that the seven Kuan brothers lived on the mountain as recluses during the Western Zhou (eleventh century–771 B.C.). Because they were worthy men, the emperor sent an emissary to invite them to the capital to help govern the country. When the emissary arrived, he only found empty straw huts. Hence, it was called the Mountain of the Straw Huts. The mountain was visited by the Jin poet Tao Yuan-ming (365–427). Its peach blossoms inspired Tang poet Bai Ju-yi to write a famous poem about spring disappearing in the plains but alive in the mountains. The first Ming emperor is supposed to have escaped with supernatural help from an enemy here.

But it was not until after the last half of the 1800s that a resort was developed. With foreign money and Chinese labor, about a hundred hotel buildings and villas were completed and used by wealthy Chinese, government officials, and foreign missionaries, business people, and diplomats. Most of these were carried by sedan chair up a steep 9-kilometer path. People still climb this path from the base in about two hours from Lian Hua Deng (Lotus Flower Hole). Chiang Kai-shek also visited Lushan when he wasn't campaigning against Mao Tse-tung at nearby Jinggang Shan. He lived in Building No. 180 in the East Valley.

During the Cultural Revolution, Lushan was closed, the furniture either destroyed by the Red Guards or moved to other locations. Reconstruction started in 1977, and tourists were encouraged to come in 1978. In that year, there were nearly eight thousand foreigners, and tourism has been growing ever since.

Lushan is highly recommended as an escape from the summer heat, as a rest stop near the end of a tour, or just as a beautiful place to visit. It is historically interesting, the views of the plains and the Yangtze are breathtaking, and it is full of lovely trees, hills, pavilions, and old Tang pagodas and temples, many still untouched by the tourists. Guides can rattle off incredible legends by the hour. It has a few small factories making water pumps, plastics, small stoves and cement, a printing plant and hydroelectric power station. The only local handicrafts are walking sticks and bamboo brush or pencil holders.

Lushan is divided into an East Valley and a West Valley, with a tunnel at Gulin. Until there is a locally based taxi service, individual travelers who do not want to hike everywhere (especially carrying their own luggage) should get a taxi in Jiujiang or Nanchang for the duration of their stay. There were no bicycles in 1979; the roads were not paved and there are many hills. This situation is bound to improve with better roads.

A tourist bus leaves downtown Gulin near the entrance to the city park whenever full. For one yuan, it stops at about three tourist sites for 30 to 50 minutes each.

Shopping: Gulin, the only shopping area, was destroyed by fire in 1947 and then rebuilt. There are two Arts and Crafts stores selling porcelain dishes and statues made in Jingdezhen, 180 kilometers away. Although Lushan is closer than Nanchang, the difficulty of mountain transportation makes the price of porcelain here about the same as in Nanchang. And there is less variety. Nevertheless, the price is higher outside the province. Other good buys are watercolors of the mountain scenery if you know how to pick them (¥15 and up). There is also a bar in Gulin.

Of Interest to Visitors

Flower Path Park has a flower and Chinese *bonsai* exhibit. The miniature trees that inspired the Tang poet are here. Nearby, in what looks like a well, are two large characters meaning Flower Path, believed to be the calligraphy of the poet Bai Ju-yi, uncovered in 1929 when the well was being dug. There is a natural rock formation beside the lake and the highway, which, with a little imagination, looks like two ends of a bridge over a ravine. The story goes that before he became the first Ming emperor in 1368, Chu Yuan-chang escaped from his rival at this spot. A dragonfly completed the bridge, making it possible for Chu and not his enemy to cross. The lake here, where there is boating, was made in 1956 and is shaped like a violin. The pavilion was built in 1979. Swimming is permitted but not encouraged.

Grotto of Taoist Immortal: Beyond the moon gate to the right is a cave, about 30 feet wide, deep, and high, where Lu Tung-pin, a famous monk, studied Taoism so successfully that he not only became immortal, but became one of the Eight Taoist Immortals. There used to be many Buddhas here, but they were destroyed by the Gang of Four. The water in the "drop by drop" spring is said to be mineral and medicinal. Note the formation over the mouth of the cave, shaped like Buddha's hand.

To the right is the Path for Visiting Fairies where, on the right of the pavilion, there are three red characters meaning Bamboo Forest Temple. This refers to a temple in the vicinity that rose bodily to heaven because an enchanted boy did not want to grant the gift of immortality to the heads of neighboring temples. To the left inside the moon gate is a stone pavilion with a stele outlining the career of a famous monk who at one point helped the first Ming emperor and his army to cross a stormy river to victory. It was built by Chu Yuan-chang.

Big Heavenly Pond: The water in this pool maintains the same height (it is said) through rain or drought and is thus said to be "made in Heaven." The pavilion behind the pond is on the site of a temple, built to commemorate the spider who saved Chu Yuan-chang's life by spinning a web to cover him while Chu was hiding in a well from his rival. The monks who lived in this temple were Taoists who tried to achieve immortality through study and meditation. As a test, they jumped off Dragon Head Cliff. If you look down, you can probably guess why they were never seen again. The climb down to Dragon Head Cliff (by no means the bottom) is about 170 steps, but the view is worth it. On the way, look for a carved step that was probably part of the old temple.

Han Bo Kou (the Mouth that Holds Poyang Lake), named after the shape of this pass in relation to the lake, is the best place to see the rising sun. The lake is one of China's largest and is 20 kilometers away here. The tallest mountain on the right is Da Han Yang, which may be climbed, but "it is dangerous." Beyond Da Han Yang is the Peak of the Nine Wonders.

It is only a short walk from Han Bo Kou to the botanical garden.

The Lushan Botanical Garden of China's Academy of Science has beautiful and healthy specimens. There are 3,700 varieties including trees, flowers, grasses, and medicinal herbs on 740 acres of land. Started in 1934, it is the only subalpine garden of the ten botanical gardens of China. Tourists are free to wander through the greenhouses, open daily from 7:30 a.m. to 6 p.m. Groups can get a guide. The most exotic plant here is the metasequoia tree, a species thought to be extinct and seen only in fossils until one was found in a primitive forest in west China and propagated here. There is a large specimen by the driveway near the parking lot.

Three Treasure Trees are said to be 1,500 years old, but botanists say 500. They are nevertheless very impressive, the highest being 40 meters tall. One is a gingko and two are cryptomeria. Within a few meters are the Yellow Dragon Pool and the Black Dragon Pool with waterfalls.

Lushan Museum has relics, rubbings, photographs, paintings, ancient handicrafts, and porcelains from many periods. Open 8–11:30 a.m. and 2:30–5:30 p.m. daily. Nearby is the 1,000-seat **People's Theater,** site of the meetings of the Party Central Committee in 1959 and 1970. Here local opera and acrobatics are performed and movies are shown.

Pavilion for Viewing Yangtze has another stunning view of the countryside below. At this point, the Yangtze River is about 15 kilometers away. To the right, you can see the historic path up which vacationers used to be carried in sedan chairs.

At the base of Lushan are the **Donglin Temple,** where Hui Yuan (334–416), a famous Buddhist monk of the Eastern Jin, paraphrased Buddhist canons, and the **White Deer Academy,** where Zhu Xi (1130–1200) of the Song once taught.

Hotels: Some of the hotels and villas are over a hundred years old. They were built to last, however. Most of them are made of stone with lots of space and high ceilings, but they have fewer services than in other cities. A villa might have two twin-bed rooms, a large sitting room, a reading room with a desk, and two antique bathrooms. Meals are taken in a central dining room. My villa at the Yun Zong reminded me of an Indian or Burmese hill station.

The best rooms in three of the hotels were renovated for foreign visitors so that a total of 200 beds were available in 1979. More rooms are expected to be upgraded for 1980 and a new 500-bed hotel built before 1985 in the East Valley.

Many of the Chinese guests visit Lushan as a reward for exemplary behavior, staying in a reception house of their work unit.

Lushan Hotel. From Gulin, go through tunnel and turn right for 2 kilometers onto Hexi Road; tel. 2932. Main building has 3 stories. Villas. In 1979, 60 beds for foreigners. British-built before Liberation; renovated afterward. Heated. Has C.I.T.S. (tel. 2497) and C.T.S. (tel. 2497) offices (Open 7:30–11:30 a.m. and 2:30–5:30 p.m.).

Lu Lin Hotel. Hexi Road, tel. 2424. 100 beds for foreigners in 1979. Built 1956. 4 stories. Farthest hotel from bus station (40-minute walk, about 5 kilometers). 3-minute walk to lake, 15-minute walk to botanical garden and 20-minute walk to Han Bo Kou. Has basketball and a sports field. From Gulin, go through tunnel and turn right.

Yun Zong (Amidst the Clouds) Hotel. Henan Road and Hsiang Shan Road; tel. 2547. In 1979, 40 beds for foreigners in 5 villas. 10-minute walk to Flower Path Park, 20-minute walk to the Taoist Grotto. About 3 kilometers to bus station. See DIRECTORY.

Future Plans: Definitely a locally based taxi service; upgrading of roads as well as hotels; possibility of helicopter service from Jiujiang airport; possibility of a club for tourists in Gulin with restaurant, coffee shop, dance hall.

NANCHANG (Southern Prosperity)

Location: 2 hours by air north of Guangzhou, 2 hours by air southeast of Shanghai, and 3 hours, 20 minutes by air south of Beijing. It is the capital of Jiangxi province.

Weather: Because it is bounded by mountains on the east, south, and west, it is like a furnace in the summer; with no northern mountains, it is very cold in winter. Coldest: minus 10°C—January–February; hottest: 40°C—July–September. Rain late April and May.

Area: 175 kilometers in a province that is 10 percent water, 10 percent city, 10 percent land and 70 percent mountain.

Population: 800,000.

Background: Originally called Yuzhang (Yuchang) and Hungdu (Hungtu), Nanchang was founded over two thousand years ago on the east bank of the

Gan River. It is best known today as the site of the first independent armed effort by the Communists on August 1, 1927, considered now the founding date of the People's Liberation Army. Industries include iron and steel, machine building, electric motors, tractors, electronics, chemicals, and textiles.

The city is built almost entirely of red brick. Its principal attractions are its revolutionary museums, and therefore it is primarily of interest to students of modern history. It is also a base from which to visit Jingdezhen, Lushan, and Jinggang Shan. The province has developed its own opera and local songs, the latter sung while picking tea. In the area grow seedless tangerines, sesame, rape, and rice.

Of Interest to Visitors

August 1st Museum: The setting here is a period masterpiece with the original furniture or reproductions. You are in the Grand Jiangxi Hotel of the 1920s! On the ground floor are old, carved mahogany and rosewood furniture and an opium chair. Bedroom no. 1 was Chou En-lai's. In the bedrooms are room dividers with stained-glass windows and light fixtures with pulleys. Everywhere are large, brass spittoons. Even if you are not interested in revolutionary history, the building itself is worth the trip. Opened in 1924, it was used as a hotel until it was closed during the Cultural Revolution. After all, it had been the headquarters of the historic uprising! In 1969, it opened again as the museum.

The galleries are numbered and labeled in Chinese. On the second floor: (1) The background of the uprising, planned during the Northern Expedition when the Communists realized there could be no coooperation with the Nationalists (and vice versa), especially after the slaughter of the Communists in several cities in April 1927. (2) Preparations for the uprising in Nanchang. Chu Teh trained the officers here; Chou En-lai was one of the leaders. Thirty thousand troops took part, some from Wuhan who arrived first by boat to Jiujiang, and then train to Nanchang. Third floor: (3) The uprising. Map with lights shows enemy headquarters in black and insurgent headquarters in red. Battle started at 2 a.m. and ended five hours later in a victory for the Communists, who held the city until August 5. (4) Withdrawal to Jinggang Shan, where Mao Tse-tung in October established a base in the mountains. After a scorched-earth campaign by Chiang Kai-shek, the Long March was started from Jinggang Shan in 1934. (See also MILESTONES IN CHINESE HISTORY.)

Exhibition Hall of Jiangxi Revolutionary History is on the main square along with the Jiangxi Provincial Museum. It concerns the Anyuan Coal Miners' Strike led by Mao Tse-tung, and Jinggang Shan, Mao's Jiangxi base.

Jiangxi Provincial Museum: Open Wednesdays, Fridays, and Sundays, 8–11 a.m. and 2–5 p.m., this small but interesting museum contains some neolithic pieces, Shang bronzes, Song porcelain, an ancient implement for ironing clothes (look for picture demonstrating use), mirrors, and some tomb figures. On the second floor is a model of a Ming tomb, that of the governor of Jiangxi, who was the sixteenth son of Ming emperor Chu Yuan-chang. This model can be taken apart. Tomb pieces here are from the 1958 excavation site about 15 kilometers north in Xinjian. It includes a jade belt, hair decorations, an army of servants, sedan chairs, and orchestra. Quite delightful!

Groups can request a demonstration of the Ming Fairy of Justice Cup, made of porcelain. This has a man inside and a hole in the bottom. When filled to the black spot on the man's chest, the cup holds liquid. When filled above the black spot, all the liquid runs out the hole in the bottom. That's justice for greedy people! There is also a bronze basin which will only respond with a foot-high spray of water when its handles are rubbed with clean hands. Must be seen to be believed (or understood).

Ba Da Shan Ren Museum: In the Qingyunpu Temple (said to be Taoist) is the museum of famous landscape painter Ba Dan Shan Ren (Man of the Eight Mountains) of the late Ming, early Qing dynasties. He is also famous for his birds and flowers. The museum has a rotating collection of his works.

Arts and Crafts Exhibition Hall of Jiangxi products: The pieces here range from a two-meter-high lacquer vase to a quarter-inch ivory stele on which are written poems by Mao Tse-tung. There are also figurines of revolutionary and historical persons, inkstands, see-through paintings on porcelain, bambooware (a new craft), delicate porcelain flowers, blue and white dinnerware, wine goblets, and lamps. Some pieces are on sale; some can be ordered.

Hundred Flower Islet is the prettiest and most interesting of the city's parks.

Store Hours: 8 a.m.–7:30 or 8 p.m.

Office Hours: 7:30–11:30 a.m.; 3–6, summer; 8–12; 1:30–5 "or so," winter.

Sample dinner for eight people at the Shi Xian Lou Restaurant (all Jiangxi specialties, including turtle soup and Three Cups of Chicken).

冷碟：十字拼盘

点心四色
冰西瓜
冰啤酒
冰汽水

炒菜：白雪炒鸡脯（南昌）
金腿拼银芽（南昌）
鸡汁溜冬菇（靖安）
文山里脊丁（吉安）

六大件：黄焖玉结鱼翅　　　　三鲜子鸡（宁都）
清燉脚鱼　　（新建）
粉醋精鱼　　（鄱阳）
冰斗白莲　　（广昌）
香酥鸭　　　（南昌）
鲜菜肉丝汤　（南昌）

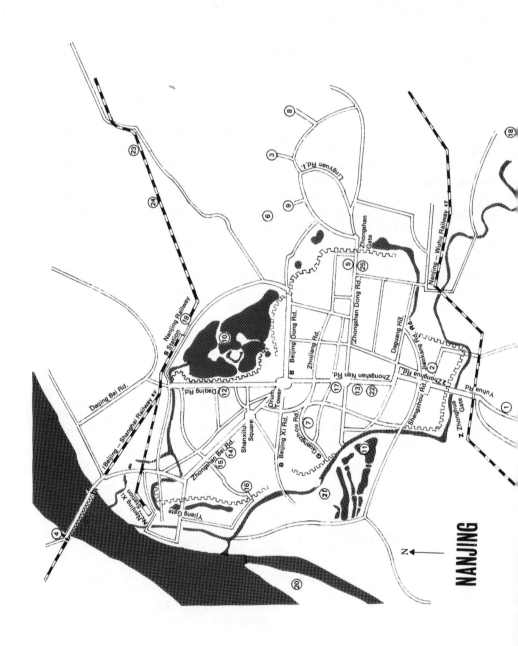

NANJING

Hotels: Jiangxi Guest House: 300 beds for foreigners. Built 1961. Large rooms. Air-conditioned. 8 stories. Beds made with straw mat on top (cooler for sleeping on in summer). C.I.T.S. and CAAC offices. Basketball. 3 restaurants. 34 kilometers from airport. Within walking distance of biggest department store and main square.

Green Mountain Lake Hotel: Planned for completion 1980–1981. 500 beds. Near People's Park and Green Mountain Lake. 15 stories. Air conditioning, heat, and swimming pool.

Other Points of Interest in Jiangxi: Please see separate listings: **Lushan—** mountain resort 180 kilometers north. **Jingdezhen (Chingtechen)—**ancient porcelain city 250 kilometers northeast. **Jinggang Shan** (Chingkang Mountains)—mountain resort and revolutionary base. **Jiujiang—**34 kilometers north of Lushan on the Yangtze.

NANJING (Nanking; Southern Capital)

Location: Southwest part of Jiangsu province on the Yangtze River, 5 hours by train or 1 hour by air (300 kilometers) northwest of Shanghai, or 16 hours by train (2¼ hours by air) southeast of Beijing. Direct flight from Hong Kong.

1. Yuhuatai People's Revolutionary Martyrs' Memorial Park
2. Museum of the Taiping Heavenly Kingdom
3. Dr. Sun Yat-sen's Mausoleum
4. Nanjing Yangtze River Bridge
5. Nanjing (also Jiangsu) Museum and Zhong Shan Hotel
6. Purple Gold Mountain Observatory
7. Wutaishan Stadium
8. Lin Gu Park
9. Ming Tomb
10. Xuanwu Lake
11. Mochou Lake
12. Nanjing Friendship Store
13. Nanjing Curios Store
14. Nanjing Hotel
15. Shuangmenlou Guest House
16. Dingshan Hotel
17. Victory Hotel
18. Nanjing Airport
19. Nanjing Railway Station
20. Egret Islet Park
21. Stone City of the Wu Dynasty
22. City of Metallurgy
23. Thousand Buddha Grottoes
24. Six Dynasties Tombs
25. Site of Former Ming Palace

Population: 3 million.

Area: 4,717 square kilometers including rural areas

Weather: Hottest: 40°C (rare)—August; coldest: minus 15°C—January.

Background: Nanjing was built more than 2,400 years ago. From A.D. 229 to 1421, it was intermittently the capital of the Wu, Eastern Jin, Song, Qi, Liang, Chen, Southern Tang, and early Ming dynasties. In 1842 the Treaty of Nanking was signed here with England, ending the First Opium War, and the city was declared an open port. In 1853, the Taiping Heavenly Kingdom made Nanjing its capital for eleven years. On January 1, 1912, it became the capital of the Sun Yat-sen government and remained so until April 5, 1912, when the capital was moved to Beijing. After a period of much confusion, Chiang Kai-shek unilaterally declared Nanjing his capital on April 18, 1927.

The Japanese captured Nanjing on Dec. 12, 1937, and massacred 100,000 civilians in what is known as the Rape of Nanking. The Nationalists' capital was moved to Chongqing but returned to Nanjing after the Japanese surrender in 1945. Most buildings survived the war. The Communists took the city on April 23, 1949, and the capital was moved to Beijing. Nanjing is still the provincial capital, and the economic and cultural center of the province.

Nanjing today is a beautiful city of broad avenues thickly lined with 240,000 trees. Central is the Drum Tower, with Daqing Road radiating north and Zhongshan Road, the main shopping street, running south. Part of Zhongshan South Road was roughly the old Imperial Way, open only for the emperor. The earlier dynasties were centered in this section of town. Xuanwu Lake dominates the northeastern sector. Above it to the east looms 450-meter Purple Gold Mountain. The magnificent Ming city wall snakes around most of the urban area.

Two thousand factories and mining enterprises involved in metallurgical and chemical equipment, coal, petroleum, radios, machine making, shipbuilding, telecommunications instruments and meters, and synthetic fibers. Zhong Xin Yuen silk factory where brocade is made, the Arts and Crafts Carving Factory (ivory and wood).

C.I.T.S. here is one of the best in the country—more eager, creative, and efficient. Try here if you can't get a visa or travel permit elsewhere. It has been organizing a Grand Canal Tour (Suzhou to Yangzhou), honeymoon tours, bicycle tours, and an interesting all-Jiangsu chartered bus. Mr. Cui Yan of Jiangsu's Travel and Tourism office, Nanjing, promised to answer all queries in English after I complained no one there was answering my letters.

Of Interest to Visitors

Sun Yat-sen Mausoleum is on an 80,000-square-meter site chosen to be better than those of the emperors the father of the Chinese republic overthrew. It is on the south side of Purple Gold Mountain. Dr. Sun

(1866–1925) was buried here in 1929. (See MILESTONES IN CHINESE HISTORY.) The mausoleum, 158 meters above sea level, has 392 steps.

Lin Gu Temple is just a building, its statues destroyed during the Taiping war when the Qing army slept here. It was built originally in the Ming without beams and is reminiscent of medieval Europe because of its arches. Nearby is a nine-story pagoda built in the 1920s to complement the area around the mausoleum 2 kilometers away.

Ming Tomb: This mausoleum is not as interesting as those in Beijing. In fact, tourists are usually shown only the Sacred Way. The tomb contains the remains of the first Ming emperor and his empress who died in 1398 and 1382 respectively. The Sacred Way has twelve pairs of life-size animals in parallel lines. Unlike other Sacred Ways, there is a bend in the line because the emperor did not want to disturb the tomb of a general in the way.

The **Botanical Garden,** with tropical and subtropical plants, is on one side of the Sacred Way.

Zijin (Tse Chin) Purple Gold Mountain (a.k.a. Bell Mountain) dominates the northeastern skyline. The observatory is on the west side and is usually combined with a visit to Xuanwu Lake. The Sun Yat-sen Mausoleum, Ming tomb, and Lin Gu Temple are on the south side, usually combined in a half-day tour.

Purple Gold Mountain Observatory, built in 1934, is a functioning observatory of the Chinese Academy of Science. Tourists usually are taken there for the magnificent view of the city and surrounding countryside and the copies of ancient instruments outside.

The armillary sphere (four dragons and spheres) was invented two thousand years ago in the Western Han and was used to locate constellations. The abridged armillary sphere (three dragons) was invented in the Yuan for the same purpose. Both these 500-year-old replicas were stolen by the Germans and French respectively in 1900. They were later returned. The gnomon column next to the abridged sphere was invented three thousand years ago and was used to survey the seasons and calculate the days of the year. It faces due south and north. In the large column is a small hole through which the sun shines at noon, casting an oval of light on the gauge below. Because of this instrument, the Chinese decided there were 365¼ days a year.

Nanjing Yangtze River Bridge is the longest in China. Including approaches it is 4,589 meters long, of which 1,577 meters are directly over the river. It has four lanes for vehicular traffic (19.5 meters wide) and, on another level, two trains side by side. Tourists are taken to an observation tower for a good view of the river, a nearby dolomite mine, and the city. The bridge was built in 1960–68.

Jiangsu Provincial Museum (a.k.a. Nanjing Museum) has exhibits ranging from the era of Peking Man to revolutionary times. The Chinese-style building was started in the 1930s, interrupted by the war, resumed in 1945, and completed in 1949. It was opened as a museum in March 1953. There are three thousand pieces on display, more in storage. Among these are a 3,000-year-old duck egg—genuine; the *jade suit* that was exhibited in Europe, Asia, and America in 1973 (Eastern Han, from Xuzhou City, Jiangsu); a sixth-century Soul Pot covered with many birds—it was put in a tomb so the birds could fly the soul of the deceased to paradise; a small bronze model of a stove (Ming) with five *woks*, also for the use of the deceased; maps of the early capitals in Nanjing from 229 to 589, so you can try to locate them in the modern city; a 20-meter scroll showing the inspection tour by Qing emperor Kang-hsi from Nanjing to Zhenjiang; the anchor from a British merchant ship lost in Zhenjiang; a photograph of a British-built electric company in 1882; a list of institutions set up by the U.S. in China with numbers of Chinese students and teachers, and of foreign teachers.

Xuanwu Lake, 15 kilometers in circumference, and now used for recreation and fish farming. One to two meters deep. Five islets. 1,100 acres, of which 121 acres is land. It was originally built in the fifth century, and several emperors have used it to train or review their navies. In 1075 (Northern Song) the emperor was persuaded to convert the lake to rice paddies. When the paddies were drained in 1953, Song tombs and pottery were discovered. In 1911 it was turned into a park and by 1949 was almost completely silted up. The new government drained and enlarged it, adding buildings. Today there is a famous pick-your-own-live-fish restaurant called the White Garden, a zoo, a theater, a playground, a swimming pool, a roller skating area, boat rides, and exhibition halls. You can walk from the railway station and take a ferry here.

Jiu Hua Hill (Monk Tang Pagoda) is south of Xuanwu Lake. With five stories and four sides, it was originally built in the Song about a thousand years ago to keep the skull of Hsuan-tsang, the monk who traveled to India in search of the Buddhist sutras and was immortalized in the novel *Pilgrimage to the Western World.* The rest of him is in Xi'an. The pagoda collapsed in the Qing. In 1942 the Japanese dug up the base, taking the skull to Japan. They built the present pagoda to house the small fragment left behind.

Drum Tower, built 1382, has a 6-foot-diameter drum and a giant stone tortoise carrying a stele added in the Qing, a report on the inspection tour of a high Qing official.

Nanjing City Wall: 12 meters high, 33.4 kilometers in circumference, and from 7.62 to 12 meters thick. Built from 1368 to 1387, it once had 13,616 cannons on top. Roughly 10 kilometers north-south by 5.62 kilometers east-west, it is said to be the longest city wall in the world. The bricks were made in five provinces, and each is inscribed with the name of the superintendent and the brickmaker, plus the date made. The mortar was lime, tung oil, and glutinous rice water. The most interesting gate is the Zhonghua Gate on the south side, which has four two-story gates in succession (in case the enemy breaks through), twelve tunnels, and room to garrison three thousand soldiers.

If you have more time or specialized interests

Ming Palace: The ruins are located in the eastern part of Nanjing and can be seen in about five minutes. Built for the first Ming emperor from 1368 to 1386, it was copied in Beijing for the Ming palace there. The Forbidden City is about the same size. The palace was partially destroyed in 1645 by Qing troops and what was left was pulled down to build the Taiping palaces. In 1911 only a gate was left standing, but in 1958 some of the relics were restored. From them you can get an idea of the original.

Former Residence of Chou En-lai. No. 30, Meiyuan Xincun. Furniture, office, clothing, and photographs as they were when he headed the Communist delegation in negotiations with the Nationalists (1946–1947).

Southern Tang Tombs: More than 30 kilometers from the city. Visitors can enter two of them and see murals, reliefs, and coffins.

Taiping Museum, near the Zhonghua Gate in the southern part of the city, Zhan Yuen Road. (See also 1853 in MILESTONES IN CHINESE HISTORY.) Building originally Ming. During the Taiping period, it was the palace of the Eastern Lord, Yang Hsin-ching. 1,000 square meters of exhibits reflecting historic events: (1) background of the revolution; (2) uprising at Jin Ting village; (3) Nanjing as capital; (4) regulations and policies; (5) insistence on armed struggle; (6) resisting aggression; (7) safeguarding the capital; (8) continuing the revolution.

Liang Tombs, on the eastern outskirts about 30 kilometers from the city wall. Only mounds, nothing excavated.

Yuhuatai People's Revolutionary Martyrs' Memorial Park: Just south of the Zhonghua Gate. It was here that 100,000 Communists and sympathizers were executed from 1927 to 1949. Now a memorial park, known also for its multicolored pebbles.

City of Metallurgy of the Eastern Jin, currently an agricultural exhibition hall but expected to revert to its origins as a place for smelting iron and making weapons.

The Stone City of the Wu dynasty: Over two thousand years old. After the Wu capital was moved here from Zhenjiang, this city was started, 10 kilometers in circumference, on what was then the banks of the Yangtze.

Thousand Buddha Grottoes: Qi dynasty. Five-story Sui pagoda with 64 statues of small Buddhas engraved on its sides. About 20 kilometers outside the city, on 313-m.-high Qixia Mountain. Of the 515 statues, the last one is a likeness of the carver himself.

Shopping: Friendship Store at 13 Hanzhong Road. Brocades, ivory and wood carving, carved red lacquer.

Food: Nanjing people say the recipe for Beijing roast duck originally was from Nanjing. So you might want to try the Nanjing version. Mandarin fish, a saltwater fish that comes up the Yangtze to spawn, is also a specialty.

Hotels: Nanjing already attracts about 40 percent of all tourists to China and is working hard at getting more. It is one of the first cities to have two-year courses for hotel attendants and drivers, with a strong emphasis on foreign-language training. The first five hundred graduated in 1980. Its hotels are all air-conditioned. It is now aiming to promote other cities in the province so visitors will stay at least a week, hopefully longer. These cities include Yangzhou, Wuxi, Suzhou, Yixing, and Hue An—Chou En-lai's birthplace, where there is now a 70-bed hotel and a Han pagoda.

Nanjing's hotels have had a few changes recently. The updates and additions are listed below.

Nanjing Hotel, Zhongshan North Rd. 100 rooms and 250-room extension. Built 1955. 3 stories. Residential area.

Dingshan Hotel. 130 rooms. Built 1977. 8 stories. Isolated on Ding Hill near the former British residency, it is surrounded by communes. From its rooftop coffee shop there is a great view of the city. A 110-room extension was built in 1980 with Australian cooperation.

Sunli (Victory) Hotel, Zhongshan South Rd. 30 rooms. 5 stories. Built before Liberation. In downtown shopping area.

Shuangmenlou Guest House. 90 rooms. Built before Liberation, on the grounds of former British consulate. By 1981 it should have 400 rooms for tourists.

Jinling Hotel. Built 1982. 800 rooms. 37 stories (the tallest in China), with revolving restaurant on top. City center.

Meiling Palace, former residence of Mme. Chiang Kai-shek. Near Sun Yat-sen Memorial. Has traditional Chinese style interior, redwood furniture and carved marble balustrades. ¥1000 a night will give you three big suites, three double rooms, one single, a dining hall, coffee shop—for up to 15 people.

Zhongshan (Bell Mountain) Hotel. 1985. Near museum.

NANNING is the capital of Guangxi Zhuang Autonomous Region in south China on the northeastern border of Vietnam. Some tours there were canceled in 1979 because of war. The city is in the southern part of the region on the Yu River and the railway line from Hanoi. Founded 1,600 years ago, it developed an industrial center after Liberation and now has a population of over 540,000. There is an institute for cultural minorities, a zoo, an art school, a botanical garden, and a museum. **Yi-Ling Cave,** a limestone cave, is 32 km. away. Twelve nationalities live in the region, of which the Zhuang form one-third. The colorful Miao and Yao live here also. The weather is subtropical. Hottest 38°C.; coldest 5°C. The city produces brocade, herbal medicines (a park displays 3,000 species), pomelo, lichee, and other fruits. Visitors can also see a Zhuang commune and swim at the Spirit Spring, 47 km. away, where the water is a constant 24°C.

Hotels: Min Yuan (160 beds); **Yong Zhou** (500 beds); **Yong River** (170 beds), downtown on riverbank; **Xi Yuan** (100 beds), former national guest house, set in garden away from town.

NINGBO (Ningpo), on the Zhejiang coast south of Shanghai, was made a treaty port, open to foreign trade and residence, in 1842. After 1860 a French military detachment was stationed there. In the vicinity is the island of Putuo Shan, the home of the Goddess of Mercy, Kuan Yin. Ningbo was reopened as a port for foreign trade in 1979 for the first time in thirty years. It has one of the oldest extant libraries in China, the **Tian Yi Ge,** built in 1561 which still has thousands of rare books. Its **Bao Guo Temple,** built in 1013, is the oldest wooden structure in South China. Both the **Tian Tong Temple** and the **Yu Wang (King Asoka) Temple** were founded in the third century, the latter with a relic of Sakyamuni himself.

Ningbo is on the Shanghai-Hangzhou railway and can also be reached by ship from Shanghai daily. The **O.C. Hotel** (1950s) has 262 beds; the **Ningbo Hotel,** 1982, 200 beds, is air-conditioned. Bookings through C.I.T.S. head office, Shanghai, and Hangzhou, or C.T.S.

QINGDAO (Tsingtao), on the southern coast of the Shandong peninsula in the Yellow Sea, is a port city and summer resort, famous for its beer. It is reached by train from Jinan. It should be put at the end of a hectic, tight schedule in summer.

Starting as a fishing village, Qingdao (pronounced Ching Dow) was once a German naval base and trading port in the nineteenth and early twentieth centuries, a fact that accounts for some of the architecture. It is now the largest city and industrial center in Shandong. The four kilometers of beaches slope gently into the sea and are protected by four large bays east from the 440-meter Qianhai Pier, a good place from which to see the sunrise. Each beach has marked swimming areas protected with shark nets, life-guards, and medical stations. There are changing facilities and fresh-water showers. Qingdao also has an aquarium and several parks. Many Chinese work units have sanitariums, which are convalescent and treatment centers for their members, in Qingdao. Its factories make steel, diesel locomotives, automobiles, tractors, machine tools, generators, TV sets, wristwatches, cameras, and precision equipment. Tourists would probably be interested in factories making Tsingtao beer and Laoshan mineral water, which are sold all over China and around the world. The beer is made from Laoshan mineral water from the mountain behind the city. The **Hiquan Hotel** (1980–1981) has 400 beds.

QINHUANGDO (Chinwangtao), population 350,000, one of China's main seaports, is at the northeastern tip of Hebei province on the Bohai Sea. The closest airport is at Shanhaiguan, 25 kilometers away. It is about 6 hours' train ride from Beijing. The city has a shellcraft and glass factory, and a 100-bed hotel for foreigners, the **Hai Bin Lu.** For excursions from here see "Great Wall" and "Beidaihe," the resort about 10 kilometers south.

QUANZHOU (Chuanchou), south of Xiamen (Amoy) in Fujian, was considered one of the two largest ports in the world by Marco Polo, who knew it as Zaiton when it exported silks and porcelain as far away as Africa and Egypt. In the Song it had a population of 500,000.

Its attractions include a 900-year-old 83-meter-long **stone bridge** and a Tang dynasty **Kai Yuan temple.** The main hall of the temple has one hundred heavy stone columns. On top of twenty-four of these are gaudy part-women-part-birds whose crowns support the beams. Indian figures, Greek-type columns, and Chinese dragons and tigers are also in the temple. Two large pagodas, the trademark of the city, are on the temple grounds. The **Zhenguo pagoda** is 48 meters high, originally built of wood in 865 but rebuilt of stone in 1238. The west **Renshou pagoda,** 44 meters high, was originally built in 916 but rebuilt in 1228.

Near the Kai Yuan temple is a special exhibition hall for a twelfth- or thirteenth-century ship 24.2 meters long and 9.15 meters wide, found in 1974 in Quanzhou Bay. At the shore itself, 30 minutes by car from the city, is the 1162-built five-story octagonal stone **Tower of the Two Sisters-in-law.** The 21-meter-high structure was originally built as a navigational aid, but its name symbolizes the loneliness of the women left behind by the emigrating Chinese workmen.

On **Lingshan Hill** outside the city's east gate is a cemetery where two Islamic missionaries are buried. They arrived in the city during the Tang; their gravestones are inscribed in Arabic with details of their lives. At one time, ten thousand foreigners from Persia, Syria, and Southeast Asia lived in the southern part of the city. In 1010 a **mosque,** copied after one in Damascus, was built by local Moslems; it was renovated in 1310.

There is also the 161-acre **Overseas Chinese University** in the mountains east of the city. In 1978 it had 180 new students, mainly from Burma, Indonesia, Singapore, Malaysia, Thailand, Taiwan, Hong Kong, and Macao.

On **Wushan Hill,** 3 kilometers from the city, is a very impressive 5-meter-high, thousand-year-old statue of Lao-tze, founder of Taoism, which used to have a temple behind it. Below are caves with Buddhist carvings.

Outside the city is **Wanshan Peak,** where there are some Manicheist remains. This religion, brought to China in the seventh century from Persia, is a combination of Zoroastrianism, Christianity, and paganism. On a stone tablet near the site of the monastery are inscribed the activities of the cult during the Song. Behind the ruins is a circular Manichean statue of a man.

The city also has a big sugar refinery and porcelain and preserved-fruit factories. Because of the cosmopolitan population, the relics here are a fascinating mix of cultures. There is even the 1326 tomb of a Franciscan bishop.

QUFU (Chufu) in southwestern Shandong province south of Jinan, with a population of 27,000, is the birthplace of Kong Fuzi (Master Kong), known to the west as Confucius, who lived from 551 to 479 B.C. In 1979 the monuments to the famous sage were just repaired and restored. Much that wasn't hidden was destroyed by the Red Guards in 1966. Visitors can see the grave (only a tumulus, not yet excavated) of the philosopher whose teachings were protected by every dynasty from the Han to the Qing. You can meet his descendants, spend the night in the family house (400 halls and a museum on 30 acres), and visit the Great Temple of Confucius, first built in 478 B.C., one of China's best ancient buildings with its 23 Ming stone inscriptions of the sage's life.

SHANGHAI (Above the Sea)

Location: This municipality, directly under the control of the central government, is located on the Huangpu River, 28 kilometers from the Yangtze River, on the east coast of China due west of the southern tip of Japan. Bordering on Jiangsu and Zhejiang provinces, it is about a 2-hour flight northeast of Guangzhou and Hong Kong and southeast of Beijing.

Weather: Sharing about the same latitude as Jacksonville, Florida, its hottest temperature is 35°C in July-August; its coldest is minus 5°C in January-February. Most rain comes in June.

Population: 11.4 million, of whom 6.1 million are in urban Shanghai.

Area: 6,182 square kilometers, of which 150 square kilometers are urban. Has ten suburban counties and twelve urban districts.

Background: Shanghai started out in the fourth century as a fishing village and became a port in the seventeenth. By 1840 its population was 500,000. In 1842 it was captured by the British, and although the Chinese paid a $300,000 ransom to keep it from being sacked, there was considerable looting both by British soldiers and Chinese thieves. The Treaty of Nanking in that year opened Shanghai to foreign trade and led to its partition into British, French, and later Japanese concessions. The British Concession eventually became the International Concession, which continued until the early 1940s. Each of the concessions had its own tax system, police, courts, buses, and electrical wattage. A criminal could escape justice just by going from one concession to another.

Shanghai thrived as a port, however, trading principally in silk, tea, and opium. Most of the foreign trade was British and one-fifth of all the opium reached China in fast American ships.

From 1853 to 1855, the walled section of Shanghai was seized by the Small Sword Society, a Cantonese-Fukinese triad, i.e., a secret society that wanted the Ming restored and opium prohibited. It was helped in its struggle by some foreign seamen, but many other foreigners helped the Qing regain the city. In 1860 the Taiping Heavenly Kingdom tried unsuccessfully to take Shanghai. In 1915 students and workers demonstrated here against the Twenty-One Demands of Japan. And in July 1921, the first Congress of the Communist Party of China was held here secretly.

In 1925 a worker striking for higher wages was killed at a Japanese factory. This led to a demonstration by workers and students in the International

Settlement, during which the British police killed several demonstrators. A rash of nationwide anti-imperialist protests followed. In April 1927 Chiang Kai-shek ordered a massacre of the Communists here, and Chou En-lai barely escaped with his life. Such was the setting of André Malraux's famous novel *Man's Fate*.

In 1932 an attack by Japan was resisted for two months and ended in a truce. China appealed to the League of Nations and the U.S., who did little to help. Japan attacked again in August 1937. The Nationalists resisted for three months before retreating to Nanjing while the Japanese stayed until 1945. In May 1949, Shanghai was taken by the Communists. During the Cultural Revolution, it was the scene of many intense political struggles, especially in January 1966.

Shanghai's cosmopolitan heritage is still reflected in the architecture and in the sophistication of many of its citizens. Its services are closest to international standards, a result of its longer, more concentrated period of dealing with fussy foreigners than any other Chinese city. It was the first to have a two-year institute of tourism for administrators in 1979. It was one of the first to have extensive courses for hotel attendants and service staff with foreign-language training. It is the first to have C.I.T.S. sub-branches at the airport (with a neon sign) and at the train station to help foreign travelers.

It is one of the biggest ports in China. Cruise ships dock almost at the foot of Nanjing Road. It is also still an important trading city and one of the biggest industrial cities. Among its industries are trucks, cars, machinery, textiles, watches, metallurgy, electromechanical equipment, chemicals, meters and instruments, and shipbuilding. Tourists might be interested in seeing factories for jade carving, embroidery, woolen carpets, and tapestries.

As an agricultural area, it is highly developed. Its own communes are among the richest in the country, completely supplying the city. It grows two crops of rice and one of wheat each year.

The city is on the north bank of the Huangpu River. Streets running east-west are named after cities and those running north-south after provinces. Its natives speak a dialect unlike that of Beijing and more akin to that of Hangzhou and Suzhou—only faster. The largest free market is at Shi Luo Pu.

Of Interest to Visitors

The site of the First National Congress of the Communist Party of China was the living room of a small rented house in Shanghai's French Concession. There, twelve representatives of the Party from all over China, including Mao Tse-tung, met secretly for four days starting July 1, 1921. Some sources say they also met at a nearby girls' school, but the guide here says they only slept there. On July 5, after a stranger burst into the room "looking for a friend," the suspicious delegates immediately left the house. Ten minutes later, the French police arrived, while the delegates went on to Jia Xing (Chia Hsing) county, 98 kilometers away in Zhejiang province, to complete their work in a rented boat in Nan Hu (lake).

The Congress adopted the first constitution and proclaimed the founding date of the Party. The house was found by the government after Liberation and restored to its modest 1921 condition. Some of the furniture is reproductions. Adjacent is a small museum with photos, history, and a model of the boat. It is at 76 Xingye Road.

Museum and tomb of Lu Hsun (pinyin, Lu Xun) and **former residence of Lu Hsun:** These are quite close to each other in the northern part of the city. Lu Hsun (1881-1936) was an author of short stories who wrote in the colloquial language about poor people, impoverished literati, and oppressed women, and he is considered a hero. He died of tuberculosis in Shanghai.

Shanghai Municipal Museum: Opened 1952. A good collection, including, on the ground floor, a demonstration of how the Shang bronzes were cast and what they looked like new (did you really think they drank out of those yucky green things?); bronze bells used as musical instruments; a knife for beheading; a model of a 2,000-year-old tomb with skeletons of slaves buried alive so they could serve the departed master; a water vat used for refrigeration; 2,000-year-old gilding on bronze; giant Ka drums; a bronze shell (i.e., money) container with tigers climbing up the sides, a slave being bound for sacrifice, and two dead cows for decoration; and two of the life-size Qin warriors and a horse from the famous Xi'an excavations. On the second floor, there is a demonstration of how pottery was made from wicker baskets, an A.D. 618 polo game, three-color Tang camels and other tomb pieces, and ancient and contemporary porcelain. On the third floor there are murals of *fat* Tang ladies (fat was fashionable); a horizontal scroll of life in eleventh-century Kaifeng—look for the bride being carried in the sedan chair; and a collection of ancient paintings—note the ones done by fingernail.

Former residence of Sun Yat-sen is in the old French Concession, an old European-style house, large by today's Chinese standards. Inside, it is as if you had stepped back into the 1920s. The master is not home yet but is obviously expected because the mahogany furniture is sparkling clean and polished. The house was bought by Chinese-Canadians for the father of the Chinese republic for 16,000 pieces of silver. He lived here with his wife intermittently from 1920 to 1924, just before his death of cancer in 1925. His widow, Soong Ching-ling, lived in the house until 1937, when the war forced her to move to Chongqing (Chungking). In October 1949 Madame Sun gave the building to the state. It was opened to the public in 1952.

In this house in 1924, Dr. Sun met Communist leader Li Ta-chao publicly for the first time to work out Nationalist-Communist cooperation and also met Lenin's representative Yue Fei. In the garden that year also, Sun held a meeting to reform the Nationalist Party, with Communist Party representatives. Sun wrote his book *International Development of China* here.

Besides the antiques, which include a Tang camel, Japanese swords, and a Victrola, there are some old photographs, a 1920 China train map, Sun's medical instruments, clothes, and glasses. The house contains his library: a 1911 Encyclopedia Britannica, biographies of Bismarck, Cicero, Lincoln,

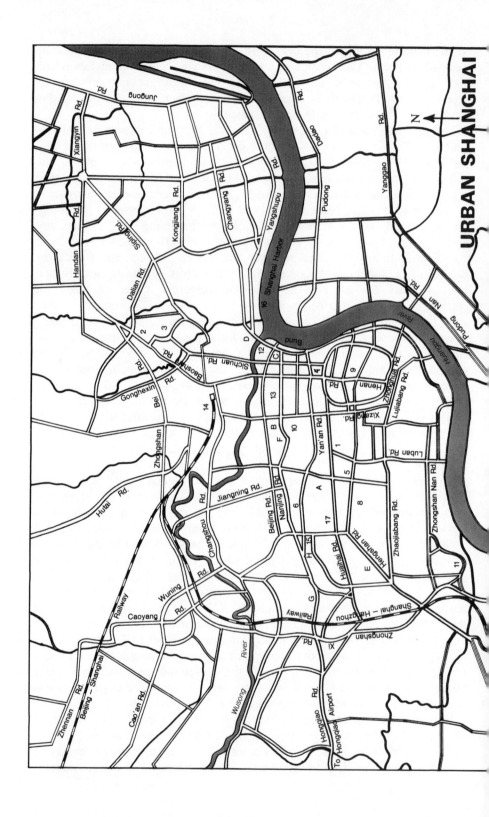

URBAN SHANGHAI

and Napoleon in English, books in Japanese, and ancient works in Chinese. Because this is a shrine, no photos are allowed.

Shanghai Industrial Exhibition Hall was completed in 1955 with Soviet help and used for exhibits from the Soviet Union, Japan, and Czechoslovakia, and from other Chinese provinces. It was closed from 1966 to 1969 (Cultural Revolution) and reopened "primarily for the exchange of technology and to tell people about the development of industry in Shanghai." For this reason products here were not "for sale," but you should be able to contact an appropriate corporation for information. There is an English-speaking guide in each hall. At press time, you could buy handicrafts at a succession of trade fairs.

Total floor space is 52,800 square meters, of which 10,000 is taken by Shanghai industries. The rest is available for foreign and other Chinese exhibitions. Exhibits include heavy industry, metals, movable toys, textiles, medical equipment, computers, watches, petroleum products, shipbuilding, and herbal medicines. There are also handicrafts and a 4-foot-high, 2-ton jade carving of the 40-man Chinese team scaling Everest.

Jade Buddha Temple was first built in 1882 in Jiangwan on the southern outskirts of Shanghai. When it was found inconvenient for adherents to visit, it was bodily moved to Shanghai in 1918 and now occupies about two acres in the western part of the city. Renovations were made in 1952, and again in the late 1970s. The temple was closed from 1966 to 1976.

In the first hall, visitors are met by a 2.6-meter gold-faced Wei Tuo. On each side are two temple guardians about 5 meters high: The Eastern King with a mandolinlike instrument using music to defend and praise Buddha; the Southern King with his dark, angry face, and sword; the Northern King, with a Chinese parasol; and the Western King, who "looks after the whole world with penetrating eyes and carries a snake which is actually a net to catch converts." Behind Wei Tuo is a 1.6-meter Laughing Buddha.

---

1. Site of the First National Congress of the Communist Party of China
2. Museum and Tomb of Lu Xun (Lu Hsun), Hung Kou Park
3. Lu Hsun's Former Residence
4. Shanghai Municipal Museum
5. Former Residence of Dr. Sun Yat-sen
6. Shanghai Industrial Exhibition Hall
7. Jade Buddha Temple
8. Shanghai Art and Handicraft Research Studio
9. Yu Yuan Garden
10. People's Square
11. Lung Hua Pagoda
12. Friendship Store
13. Main Shopping area
14. Shanghai Railway Station
15. International Club
16. Foreign Passenger Quay
17. U.S., Japanese, and French consulates

Hotels
A. Jing Jiang (Chin Chiang)
B. Huaqiao [Overseas Chinese]
C. He Ping [Peace]
D. Shanghai Da Sha [Shanghai Mansions]
E. Heng Shan
F. Guo Ji [Park]
G. Da Hua Guest House
H. Shanghai and Jing'an

In the courtyard is an incense burner made of iron and bronze cast in 1922. On it are the names of believers and some of their deceased relatives. Inside the next parallel building is a giant red wooden knocker. The bell is Qing, made in Wuxi. The three largest figures are Sakyamuni (center), to his right the Amitaba Buddha (with lotus), and the Yuese Buddha carrying the Buddhist wheel of law. Along the sides are the twenty guardians of heaven. Kuan Yin is centered behind the three main Buddhas. Note the very thin Sakyamuni above paying homage, and the eighteen *arhats*. The bases and supports are made of cement and clay, but the statues are sandalwood.

In the building of the Jade Buddha, one changes into slippers and observes the "no photos" sign. The seated Buddha, 1.9 meters high and carved from one piece of white jade in Burma, was brought to China in 1882. The shelves on both sides of the room contain 7,240 volumes of Buddhist scriptures, each about 12 by 5 inches and printed in the Qing dynasty two hundred years ago. They are mothproof and similar to the book under the glass.

In another building is a Reclining Buddha about 40 inches long, also of white jade, depicting Sakyamuni breathing his last. Also in the temple complex are a retail store of religious relics, a small museum with a 5-foot wooden Kuan Yin, a sixth- and a seventh-century stone Kuan Yin (looking male and Indian here), a bronze Buddha (date 491), a tiny child Sakyamuni with his right hand up, left hand down, said to be proclaiming his Buddhahood (which was not possible historically, but never mind!); two 1,400-year-old stone Buddhas; and a scepter. There are also a vegetarian restaurant, a small antique store where you could buy your very own carved, gold-painted, 5-foot sandalwood screen for ¥20,000, and an Arts and Crafts Store.

Shanghai Arts and Handicrafts Research Studio is more interesting than most factories of the same nature because of the development of new crafts here. Demonstrations of paper cutting and dough figure-making.

Yu Yuan Garden (open 8:30 a.m.–4 p.m.) is considered a National Cultural Treasure by the State Council. I can't decide whether or not to recommend it if you are also going to see the gardens of Suzhou. It depends on how much you like gardens, and this one is worth seeing. It was originally built between 1559 and 1577 by a financial official from Sichuan and now covers 20,000 square meters. About a hundred years ago, part was sold to merchants and this now is the site of the 98-shop Yu Yuan Market, once the busiest in the city. There you can get dressmaking patterns (six sizes in one pattern) and novelties and watch *jiao tze* being made. The large new Shanghai Old Restaurant (at the parking lot) is famous.

From 1853 to 1854 the garden was used as the headquarters of the Small Sword Society, which staged an armed uprising and held part of Shanghai for eighteen months. It was a blow at the Qing. The pavilion opposite the exquisite stage is now a museum.

Other points of interest: the top of Rockery Hill, which is an artificial mountain made with rocks carried from Jiangxi province. Until it was dwarfed by Shanghai's skyscrapers, this was the highest point in the city from which you could see and hear the Huangpu River nearby; the five dragon walls winding concentrically around the garden—look for their heads; the unusually shaped doors; the Pavilion to See the Reflection of the Water on the Opposite Side (these names are really something!); and the stepover doorways. There are also the 400-year-old ginkgo tree, the 200-year-old magnolia; the cedars; the poem written on a grain of rice. The south side of the garden was for women; aristocratic women were usually kept out of sight from all but family members. There is a snack bar and an antique store.

Huangpu Park, built in 1868 by the British next to the Suzhou River near the Shanghai Mansions, once had the sign "No Dogs and Chinese Allowed." Now open from 5 a.m. to 10 p.m., even for foreign tourists. The **zoo** has 350 species and over 2,000 animals on 173 acres of a former golf course.

People's Square: 467 × 100 meters. 1951.

Visit the **Botanical Gardens,** built 1954, 70 hectares. Its specialities are potted ancient miniature trees and rock gardens. Also, the **Tomb of Soong Ching Ling,** Mme. Sun Yat-sen, the widow of the founder of republican China and a humanitarian in her own right who died in May 1981.

Lunghua Pagoda and Temple in southwest Shanghai was built in 247 A.D. and rebuilt in 1977 and the early 80s. The pagoda stands about 40 m. high with seven stories. The statues in the temple, currently looking like something out of Disneyland, should look better with age and dust. Huge temple guardians protect some impressive carved boxwood furniture, a fine jade pagoda, and a small museum inside.

Jing Jiang Club, former French Club next to Jing Jiang Hotel has live music, billiards, heated indoor pool, occasional dance party, tennis, restaurants, bar, games, bowling alley. Many foreign residents belong. Foreign visitors can buy cheap membership and use facilities such as the Service Center (telex, typists, translators, help in contacting trading corporations, booking airplane tickets, and taking messages).

International Club has outdoor pool and tennis courts.

Jia Ding County. Confucian Temple (1219) boasts five dragons (i.e., streams) that come together in front attempting to seize a pearl (the hill). **Guyi Garden** at Nanxiang, first built in 1566, then renovated in 1746, has two stone pillars inside over a thousand years old inscribed with Buddhist sutras.

Song Jiang County. About 40 km. southwest of the city, it is usually seen in a full day. Rare **square pagoda,** 48.5 m. high, first erected in 1066, still has some original brick. Its nine stories lean slightly seaward to compensate for prevailing winds. The screen in front is oldest brick carving in the area, erected in 1370. Very well preserved, the mythical animal is a *tuan,* greedily eating everything in sight (note money in mouth). The story goes that the *tuan* saw the sun reflected in the pool below, jumped in, and drowned. A 174-hectare garden also contains newly built Qing-style administrative buildings, teahouse, and a Qing Buddhist temple moved from downtown Shanghai in 1981. Possibility of guides on site in period costume.

Also in Song Jiang County is the **Zui Bai Ci Pond Garden,** first built in 1652 and expanded in 1958. The lotus flowers in the pond are said to date from that time. Highlights include stone etchings of 91 leading Ming Songjiang citizens, and a small museum. The oldest relic in Shanghai is a **Tang stone pillar** (859 A.D.) with some Buddhist inscriptions just barely visible, some lions, and part of a dragon. Currently in the playground of the Zhong Shan Primary School. Visitors are also taken to a **retirement home** with 2,000 residents. Song Jiang is also noted for its fine embroidery and Moslem hats.

Huangpu River boat trip: This 3½-hour trip is usually offered as a ¥8 option for prepaid tourists. It goes to the Yangtze River and back, 8:30 a.m. and 1:15 p.m.

Passenger Service by Ship available nonstop between Shanghai and Hong Kong. Book through C.I.T.S. or China Ocean Shipping Agency, Huangpu Hotel, 255 Jiangxi Rd. Prices range from HK$260 to $845, including food. Service also to Dalian, Qingdao, Ningbo, Chongqing, Wenzhou, and Hankou (Wuhan).

Visitors are taken to **Children's Palaces,** an after-school program for 7–16-year-olds. They are also taken to some model residential areas. Ask if you can visit a home. Optional tours to **Hangzhou, Suzhou** and **Wuxi** can be arranged from Shanghai in less busy seasons, esp. winter.

Shopping in Shanghai is the best in China for variety and quality of goods. There are several department stores along Nanjing Road in between the Peace and Park Hotels. Carpets, tapestries, jade carving, and all kinds of arts and crafts are sold here. Also now open for antiques are the Friendship Store (Antique and Curio Branch), 694 Nanjing Xi Rd. and the Shanghai Antique and Curio Store at 218 Guangdong Rd. Also the Shanghai Jewelry and Jadeware Store at 438 Nanjing Dong Road and the Shanghai Arts and Crafts Trade Fair at 1000 Yan'an Zhong Rd. The Duo Yun Xuan at 422 Nanjing Dong Rd. is for calligraphy and paintings, a highly specialized store.

Friendship Store, one of the largest in China, is near Huangpu Park, the Shanghai Mansions, and Peace Hotels. Purchases can be crated and shipped. Antique store also on premises. The store is on the grounds of the former British Consulate.

Shanghai food is sweeter, lighter, and prettier than other Chinese foods. Most hotel restaurants here are good, especially the **Jing Jiang** and **Peace.** For Western food, there is also the **De Da Restaurant** at the corner of Sichuan and Nanjing Roads (crowded), and the **Red House** (room reserved for foreigners).

Hotels: At the present time most of the hotels for foreigners and Overseas

Chinese, etc., were built before Liberation—big lobbies and relatively elegant restaurants, neon signs. Most rooms are carpeted, renovated and air-conditioned, and have televisions. Live music at the Peace Hotel, Shanghai Mansions, and Jing Jiang Club. **Jing'an Hotel.** Residential district. Spanish exterior. Garden. 109 rooms from ¥36 to ¥76. High food prices. Pan Am office. Electronic games. Same compound as Shanghai Hotel and International Club for swimming and tennis. **Guoji (Park) Hotel,** Nanjing Road, tel. 225225. Built 1934. 166 rooms, 24 stories. For Overseas Chinese, etc. and foreign tourists. Excellent location across from People's Park. To the right as you leave is the Antique and Curio Store and the winter theater of the Shanghai Acrobats. To the left is the main Nanjing Road shopping area.

Da Hua Guest House. Built 1937. 90 rooms, 9 stories. Not convenient to downtown. Originally an apartment building. Near Jade Buddha.

Overseas Chinese Hotel, Nanjing Road, 2 doors east of the Park Hotel. Over 90 rooms. Used primarily for Overseas Chinese, etc. China Travel Service office on premises. Grubby but staff helpful.

Shanghai Mansions. Built 1934. 254 rooms (508 beds) 22 stories. Closest hotel to Friendship Store. Very close to noisy river and harbor but a little farther to other shops.

Heng Shan Hotel. About 87 apartments, 15 stories. Not as many services as other hotels. However, very pleasant, though far out in the western part of the city near the International Club and Temple of the Jade Buddha.

He Ping (Peace) Hotel, Nanjing Road at waterfront. 334 rooms total. Most convenient to Nanjing Road shops, Friendship Store, foreign trade offices, and terminal for the Yangtze/Huangpu River Tour Boat. Has booking office for C.I.T.S. tours, planes, and trains in lobby of North Bldg., which also has the fanciest restaurant in town. One of the best for business people. Disco.

Jing Jiang (Chinchiang) Hotel. 750 rooms. This is the biggest hotel with the most services (including twelve self-punch telexes), two coffee shops, and five restaurants. Four buildings. In western part of the city close to parks and a small shopping area. Has 250-seat movie theater/meeting hall and large garden. One of the best. Handy to Jing Jiang Club and U.S. Consulate.

Other Hotels: Shanghai Hotel. Plans to open 1982–83. 600 rooms, 25 stories. Next to International Club where guests can swim and play tennis. **Lungpa Hotel** (a.k.a. **Hongqiao**) near airport. The Chinese hope it will be used primarily for foreign petroleum offices and residences. Small. The **Airport Hotel** is tiny, dumpy, and has no restaurant. The **Shenjiang Hotel** on People's Park has nine stories—190 rooms, 6 suites.

SHANTOU (a.k.a. Swatow) Guangdong province, a port city, 350 air kilometers north of Guangzhou, is the ancestral home of many Chinese emigrants to South and Southeast Asia, Japan, and Africa. Many Chinese were also kidnapped here and sent to Cuba in the late 1800s. Today about 15 percent of the population receives remittances from overseas.

Shantou is famous for its port, which at one time was used by the Europeans for the importation of opium to China. The city is also famous for its embroidery, lace, wood carving, lacquer carving, silver and gold jewelry, but has other industries, notably the Shantou Photographic Chemicals Plant and the Shantou Ultrasonic Instruments Factory.

Among its attractions are: **Maya Islet**, 6 km. from the city, for swimming, and the **Tian Hou (Heavenly Queen) Temple,** a famous landmark from the Ming (restored in the Qing) for fishermen and emigrants from the area. **Zhongshan Park** has an artificial hill, a small lake, and "gardens within gardens." The city also has a museum.

About 30 km. from Shantou is **Chaozhou,** a 2000 yr. old town to which disgraced officers of the Tang were exiled, notably Yan Hu, who objected to his Emperor spending so much money on Buddhist structures. **Ling Shan Temple** (Tang) has a record of his dispute with the founder of the temple and the founder's grave. **Kai Yun Temple** (also Tang) has a rare set of Buddhist sutras presented by the Qing emperor. **Chaoyang,** about 30 km. away, has two hills, with Tang Taoist and Buddhist temples. Shantou has an Overseas Chinese **Hotel** and 100 tourist beds in a government reception house. It plans to open new hotels in 1982 and 1983.

Shantou is one of the new special foreign trade areas. The plane is usually booked well in advance. A bus from Guangzhou takes 10 hours and a taxi eight.

SHAOSHAN, the village birthplace of Chairman Mao Tse-tung, is worth visiting. It is 2½ hours by tour bus (104 kilometers) southwest of Changsha; there is also a train. The countryside grows tea, oranges, camphor, and rice.

Mao's Birthplace: In this most famous of mud-brick farm houses, Mao was born on December 26, 1893. He lived here until 1910 when he left for studies in Changsha. He returned briefly several times, holding meetings and conducting revolutionary activities. The original house was confiscated and destroyed by the Nationalists in 1929, but after Liberation, it was rebuilt along the original lines. It was shared by two families, the section on the left as you enter being the Chairman's, very sparsely furnished. The kitchen has two large woks, a rice steamer, and a fireplace. The dining room still has the original small table. His parents' bedroom has portraits of his parents and the bed in which he was born. Another room holds original farm tools.

The **Museum,** with ten large galleries, is a 10-minute walk from the farmhouse. It is full of exhibits depicting events in the life of the leader, although Mao's deposed wife Chiang Ching and Lin Piao don't appear at all.

Shaoshan Hotel is 5 minutes' walk from the museum. Built during the Cultural Revolution, it has about 300 beds and a retail store.

SHASHI (Shashih, Shasi), on the north side of the Yangtze River west of Wuhan in Hebei, is passed on the Yangtze Gorges boat trip. It is an industrial city of

180,000 people making mini-bicycles, refrigerators, electronics, building materials, meters, textiles, and light industrial products. Shashi is a centuries-old transshipment port. In 1895 it was opened to foreign trade under the Treaty of Shimonoseki. Over 2000 years old, the city has such relics as **Zhanghua Temple** (Ming) and a Ming longevity pagoda built for an Empress Dowager's 60th birthday. There is also a gate built by Kuan Yu of the Three Kingdom's Period. 7½ km. away is **Jingzhou** with more relics from the same period and a well-preserved Han mummy.

SHEKOU, Guangdong, is 20 nautical miles (40 min. by hover-ferry) from Hong Kong on the Chinese side of Deep Bay. It is part of the Shenzhen Special Economic Zone. In addition to its industrial district, it has a tourist hotel and plans for seaside villas to be sold or rented to tourists.

SHENYANG, formerly known as Mukden, is the capital of Liaoning province, which borders on Korea. It is the biggest industrial city of this region, which was formerly Japanese-held Manchuria, and in winter it is cold, cold, cold (minus 30°C). The population is about 4 million.

The city was recorded over two thousand years ago. From 1625 to 1644 it was the Manchu capital (until the capital was moved to Beijing). This was time enough to build an **imperial palace,** which is now restored to its original gaudy splendor, in an area of almost 60,000 square meters. It is one of the best museums in China.

The **Beiling Tombs (Zhaoling)** north of the city are of Qing Emperor Huang Tai Chi and Empress Poerhchichiteh. Begun in 1643, the tombs were completed in 1651 in a total area of 4,500,000 square meters, of which the graves occupy 160,000. The **Dongling Tomb (Fuling),** east of the city, is that of the first Qing emperor and his wife.

The Mukden Incident on September 18, 1931, a surprise attack on the Chinese army stationed in Shenyang (Mukden), marked the beginning of Japanese aggression in China.

Shenyang is a cultural center with institutions of higher learning and research. It is the home base of the Shenyang Acrobats, some of China's best, the first cultural troupe from the PRC to tour the U.S. and Canada in 1972–73.

SHENZHEN (Shumchun), on the Hong Kong border, is presently a Special Economic Zone with 600 projects underway. It is also a recreation area for crowded Hong Kong, with a lake for swimming and boating, and China's first golf course, to open 1982.

Already opened are a campsite for tents beside the reservoir; the **East Lake Hotel,** near the reservoir, eventually with mini-golf, shooting range, sauna, tennis, swimming pool, convention center, holiday resort; the **Bamboo Garden Hotel,** 1000 rooms when finished; possibly a **Holiday Inn,** 500 rooms with swimming pool. An international airport is expected here.

Shenzhen can be reached by day-tours from Hong Kong. Be aware that some tours are partially by bus then train; some pick you up at a hotel. Others have you meet at the train station.

SHIHEZI (Shihhotzu), in the far western province of Xinjiang, is a city reclaimed from the Gobi Desert, at the northern base of the Tianshan Mountains, 150 kilometers northwest of Urumqi. It has a population of 100,000 and a woolen mill, sugar refinery, oil-pressing mill, flour mill, and agricultural machinery plant. The area grows grain and cotton.

SHIJIAZHUANG (Shihchiachuang, Shihkiachwang), a few hours by train south of Beijing in Hebei, on the main line to Guangzhou, is east of the Taihang Mountains on the Hebei Plain. It is an industrial city of importance to Chinese revolutionary history as the burial place of the Canadian who became a Chinese hero. Dr. Norman Bethune, the son of a Gravenhurst, Ontario, clergyman arrived in China in 1938 to help fight the Japanese. Working almost in the front lines, he died of blood poisoning on November 12, 1939, in Huangshikou village, Tangxian county, in Hebei. On December 21 of that year, Chairman Mao wrote an article, "In Memory of Norman Bethune," pointing him out as an example of "utter devotion to others without any thought of self." He became known to every schoolchild, and statues were made of him all over China. Several films and biographies have been made about him. In Shijiazhuang is the **Bethune International Peace Hospital** and the **Bethune Exhibition Hall and Museum.** He is buried in the western part of the North China Revolutionary Martyrs' Cemetery.

Shijiazhuang is also known for its famous **Zhaozhou Bridge,** still serviceable although it was built between 605 and 610. It is in Zhaoxian county, southeast of the city. The bridge is 50.82 meters long and 9 meters wide with a single stone arch. New hotel, **Hebei Guest House,** 380 beds.

SUZHOU (Soochow)

Location: Yangtze basin, Jiangsu province, about one hour (86 kilometers) west by train from Shanghai and 219 kilometers southeast of Nanjing, on the Beijing-Shanghai railway line. No civil airport.

Weather: Hottest: 36°C—late July, early August; coldest: end of January. Snow once or twice a year. Winter usually 5°C–7°C. Rain: May–July.

Population: 600,000 **Area:** 119 square kilometers

Background: Suzhou was founded by Ho Lu, King of Wu, as his capital in the sixth century B.C. Iron was smelted here more than 2,400 years ago. Silk weaving was well developed in the Tang and Song. It was an early stronghold of Buddhism. Suzhou was visited by Marco Polo in the latter half of the thirteenth century. During the Ming, it was very strong in textile manufacturing. From 1860 to 1863, it was held by 40,000 troops of the Taiping Heavenly

Kingdom movement. During the Japanese occupation, the Suzhou puppet government had its headquarters in the Humble Administrator's Garden.

The people here speak the Wu dialect, which is similar to that of Shanghai, only with softer tones and more adjectives. Industries include mining, metallurgy, chemicals, machine building, electronics, meters, and instruments. Tourists would probably be interested in seeing the various factories that weave silk, print silk, make sandalwood and silk fans, and make one of the three most famous embroideries in China. The communes here raise silkworms, jasmine for jasmine tea, shrimp, and tangerines and are therefore particularly interesting to visit.

The city is about 3 by 5 kilometers and is crisscrossed by many canals. The western and southern moats are actually part of the famous Grand Canal (A.D. 610) extending from Hangzhou to the Yangtze and beyond. The city wall was built in 516 B.C., and remnants, including a gate, remain. Also remaining is one out of eight water gates, which used to be closed at night.

Suzhou is one of the prettiest towns in China, its streets thickly lined with plane trees and its tiny whitewashed houses of uniform design. Unlike many other Chinese communities, there was little damage during the Japanese war. It is known primarily as a cultural and scenic city, similar in this respect to Japan's Kyoto. Its classical gardens are among the best in China.

The main street, Renmin (People's) Road, runs north-south; Jingde and Guanqian Roads (actually the same) run east-west, meeting with Renmin almost in the center of the city.

Of Interest to Visitors: (See also "Chinese Garden" in chapter 10.)

Shizilin (Shih Tzu Lin; Lion Forest) Garden was built in A.D. 1350 during the Yuan and so named because the teacher of the monk who built it lived on Lion Rock Mountain. Some of the rockeries are shaped like lions. Six acres. Compact. Guides say that it was once owned by the grandfather of the famous American architect I.M. Pei. Notable are the maze inside the rockeries at the entrance; the rocks, some shaped naturally, others carved and then weathered in Taihu Lake for seventy years; the rock structure above the stone boat prepared for a waterfall, which in the early days was hand-poured (and therefore no longer operating); the rocks in one of the courtyards, which with a great deal of imagination, look like a cow, crab (note claw), and a lion.

There is also the Standing in the Snow Reading Room (pavilion), so named because a student once went to visit his teacher there and, too polite to awaken him, stood in the snow. Moved by his spirit, the teacher renamed the pavilion. Note also the Lingering and Listening Hall for listening (of course) to the raindrops on the lotus leaves; the ramps instead of stairs; the wood carving; and the cloud designs on the glass. There is some excellent Peng Jing (Chinese bonsai), including a 200-year-old miniature pomegranate tree.

Chang Lang (Gentle Wave) Pavilion, about two acres, is the only garden

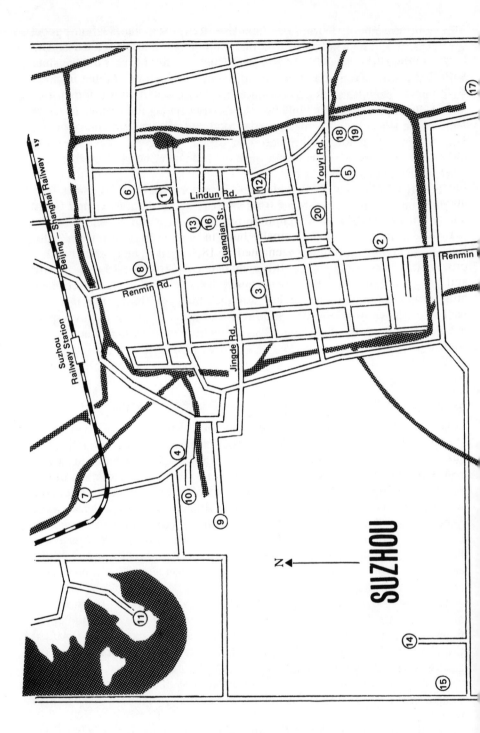

that is not surrounded completely by a view-blocking wall. There is a pond outside and a View-Borrowing Pavilion from which you can enjoy it. The stones in the rockeries here are also from Taihu Lake. There is a large stele with the images of five hundred Tang to Qing sages carved in relief in 1840, their deeds described in sixteen characters each. The garden was founded in 1044 (Song) by poet Su Tzu-chien. In the Yuan and early Ming, it was a Buddhist nunnery. The courtyard outside the Bright Hall for Giving Lectures was once gilded. Note the different eave tiles. I did not find this garden as spectacular as the others, so if you're short of time, skip it.

Yi (Joyous) Garden was built by a Qing official and at a hundred years, it is the newest. It has taken the best of all the gardens, concentrating them into about an acre. The rockeries are from other older gardens. The dry boat is an imitation of the one in the Humble Administrator's.

Liu (Lingering) Garden, originally built in 1525 (Ming) and named the East Garden, was rebuilt and renamed in 1876. It is a National Treasure protected by the State Council. It is eight acres. The garden consists of halls and studios in the east sector, ponds and hills in the central, and woods and hills in the western section. In late autumn, these woods are red. As you walk by the two hundred different flower windows, look out at each scene. It is a living picture gallery. A huge 2-ton, 6-meter high rock from Taihu Lake stands in the eastern section.

Wangshih (Garden of the Master of Nets), built in 1140 (Southern Song), is one of the best. The Metropolitan Museum of Art in New York City has reproduced part of it as the Astor Chinese Garden Court and Ming Furniture Room. This garden is very pretty, especially when decorated with colorful palace lanterns. It is open summer evenings for this exotic experience.

Zhuozheng (Chocheng; Humble Administrator's) Garden, the largest in Suzhou, was laid out in 1522 (Ming) by a humble administrator (i.e., dismissed official) and later split into three after the owner lost it gambling. It was restored in 1953 and is now a National Treasure protected by the State Council. It is the largest and most open of the gardens, water making up three-fifths of its total area, and is reminiscent of the water country south of

---

the Yangtze. Almost all buildings are close to water, much of the water filled with shore-to-shore lotus flowers in summer. The central part is the most interesting, with its two-story stone "dry boat" complete with gangplank, "deck," and "cabin." The Mandarin Duck Hall has blue windows and furniture made from mahogany tree roots that look like chocolate-covered peanuts. Loquat fruit trees ripen in June. There is a garden within a garden and Fragrant Island. The covered walkway in the western section follows the natural contours of the land. There are also the Small Flying Rainbow Bridge, the Pavilion of Expecting Frost, and Pavilion of Fragrant Snow and Azure Clouds. In November and December, there is a chrysanthemum show here with life-size wax figures of characters from the *Dream of the Red Chamber* in costume.

Hu Qiu (Huchiu; Tiger) Hill is important for tourists. The 45-acre site is northwest of the city outside the moat. It is a National Treasure protected by the State Council. The grounds were an island many years ago and originally were called Hill of Emergence from the Sea. It is now about 100 kilometers from the South China Sea. It was named Tiger Hill because a white tiger appeared here at one time, and now the entrance (the head), the pagoda (the tail), and what is in between are considered parts of the tiger. On the right after entering is the Sword Testing Rock which Ho Lu, King of Wu, was supposed to have broken in the sixth century. The sword is now in the Jinan museum in Shandong. On the left is a large magic rock. If the stone you throw stays on top, you will give birth to sons—or so the story goes. On the right is a pavilion with red characters, the Tomb of the Good Wife. It commemorates a widow sold by the brothers of her deceased husband to another man. Forced by that man to be a courtesan, she committed suicide. Well, wouldn't you?

Here is also the place where Fu Tsai, King of the State of Wu, is said to have built a tomb for his father Ho Lu in the early fifth century B.C., after which the tomb builders were slaughtered to keep the location a secret. Hence, no one is sure if this is indeed the right place. If you look carefully you can still see the red of the blood on the large flat rock. Oh, come on! From the carved stone Fairy Pavilion above the "bloodied" rock, Buddhist monk Sung Gong preached so well that his disciples nodded in agreement and so did the rock to the right in the adjacent pond, now called Nodding Head Stone.

Beyond the moon gate is where the tomb of Ho Lu is supposed to be. In 1956 attempts were made to enter it. They were abandoned because of the danger to the foundation of the pagoda. Inside are supposed to be three thousand iron and steel swords. You can see the cave, blocked by large, cut stones, from the bridge to the pagoda. Is it or isn't it a 2,500-year-old tomb? The two holes on the bridge were to let down buckets for water.

The pagoda of the Yunyen Temple was built originally in A.D. 961 (Northern Song). It was burned down three times. The latest repairs were made in 1956, 1979, and 1981, when its foundation was fixed. It tends to tilt to the northwest. At one time it had wooden eaves. It is 47.5 meters high. Pilgrims used to climb the 53 steps here on their knees. Note Indian arches.

The **North Temple Pagoda** at the north end of Renmin Road, nine stories and said to be 76 meters tall, was built during the Three Kingdoms by Sun Chuan, King of Wu, for his mother. The pagoda was first built in the 10th century and rebuilt in the 12th.

Han Shan Temple, west of the city, was the home of two Tang monks, Han Shan and Shih Te. They are said to have taken Buddhism and Chinese culture to Japan. You might see rubbings made here of the steles. If you buy them here they are more expensive than at the Friendship Store because they have the red chop (seal) to prove you got them at the temple! To the right of the central, gold Sakyamuni Buddha is Ar Nai, the young disciple who wrote the sutras; the older man is disciple Ja Yeh. The original bell was stolen by Japanese pirates but replaced with a bell cast in 1906 as a gift from Japan. Originally built in the Liang dynasty (sixth century), the temple here now was rebuilt at the end of the Qing.

Xiyuan (Hsi Yuan; West Garden) Temple is a very exciting temple, my favorite Suzhou site, because it is so rich in beauty. Near the Han Shan Temple, it was originally built in the sixteenth century (Ming), but was destroyed by fire, and rebuilt in 1892. The temple guardians here are surnamed Ma Li, though basically they look like temple guardians from other temples with other names. Here Ma Li Blue is dark and angry and carries a sword. Ma Li Red carries an umbrella. Ma Li Sea holds a pipa, a musical instrument. Ma Li Long Life is holding a dragon, though it looks like a snake, a magic weapon.

The ceiling in the main building is magnificent—bats (long life) and cranes (happiness) as in Beijing's Forbidden City. The central Buddhas are 7 meters tall, including base and mandala. On both sides are twenty devas, gods in charge of natural phenomena such as the sun, moon, and rain. Behind them to the right is the Bodhisattva of Wisdom with a crown on his head. To the left is the Bodhisattva of Universal Benevolence.

The five hundred *arhats* here—all men—are very interesting, each face real, expressive, profound, individual. Outstanding is Chikung, the crazy monk who can look sad, happy, or wry, depending on the angle you look at him. Enjoy those incense burners. At the time of the Great Leap Forward (1958–1960) and backyard furnaces, they were supposed to be smelted. But the C.I.T.S. director said No!

Purple Gold Nunnery on East Hill, 35 kilometers from Suzhou, is famous for its sixteen *arhats,* who are said to be older (Song) and better than those in West Garden Temple.

Twin Pagodas, almost in the middle of Suzhou, are known as the big (30 meters) and small (25 meters) "brushes." They were built in the Song in commemoration of Confucius.

The **Xuan Miao Guan** (Mysterious Wonder Taoist Temple, Song) behind the Friendship Store (look out the third-floor window) has been described as the tallest, most magnificent temple in the area and probably in China. There are three giant, gilded sculptures of the founders of Taoism.

Confucius Temple: This looks very big and impressive too. It is already repaired and may be opened by the time you arrive.

Sky High Hill is 14 kilometers west of Suzhou. At its foot is the tomb of the famous Song writer Fan Chung-yen. The mountain is famous for its scenery. A narrow path is aptly named One Thread to the Sky Path, and the pavilion on top, the highest spot in the area, is Middle of the White Clouds Pavilion.

Divine Cliff Hill is about 13 kilometers west of Suzhou and topped by a seven-story pagoda, probably Qing or slightly earlier. It is at the site of the palace of Ho Lu and his beautiful queen, Hsi Shih. At the foot of the hill is the ancient town of Mu Tu, built during the Wu period.

The **Suzhou Embroidery Research Institute** is not a factory. It does, however, train young people to do embroidery, develops new embroideries (new stitches, new materials, e.g. human hair), and produces embroidery pieces for places like Beijing's Great Hall of the People.

Boat ride from Jin Gate to Tiger Hill for tourists. This is being planned and may be available when you arrive. Ask about it. It should be fun, especially if ancient-style boats are used.

Shopping: Friendship Store is on the main shopping street of Guanqian Road. It is large, with a good selection of inkstones, brushes, iron reproductions of ancient relics, reproductions of some of the *arhats,* jewelry, embroideries, silks, and antiques. This is one of the best places to buy sandalwood fans (always smell them to be sure) and rubbings (see note on rubbings in chapter 9, SHOPPING). Hours are 8:30 a.m.–6 p.m. Other stores 7:30 or 8:30 a.m.–6 or 7 p.m.

Recommended Restaurants

Pine and Crane Restaurant	松鹤楼
Nanlin Hotel Restaurant	南林饭店
Suzhou Hotel Restaurant	苏州饭店
New Bumper Harvest Restaurant	新聚丰

Recommended dishes—local:

sautéed shrimp meat	清炒虾仁
squirrel Mandarin fish	松鼠桂鱼
stewed turtle	清蒸元鱼
stir-fried eel	生炒鳝贝
fried crisp duck	香酥肥鸭
water-shield soup with floating Mandarin duck	鸳鸯莼菜汤
snow-white crab in shell	白雪蟹斗
pickled duck	苏州酱鸭

Suggested banquet for four to six people at Nanlin Hotel Restaurant, Suzhou (mainly local dishes):

荷　花　冷　盆
辣　味　小　碟
虾　虫　两　鲜
松　子　火　爽　鸡
松　鼠　桂　鱼
香　菇　点　心　汤
鸳　鸯　炖　汤　点
什　锦　船　点　笼
灌　汤　小　笼　饼
葱　油　酥　饼　酥
花　生　香　酥　合
蒲　荷　百　合

Hotels

Suzhou (Soochow) Hotel, Youyi Road, tel. 4646. Section with 100-plus beds for foreigners built 1958; section with 310 beds built 1979. 9 stories. About 400 meters from Garden of the Master of Nets, and within 600 meters of the Nanlin Hotel in the southeast section of the city. Has theater/cinema seating 550 people with simultaneous interpretation equipment. **Nanlin Hotel,** Youyi Road. 104 rooms built 1977. 3 stories. Three smaller buildings have 30 rooms, built 1959. New 200-room extension planned. **Gusu (Ancient Suzhou) Hotel.** Built 1980. 110 rooms, 2 stories built in cooperation with an Australian group. Located on Suzhou Hotel grounds. **Nanyuan Guest House** also being used.

TAI'AN, about 60 kilometers south of Jinan in Shandong, is where you get off the train to start climbing 1,524-meter-high Mount Tai, one of China's Five Famous Mountains. The mountain was regarded as sacred in ancient times, and the emperors offered sacrifices here to Earth and to Heaven. Climbers should be in good shape, for they may have to carry their own luggage for about five hours to the top. Each route is well-marked by a wide stone staircase and there are occasional soft-drink stands. Visitors usually go up the eastern (9 km.) route which goes by interesting temples. The mountain has about thirty temples and modest hotels on top. From the top you can see the rising sun, the sunset, and the Yellow River. A 2,000-meter cable car here, too.

TAISHAN (Cantonese, Toishan), in Guangdong province, is the county seat of the area from which many Chinese left their families for the Chinatowns of the U.S. and Canada. It is little more than a half-day's ride by public bus (101 kilometers south) from Guangzhou, during which three wide rivers are crossed by ferries and over an hour is spent for lunch. An air-conditioned bus leaves twice a day from Guangzhou. See chapter 12, SPECIAL FOR OVERSEAS

CHINESE. Taishan is technically only open for Overseas Chinese, etc. Foreigners wanting a people-to-people experience should stay at the unique new (1981) **Stone Flower Mountain Inn** nearby (¥22 for a double) built in the old black brick village-styled architecture with solar heat and nature-cooled air. Arrangements can be made through the Chinamerican Corp. of Sonoma, California, or by getting a visa to Taishan (which must not be confused with the famous mountain).

In the area is a hot-spring resort with a 100-room extension built in 1979. The **Overseas Chinese Hotel** (1970) is adequate and the 6th floor of the **Hubin Hotel,** both on the main street next to the park, is good. The park has a tiny zoo and boat rides. During my visit, three fish jumped into our boat unsolicited. Visitors can also see tractor and porcelain factories and get bicycles from the Stone Flower Mountain Inn. There is a Taishan Travel Service in Room 251 of the Overseas Chinese Mansion in Guangzhou.

See also chapter 12 and IMPORTANT ADDRESSES.

TAIYUAN, in the center of Shanxi province, of which it is the capital, is a little over an hour's flight southwest of Beijing. The city was founded more than two thousand years ago and was a silk center under the Sui. It also has been growing grapes for a thousand years. It now has an urban population of one million and metallurgical, coal, chemical, and power industries.

The city is most famous for the **Jin Temple,** 25 kilometers S.W. of the city, at the foot of Xuangweng Mountain. Started in the Northern Wei (386–535) in memory of the second son of King Wu of the Western Chou, the Jin Temple was renovated with additions in 1102 during the Northern Song. It is the oldest wooden structure in Taiyuan. Forty-three statues inside from the Song, thirty of these pretty young maids-in-waiting, all different and still retaining much color. Important also are a bridge from the same period on the grounds, the Nanlao Spring, and a cypress planted in the Western Zhou. The **Chongshan Monastery** in the city itself, believed to have been a Sui palace, and the **Shuangta Monastery,** with two pagodas, are also of note.

Hotels: Yencai; and **Jinsi** is the better one, near the Jin Temple.

TANGSHAN in Hebei province northeast of Tianjin was almost completely destroyed by an earthquake in 1976. Much has since been rebuilt and it is back in business as an industrial center, open to foreign visitors.

TIANJIN (Tientsin; Ferry to the Imperial Capital)

Location: In north China on the banks of the Hai River where five tributaries converge. Over 2 hours (137 kilometers) by train southeast of Beijing, 70 kilometers from the Bohai Sea. On the Beijing-Shanghai and the Beijing-Harbin railway lines. Direct flights from Hong Kong.

Weather: Coldest: January—minus 22°C; hottest: 40°C—July. Most rain, June–August.

Population: 7 million (of whom one half are urban) **Area:** 11,204 square kilometers

Background: Tianjin developed as a port starting in the Yuan. It was given its current name in 1404 by Ming Emperor Cheng-tse, then Duke of Yen, who crossed the Haiho River here on a military expedition. The walls were also built in 1404. Tianjin was invaded by the British and French in 1840. In June 1858 the Treaty of Tientsin was signed in which ten more treaty ports were opened to foreign trade. Christian missionaries were given freedom of movement and the Chinese were forced to guarantee the protection of missionaries because "the Christian religion as professed by Protestants and Roman Catholics inculcates the practices of virtue, and teaches man to do as he would be done by." In 1860 British and French troops from Tianjin marched on Beijing. They forced the Qing rulers to ratify the Treaty of Tientsin and burned down the Summer Palace. The resulting Treaty of Peking opened Tianjin and nine other ports to foreign trade.

Nine countries eventually controlled over 3,500 acres of the city: Britain (with over 1,000 acres), France, Germany, Japan, Russia, Italy, Belgium, Austria, and the U.S. The concessions lasted from twenty to eighty years and, as in Shanghai, left the Chinese some very interesting old European architecture as well as bitter memories. The Treaty of Peking also forced the Chinese to permit French missionaries to own or rent property anywhere, and further helped to inflame smoldering anti-Christian and anti-foreign feelings.

Many of these feelings resulted from Christian arrogance that insisted that their God was the only true God. Added to this were cultural misunderstandings. Quite a few Chinese actually believed that the children in Catholic orphanages were either eaten by nuns or ground up for medicine. The French Catholics, with good intentions, did pay money for female babies (to keep them from being killed). By 1870 the atmosphere was so tense that after the French consul fired at a minor Chinese official he was immediately hacked to death. Ten nuns, two priests, and another French official were also brutally killed in what is now known as the Tientsin Massacre, or what the Chinese like to call the Tientsin Revolt. The tragedy might not have happened if all Christian missionaries had refused to become arms of Western imperialism.

On January 15, 1949, Tianjin was taken by the Communists. In 1976 it was severely damaged by an earthquake centered in nearby Tangshan. The temporary shelters along many of the streets, especially around the Friendship Hotel, are from that time. They will probably remain until the city can provide alternative housing.

Tianjin today has one of the largest ports in China. It is an important industrial and commercial city, and like Beijing and Shanghai, a municipality directly under the central government. It has eight urban and four rural districts and five suburban counties. Its factories make machine tools, Flying Pigeon bicycles, Seagull watches, petrochemicals, cotton and wool textiles, tractors, diesel engines, etc. The Dagang Oil Field is 60 kilometers away. Tourists would probably be interested in seeing its factories making carpets (by hand), silk and paper kites, jade, ivory and shell carvings, clay sculptures, wood-block prints, feather pictures, and New Year's pictures. (See section on New Year's Pictures in the SHOPPING chapter.) Its communes are noted for walnuts, chestnuts, dates, Xiaozhan rice, and prawns. Cultural presentations here sometimes include traditional opera, Beijing Opera, Tianjin ballet, singing and dancing, Tianjin acrobats, and puppets.

The city sprawls on both sides of the Hai River. The area immediately southwest of Jiefang (Liberation) Bridge was formerly French. The section south of that, around the Tianjin Hotel, was formerly British. Liberation Road was Victoria Road. Tianjin in 1981 had little to offer the average tourist. It is industrial and very smoggy, of interest primarily to business people and to fans of old European architecture, modern history, and handicrafts. It makes some of China's best carpets. Cruise ships berth in its harbor and their passengers sleep in its hotels—but then commute to Beijing. It is being promoted as a base from which to see the Qing tombs, Chengde, Beidaihe, etc. Like many other Chinese cities in the early 1980s, it is serious about tourism and is in the process of upgrading its attractions, roads, services, and air quality.

Of Interest to Visitors

The Water Park: Built 1951. About 500 acres, half land, half lake. Rowboats, zoo, fish farm, lotus, open-air theater, library, Dengyinglou Restaurant, swimming pool, and roller-skating rink. Pleasant but not very exciting.

Zhou Enlai (Chou En-lai) Museum (1977): The former premier studied at the Nankai Middle School here from 1913 to 1917 and briefly at Nankai University (1919), where he led student uprisings before going to France in 1920.

Art Gallery, a.k.a. Museum of Art collects, analyzes and displays traditional works of art from ancient times. New building planned.

No. 1 Carpet Factory, the biggest of nine carpet factories here, makes Junco-brand carpets. Carpets have been made for more than a hundred years in Tianjin; this factory opened in 1958. Thick carpets are made out of pure wool, with no synthetics. Knots are made by hand, either 70 rows per square foot (ordinary) or 120 rows (refined). Embossing is also done by hand. Washing in a chemical solution adds gloss. Exports mainly to U.S. Staff of 1,400. (Silk carpets are made in Wuqing county, about 28 kilometers north.) Visitors here should not be allergic to dust or wool. Retail shop sells only small squares. Try the Friendship Store.

The **International Club** (1925) is frequently used to give visitors a real Tianjin meal. It is open to both Chinese and foreigners. Formerly the Tientsin Club, it reeks of Britain in the early 1900s, with beautiful high mahogany paneling and a drab, dismal interior. There are billiards, badminton, tennis, table tennis, four bowling lanes (duck pins and ten pins), a 1,300-seat theater, a 500–600 seat banquet hall, and a ballroom with an "elastic" wooden floor. (Real springs are under it. It is big enough for 500, but so far no dancing.) Swimmers in the 33°C pool (¥1.50) need a medical certificate, but you might try arguing if you haven't got one.

Future Plans: Renovations to the famous old Catholic church, which you can see to the right as you leave the Friendship Hotel, "where resources are available." Estimated cost ¥ one million. Repairs also to the Drum Tower and city temples. And hopefully, a park and tour boat rides along the Hai River. Ask about these when you get there.

Tianjin Food: Not spicy hot, not fat, no starches in the sauces, thin soups, and beautiful, cheerful colors. Especially famous is Crystal Shrimp, flowers carved out of vegetables, and a banquet of only fish. The Baozi Restaurant here is very famous. People even come from Beijing, it is said, to eat Tianjin's meat or bean dumplings.

Shopping: Friendship Store sells carpets, jewelry, jade, ivory, kites (¥38), fur coats (mink, fur, wolf), fur hats, suede coats, padded silk jackets, men's suiting, shell work, cloisonné, carved lacquer, screens, inlaid chests, cork, and boxwood carvings. Shipments can be made internationally.

There are good prices for scrolls (¥17 and up) and prints (¥8 for a 12″ × 18″) at the **Yangliuching New Year's Picture Studio.** This is the cheapest place I've found in China for a Chi Pai-shih (prawns, monkeys) reproduction (from ¥20).

Hotels

Youyi (Friendship) Hotel. Shengli Road. Built 1975. 168 rooms and 20 suites, 9 stories. Second-floor restaurant specializes in local food. Located close to the Foreign Trade Building and some good restaurants. In residential district.

Tianjin (Tientsin) Hotel. Built 1924. 74 rooms, 4 suites, 3 stories. Mahogany-paneled lobby. British-built. Located very close to the Hai River, Friendship Store, and Overseas Chinese Hotel. Relatively close to the railway station.

Tianjin Grand Hotel (a.k.a. **Tianjin Guest House**), Friendship Road. Built 1960. 199 rooms, 40 two-room suites and 8 three-room suites for foreign tourists. This giant of a hotel is on an immense lot and is surrounded by parks in the southern edge of the city, close to the Friendship Club. The hotel has two main buildings, the tallest 7 stories. It has a 1,057-seat theater and a conference building with a smaller theater also. Its huge dining room can seat 1,700 people (over twenty cooks, 120 to 130 waiters).

No. 1 Hostel, a posh state guest house with mostly suites, is expected to be opened for foreign tourists soon. It has a lake, apple orchard, and gardens, and is on the southern edge of the city near the Friendship Club.

Overseas Chinese Hotel (a.k.a. **Tianjin No. 1 Hotel**) is close to the Tianjin Hotel and the Friendship Store. It has 74 rooms and 12 suites.

New Hotel: Planned are 2,000 rooms built in stages; near the Tianjin Grand Hotel; as yet unnamed.

Excursions

Qing Tombs—see "Zunhua." About 3 hours' drive northeast.

Beidaihe—see separate listing. Seaside resort 3½ hours northeast by train.

Chengde, a.k.a. Jehol—Qing imperial mountain retreat. See separate listing.

Mt. Panshan (Screen of Green). About 100 kilometers north in **Jixian,** this was opened to foreign tourists in 1980. It has been a mountain resort since the Tang. Highest peak is Moon-Hanging Peak, 1,000 meters above sea level, on top of which is a pagoda said to contain a tooth of Buddha. Other peaks are called Sword-Playing Peak, Zhi-lai Peak, Jiu-hua Peak, and Purple Canopy Peak. Famous for its scenery, unusual rocks, and pines, it also has a lake. Its seventy Buddhist temples were burned by the Japanese during World War II. Some of the buildings have just been replaced or renovated.

Dule (Temple of Solitary Joy), 120 kilometers north, about 2 hours' drive, in the western part of **Jixian** city. It is also listed as an important cultural monument by the State Council. It is said to have been first built in the Tang. Its Kuan Yin Hall and Gate to the Temple were rebuilt in A.D. 984 (Liao). The magnificent Kuan Yin Hall, 23 meters high, is the oldest existing multistoried wooden structure in China. The 16-meter high, eleven-headed Goddess of Mercy is one of the largest clay sculptures in China. The murals are Ming; the colored clay bodhisattvas are Liao. There is a new 100-room hotel in Jixian.

TURPAN (Turfan) in Xinjiang was once an oasis on the Silk Road. It is supposed to be the hottest spot in the country. A 4-hour bumpy ride by bus from Urumqi. It exists because of subterranean water. Uygur, Han, and Hui nationalities live here, growing grapes, cotton, and hami melons. The area has many ancient tombs, Buddhist art grottos, and the ruins of ancient cities. The ghost city of **Gaochang,** 40 km. southwest of Turpan reached its peak in the 9th century, flourishing for 1,500 years. There were once 30 to 40 monasteries there. Another abandoned town is **Jiaohe,** 10 km. west of Turpan, which existed from the second century, B.C. to the 14th A.D. Its buildings are better preserved than Gaochang's.

Close to Gaochang are the 500 mummies of **Astana,** dating from the third century to about the eighth A.D., plus their belongings. The 44-meter **Imin Minaret,** 200 years old, stands two km. east of Turpan.

URUMQI (Urumchi) is the capital of China's largest autonomous region, Xinjiang, in the extreme western part of the country. It is four hours by air from Beijing and is the home of thirteen nationalities. Of these, the largest group are the Uighur, of Turkish origin. The population of Urumqi is 830,000. The city dates from the Han. Summer days are hot, the nights chilly. The winter lasts about five months, the coldest temperature being minus 41.5°C. The food is mainly mutton. At an altitude of 900 meters, it is surrounded by mountains.

The tourist attractions are mainly scenic. **Tianzi** (Lake of Heaven) is about 1,950 meters above sea level. It is 5 square kilometers and 100 meters deep, and is reachable by horseback if you wish. There is also an ancient **glacier** about 100 meters thick, 5,000 meters long, and 2,000 meters wide with ice caves and lakes below. About 50 kilometers south of Urumqi is the **Nanshan Pasture**—mountains, valleys, fountains, waterfalls, and cypress and pine trees. Horseback riding, mountaineering, and digging for valuable ginseng roots are listed among the attractions. The city also has the nine-story **Red Hill Pagoda** from the Tang.

Urumqi produces good carpets, embroidered skullcaps (¥5–¥7), jade carvings, and musical instruments. The Xinjiang Museum has a Mummies Hall with a 3,000 year old female.

WUHAN, capital of Hubei province, is really three cities: Hankou (Hankow), Hanyang, and Wuchang, separated by the Yangtze and Han Rivers. It is now visited mainly by tourists at the end of the boat ride through the Yangtze Gorges. It is on the main Beijing-Guangzhou railway line.

The city itself dates from the eleventh century B.C. It was made a walled city in A.D. 221 by Sun Chuan, King of Wu. There were ports here two thousand years ago. Several foreign nations had concessions after the Opium War and some of the architecture still reflects this. In 1923 the Communists led a successful general strike; in 1927 Mao Tse-tung set up a Peasant Movement Institute in Wuchang. Wuhan was the headquarters of the left wing of the Nationalist party. Historically, Wuchang is famous because on October 10, 1911, the first victory of the Sun Yat-sen revolution took place here, although Sun himself was absent. The site can be seen on Shouyi Road, marked by a bronze statue of Dr. Sun.

The city was liberated in May 1949. During the Cultural Revolution it experienced some of the heaviest fighting between factions. Chou En-lai narrowly escaped being captured by one group. Wuhan is today one of China's most important industrial centers, the home of the Wuhan Iron and Steel Works. Other industries include metallurgy, machine building, electric power, electronics, chemistry, textiles, and food.

Among the tourist attractions is **East Lake** in the eastern suburbs, where boats can be hired. Here is the **Muse-Humming Pavilion** commemorating Qu Yuan, the famous Warring States (475–221 B.C.) poet and patriot, and the **Nine Heroines' Mound,** the 1855 burial site of nine women who fought the Manchus during the Taiping Heavenly Kingdom rebellion; the women were captured and executed. There are also **Moon Lake, Chibi,** which is the site of a famous Three Kingdoms battle, the **Bridge over the Yangtze** (smaller than Nanjing's), a factory for traditional paintings, and some temples. The famous **Yellow Crane Pavilion,** rebuilt many times since its origin in 223 A.D., is being rebuilt again. Also, the 17th-century **Guiyan Temple** in Hanyang. A new airport big enough for 747s was started in 1979. The urban population is 3,830,000.

Hottest weather: July–August—39°C; coldest: January–February—minus 5°C.

Outside the city are the **Wuzu Temple** in Huangmei County, originally built in the 7th Century, and **Jingzhou City** whose 1187 city wall was rebuilt in 1646, 9-m.-high and 9 km. in circumference with 6 gates. The museum at the West Gate has a male 2,100-year-old cadaver, and a famous sword, the Goujian, used in the Spring and Autumn Period.

Jinan City is 5 km. north of Jingzhou, the capital of the Kingdom of Chu in 689 B.C. **Yuquan Temple** at the eastern base of Yuquan Mountain near Dangyang County city was built in the Eastern Han. It has an iron pagoda dating from 1061 and a temple from the Southern Song. The **Wudang Mountain** is the most important to see. A center of Taoism mostly built in the Ming, it includes eight palaces, two temples, 36 nunneries, and 72 grotto temples, all along a 30-km. or so mountain path. The highest point Tianzhu Peak reaches is over 1,600 m.

WUXI (Wusih), on the northern shore of Lake Taihu in southern Jiangsu province, is an industrial and resort city straddling the ancient Grand Canal (Sui). It is less than an hour by train from Suzhou, just west of Shanghai. As a beauty spot it has classical Chinese gardens—**Liyuan and Meiyuan (Plum Garden)** and the **Yuantouzhu (Turtle Head) Islet.** Historical sites include **Xihui Park** west of the city, with its Heavenly Second Spring (Tang), and **Jichang Garden** (for Relaxing the Mind) and the **Longguang Pagoda,** both from the Ming. The city itself was founded during the Zhou. It is a silk-producing center, the hills around it filled with mulberry trees. There is also the famous **Hui Shan Clay Figures Factory.** Boat trips with lunch on Lake Taihu, and trips on the Grand Canal.

Hotels: Taihu, former university, 300 beds. **Hubin,** by lake, 300 beds. Older part known as **Lihu Hotel** (best for Foreign Friends). **Shuixiu Hotel,** 220 rooms.

XIAGUAN. At an altitude of 2,000 m., it is the capital of Dali County, Yunnan province. Located at the southern tip of 41-km.-long Lake Erhai, a 12-hr., 400-km. drive (with rest and lunch stops), west and slightly north of Kunming. Part of it lies on the famed Burma Road. Xiaguan merits a visit because of its colorful national minorities, old cities, historical monuments, and views of year-round snowcapped mountains. Reached by only a trickle of foreign visitors on special interest tours, it is for those who prefer to get well off the beaten track.

The two guest houses in Xiaguan have no private toilets, no showers, or baths. You wash from basins. The guest houses are the best in the area; use them as bases for day trips. The bathing is great at the hot springs four km. away.

Before you go, read C.P. Fitzgerald's *Tower of Five Glories* about his experiences there in the 1930s. One recent visitor didn't think much had changed since then.

The natives of different national minorities are mainly Bai, Yi, and Naxi. The women wear brightly colored embroidered and handwoven clothes. The architecture resembles a mix of Hong Kong's posh Kowloon Tong, old walled towns, houses with fine Moslem-style carvings, gateways, and gables different from other parts of China.

The history goes back over 2,000 years. In the 8th century, this area made part of the vast Nanzhou empire which refused to submit to the Tang, although it was later subdued by the Mongols.

Among the day trips: Dali, 10 km. north, an old walled town with marble factories and some of the best marble in China. See a large obelisk erected by conquerer Kublai Khan in the 13th century; **Xizhou,** for its "remarkable architecture;" **Shizhong Shan** a.k.a. Shibao Shan (7-hour trip), has a unique Buddhist Grotto reached by a steep 45-minute climb. It has 3½-ft. stone female genitalia which women rub for fertility and boys for courage. Also some of the earliest Buddhist carvings in China—several styles, including some humans pictured with long curly hair. At the base of this mountain lies an exotic old monastery.

San Ta Si (Three Pagoda Temple) on the west shore of Lake Erhai outside the northwest gate of Dali was built in the Nanzhao/Tang period and recently renovated. The view of the lake, the three towers, and the mountains behind are famous.

Butterfly Pool on the northern tip of the lake is a natural spring with one huge tree covering it. In May strings of different kinds of butterflies appear. **Xiaguan** itself has a tea brick factory worth visiting and a temple to the Tang general who failed to conquer.

This is frontier country, especially with the caravans of horses and mules arriving for the **Third Moon Market,** the 15th to 24th day of their third lunar month. It is the most important market for traditional medicines. About 60,000 people take part from Burma, Laos, and all provinces except Taiwan. It is also a livestock market enlivened by races and perhaps gambling. This famous market is on the former KMT execution grounds.

XIAMEN (Hsiamen, Amoy) is on the coast of Fujian a few hundred yards from Quemoy, the Nationalist-held island. Xiamen was the base of Cheng Cheng-kung, known as Koxinga, who captured Taiwan in 1661. It was opened to foreign trade in 1842 and by midcentury, American and British merchants had dockyards here. In late 1979, it was made a Special Economic Zone.

XI'AN (Sian; Western Peace)

Location: Central China, 1¾-hour flight southwest (1,165 kilometers) of Beijing. Eight-hour train ride west of Luoyang. Eight-hour drive south of Yan'an. Capital of Shaanxi province on the 340-kilometer-long Guanzhong Plain, it borders on the Loess Plateau to the north and the Qinling Mountains to the south.

Weather: Hottest: 40°C—July; coldest: minus 10°C—two weeks in January. Rain all the year round, but especially August–early September. Altitude: 400 meters above sea level.

Population: 2.8 million, of whom 1.4 million are urban.

Area: 2,283 square kilometers (both urban and rural).

Background: Next to Beijing, Xi'an is the most important place to visit in China if you are interested in ancient Chinese history, traditional culture, and archaeology. A full week is needed just to *see* each of the essential places. It is an important neolithic site and was capital intermittently for 1,087 years (eleven dynasties including the Zhou, Qin, Han, Sui and Tang) from the eleventh century B.C. to the early tenth A.D. From the second century B.C. (Han) to the fourteenth century A.D. it was the eastern end of the Silk Road. Foreign traders visited here when it was first called Changan (Everlasting Peace) and especially in the Tang at the height of its prosperity, when thousands of foreigners lived in the Western Market, the city then having a total population of one million. (See also Silk Road in MILESTONES IN CHINESE HISTORY.)

The Xi'an Incident, on December 12, 1936, was the kidnapping of Generalissimo Chiang Kai-shek at the Huaqing Hot Spring resort by one of his own generals in order to force him to cooperate with the Communists against the Japanese. (See 1936 in MILESTONES IN CHINESE HISTORY.) After the settlement, the Communists set up a liaison office here, the Eighth Route Army Xi'an Office, which is now the Museum of the Eighth Route Army. On May 20, 1949, the Communists took over the city.

Today, Xi'an is an important textile center (wool and cotton) and has over a thousand factories making also super-high-voltage transmission electrical equipment, watches, aluminum and enamelware, and Chinese and Western medicines. Visitors might be interested in the arts and crafts factories that make shell products, inlaid lacquer, cloisonné, stone and jade carvings, gold and silver jewelry, and reproductions of ancient relics.

Xi'an's 282,990 acres of cultivated land grow cotton, maize, wheat, vegetables, pomegranates, and persimmons. Its peasant painters of nearby Huxian (county) have exhibited internationally. The Daming Palace Commune still has remains of the old Tang palace.

Many of the area's houses and walls are made of the loess soil mixed with straw that won't wash away in the rain. If cared for properly, i.e., protected with bricks on top, the mud walls could last a hundred years. Cheap too!

The city today still has its 600-year-old Ming wall, one of the best in China. Many of the historic buildings have been restored and are opened to foreign visitors. The map shows the sites of the different ancient cities.

Of Interest to Visitors

The Qin Army Vault Museum, 40 kilometers northeast of the city, is the most spectacular and important place to visit here because it is the site of a 2,180-year-old painted ceramic army of more than eight thousand life-size soldiers buried to "protect" the tomb of the first Qin emperor. If you want to take a photo here, there's a ¥100 fee or risk having your film confiscated.

The relics were discovered in March 1974 by local peasants digging a well. They are a great puzzle because the Qin left no record of their existence. Excavation started in 1976 and is still going on, but there is enough to see now, including an exhibition hall and some figures or pieces of figures emerging from the earth.

There are three vaults. No. 1 is 62 × 230 × 5 meters deep—14,260 square meters. Most of the army was found facing east toward the tomb, 1½ kilometers away. The soldiers were in lines of 70 across and 150 deep, separated by ten partition walls and eleven corridors. One line at each edge also faced south, west, and north. The figures are hollow from the thigh up and made in two parts; they are 1.78–1.87 meters tall. Soldiers in front had crossbows; also in front were two bells and drums. Officers can be distinguished from soldiers by their clothing and armor. Charioteers had their hands out in front as if holding on to reins. The horses originally wore harnesses with brass ornaments and are identified as a breed from Hechu in Gansu. Researchers believe that the kiln was built around the molded figures

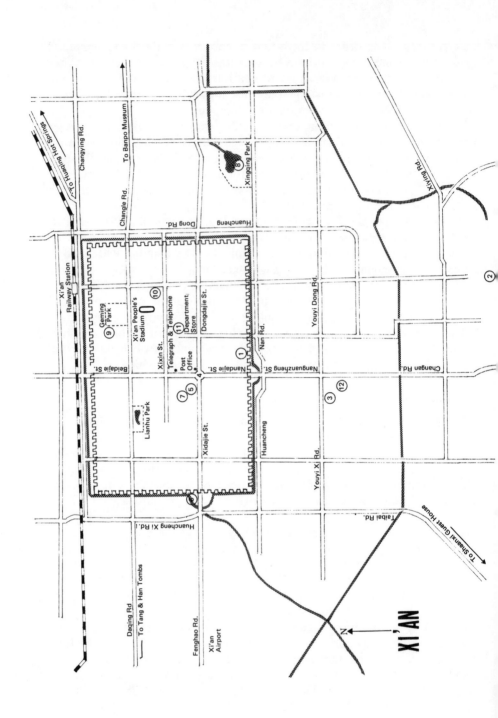

(probably two horses at a time) and destroyed after firing. There are remains of thirty chariots, which were made of wood and did not survive as well.

The Chinese consider this their most important archaeological site and in 1979 had thirty scholars (for study and investigation) and over seventy technicians (photographers, repairmen, and artists) employed here. The site is covered by a quonset hut-type structure. It was officially opened October 1, 1979, but visitors were allowed before then. The Chinese plan to open another museum over vaults nos. 2 and 3 and enter the main tomb in 1985. Tourists will be able to walk through the corridors. In 1980, two bronze chariots were uncovered 17 meters west of the tomb of Shih Huang-ti, the earliest bronze chariots found in China.

Tomb of Emperor Chin Shih Huang-ti, first emperor of the Qin dynasty, first builder of the Great Wall, and first unifier of the Chinese nation (259-210 B.C.), Lintong county. Now all that can be seen is a tumulus 6 kilometers in circumference and 40 meters high covered with pomegranate trees. Over 700,000 people built it between 247 and 211 B.C., and it is said to contain a deep and magnificent underground palace. When excavated in 1985, it may give reason for another trip back to Xi'an.

The Huaqing Hot Springs have been so overshadowed by modern history that their ancient history is frequently forgotten. At the base of Lishan Hill, 30 kilometers northeast of Xi'an, it can be combined with the Qin Army Vault and the Tomb of Chin Shih Huang-ti in a half-day excursion. The site has been used for the last three thousand years as an imperial resort, most notably by the famous Tang couple, Emperor Hsuan-tsung and his beloved Yang Kuei-fei. They used to live here in the winter because it was warmer than Xi'an, and bathe in the Nine Dragon Hot Spring and the Kuei-fei Hot Spring. But now, so can you! Foreigners pay ¥1.20 and Chinese pay ¥.30 for a 40-minute soak in 43°C mineral water (sodium, sulphur, and magnesium), said to be good for rheumatism and skin disorders. The original buildings were all destroyed and most of the current ones were built since Liberation. You can also trace the flight of Chiang Kai-shek as he ran with one shoe leaving his false teeth behind at 5 a.m., up the hill where he was captured. A pavilion today marks the spot.

The Big Wild Goose Pagoda of the Da Chi Eng temple, along with the Little Wild Goose Pagoda, are the most famous pagodas in China because of their age and their important historical connections. They are not, however, the most beautiful or spectacular. The Big Wild Goose Pagoda was built to house the sutras and images brought back from India in A.D. 652 (Tang) by the famous monk Hsuan-tsang (see Jiu Hua Hill under "Nanjing"). It was

---

1. Shaanxi Provincial Museum	7. Great Mosque
2. Big Wild Goose Pagoda	8. Xingqing Park
3. Little Wild Goose Pagoda	9. Museum of the Eighth Route Army
4. Bell Tower	10. Renmin Hotel
5. Drum Tower	11. Friendship Store
6. West City Gate	12. New Hotel

named in memory of the temple in India where he lived on a hill shaped like a goose. Another story says that once some monks were starving and the Buddha in the form of a wild goose dropped down close to them. The monks, being vegetarians, refused to eat it.

The pagoda has seven stories, 248 steps, and a great view from the top. In the temple are painted statues of eighteen *arhats* (Ming) made of clay on a wooden frame, most with strong Indian rather than Chinese features. One gets the impression that the sculptor must have been playing a joke, the faces are so funny. The Japanese lantern was presented in 1974 in honor of the first Chinese monk who went to Japan in the eighth century.

The Shaanxi Provincial Historical Museum is an old (Qing and Ming) Confucian temple where officials used to get off their sedan chairs and kowtow in respect as they passed by. The collection has some very excellent pieces, labeled in English and Chinese: (1) an eighth-century B.C. stone drum, believed to be the earliest stone tablet in China, with writing (about a hunting expedition); (2) a bronze gate hinge from the Qin; (3) the standardizations of weights, measures, and currency by the first Qin emperor; (4) a wooden model of a bronze seismograph (eight dragons) from the first or second century B.C.; (5) giant stone carvings, the largest from the eastern Han, including a life-size rhinoceros and ostrich (the original live animals had been tribute gifts). The horses on the wall are copies, the originals said to be in Philadelphia; (6) the most important collection of steles in China with over a thousand from the Han through the Qing, including twelve Tang engravings of the Confucian classics. These have been used by scholars to copy and study for content as well as calligraphy. You can probably watch rubbings being made; (7) gold and silver inlaid dishes and ancient Byzantine and Persian coins found in the Western Market where the foreigners lived (Tang).

Bell Tower was first built in 1384 (Ming) in another location and moved here two hundred years later. It was renovated in 1739 and again in 1953–54, and apparently once more in the late 1970s. There are three sets of eaves "to weaken the force of the rainfall" but actually two stories. It is 36 meters tall and made of brick and wood, with no nails. Glass windows were installed in 1950—previous windows were paper. The furniture is gorgeous (Qing), and there is a very fancy traditional Ming ceiling. The bell was where the giant lantern is now. From the second story you can see all four gates of Xi'an.

The Great Mosque, the largest in Xi'an, was built as a mosque in 742 (Tang) with additions in subsequent dynasties. It is unlike other mosques in the world, except probably in China, a good example of the Sinification of foreign architecture. The minaret is a pagoda with Chinese eaves. The interiors are Chinese right down to the bats, dragons, unicorns, marble-top tables, and mother-of-pearl inlaid furniture (note the bed). The Great Hall (Ming) is Moslem, however, the writing Arabic, the arches and flowers West Asian. Shoes are removed. Prayers five times a day. Moslems first came here from Xinjiang (Sinkiang) and Guangzhou (Canton) and started the mosque

Locations in different historical periods
1. W. Han—Fengjing
2. W. Han—Haojing
3. Chin—Xianyang
4. Han—Changan
5. Ming and Ching—Xi'an
6. Sui—Daxing
7. Tang—Changan
8. Xi'an today

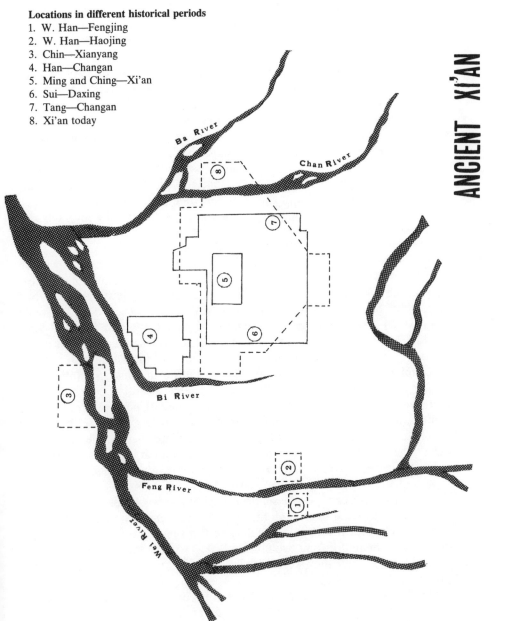

ANCIENT XI'AN

with support from the Tang emperors. There is a small store at the mosque.

Banpo (Panpo) Museum in the eastern suburbs of Xi'an (10 kilometers from the People's Hotel) is the actual archaeological site of a 6,000-year-old Neolithic village. English as well as Chinese titling. The site covers 50,000 square meters, of which the museum encloses 3,000—living quarters, pottery kiln, and graveyard.

The remains were discovered in 1953 and excavations made 1954–57. The building was completed in 1958. Shown are living quarters (including a reproduction of a hut) and one of the earliest kilns in China. To find the kiln you have to go outside again after you enter the main chamber. A communal storage area, moat, graveyard (skeletons with cooking pots and water vessels under glass), post holes, and fireplaces are also here.

In the museum are a bow drill, a clay basin painted with a fish, a barbed fish hook, clay pots (coil method), a pottery whistle believed to be the earliest musical instrument in China, ornaments, hairpins, stone axes, and a pot with holes in the bottom believed used as a steamer. The museum also has a narrow-necked, narrow-based water jug with two handles similar to the amphora used by the ancient Greeks and Romans!

Guides will tell you this was a matriarchal culture but they probably mean matrilineal. The matriarchal label is used because (1) of the burial customs. Most of the 174 Banpo graves had one skeleton each; the few graves that had more than one had those of the same sex. There were no male-female couples. (2) The women gathered wild food at first, the men hunted. After the women discovered how to plant seeds, land became valuable and it was passed on from mother to daughter. (3) Because of the burial system (with no couples) and knowledge of an existing culture in Yunnan (Nahsi) with similar implements, village layout, customs, etc., scientists concluded that there were no fixed marriages. Besides, did the neolithic people know where babies came from? (4) The village consisted of one big house in the center for old and young, and smaller houses for visiting males. The men kept their belongings and were buried in their native villages. Farming tools were kept in the communal storage pit and were not buried with the dead.

As agriculture developed, men started to pursue it too. As surpluses were collected (and probably the basic principles of physiology discovered), fixed families started. In a later neolithic gravesite in Gansu, the male was found lying straight and the female kneeling in the same grave. In another, the male was in the middle and two females were kneeling toward him. Since the women were bound, they were probably buried alive with him. So much for women's lib!

Maoling, on a plateau north of the Wei River, 40 kilometers from Xi'an, has more than ten tombs, small grassy pyramids, about 46.5 meters high. The main tomb is that of the fifth Han emperor, built 139–87 B.C. According to records, it contains a jade suit with gold threads (seems to be a Han fad) and in a gold box, more than 190 different birds and animals, plus jade, gold, silver, pearls, rubies, and a jade walking stick. The other identified tombs are of his favorite concubine (Madame Li); General Ho Qubing (who fought the Huns); General Wei Qing; his horse breeder Jing Min Ji, who remained faithful after Jing's tribe was defeated by the emperor; and General Ho Guang.

Some of the earliest and therefore most primitive massive stone carvings, originally placed in front of the tombs, are here in a small museum: a giant toad (with teeth!), a reclining elephant, a leaping horse (about 2 meters long), a horse trotting over a Hun aristocrat, a fat cow—each a few lines added to the natural shape of a rock. Also in the museum are Han artifacts found by peasants: an irrigation pipe, a pottery grinding stone, pottery animal figures, metal mirrors, coins, pavement bricks notched to fit together, a bronze rhinoceros wine container, a bear-shaped ceramic brush holder, and replicas of tile faces. Genuine rubbings are on sale here for ¥20 and ¥40. Near Maoling is the **Xianyang Museum** which has the 3000 painted terracotta warrior and horse figures from the Western Han (206 B.C.–A.D. 24). They are each between 55 cm. and 68 cm. high.

Xin Jiao Temple (30 kilometers south of the People's Hotel) is an interesting temple in the country on a hillside, which, with a little mist, could look like the lonely setting for the famous Japanese movie *Rashomon.* The place oozes with atmosphere because it is old. In 1979 it was not freshly painted, except for the gilding of some of the Buddhas. The religious statuary tends to be eclectic in style: a white jade Buddha from Burma, a scroll with images of the eighteen *arhats,* a Kuan Yin with eight pairs of arms, a Ming Kuan Yin with a bird on her shoulder, a Sui Kuan Yin in stone, a bronze Sakyamuni, a porcelain Laughing Buddha (with children). It is an important functioning temple. The remains (at least some of them—see "Nanjing") of the famous monk Hsuan-tsang, who first walked to India day and night and brought back the sutras, are buried in the small, five-story pagoda here. A map shows his route. The two smaller pagodas hold the remains of his disciples. The temple also has six palm-leaf pages of a Sung copy of Hsuan-tsang's original sutras.

City Wall, built 1374–1378 (Ming). 3.4 (north-south) × 2.6 kilometers (east-west); 12 meters high, 12–14 meters thick on top, 15–18 meters thick on bottom. Four gates, the most imposing of which, the **West City Gate,** should be opened now for tourists to climb.

If you have more than three days or specialized interest:

Qian Ling: Tomb of Tang Emperor Kao-tsung and the Empress Wu (she was almost as ruthless and outrageous as Qing Empress Dowager Tsu Hsi but a more successful ruler). He died in A.D. 683 and she in 705. It is 80 kilometers outside the city and it's a full day's excursion, usually offered as an "optional tour" for additional payment. While earlier tombs were built creating their own artifical hills on the plains, the Tang tombs were built into natural hills. This one is 400 meters high, 1,049 meters above sea level.

Outside are life-size statues of horses, ostriches, guards, foreign diplomats who took part in the funeral (now without heads—look for the names on their backs. One was from Afghanistan). The wall around the tomb is 1,450 meters long (north and south), 1,582 meters on the east, and 1,438 meters on the west. Some of the minor tombs are excavated, and visitors can go underground to see the coffin and murals in the tomb of Princess Yong-tai. Although a great number of structures here were destroyed in the war at the end of the Tang, there is a museum with about four thousand pieces—three-colored Tang porcelain, burial pieces, pottery utensils, animals, gold and jade carvings, bronze mirrors, etc.

Huxian County: Here you can visit peasant homes and watch painting in progress. There are about two thousand painters here; some have exhibited abroad. Nearby is the thatched-cottage temple named **Chao Tang Temple** (Tang), where Indian monk Chi Mo Lo Shi translated the sutras and was later buried.

Horse and Chariot Pit can be combined with Huxian county for a half-day tour. It is the burial site of two chariots, six horses, and one slave (eleventh century B.C.—Western Zhou) and is the best of seven such pits found.

Little Wild Goose Pagoda, 45 meters high and made of brick, was built after the Big Wild Goose Pagoda, in A.D. 684. Thirteen stories high, this is the original building minus two of its original stories, which were destroyed in serious earthquakes in 1555.

Drum Tower, built 1384, was opened to tourists only in 1979. This is the original building. An extensive antique store on the second floor also sells reproductions. Drums were beaten about 800 times (about ten minutes) before the city gate was closed for the night.

Xingqing Park was the site of one of the palaces of Tang Emperor Hsuan-tsung, who also had a palace at the Hot Springs. The original pavilion was of sandalwood but was replaced with "ordinary" wood. There is a post-Liberation copy of the original tower where the emperor once a year stayed overnight with his four brothers to flatter them out of rebelling against him.

Zhaoling is the tomb of the second Tang emperor and is also built inside a mountain. There are more than a hundred minor tombs in the area (children, wives, generals) and a small museum with three-color Tang pottery, stone tablets, and murals.

Huangling County: Tomb of Yellow Emperor—see "Yan'an."

Hua Shan Mountain (150 kilometers east of Xi'an), highest peak 2,100 meters. C.I.T.S. is planning to build a small hotel at the foot and cable cars. In the meantime, one climbs the 90-degree cliffs helped by iron chains and the "1,000-Foot-Long Flight of Stone Steps" and squeezes through the "100-Foot-Long Gorge." Famous as one of the Five Sacred Mountains, it has some old temples.

Binxian (about 90 kilometers northwest of the city) has enormous Buddhist statues (Tang), the largest about 25 meters tall.

Tomb of Tang Concubine Yang Kuei-fei.

Shopping: The main shopping area is east of the Bell Tower on Dong Da Jie. Most stores are open 7 or 9 a.m.–8 or 9 p.m.

The **Friendship Store** sells Kodak film and says processing for Ektachrome can be done in 24 hours, but they have no mounts for slides.

Your best bargains are things that are made here: rubbings are ¥3.60–¥300 (see chapter 9, SHOPPING), a foot-high copy of the famous three-color Tang camel with five musicians is ¥100, and pottery reproductions of Qin Army soldiers are ¥11. There are also shell models of pavilions, the Bell Tower, the Big Wild Goose Pagoda, brass hot pots (a place for charcoal in the center) for cooking soup at the table, purses, jewelry, jade carving, cloisonné, carved red lacquer, carved boxwood balls within balls within balls, fur coats (wolf and fox), wool rugs, musical instruments, T-shirts, embroideries, silks, paintings, suitcases, reproductions of Shang bronzes, and a book of tile face rubbings for ¥1,000.

In 1979 there were still problems here about shipping purchases overseas, which may be solved by the time you arrive. But you can have crates made. The Friendship Store is open 11 a.m.–8 p.m.

Food: Xi'an food is similar to that of Beijing, somewhat bland. Its famous local dishes are crisp fried chicken or duck, and fried fish shaped like grapes. There are two famous wines here—one is thick and sweet and looks like milk. Served hot, Chou Jiu wine inspired Tang poet Li Po, who drank a thousand cups and wrote more than a hundred poems. Another wine made in nearby Fengxiang county is Xifeng (Hsi Feng) Jiu, a blend of sour, sweet, bitter, and spicy. It is one of the eight most famous wines in China.

Sample menu: for ten people at the Dongya Restaurant, Xi'an.

1. Assorted cold dishes in the shape of a phoenix　凤凰拼饼
2. Four small cold dishes　四围碟
3. Sea cucumber in the shape and color of hibiscus　芙蓉海参
4. Crisp fried duck　香酥鸭
5. Mushrooms with the Three Delicacies　口蘑三样
6. Fried fillet of chicken　炸鸡排
7. Sharks' fins with three kinds of slices (pork, bamboo shoots, and chicken)　三丝鱼翅
8. Fried fish shaped like grapes　鸡丝拉皮
9. Steamed carp　清蒸鲤鱼
10. White fungus with pineapple　菠萝银耳
11. and 12. Dessert—cakes and pastries　点心　冰淇淋

Hotels

Renmin (People's) Hotel in walled city. Front section built 1954; back section 1957. Over 200 rooms for tourists now being renovated and increased. Within walking distance to main square and Friendship Store.

Lintong Hot Spring Hotel, 40 kilometers away. Closer to Qin Army Vault Museum. 40 beds.

Shaanxi Guest House, an old hotel, transformed in 1979 for foreign tourists. Small hostels built by three collectives in countryside: Zhuque, Fanchuan, and Chingdu. Tourists are also staying in the Huaqing Hot Spring Guest House, an exotic experience.

The **Xi'an Guest House,** 500-bed, 14-story, air-conditioned hotel to be finished in 1982, near the Little Wild Goose Pagoda.

XINHUI (Hsinhui; Cantonese, Sunwai) is a small city (population 80,000) about 130 kilometers southwest of Guangzhou in Guangdong province in the heart of fan-palm country. Every spare inch seems to have these trees, whose leaves are woven into baskets, fans, and mats. Xinhui is also the ancestral home of many Overseas Chinese. The city is usually combined with Jiangmen in a 2- or 3-day tour. Both are about a 4-hour tour bus or a half-day bumpy public bus ride from Guangzhou. The road is interrupted by three very wide rivers crossed by ferry. The route preferred by some travelers is the overnight boat to Jiangmen and then a half-hour public bus ride to Xinhui. Visitors can see the fan-palm factory or relax on a very pretty nearby mountain on top of which is Yuhu Lake. This artificial lake has a changing room for swimming, the usual pavilions, and a restaurant. In another direction from the city, there is a magnificent old tree called Birds' Paradise where cranes came at night to roost. The Overseas Chinese Hotel is on the main street and the **Yu Hu Guest House** is at the foot of Guifeng Hill.

YAN'AN (Yenan)

Location: 2½ hours by air (stopover in Taiyuan) southwest of Beijing; 1 hour by air or 8½-hour drive north of Xi'an. No rail connection. Northern Shaanxi in the Loess Plateau.

Weather: Hottest: 35°C—July; coldest: minus 25°C—January. Rainy season: August–September. The best time to visit is late September–October. Altitude in the city is 800–1,000 meters. C.I.T.S. has extra coats but no warm trousers for guests, who usually find it colder than they expected. During the rainy season, planes may not be on time.

Population: 220,000 (of whom 50,000 are urban). **Area:** 5 sq. km.—urban only.

Background: Yan'an was a small administrative town a thousand years ago. In 1936 it had a population of three thousand. It became the most important revolutionary site in China in January 1937 after the end of the Long March. It was chosen because of its rugged mountain terrain, which made it impossible for the Nationalists to dislodge the Communists for the next ten years. It was also chosen because it was the only existing Communist base big enough to accommodate a large army and close enough to inflict damage on the Japanese. Here, until March 1947, the Communists trained leaders, developed policies, organized the peasants, and planned military strategy against the Nationalists and Japanese. In 1945 the population was 100,000. Chiang Kai-shek finally succeeded in capturing the city without a fight and holding it until April 1948, while Mao Tse-tung went on to take the whole of China.

Today Yan'an is primarily of interest to students of modern history and architecture. It has only a Tang pagoda famous primarily because of Yan'an's fame, and a tiny cave of 10,000 Buddhas. Four hours' drive away is the 2,000-year-old tomb of the legendary Yellow Emperor at Huangling, which can just as easily be reached from Xi'an.

The city, clinging to the mountainsides, stretches along both sides of the Yan River and the South and Dufu Streams. In July 1977 the river flooded the lower parts of the city. The soil is loess, excellent for construction. Most of the area houses are quonset-hut-shaped "caves" either freestanding or dug into a mountain. They are said to be cozy and dry in the winter, cool in the summer. Even the university is built in this style, and the villages are fascinating.

The city is now largely industrial—factories making steel, chemical fertilizers, cement, diesel engines, watches, radios, matches, carpets, silk, and knitwear. There are oil wells and coal mines. It is a little startling to find meter-high mounds of large black chunks of coal piled here and there. The area communes grow apples, dates, peaches, pears, grapes, apricots, millet, corn, wheat, buckwheat, beans, potatoes, and a little rice. For those interested in visiting a commune here, read Jan Myrdal's *Report from a Chinese Village,* about the Liu Lin Production Brigade here in the 1960s.

The middle school rates a visit insofar as it was started after the Long March, whose leaders visited often to oversee the curriculum. Classes were first held in caves. As the Nationalists advanced on the city, some of the students left to follow the Red Army, serving in its hospitals; others went with the Central Committee. Now it is like any other school. See also MILESTONES IN CHINESE HISTORY.

Of Interest to Visitors: Yan'an Revolutionary Memorial Hall (a.k.a. Museum of Chairman Mao's Leadership of the Chinese Revolution from Yan'an): This excellent museum has a giant map outlining the route of the Long March in neon. Titles are in English and Chinese. Exhibits also include a fascinating model of tunnel warfare, Communist banknotes, and Chairman Mao's horse (stuffed).

Residences of Chairman Mao are also museums, furnished as simply as they were then, all of them "caves":

241

(1) Foot of Fenghuang (Phoenix) Hill. January 1937–November 1938. Here Mao wrote his important articles on "contradiction" and "protracted war." The photo in front of the cave was taken in 1937 here, just after Chou En-lai returned from settling the Xi'an Incident. Mao left this cave because of the Japanese bombing. Chu Teh, commander of the Red Army, and Chou En-lai, Mao's chief negotiator, lived close by.

(2) Yangjialing. November 1938–January 1943. Chu Teh had a tunnel here to Mao's cave. The auditorium was the site of several party Central Committee meetings and the Seventh National Congress of the Party in 1945, delegates risking their lives to come from and return to the Nationalist-held areas. This is where Mao made his "Foolish Old Man Who Removed the Mountains" speech. Here also was the site of the Yenan Forum on Arts and Literature to encourage musicians, writers, and painters to "make art and literature serve the workers and peasants better." Mao directed the Great Rectification Movement, which imbued his men with a working knowledge of Marxist-Leninism, from his cave home up the hill. He left because it was too noisy; he needed quiet to prepare for the Congress.

(3) Zaoyuan (Date Orchard). January 1943–end of 1945. The Secretariat was close by. The lilac tree in front was planted by Mao. Mao wrote twenty-eight articles and several other works. On his desk is the first iron bar made in the local foundry with which he exercised his hand to avoid writer's cramp. Here is where Chu Teh, then over sixty, played basketball. From here Chou En-lai flew to Chongqing (Chungking) to negotiate with Chiang, an American-instigated effort to avoid civil war.

(4) No. 4 Wangjiaping. January 1946–March 1947. Headquarters of the Eighth Route Army. Dances were held in the garden. The civil war resumed and here Mao argued with his military commanders about withdrawing from Yan'an in the face of an enormous Nationalist campaign in March 1947. While his commanders wanted to defend the city, Mao argued, "We must not concentrate on hanging on to places. Our main purpose is to wipe out the enemy's effective forces . . . there are only a few caves here. If they destroy the caves, it is good. We can build high buildings when we come back." The city was regained on April 22, 1948, but Mao did not return then. The guides here insist that the Nationalists at this assault were backed by U.S. imperialism, but Truman had stopped all aid to the Nationalists in 1946 after his failure to reconcile the two.

Baota (Precious Pagoda), a.k.a. Yan'an Pagoda: 44 meters, 9 stories; 1,300 years old (Tang)—original building. Stairs from the first to second story, a ladder the rest of the way. Usually locked but you can hike up the hill or around the park for a good view of the city. The bell is Ming.

Wanfo Dong (Cave of the 10,000 Buddhas) is right in town below the pagoda and relatively close to Wangjiaping, dates from the Song and Jin. Most of the Buddhas are tiny, some in good condition. The cave was used to house the printing presses of the Central Committee. Up the hill is a Laughing Buddha carved on the hillside, now the back wall of a house. It can be seen through the front window. During the Cultural Revolution, it was hidden by a cloth, which saved it from the Red Guards.

If you have more time

Nanniwan, 45 kilometers south, was turned from a wasteland into a productive area in 1941–43 by the 359 Brigade of the revolutionary army. It is now a commune with a small museum.

Huangling County: Just about halfway on the road between Xi'an and Yan'an, 4 hours' drive from each, Huangling makes an interesting break and for Chinese history buffs a very important stop. There is a hotel, built 1978.

Tomb of the Yellow Emperor Xuan Yuan: 3.6 meters high and 50 meters in circumference. Originally built in the Han but moved to its present site in the Song. The Yellow Emperor is the legendary ancestor of the Chinese people believed to have lived about 2000 B.C. The tomb is at the top of Qiaoshan (hill), 1 kilometer north of Huangling town. At the base is Xuan Yuan temple. There are 63,000 cypress trees, one of which, said to have been planted by the Yellow Emperor himself, is the largest known ancient cypress in China. In 1979 there were no plans yet to open the tomb. In front of the tomb is the Platform of Immortality built by Emperor Han Wu (156–87 B.C.) to announce his victory over his enemy and to pray for longevity. The temple of Xuan Yuan was built in the Han, the many steles recording the sacrifices offered, memorials about the repair work done by subsequent dynasties, and orders for the tomb's protection. The throne stands in the middle with information about his life on both sides. In ancient times, travelers had to dismount from their horses and pay respect to their First Ancestor as they passed by.

The Cave Temple of a Thousand Buddhas (Tang) is halfway up Ziwu Hill in the western part of Huangling county.

Liu Lin Production Brigade: Here is a yardstick with which to compare any commune you will see. In 1979 this production brigade had a population of 1,003 people (203 households), six production teams based on four villages, 9,000 mou of land of which 3,600 was cultivated, plus 2,000 mou of forest (of which 400 mou is orchard). There were 182 draft animals, 1,000 sheep and goats, 500 pigs, and two bulldozers, two trucks, two large tractors, and six hand tractors—total, over 60 machines, also including those for grass cutting and grain processing and water pumps, etc. There were three televisions.

In 1979 it produced 104,000,000 jin of wheat of which 20 to 30 percent went to the State. Average yearly income per worker was ¥160, ranging from ¥80 to ¥300. The commune has 250,000 jin of grain in storage belonging to the whole brigade.

The cooperative medical station charged ¥1.50 a year for free medical treatment. Eight new babies were allowed per year; who the mothers would be was decided by the Women's Association. Since there are as yet no rural pensions, most peasants want children, preferring sons. Most of the people live in new houses. Fifty percent of the households have radios and bicycles.

By 1985 the average income per worker is expected to reach ¥200 a year. The houses are 20.46-square-meter "caves." A peasant can pay ¥1.00 a month rent or build his own house on commune land according to an overall plan. He can borrow money for the materials and build with help from other team members. Material for a stone "cave" cost ¥500 to ¥600.

Three to five percent of the total cultivated land is set aside for private plots where team members can grow their own vegetables to eat or sell. Each person gets .15 mou, of which .05 mou is valley land and .10 mou is hillside. A family of five would thus get .75 mou (about one-tenth of an acre). This commune has a lower annual cash income than many others, probably because of the hilly terrain and also because money is being put into mechanization. It aims to mechanize even more to free manpower to diversify its income (animals, orchards, etc.).

Food: If the 1979 cook is still at the Yan'an Guest House (see below), this is one of the best places to eat in China.

Interesting local foods:	
fried spring roll	炸春卷
buckwheat noodles	乔呂饸铬
fried millet cake with sugar	油炸软米羔
millet drink (nonalcoholic)	米酒
mutton and egg, fried crisply	锅烧羊肉
fragrant, crisp chicken	香酥鸭
thin pancakes with meat and vegetables	煎并
fried potatoes with syrup	拔丝土豆
potato balls	油炸土豆丸子
eight-jewel pumpkin	八宝蜜汁南瓜

Hotel

Yan'an Guest House, tel. 2767, 2252. Built 1965. 110 beds, 3 stories. 10 kilometers from new airport (1979). Short walk to shopping, downtown, cinema, pagoda. Next door to No. 1 Mao Residence. 250-bed extension was completed 1980. The hotel has 40 minutes of documentary films of historical interest showing Mao giving his lecture "on practice" and "on contradiction," the Lu Hsun Academy of Arts (at the old church on the way to the airport), and Nanniwan. These can be shown on request.

YANGTZE GORGES. The boat trip through 204 kilometers of gorges and on the mighty river itself to or from Chongqing is highly recommended not just for its spectacular scenery but for its history. Do bring binoculars, a telephoto lens if you're a camera bug, and reading material. The scenery includes sheer cliffs rising up to 400 meters on either side of narrow rushing water, mountains up to 1,000 meters, old towns above lines of stone steps, and a mountain lined from top to bottom with pagodas. The Yangtze River is also a busy highway now being harnessed even more for flood control, irrigation, and hydroelectric power.

The history is still alive in much of what you experience here: the chant of men pulling heavy loads "wei wei li hou," the towpaths cut out of the sides of sheer cliffs, the towing of boats upstream by manual labor, the lives lived on the water, the twelve-man-powered sampan-junks, and the architecture. Guides will tell you stories of the Three Kingdoms, but do bring your own history books along, or a copy of *The Sand Pebbles* or *Yangtze Patrol: The U.S. Navy in China.* If you don't have a guide, maybe the steward or cook can point out landmarks. The Yangtze was also central to the foreign merchants, gunboats, and missionaries in the late 1800s and early 1900s.

The trip is usually two nights on board ship and three days on the water from Chongqing to Wuhan. The ships are either regular ferries or tourist boats, so you get a good look at life on the river. They make stops at towns along the way for a few minutes up to several hours. Take your own soap and towel. Each ferry has about 24 second-class cabins (the best) with two to a room, shared toilets and showers. The third class has four to a room, no curtains. None have much privacy. Some even lower class passengers sleep on the floor in the hallways. This is all part of the Chinese experience, if that's what you want. Second class from Chongqing to Wuhan is ¥56.10; third is ¥45.20, food included. It is better to get on only between the gorges and Chongqing since the stretch between Yichang and Wuhan, a whole day's ride, isn't all that interesting. One can get off (on the downstream trip) at Chenglingji and spend a day at Yueyang and then by train to Changsha, or go on to Wuhan.

For those who prefer comfort to color, there are three air-conditioned tourist boats (not all have private baths though), each chartered exclusively by Lindblad Travel, Club Universe, or an Australian agency headed by Wim Bannink. These are much more expensive, but they are meant for tourists, not travelers. First-class cabins. Some do make stops at interesting places like Lushan, Jingzhou, and Shibaozhai long enough for you to enjoy these. You don't have to line up for a toilet nor be awakened at 6 a.m. by a noisy loudspeaker. The choice is yours.

On the ferry, the stops depend on which one you take. They are not all the same.

Ferry Downstream—Day 1. Leave Chongqing early (about 7 a.m.) in the morning. Note white pagoda on north bank at Changshou. At about 3 hours out, Fuling. At 8½ hours out, Zhongxian. At 10 hours out, pass Shibaozhou; look for the 13-story pagoda.

At 12½ hours, overnight stop at Wanxian (Wanhsien), the site of one of the first successful assertions of Chinese power against the imperialist gunboats during the Northern Expedition. There was a lot of shooting here in the late 1920s. Tourists climb about 85 steps to town for a tour of a silk factory and the 700,000-inhabitant town. There is a Friendship Store, but baskets are cheaper from children outside—especially on the way back to the ship.

Day 2. The ship leaves early (about 2:30 a.m.) to reach the first gorge 4½ hours later at daylight. Near the entrance on the north bank is a two-story pavilion with red lacquer columns, the Pai Ti Ch'eng, which marks the beginning of the gorges. On the south side of Kui Men Gate are two stone towers and five Chinese characters, "Kui Men Tian Xia Xiong," which mean "The Kui Men Gate is an unmatched pass." You may leave a little earlier or later, depending on the current.

The **Qutang (Chutang) Gorge** is 8 kilometers long and takes about an hour to pass through. It is the "most imposing" of the gorges, only 100 to 150 meters wide. Prepare for a very windy passage as the wind as well as the water is funneled between the cliffs.

The **Wuxia** (Wuhsia), or just Wu Gorge, starts 30 minutes after you leave the Qutang. It is 44 kilometers long and takes about 1½ hours. Look for the Twelve Peaks Enshrouded in Rain and Mist, of which you can see six on the north bank and three on the south. Of these, the Peak of the Goddess is the highest at over 1,000 meters. It has a tall stone column on top that looks like "a strongly built young woman gazing from high up in the sky at the waterway down below." Look for a tablet-shaped rock with six Chinese characters meaning "The Wu Gorge boasts craggy cliffs," said to be written by a prime minister of the Shu Kingdom in the third century. Ask also about Xiang Xi (Fragrant Stream), where a lady-in-waiting of a Han emperor dropped her pearls accidentally. The water here is said to be "limpid and fragrant" as a result.

About 20 minutes after leaving the Wuxia Gorge, there is the town of Badong, where in season pomelos, oranges, and persimmons are for sale on shore. Look for a temple high on a hill.

About 1 hour from Badong is the 75-kilometer long **Xiling** (Hsiling) **Gorge,** which takes about 1½ hours to pass through. It is the longest and most treacherous of the three. Oranges grow on some of the hillsides. Thirty minutes beyond the entrance, on the south side, is Kuang Ming village, with a large temple, Huang Ling Miao. Then come Five Sisters Peaks, Three Brothers Rocks, and the Needle. Toward the end of this gorge are unsightly sandstone quarries, and then the locks at Gezhouba. After that is Ichang, an industrial city in the plains. This is the end of the spectacular scenery. From here read or get to know some of the 500 other passengers. If you stay on board, you arrive late afternoon the next day in Wuhan.

YANGZHOU (Yangchow), north of the Yangtze on the Grand Canal in Jiangsu province, is 2,400 years old and famous for its gardens and pavilions. Because of its location, it was an important port after the Sui dynasty that built the canal, and at one time was the residence of many Persian merchants. One of Prophet Mohammed's descendants is buried here, and Marco Polo is said to have spent three years as governor-general. It is now reached by ferry and bus from Zhenjiang on the south shore, two hour's bus ride from Nanjing or by boat along the Yangtze. Its hottest temperature is 38.6°C in July–August; its coldest minus 15.7°C in January–February.

The most important tourist attraction is **Shouxihu (Lean West Lake)** and the surrounding area. Originally a stream, the lake has been dredged and the park landscaped since the eighth century. The lake is now 4.3 kilometers long and is surrounded by the Rainbow Bridge, White Pagoda, Jade Pavilion Bridge, Moon Taoist Temple, and Happiness Terrace. The Miniature Gold Hill, first built in the Qing with soil from the lake, is the most important.

Other attractions include the **Fajing Temple, Pingshan Hall, Guanyin Hall, Ge Garden (Qing), He Ja Garden (Song), Siwang Pavilion (Song), Wenchang Pagoda (Tang), Stone Pagoda (Tang).** The **Memorial Hall for Monk Jianzhen** (687–783) was built in 1973 to mark the Tang monk's contribution to Sino-Japanese friendship and cultural exchange. The main hall resembles the one Jianzhen had built in Nara, Japan, and is located in the Da Ming Zi Temple (Tang) in the western suburbs.

Tourists can take a boat trip on the Grand Canal and also visit nearby **Changzhou,** also over 2,500 years old. Attractions there are the Tianning Temple (Tang, restored 1981), Wenfeng Pagoda, and the Hung Mei (Red Plum Tower).

Yangzhou's handicrafts include lacquerware, jade, and velvet flowers.

YIXING (Yihsing, Ihsing, Yising) is due west of Shanghai and Suzhou, on the west side of Taihu Lake in southeast Jiangsu province. Best known for its famous purple stoneware pottery, it also has limestone caves, the most famous of which are Shanjuan, about 25 kilometers away, and Zhanggong, 22 kilometers southwest, all full of legends and grotesque formations.

Shanjuan is named after a poet who lived there after refusing to take over government responsibilities. There are historical records of this cave starting two thousand years ago (Spring and Autumn). It totals 5,000 square meters and consists of a foggy (23°C) upper cave, a spacious middle cavern with a 50-by-20 meter chamber and a "lion" and an "elephant," and a lower, narrow cavern where you can hire a rowboat on a 120-meter-long underground river. At one entrance is the grave of Liang Hsienpo and Chu Yingtai, the principals of a Chinese star-crossed lovers story, only here the man died first, and the girl was allowed to visit his tomb before her forced marriage to another man. Amid thunder and lightning, the tomb opened and the girl jumped in, and two became a pair of butterflies. The **Zhanggong Cave** has 72 caverns linked together. Total area is about 3,000 square meters. The **Lingguo Cave,** about the same size as the Shanjuan, is nearby.

A 100-room hotel for foreign tourists was built in 1980.

YUEYANG (Yoyang, Yochow), on the north shore of Lake Dongting (Tungting) in northern Hunan, just south of the Yangtze, is sometimes a side-trip from Changsha, but it's worth a day's visit.

Yueyang Tower was first built in 716 in the Tang where many soldiers were buried during the Warring States. It was destroyed and rebuilt many times, the latest time in 1867, when it became the west gate of the city. It is made of wood, is 19 meters high, and covers 240 square meters. One of the eight Taoist genii—Lu Tung-pin with the supernatural sword—was a Tang scholar who became a priest after failing the imperial examinations. He is said to have magically saved the original tower from collapsing. He is also said to be responsible for the creation of the long silver-white fish in Lake Dongting. On the right of the tower is the Drunk Three Times Pavilion, named after the occasions Lu Tung-pin became drunk there; on the left is the Fairy Plum Pavilion, named because a stone slab with imprints was found under the foundation during renovations in the Ming. The main tower is now a museum. Around the tower are forty stone tablets inscribed with ancient poems praising the building. In 1962 a pavilion was built nearby to commemorate the 1250th birthday of the famous Tang poet Tu Fu. Look for a finger-painting demonstration. A hotel for tourists was built in 1981.

Junshan Island, 15 kilometers west across the lake, has 72 hills on 247 acres of land. The highest hill has a celebrated view of the 740,000-acre lake which is one of the settings of *The Sand Pebbles*. The island grows the famous Chunshan Silver Needles Tea, many species of bamboo, and a tree with red leaves on one side and green on the other. It is a bird-watcher's paradise. The island abounds in myths, so expect your guide to tell you many of the stories as you sip tea made from Liu Yi well water. Try to imagine the time during the Song when ten thousand troops were stationed here.

ZHANGZHOU (Chengchow) in Fujian is in the best rice area in the province and is famous for its narcissus flowers, streets lined with magnolia trees, and its many plants for industrial and medicinal uses. Zhangzhou also grows a lot of fruit and makes fruit wines. At the Zhangzhou Handicrafts Factory, the famous Longxi puppets are manufactured.

ZHAOQING (Chaoching), Guangdong province, located 110 kilometers from Guangzhou, is famous for its scenery and Duan inkstones.

Seven Star Crags, so named because they appear placed like the seven stars of the Big Dipper, has been described by one tourist as "prettier than Hangzhou." The mountains are very much like those of Guilin, with grotesque limestone formations and an underground stream for boat riding. Known since ancient times, it was not really developed as a resort until work was started in 1955. Star Lake was created for irrigation, fish breeding, and scenery. Walkways, bridges and lights were set up in the caves. The seven crags are named Langfeng (Lofty Wind), Yuping (Jade Screen), Shishi (Stone Chamber), Tianzhu (Pillar of Heaven), Chanchu (Toad), Shizhang (Stone Palm), and Apo (Hill Slope). The biggest cave is at the foot of Apo Crag and can be entered by boat. If you hit the rocks at Instrument Music Rock, you get different musical notes. Zhoqing also boasts a Ming temple, the **Qingyun. Mt. Dinghu (Tripod)**, 20 km. east has an old temple, the **Plum Monastery.**

Star Lake Hotel was built in 1978. There are also restaurants, swimming pools, and an art gallery.

ZHENGZHOU (Chengchow), the capital of Henan province, is on both the Beijing-Guangzhou and the Shanghai-Xi'an railway lines. It is a 2-hour flight south of Beijing.

It is historically important as one of the first cities to be built in China during the Shang dynasty three thousand years ago. Its museum has artifacts from that and succeeding periods found locally. Historically it is also known as the site of the February 7th Beijing-Hankou Railway Workers General Strike of 1923, part of a larger workers' movement for better wages and conditions. Over a hundred railroad workers were killed. The strike is commemorated with a monument in February 7th Square.

The **Zhengzhou Mangshan Pumping Station** in the suburbs, built between 1970 and 1972, is a very impressive system raising water from the muddy Yellow River 86 meters up the mountain to a reservoir for cleaning before 60 percent is used by the city and the rest for irrigation. The main canal is 40 kilometers long, passing through six tunnels and along three aqueducts. The system has more than one hundred bridges, underground passages, sluice gates, and dams. A trip there is impressive also for the terracing on the hills.

Near Zhengzhou are the **tomb of the Tang poet Tu Fu,** the ancient capital of **Kaifeng,** and the famous **Shaolin Monastery,** sacred to all Kung-fu and martial arts fans. Shaolin is 75 km. southwest of Zhengzhou on Mt. Song, which also is the home of the **Zhong Temple** (the earliest Taoist temple in China) and the Songyang Academy of Classical Learning. Kaifeng is relatively easy to get to, but the others are rough, long trips. You will probably have to pay considerably extra for these side trips, but they have been done by public bus by youthful, adventurous souls.

ZHENJIANG (Chinkiang, Chenchiang, Chenkiang; To pacify the river)

Location: In central Jiangsu province, where the Grand Canal meets the south bank of the Yangtze. About 1 hour by train (90 kilometers) northeast of Nanjing, and about 3 hours (220 kilometers) northwest of Shanghai. It is a historic old city, its streets lined with plane trees, some of its houses small and whitewashed like Suzhou's, others black brick with courtyards. It is bounded on three sides by hills and the north by the Yangtze River.

Weather: Coldest: minus 8°C—mid-January–end of January; hottest: 38°C—July and August with breezes from Yangtze. Rain in July.

Population: 270,000

Area: 92 square kilometers

Background: Zhenjiang was founded in the Zhou, when it was called Guyang and then Dantu. It boasts 2,500 years of history, including seven as capital of the Eastern Wu (third century), when it was called Jingko (entrance to Nanjing). Many battles were fought in the area from the third to fifteenth centuries, and the city is mentioned in *The Romance of the Three Kingdoms.*

During the Yuan, it was visited by Marco Polo. The first British missionaries arrived in the seventeenth century. Toward the end of the First Opium War, it was the only city that strongly resisted the imperialists. After that failed, however, about a thousand foreigners, mainly merchants and missionaries from Britain, Germany and the U.S., lived here. The foreigners left their mark on the architecture.

In 1938 Marshall Chen Yi's New Fourth Army was stationed about 50 kilometers away, and some skirmishes with the Japanese took place in the area. In April 1949, the British warship H.M.S. *Amethyst,* while rescuing British citizens upriver, was caught in the crossing of the Yangtze by the PLA and held for over three months here. The captain refused to cooperate or admit his ship fired first. Under cover of a passing passenger boat, it finally escaped.

Today Zhenjiang has three hundred factories and mines, and makes industrial chemicals, textiles, silk, and paper (from rice stocks) for export. *Dashikou* is its main shopping area—department store, antique stores, and arts and crafts. Its factories make elaborate palace lanterns, and it is famous for its *mei jui shiao* "crystal" meat and vinegar. Its communes grow rice, wheat, and silkworms. You can visit the national government Silk and Mulberry Research Institute. Also made in the city are jade carvings, paper cuttings, and cotton birds.

Of Interest to Visitors

Bei Gu (North Consolidated) Hill is the site of the temple where Liu Pei, founder of the Shu Han dynasty and hero of *The Romance of the Three Kingdoms,* was married to the sister of Sun Chuan. After he died, his wife mourned for him at the pavilion on top of the hill now called Mourning over the River Pavilion. On this hill also is a ninth-century Iron Pagoda (Northern Song) originally nine stories. Struck by lightning several times, it was repaired in 1960 and now has only its first, second, fifth, and sixth stories.

Jiao Hill (150 meters high) on an island less than half a kilometer from the city, is named after an Eastern Han scholar, Jiao Guan. A slightly larger than life-size white statue of the hermit meditating in the dim light of the actual cave is at the base. Two hundred and fifty steps later is a magnificent view of the Yangtze—all three of Zhenjiang's hills have magnificent views of the Yangtze—and one can see the place where the *Amethyst* was held and where she fought her way out.

Back at the base, you can look at the **Battery,** which was used against the British in 1842. It was originally on the river. Also below is the **Din Hui Temple** with steles of many calligraphers, including that of the father of modern calligraphy, Wang Hsi-chih, written 1,500 years ago. The original tablet was broken but retrieved from the river in 1713. There is also a loquat orchard and a Buddhist temple building where most of the Ming statues were destroyed by the Red Guards. The existing statues were made in 1979.

Jin Shan Pagoda looks better from afar than close up. The temple here was first built 1,400 years ago (Song) and rebuilt several times since, a victim of lightning, fire, and weather. Parts have never been rebuilt. The current pagoda was finished in 1900 with crude animal carvings in time for the Empress Dowager's birthday. It reflects her tastes. Seven stories tall, 30 meters high, it is easier climbing up the 119 steps than down because of the thin steps.

But there are some fun **caves,** all the more interesting because of the presence in one of the white, life-size figure of the founding monk, Fa Hai, and in another of the two beautiful women said to be the White Snake and the Blue Snake, both fairies. The cave is said to reach Hangzhou.

The mythology is in a way new to China, in a way very old. Guides avoided telling such traditional stories in the late 1960s, and it has only been in the late 1970s that one hears stories like the White Snake's. It is also the plot of a Beijing opera. Briefly, it is about a 1,000-year-old White Snake from Mount Emei (the Blue Snake is incidental) who becomes a beautiful woman and goes to Hangzhou. There she falls in love with a man, and eventually the two marry. The White Snake, using her magic powers, takes money from a government official to build a house, but because the official's seal is still on it, the young man is arrested and ordered beaten for theft. The White Snake again uses her magic so that whenever her husband is beaten, the official's wife feels the pain. Consequently, the young man is expelled to Zhenjiang. After his arrival, the monk master tries to separate the couple, but the White Snake floods the area, including Jin Shan temple. The monk master retaliates by imprisoning the White Snake under the Lei Feng pagoda in Hangzhou. There she gives birth to a boy whose tears for his mother's fate move the gods deeply. The pagoda collapses, freeing her. The White Snake, her husband and her son are reunited and live happily ever after.

Museum: Housed in the former British consulate building next door to the former Southern Baptist Convention buildings, this museum was opened in 1958. Its permanent collection includes an anchor from the British ship *Amethyst* and a land lease dated 1933 referring to the "former British Concession lot." It has the well-preserved 720-year-old corpse of a scholar, buried with his precious Imperial University entrance certificate in hand. There is also a tiny silver coffin containing two gold coffins and the ashes of a Buddhist saint, found under the nearby Iron Pagoda, and a Song porcelain pillow in the shape of a sleeping child.

Boat trip on the Yangtze: ¥10 for 1½ hours.

Other Places of Interest

Yangzhou, ancient city, 25 kilometers away. From the bus station there is a bus that goes on the ferry across the Yangtze.

Grand Canal, built in the seventh century (Sui); 16 kilometers from hotel.

Yixing: Famous caves and porcelain. See separate listing. About 150 kilometers away.

Local Food: Crab cream bun, a steamed meat pastry, is a specialty. Make a hole first and slurp out the soup inside. Food here is concerned with fragrance, shape, and color, and is not too sweet or salty. You may find your hors d'oeuvres looking like butterflies, peacocks, or fans. Everything can be dipped in vinegar.

Hotels: Zhenjiang was opened to foreign tourists in June 1978. The hotels for foreigners here are centered around the 25-acre Shadow of the Pagoda Lake in the western suburbs of town, 6.5 kilometers from the railway station. The setting is sylvan. You can borrow a fishing rod.

Jingko Guest House. Built 1960. 50 rooms (100 beds). Antiquated but pleasant. Extension built 1981.

Jin Shan Hotel. Built 1979. 110 rooms (220 beds). This is one of the Australian-built hotels with air conditioning, television, room refrigerators, and individual telephones. Closest to town.

ZHONGSHAN AND ZUHAI COUNTIES, adjacent to the Portuguese colony of Macao across the Pearl River delta south of Hong Kong, were opened to foreign tourists in 1979. Tours are arranged through C.T.S., any other travel agent, or the International Tourism and Trade Development Corporation of Hong Kong (see chapter 1).

The ITTDC's tour from Hong Kong includes an afternoon and evening in Macao. In China you visit the former residence of Dr. Sun Yat-sen in Cuuiheng village. The house was designed by the father of the Chinese republic himself in the Chinese style. There is also a visit to the Sun Yat-sen Memorial Middle School and the town. After lunch in Shek Ket, there is a visit to Long Rui Production Brigade before returning to Macao. C.T.S. tours do it in one day from Hong Kong.

The county also has two hot spring resorts mainly for Hong Kong Compatriots who need no visas for entry. Foreigners and Overseas Chinese have to go the usual route unless they want to buy an expensive package tour (HK$1,450 for one from Hong Kong for one night all inclusive; HK$650 each if in a group of five) at the **Shi Ching Shan Tourist Center** where the rooms themselves are HK$200 for a twin. But try if you want. Ask for Dennis at the Golden Star Tourism Corp., 469 Nathan Rd., Sun Beam Commercial Bldg. No. 1009, Yaumati, Kowloon, Hong Kong. The Center, which is a 20 minute drive from the Macau border, has boating, tennis, shooting gallery, horses, and a swimming pool.

The **Zhongshan (Chungshan) Hot Spring Resort** is 30 km. from the border. Sintra Tours which books it from Macau has its tour lunches there. The resort has 200 rooms, tennis, shooting gallery, a swimming pool, and a fishing lake.

Shiqi (Shekki, Shekket) has a 180 room hotel built by C.T.S. in 1980.

ZIBO, in Shandong on the Beijing-Shanghai express train route or by air via Jinan, is near **Linzi,** the capital of Qi (859–221 B.C.) where 150 ancient tombs have yielded a large mirror, bronzes, crossbows, and bronze coins from that era. Zibo itself makes porcelain, artistic pottery and glassware, and silk.

ZUNHUA (Tsunhua), about 125 kilometers northeast of Tianjin and 150 kilometers east of Beijing, is the site of five of the Qing Imperial tombs. That of the Chien Lung Emperor, who is known to many collectors of Chinese porcelain, and that of the Empress Dowager Tzu Hsi can both be seen. The Empress Dowager was the fascinating, outrageous, scheming, brilliant, scandalous but shortsighted woman who built the Summer Palace in Beijing. Her tomb, covered with phoenixes, was completed in 1881 and renovated in 1895 with an additional 4,590 taels of gold as decoration. She died in 1908.

Like the Ming tombs, there is also a Sacred Way of animals. The Qing carving is more elaborate than the Ming, with Buddhist sutras carved inside. The Western Tombs are 120 kilometers from Beijing at Yihsian, and contain four emperors. The Eastern Tombs at Zunhua, however, are more interesting.

12

SPECIAL FOR OVERSEAS CHINESE

A Hong Kong Chinese presented a Hong Kong British passport to a Chinese immigration officer a few years back. The Chinese official tore it up. "You are Chinese; you are not British!" he said.

Overseas Chinese with other passports, however, are something else. Sometimes in China we are treated like visiting family; sometimes like foreigners. It depends on who is doing the treating, and the decision is made when we ourselves choose to go with China Travel Service or China International Travel Service.

I have gone to China both ways. Emotionally, it's a strain because sometimes when I'm with one group, I want to be with the other. It is part of the conflict of living in two worlds. In China it is not so easy to pass from one to the other.

I think people of Chinese ancestry in particular should visit China. If you feel this bicultural conflict as many of us do, it would be good to explore the Chinese part of your roots. If nothing else, it will help you understand your parents, your grandparents, and your great-grandparents. It might even help you understand things about yourself.

I highly recommend a visit to your ancestral village. Even if you have no relatives there, at least you can look around and see how you would have lived if your ancestors had not emigrated. And you might find your name, if you're male, in a family history book. Part of my novel is about this experience, which can be traumatic.

But you don't have money to take expensive presents? Don't be silly! People outside China send back presents to relatives inside partly to show off. They also send because they feel a strong family obligation. People in China ask for expensive luxury presents like color televisions and Omega watches because they do not really know how much these things cost outside. They think these are cheap. And they want to keep up with the Wongs. So what do you think will happen if you don't take them a sewing machine? Do you think your relatives are going to be rude to you? Of course not. Forget foolish pride. If they ask, tell them you couldn't afford it. Making friends and learning about China are much more important. The Overseas Chinese is in a much better position to do this than the average traveler with C.I.T.S.

You should take some presents. Cotton cloth bought in Hong Kong at Chinese Products Store is less than US$1 a yard. Peanut oil, cashews, bean threads, soap, and cookies won't cost you more than US$10 and these are much appreciated. My relatives were pleased with the US$20 watch I took in once, especially after I showed them the $16 Timex I usually wear myself. If you can afford to go to China from the U.S., you can at least afford something like that. Besides, they may reimburse you for some "gifts."

You may find you have nothing in common with the Chinese people. On the other hand, you may find that you do. You may find no feelings of obligation to these people, dismissing their comparative poverty as their, not your, bad luck. So be it. At least you went and had a look.

For those who do feel pangs of conscience, I think you should be sensitive to opportunities to help. Many officials are stifled by a "lingering fear" of trying anything new in case they may end up getting demoted or severely criticized if the scheme goes badly. Besides, they may not know you. Can you be trusted? Do you truly want to help? Do you have ulterior motives? And what can you do? It boggles their minds.

Developing industries now has high priority, but there are proper channels and it may take years to go through them. Offering to work as a "foreign expert" is also very slow to arrange, but try if you want (see chapter 1 for this and academic channels). Do not expect anything done in China to happen in a hurry. The bureaucracy can be deadly. If you have good relations with responsible Chinese officials already, especially if they're relatives, do talk to them about how you can help. If you're visiting a school or factory, talk about its problems. If it's appropriate and especially if these officials ask, make suggestions. If they seem more than politely interested in what you say, bring up the question of ways you can help even more. Tell them the names of important Chinese people who know you to help allay their fears. Since fear of making decisions is one of the biggest obstacles on lower levels, try for the higher levels. Write to the Premier, Vice-Premiers, Ministers, and high party officials with concrete proposals.

At the same time, I think your best bet is on the village level, especially your own ancestral village where you are known. But don't rush it. Look around. Don't put on the high and mighty act and tell your country cousins "you should do this . . . you should do that . . ." That will antagonize them. Stay with them at least a week. Go out into the fields and work with them their way—yes, with your hands! If you're mechanically minded, help them fix their tractor. You may learn something about improvising parts. What they don't need on this level is a lot of sophisticated machinery dependent on foreign exchange for maintainence. What they might need is help in marketing handicrafts or creating designs that would appeal to the foreign market, or capital—to get a project started. Listen to their problems. Make suggestions. Listen to their reactions. Make another visit next year after you've learned more Chinese and done some reading on community development projects. Feel them out again. Remember, they have been isolated for years and know little about the world outside China.

It may be that teaching English and sending them scientific and technical books and journals will be the only useful help you can give them. Sending money to support relatives is important for foreign exchange but unless it is making education possible or developing cooperatives, I think it is only encouraging an elite that is doing nothing to help develop the country.

One Overseas Chinese I met with a British passport, but not from Hong Kong, entered China as "Returned Overseas Chinese." This also took a lot of letter writing to prove his sincerity, and contacts with the U.S.-China People's Friendship Association. He is doing research in chemical engineering now, and making only slightly more than an average Chinese salary. He is also living in two rooms, even though he is single. Two rooms are usually assigned to a family of four. In America he used to work just for a fat salary. Now he gets a lot more satisfaction working "for China." Of course, this takes a special kind of person, one with a great deal of patience and particularly a good sense of humor. It is not easy for someone used to Western affluence to adapt to Chinese standards, but some do. My novel deals with this too.

It is also possible now to sponsor a Chinese student to study abroad. For China's sake, please make sure he returns. Nothing is really solved if this results in his sending back only foreign exchange to his family. China needs scientists and technicians *in China.*

I think Overseas Chinese are in a much better position than other foreigners to help China. And for the first time in recent history, China is open to outside help. But the openness is only comparative.

13

SPECIAL FOR BUSINESS PEOPLE

Advice: Trading with China is not like trading with other countries. As one trade official put it, "If you want to play in the Chinese sand pile, you have to play by Chinese rules."

These rules are much too complicated to put into a travel guide. There are lots of books, business guides, and experienced people to give advice. But to get you started: Trading with China is done primarily through foreign trading corporations, a list of which is in the IMPORTANT ADDRESSES with details of their specialties. Joint ventures are negotiated through the China International Trust and Investment Corporation.

K. G. Ramsay, former Commercial Counsellor at the Canadian embassy in Beijing also says:

1. It is possible sometimes for a member of a tour group to get a business appointment.

2. Don't come with the attitude, "We're going to liberate the Chinese." These aren't Chinese laundrymen you're talking to. They'll ask you questions like "Why did you reduce the number of your employees from 500 to 200 last year?" Be prepared. The Chinese know b.s. when they hear it.

3. The Chinese want specific proposals. Don't give them general statements. However, whatever proposal you make won't be accepted anyway. Do not quote rock-bottom figures. The Chinese like to negotiate.

4. Be patient. If you lose patience, you've lost the negotiating battle.

5. Keep accurate notes. The Chinese do. But no tape recorders. The Chinese use interpreters even though they can speak good English. There is plenty of time to make notes. Record who is present, dates, and what was said. Later the Chinese may say to you, "On such a date you said . . . Why are you now saying. . . ?"

6. There is no need to take your own interpreter—too expensive. Chinese interpreters are competent.

7. A Memorandum of Understanding means two parties have identified a field where there is reason to believe there are grounds for possible future

259

negotiations, which, if exploited, should lead to a possible contract. It is not a contract, even if it mentions prices.

8. If the Chinese give you a welcoming banquet, you should return a banquet. It is not necessary to pay more than ¥15 a head. Get help from your embassy.

9. Gifts must be modest: a good ballpoint pen or a small calculator. You may want to say, "Would it cause you any embarrassment if I gave you a small token of my esteem. . . ?" Cash is out, but the Japanese have been giving television sets.

To this, let me add that the atmosphere in China among foreign traders is very informal and friendly. Fairs are among the best places to get advice from fellow traders unless you happen to meet a competitor. Try also the Chinese embassy nearest you or, in Hong Kong, China Resources. Your own government's department of trade probably has a free booklet on the subject. If you are in Hong Kong or Beijing, contact the trade representative at your country's mission.
See also INTRODUCTION.

Best News Sources on Trade with China: *Asian Wall Street Journal* (daily); *South China Morning Post* (Hong Kong daily); *Asian Wall Street Journal Weekly; Far Eastern Economic Review* (weekly).

Very Helpful: "China Trade Report" (monthly), *Far Eastern Economic Review; The China Business Review* (bimonthly), National Council on U.S.-China Trade; *Business China* (bimonthly); *China Trader Weekly Bulletin; China Briefing* (quarterly and free), Hongkong Shanghai Banking Corporation; *Amcham Magazine* (of the American Chamber of Commerce, Hong Kong, a monthly that focuses several times a year on China); *China Trader.*

Also Helpful: *Economic Reporter,* English Supplement; *China's Foreign Trade; Ta Kung Pao Weekly.*

Some Banks Experienced with China Trade: See IMPORTANT ADDRESSES. Their branches in Hong Kong should be in the best position to give advice. Some also have branches and representative offices in China.

Guides: *China,* Business Profile Services. The Hong Kong and Shanghai Banking Corporation, Hong Kong; anything from the National Council for U.S.-China Trade. Also, *The China Phone Book,* updated every October.

Trade Councils: The National Council for U.S.-China Trade is a private, not-for-profit membership organization of more than 620 large and small firms, financed by membership dues, with its main office in Washington, D.C. A staff representative is available to assist members in Beijing. Among its members are Allied Chemical, Boeing, Coca-Cola, and Pan American World Airways. The Canadian equivalent is the China-Canada Trade Council, and the British, the Sino-British Trade Council. See also chapter 1, "Individually as a Business Person," and INTRODUCTION.

Garden of the Master of Nets in Suzhou. *(Photo by the author)*

Boats plying the waters of a Suzhou canal. *(Photo by the author)*

Carpet making in a factory in Tianjin. (*Photo by the author*)

The view down the Bund in Shanghai. *(Photo by the author)*

The famous Democracy Wall in Beijing. (*Photo by the author*)

Workers repairing the Great Wall in Shanghaiguan. (*Photo by the author*)

A pagoda in Beijing. *(Photo by the author)*

The dining car of a Chinese train. (*Photo by the author*)

❊❊14❊❊

USEFUL PHRASES

These are designed so you will be able to communicate with people who speak only Chinese. In most cases you need only point to the Chinese and you will get a "yes" (shi de) or "no" (bu shi) answer or a reassuring smile or an attempt to look up an answer from this book.

Read through the phrases at your leisure so you will know what is available. If you think you need other phrases, get a Chinese-writing friend to do them for you.

TRAVEL

Arrivals

I am looking for the interpreter who is supposed to meet me.
我正在找一位翻译，他是来接我的。
He is from———.　　　他是＿＿＿＿＿＿＿＿的人。
　C.I.T.S.　　　　　　中国国际旅行社。
　the Foreign Ministry　　外交部
　Foreign Trade Corporation　外贸公司
　Academy of Sciences　　科学院
　All-China Sports Federation　中华全国体育总会
　Committee for Cultural Relations with Foreign Countries
　　　　对外文委
　Chinese People's Association for Friendship with Foreign Countries
　　　　对外友协
　People's Institute for Foreign Affairs
　　　　中国人民外交学会
When do I get my passport back?
什么时候能将护照还给我？
Where do I get my checked luggage?
我托运的行李在那里取？

269

That bag is mine. Please give it to me.

那个手提包是我的。请递给我。

Is there someone here who can carry my bag for me?

有没有人可以帮我拿手提包？

Please call a taxi for me.

请代我叫一辆出租汽车。

How long will it take for the taxi to get here?

出租汽车要多久才能到达这里？

minutes 分钟   hours 小时

Is there a bus I can take to the city?

有进城的公共汽车吗？

How can I get to the city?

我怎样可以到城里去？

City Travel

Do you have a map of this city in English?

你有一张这个城市的英文地图吗？

    . . . with city bus routes?   有公共汽车路线图的？

I want to go to ———.   我要去_____。

China International Travel
                   Service 中国国际旅行社

CAAC office   中国航空公司

Bank of China   中国银行

hotel   旅馆

hovercraft terminal   气垫船终点站

train station   火车站

ferry terminal   渡船码头

airport   飞机场

bus station   公共汽车站

trade center (as planned for
           Beijing) 商业中心（像为北京设计的）

Guangzhou (Canton) Export
        Commodities Fair 广州出口商品交易会

Where can I get a ———? 我在哪里可以叫／乘_____?

taxi 一辆出租汽车   motorscooter 摩托车

bicycle rickshaw 三轮车   city bus 市内公共汽车

subway 地下铁道列车

About how much would it cost? 大约要多少钱？

City Bus

What number city bus do I take to go from here to ———?

我从这里到＿＿＿＿＿应该乘那一路公共汽车？

Please show me where I can get that bus.

请告诉我在那里上车。

Across the street?

过街？

This side?

这一边？

Please tell me where I get off for ———.

请告诉我到＿＿＿＿去应该在那儿下车。

Do I need to change to another bus?

我要不要换车？

What number?

几路？

Taxi

Please drive more slowly.

请开的慢一些。

Please drive faster.

请开的快一些。

Please wait for me.

请等我一会。

I will be about ——— minutes.

我要耽搁＿＿＿＿分钟。

How much does it cost for you to wait?

等我得付多少钱？

An hour?

一小时？

Where will you wait?

你在哪里等我？

I want to be sure there is a taxi for me early tomorrow morning at ———
o'clock. 我要确定能在明天早晨＿＿＿点种叫到一辆出租
汽车。

Could you order a taxi for me for that time?

你能为我订一辆那个时候要的出租汽车吗？

Buying a Ticket (see also Permission)

I want to buy a ticket to go to ———.

我要买一张到＿＿＿＿去的车票。

One-way 单程 Return 来回

Can I make the return reservation now?

现在我能订回来的票吗？

I want to go ——. 我要在_____走。

in the morning	早晨	in the afternoon	下午
in the evening	晚上	today	今天
tomorrow	明天	the day after tomorrow	后天
next week	下星期	earlier	早一些
later	晚一些	as soon as possible	尽早地
soft class	软席	hard class	硬席
berth	卧铺	seat	座位

What times does it leave?

什么时候开车？

What time does it arrive?

什么时候到？

Where does it leave from?

车从哪儿开出？

Please write that address here.

请你把地址写在这里。

What time should I be there?

我应该在什么时候到那里？

How much is it?

多少钱？

Do you have a schedule in English?

你有一个英语时间表吗？

Cancellations

Do you think someone might cancel a ticket later?

你想等一等会有人退票吗？

Could I take his place?

能把他的位子给我吗？

When should I try again?

我应该什么时候再来问？

Can I exchange this reservation for another time?

我能把订的这张票换一个别的时间的吗？

Is there a service charge?

要付服务费吗？

I would like to cancel this ticket and get a refund.

我想把这张票退掉。

If I wait here, is there a possibility I can get a ticket?

如果我等在这里，有可能买到一张票吗？

Someone may not show up.

可能有人不来。

It is an emergency.

这是一个紧急情况。

(For waiting list, see Hotel section of this chapter.)

Private Car

Checkpoint 检查站

Do you have permission to pass here?

你有通行证吗？

I didn't know we needed permission.

我不知道我们需要办通行证。

I didn't see a sign.

我没有看见牌子。

We are only sightseeing.

我们只是在观光。

We are traveling from ——— to———.

我们是从_____旅行到_____。

We are lost.

我们迷路了。

Could you please tell me how to go from ——— to ———?

请告诉我从_____到_____怎么走。

How far is it from here?

从这里去有多远？

Please mark where we are now on this map.

请在地图上把我们现在所在的地方做个记号。

Please draw a map for us.

请给我们画个地图。

here   there

这里   那里

Do you have a telephone?

你有电话吗？

We are ———. 我们是。_____。

    diplomats 外交官

    guests of the China International Travel Service

      中国国际旅行社的客人

    Overseas Chinese 华侨

    foreign experts   外国专家

Where can we find a(n) ——— 哪里有_____?

    gas station?   加油站

    restaurant?   饭馆

lavatory? 厕所

hotel? 旅馆

English-speaking person? 会说英语的人

Please circle the location on this map.

请在这个地图把那个位置圈一下。

Permission

Is permission necessary?

需不需要先申请？

Do I need permission to come back to this city?

再回这个城市我还需要先申请吗？

Where do I get permission to go there?

到哪里办申请？

Please write that address down here.

请把地址写在这里。

Internal Visas

Where is the office of the Security Police? I want to get permission to go to the following cities:

公安局在哪里？我要申请到以下几个城市去：

When? 什么时候？

Passport? 护照？

What hotel are you staying in? 你住在哪一个旅馆？

Who invited you to China? 谁邀请你来中国的？

Come back tomorrow. 请明天再来。

Come back in two days. 两天后再来。

What time? 什么时间？

Is there any charge? 要付钱吗？

Departures (see also City travel)

Is it time to board yet?

还不该上车吗？

Which platform?

哪一个站台？

Which coach?

哪一辆车箱？

Where is the ———?

_____在哪里？

waiting room 侯车室

schedule in English 英语时间表

restaurant 餐馆

retail store 商店

ticket 车／船／飞机票　　passport 护照

customs declaration form
海关报税单

foreign exchange receipt
外汇兑换收据

identification badge
身份证章

Lost and Found

I have lost my———,
我的_____丢了。或：我找不到我的_____。

spouse	丈夫／妻子	luggage	行李
tour group	旅行团	watch	手表
glasses	眼镜	wallet	皮夹子
umbrella	伞	camera	照像机
purse	钱包	tape recorder	录音机
typewriter	打字机	shoe	鞋
luggage wheels	推行李的小车	package	包裹

Have you seen it? 你看见了吗？

Is there a lost-and-found here? 这儿有失物招领柜吗？

If someone finds it, could you 如果有人找到了，

please mail it to me at this address? 请寄到这个地址给我。

HOTEL

General Information

Where do I register? 我在哪儿登记？

I have a reservation for today. 我已经订了今天的房间。

single 单人房　　　double 双人房　　　suite 套房

——— persons _____个人。

cheapest 最便宜的　　whatever is available

most expensive 最贵的　　　不管有什么都行

old wing 老厅　　　　　　in between 中间的

private bath or shower 私人浴室或淋浴　　new wing 新厅

air-conditioned 有冷气的　　not air-conditioned 没有冷气的

better view 看出去风景较好的。

Can I wait in the lobby until a room is available?
我在前门大厅等到有房间空出来行不行？

Please put me on the waiting list.
请把我的名字登记上。

275

I will check with you tomorrow morning.

明天早上我再来问。

I would like to make a reservation for a future date.

我想订一个房间。

I am looking for a friend.

我在找一个朋友。

Please show me the registration forms so I can find his room number.

请将登记本给我查一下他的房间号数。

His nationality?

他的国籍？

Is there someone to carry my bags to my room?

有人帮我把行李拿到房间里去吗？

Where is ———?

_____ 在哪儿？

barber shop	理发店
hairdresser	理发师
masseur	按摩师
bank	银行
post office	邮局
cable office	电报局
Telex	用户电报
clinic	诊疗所
retail store	零售商店
bar	酒吧间
coffee shop	咖啡馆

When does it open? 什么时候开门？

When does it close? 什么时候关门？

Do you have ———? 你有_____ 吗？ Where? 在那里？

ping-pong	乒乓
billiards	台球
badminton	羽毛球
racket	拍子
bird	羽毛球
net	球纲
volleyball	排球
swimming pool	游泳池
hot spring	温泉
nearby park for jogging	附近可供步行锻练的公园
scales for weighing luggage	秤行李用的磅秤

276

English-language newssheet (Xin Hua)
新华社英语报纸
Chinese newspaper
中国报纸
typewriter
打字机
meeting room for ——— people
_____人开会用的会议室
professional photographer
职业摄影师。
simultaneous translation equipment
同声翻译设备
interpreter
翻译

movie projector	放影机	
35 mm.	35毫米	
8 mm.	8毫米	
super 8	超8	
slide projector	幻灯机	
tape recorder	录音机	
spool	录音胶带	
cassette	暗盒	
8-track	八声道	
microphone	扩音机	
megaphone	传声筒	
refrigerator	冰箱	
freezer	致冷器	

What is the rental price?
租金多少？
Can you organize a cocktail party for ——— people?
你能为_____人安排一个鸡尾酒会吗？
Please show me the room.
请你让我看看那个房间。
How much for hors d'œuvres and canapes?
小吃多少钱？
How much for liquor?
酒多少钱？
How much if we supply our own liquor and you supply the ice and glasses,
waiters, and bartender? 我们带自己的酒，你供应冰块、
玻璃环、服务员和酒吧间招待员，要多少钱？

What is your cable address?

你的电报挂号是什么？

What is your telephone number?

你的电话号码是什么？

Dining Room

Where is the dining room?

餐厅在哪里？

Chinese food

中餐

Western food

西餐

upstairs?

楼上

downstairs?

楼下

What time does it open? close? 餐厅什么时候开？关？

Laundry

If I give you my laundry now when will it be done?

如果我现在把要洗的东西给你，什么时候可以洗好？

I must have it by tomorrow morning. I am leaving at ———.

我明天早上一定要。我＿＿＿＿点钟动身。

Where is my laundry? I gave it to the attendant yesterday and he promised to have it done now. 我交去洗的东西在哪里？

我是昨天交给服务员的，他答应我现在可以洗好。

man's	男人的
woman's	女人的
child's	小孩的
shirt	男式衬衫
trousers	长裤
blouse	女人衬衫
underpants	内裤
undershirt	内衣
socks	短袜
dress	衣裙
pajamas	睡衣
tie	领带
suit (man's)	西装
dry cleaning	干洗

I am leaving this morning. 我今天早上走。
I don't have anything else to wear. 我没有别的衣服可穿了。
I need it today. 我今天要。
I need it right now. 我现在就要。

Rooms

There are mosquitoes in this room. Can you give me an incense coil to burn?
这个房间里有蚊子。你能给我一盘蚊香吗？
Do you have a mosquito net?
你有蚊帐吗？
extra blanket?
你还有毯子吗？
Please give me some hot water in a thermos.
请给我一暖瓶热水。
I need enough hot water for a bath.
我需要足够洗一个澡的热水。
Please bring me ———. 请给我拿_____来。

ice	冰	beer	啤酒	tea	茶
orange soda	橘子汽水	Coke	可口可乐	glasses	玻璃杯
cup	杯子	towel	毛巾	soap	肥皂
clean	干净的	fan	电风扇／扇子		

Something is broken in my room. 我房间的_____坏了。

toilet	厕所	light	电灯
telephone	电话	chair	椅子
bed	床	air conditioner	冷气机
fan	电风扇	mosquito net	蚊帐
television	电视机	radiator	暖气

There isn't enough heat. 不够热
This is dirty. 这个不干净
Could someone fix it immediately?
能叫人立刻来修吗？
No.不能   Yes. 能   I will try.我试试看
I will ask my director.
我问一下主任。
Can I get a discount on my room if it is not fixed before I leave?
如果在我离开以前没有修好，我是否可以少付房钱？
Can I have a hot water bottle?
能给我一个热水袋吗？

279

Telephones

How do I get an outside line on the telephone?
我怎样打外线电话？

Please telephone this person and ask him/her to meet me at the hotel
请你给这个人打一个电话，让他／她在＿＿＿点钟到

at ——— o'clock. My name is ——— and my room number
旅馆来找我。我叫＿＿＿＿住在＿＿＿＿号房间。

is———.

I would like to make an international telephone call.
我想和国外通一个电话。

I would like to call long distance in China.
我想打个中国国内的长途电话。

Can I take it in my room?
我能在我房间里接吗？

Can I pay for it with a credit card?
我能用信用卡付款吗？

collect call
收话人付款的长途电话。

FOOD

Banquets 宴会

(Arrangements can be made at service counter at hotel.)

Can you recommend a good restaurant for me?
你能推荐一家好的餐馆吗？

One noted for good food, moderate prices. I don't care what it looks like.
一家菜闻名，而价钱公道的，我不在乎餐馆的样子
如何。

One noted for beautiful surroundings and good food.
一家环境优美，菜又好的餐馆。

Could you please make a reservation for me for ——— people
a. at ——— each. b. The chef can decide the menu.
请你代我订＿＿＿人一桌的菜。每人＿＿＿元的。
菜单由厨师决定。

Yes, I understand we have to pay extra for drinks.
对，我知道喝的要另外算。

Can we bring our own bottles of liquor?
我们能自己带酒吗？

Is it possible to include one dish of ——— for that price?
这个价钱能不能有个＿＿＿菜？

Please make the reservation for ——— o'clock

请代我订在＿＿＿点钟。

today. 今天

tomorrow 明天

the day after tomorrow. 后天

Please write down the name and address for the taxi driver.

请将名字和地址写给司机。

Small Noodle or Bun Shops (food is usually in sight)

I understand Foreign Friends and Overseas Chinese do not have to give ration coupons.

我听说外国朋友和华侨不需要给粮票。

Please, I would prefer to stand in line with everyone else.

啊，我愿意和大家排在一起。

Hotel Dining Rooms and Other Restaurants

I am in a hurry. 我有急事，请你快一点。

Please bring me ———. 请给我＿＿＿＿。

a bowl of noodle soup 一碗汤面

fried noodles 炒面

fried rice 炒饭

an assortment of meat dumplings 肉馅饺子／馄饨

a dish of meat 一盘肉菜

anything that can be

prepared quickly 任何快餐都行。

I would like a Chinese breakfast. 我要一份中式早餐

rice congee	大米粥	baked buns	烧饼
pickles	泡菜	oil sticks	油条
salted eggs	咸蛋	dim sum	点心
peanuts	花生米	soy milk	豆浆
tea	茶		

I would like a Western breakfast. 我要一份西式早点

fruit or juice	水果或水果汁		
toast or buns	烤面包或小园面包		
eggs	鸡蛋	butter	黄油
bacon or ham	咸肉或火腿	coffee	咖啡
jam	果酱	milk	牛奶
sugar	糖		

If you have a menu in English, please bring it.

如果你有英语菜单，请拿给我看一看。

What do you recommend that is good but not expensive?

你可以介绍什么好而又不贵的菜吗？

What is the specialty of this restaurant?

这里的特菜是什么？

Please bring enough food for one person.

请你给够我一个人吃的饭菜。

Please bring enough food for all of us. Total cost no more than ——— per person.

请你给够我们大家吃的饭菜，每人不超过_____。

Please bring me one order of———.

请你给我一份_____。

beef	牛肉	vegetables	蔬菜	菜
chicken	鸡	celery cabbage	芹	豆
pigeon	鸽子	green beans	青	
goose	鹅	green onions	葱	
pork	猪肉	bean sprouts	豆	芽笋
fish	鱼	bamboo shoots	竹	荸
crab	螃蟹	water chestnuts	荸	芹菜
lobster	龙虾	watercress	水菜	
shrimp	虾	cabbage	白	菇
sea cucumber (or slug)	海参	mushrooms	蘑	耳
bean curd	豆腐	cloud's ears (fungus)	银	
Beijing (Peking) duck	北京鸭	pine nuts	松子	
duck	鸭子			
monkey	猴子	cashews	枦	如树果
snake	蛇	peanuts	花	生桃
dog	狗	walnuts	核	
frogs' legs	蛙腿	eggs	蛋	
civet cat	香猫	caviar	鱼子	
turtle	甲鱼	hors d'œuvre	小吃	
lotus seed	莲子	black or yellow bean	黑或黄豆	
heart	心	gizzard	胗	
liver	肝	kidney	腰子	
brains	脑	spareribs	排骨	
hocks	蹄膀	tongue	舌	
steak	牛排	fillet (boneless)	里几	
slices	肉片	balls	丸子	
soup	汤	stomach	肚子	

282

minced	剁碎的	shark's fins	鱼翅
bird's nest	燕窝		

stir-fried	快炒	roasted	烤
deep-fried (in batter)	炸(裹鸡蛋面)	cooked in wine	酒焖的
poached	烫熟的	barbecued	烧烤
steamed	蒸的	baked	烘烤
fried in paper	包纸炸的	baked in mud	泥烤
scrambled	炒	baked in salt	盐烤
boiled (hard)	煮（老的）	boiled (soft)	煮（嫩的）

sweet and sour sauce	糖醋汁		
hoisin sauce	甜面酱	bland	淡的
oyster sauce	牝蛎酱	no salt	无盐的
soy sauce	酱油	sour	酸
mustard	芥茉	spicy hot	麻辣
hot pepper	辣椒	sweet	甜
plum sauce	梅子酱	no sugar	无糖
sesame oil	芝麻油／香油	salty	咸
peanut oil	花生油	1000-year-old eggs	皮蛋
coriander	芫荽	white rice	白米饭
honey	蜂蜜	ginger	薑
salt	盐	garlic	蒜
vinegar	醋		

canned	罐头的	fresh	新鲜的
sweet cakes	甜饼	apples	苹果子
bananas	香蕉	oranges	橘子
apricots	杏子	plums	李子
olives	橄榄	kumquats	金橘
pomelo	柚子	lichees	荔枝
pineapple	菠萝		

What kind of tea do you have?

你们有什么茶？

jasmine	茉莉花茶	lung ching	龙井茶
woo lung	乌龙茶	bo ni	普洱茶
chrysanthemum	菊花茶	ginseng	人参茶

milk (hot)	热牛奶	milk (cold)	冷牛奶
unsweetened	未加糖的	soft drink	
beer	啤酒	Coca Cola	饮料
red wine	红酒	fruit juice	可口可乐
white wine	白酒	fermented	果子汁
mao tai	茅台酒	mare's milk	发酵的马奶
mineral water	矿泉水	buttered tea	油茶
cold drinking water	冷开水	cocoa	可可

This tastes terrible. Please bring me something else.
这个很难吃／喝。　请给我来点别的。

Enough! 够了！

We cannot eat any more. Please cancel the other dishes.
我们吃不下了，请把别的菜取消罢！

Western food
西餐

bread	面包	hot dog	热狗
sandwich	三文治	hamburger	面包夹牛肉饼
ice cream	冰淇淋	popsicle	冰棍

Please write down the name of this dish so I can order it again.
请将这个菜名写下来，我以后好再要。

I am a strict vegetarian. I would like to order a dish of only vegetables, cooked in vegetable oil. What do you recommend?
我是一个真正的素食者。我想要一个素油炒的蔬菜。你能给我介绍几个这样的菜吗？

I am a Moslem. I do not eat pork or anything cooked in lard. What do you recommend?
我信伊斯兰教。我不吃猪肉或猪油烧的东西。你有什么我可以吃的呢？

I am a diabetic. I cannot eat anything with sugar in it.
我有糖尿病，我不能吃任何有糖的东西。

TELEPHONE (see also Hotel Telephones)

Finding a Public Telephone

Please show me where I can find a telephone.
请告诉我哪里有电话？

How much for using the telephone?
打一次电话多少钱？

Can you find out the telephone number for ———?

你能帮我找一找 _____的电话号码吗？

      the China International Travel Service in this city?

      这里的中国国际旅行社？

      the CAAC office in this city?

      这里的中国航空公司？

      someone who speaks English?

      会说英语的人。

Please telephone this person. I want to talk to him.

请给这个人打一个电话。我要和他说话。

I want to make ———. 我要一个_____。

      a long-distance call in China 中国境内的长途电话。

      an international telephone call 国际长途电话。

Can I take the call in my room?

我能在我房间里接吗？

Can I pay for it with a credit card?

我能用信用卡付款吗？

collect call

收话人付款的长途电话。

How long will it take?

要多久可以接通？

EMERGENCIES

If Lost

Help! 救命！

Excuse me. 对不起。

I am lost. Which way to this
address?

我迷路了，到这个地址去走那一条路？

      the closest hotel?

      最近的旅馆在哪里？

      the nearest English-speaking person?

      在哪个最近的地方可以找到会说英语的人？

Can you ask someone to take me there?

你能叫人带我去吗？

I am very tired.

我很累。

Please don't push me.

请不要推我。

Where can I find a telephone?

哪里有电话？

Is there any charge for the call?

打这个电话要付钱吗？

Embassies

Please contact the embassy of ———.

请你和＿＿＿＿＿＿大使馆接个电话。

I will speak to them on the telephone.

我要和他们说话。

Please tell their representative to come here.

请告诉他们的代表到这儿来。

Australia	澳大利亚
Belgium	比利时
Britain	英国
Canada	加拿大
France	法国
India	印度
Indonesia	印尼
Italy	意大利
Japan	日本
Malaysia	马来西亚
Mexico	墨西哥
Netherlands	荷兰
New Zealand	新西兰
Pakistan	巴基斯坦
Philippines	菲律宾
Portugal	葡萄牙
Singapore	新加坡
Spain	西班牙
The Federal Republic of Germany	德意志联邦共和国
The German Democratic Republic	德意志民主共和国
Switzerland	瑞士国
Thailand	泰国
U.S.A.	美国

Miscellaneous Emergencies

Stop, please.

请停下来。

I need a lavatory. Please show me the closest one.

我需要上厕所。请告诉我最近的一个在哪里。

| women's | 女人的 | （如指厕所则是：女厕） |
| men's | 男人的 | 男厕 |

Stay away! 站开点！

Danger! 危险！

Run away! 跑开！

Follow me! 跟着我！

Please hurry! 快些！

air attack 空袭

air-raid shelter 防空洞

boat sinking 船在沉

Fire! 失火了！

Explosion! 爆炸了！

Earthquake! 地震了！

Get outside, away from falling debris.

到外面去，躲开掉下来的碎砾。

Riot! 暴动！

accident 意外。

flood 水灾。

Please call someone who speaks English.

请叫一位能说英语的来。

Please call the China International Travel Service.

请叫中国国际旅行社的人来。

Medical Emergencies

Is anyone hurt? 有人受伤吗？

Is there someone here who can help us?

这里有那一位能帮助我们吗？

Please ask people to stand back and give us some air.

请你叫人们靠后站，使我们能吸到些空气。

Please call a doctor.

请叫一位医生来。

Please bring ———. 请你拿_____来。

blanket	一床毯子
stretcher	一个担架
oxygen	氧气
ice	冰
splints	夹板
bandages	绷带
drinking water	喝的水

Stop the bleeding.	止血
Call an ambulance.	叫救护车来
Get him to a hospital.	送他去医院
Hurry.	快！
Help him breathe.	帮助他呼吸
A bone caught in the throat.	喉咙里卡了一根骨头。
Help him lie down.	帮他躺下。
Raise his head.	把他的头抬起来。
Lower his head.	把他的头放下去。
Raise his feet.	把他的脚抬起来。
Give heart massage.	给他按摩心脏。
Give mouth-to-mouth resuscitation.	做口对口的呼吸急救。
Get him cool.	让他凉快凉快。
Fan him.	给他扇一扇。
appendicitis	阑尾炎
bleeding	流血
Broken bone. Do not move it.	骨头断了，不要挪动。
burn	烧伤
diabetic	糖尿病
drowned	淹了
drunk	喝醉了
epileptic fit	癫痫发作
heart attack	心脏病发作
high fever	高烧
insect bite	虫咬了
poisoned	中毒了
snake bite	蛇咬了
stroke	中风
vomit	呕吐

Medical (see also Medical Emergencies)

Where can I find a doctor to treat this ———?

在哪里能找到一位医生治这_____？

itch	痒
pain here	这儿痛
bleeding here	这儿流血
common cold	受凉感冒
diarrhea	腹泻
cough	咳嗽
headache	头痛

fever	发烧
difficulty in breathing	呼吸困难
hives	荨麻疹
sore throat	喉咙痛

acupuncture	针刺治疗
compress	纱布垫
injection	打针
soak	浸湿
bandage	用绷带包扎
Go to the hospital.	去医院
How long bed rest?	要卧床多久？
When can he continue on his journey?	他什么时候可以继续旅行？
What is his temperature?	他的体温是多少？
What is that in Fahrenheit?	华氏多少度？
Is it a high fever?	体温高吗？
Is it normal?	正常不正常？

Dental

dental	牙齿的。
I have a pain here.	我这儿痛。
I think I have lost a filling.	我想我有一个牙齿的充填物掉了。
Can you give me a temporary filling?	能给我临时补一下吗？
Please do not pull out the tooth.	请不要把那个牙拔掉。
Please pull out this tooth.	请把这个牙拔掉。
Can you give me something to ease the pain?	你能给我什么止痛的药吗？

Pharmacy (see also Medical)

traditional Chinese herbal medicine	中国草药
Western medicine	西药
allergy to antibiotics	对抗生素过敏
aspirin	阿司匹灵
insulin for diabetic	治疗糖尿病的胰岛素。
How many teaspoons a day?	一天服几匙？
How many times a day?	一天服几次？
How many pills?	几丸？
For how long?	服多久？
How much water?	多少水？

Boil and drink like tea?	熬后像喝茶一样喝下去吗？
All of it?	全喝吗？
With sugar?	加糖吗？
Is it bitter?	苦不苦？
Any more injections?	还要打针吗？
aphrodisiac	催欲剂
ginseng	人参
sea horse	海马
pearl	珍珠
sleeping pill	安眠药
snake	蛇
insects	昆虫
herb	草药
mineral	矿石
animal	动物
deer horn	鹿角

WEATHER

What is the temperature today?	今天的温度是多少？
Is it hot?	今天热吗？
cold?	冷
rainy?	有雨
snowing?	下雪
sunny?	晴
Do I need to take a ———?	我需要带_____。
coat	一件外套
sweater	一件毛衣
umbrella	一把伞
swimming suit	游泳衣
suntan lotion	一瓶防晒油

RENTALS

Where can I rent a ———?	哪里可以租_____？
bicycle	一辆自行车
rowboat	一条划艇
tennis racket	一个纲球拍
car (with driver)	一辆有司机开的汽车

How much for an hour? 多少钱一小时？

      a day? 一天？

      deposit? 押金多少？

I will return it in about ——

hours. 我大概在＿＿小时后送还。

CONVERSATIONS

Courtesies

Hello!	你好！ Ni hao.	
Good-bye!	再见！ Zai jian.	
I'm sorry. (or) Excuse me!	对不起（或）请原谅！ Dui bu qi (or)	
Please.	请 Qing.	Qing yan liang.
Thank you.	谢谢你！ Xie xie ni.	
You're welcome.	不客气。Bu ke qi.	
Yes.	是。 Shi de.	
No.	不是。 Bu shi.	
Maybe.	可能。 Ke neng.	
Wait awhile.	等一会。 Deng yi hui.	

Please tell me how to say this in Chinese.

请告诉我这个用中国话怎么说。

Please say it again slowly.

请再慢一些说一遍。

Would you feel offended if I gave you a small token of my appreciation?

如果我送你一件小纪念品以表示我的谢意，你会不
会不高兴？

It is not necessary.

你不需要这样做。

But you have been so kind and I feel I will be indebted to you for the rest

of my life. 但是你对我这样好，使我觉得此生欠了你很大
的情份。

It is not convenient.

我不便接受。

In that case, I will not feel offended.

如果是这样的话，我就不会不高兴了。

Meeting Strangers (Please have someone fill in the blanks beforehand in Chinese.)

Hello.

I am sorry, I do not speak Chinese. 对不起，我不会说中文。

I speak English. 我说英文。

My name is ———.	我的名字是＿＿＿＿＿。
I am from ———.	我是＿＿＿＿人。
I am in China for ——— weeks.	我要在中国＿＿＿＿周。
——— months.	＿＿＿＿个月。
I arrived ———.	我是在＿＿＿＿到的。
I expect to leave ———.	我预定在＿＿＿＿离开。
Please write that down and I will have someone translate it later.	请把它写下来，以后我再找人翻译。
I am visiting ———, ———, ———, ———, ———, and ———.	我将到＿＿＿ ＿＿＿ ＿＿＿ ＿＿＿＿＿＿＿去观光。
Where do you work?	你在哪里工作？
factory	工厂
commune	公社
hospital	医院
office	办公室
restaurant	饭馆
transportation	运输部门
hotel	旅馆
school	学校
cultural organization	文化机构
government organization	政府机构
I am a ———. (profession)	我是一个＿＿＿＿＿（职业）
Do you work in this city?	你在这个城市工作吗？
Where were you born?	你出生在哪里？
How many children do you have?	你有几个孩子？
Are they all in school?	他们都进学校了吗？
How old are they?	他们多大？
How much money do you make a month?	你一个月赚多少钱？
How much do you pay for rent?	你的房租多少？
for food?	你吃饭花多少钱？
What hours do you work?	你什么时间上班和下班？
Do you have any relatives in my country?	你有亲属在我的国家吗？
Do you have any friends in my country?	你有朋友在我的国家吗？
How many years of schooling have you had?	你曾在学校读过多少年书？

How much time have you spent doing manual labor in the countryside?

你下乡干体力劳动的时间有多久？

When was the last time and for how long?

你最后一次是什么时候去的，去了多久？

Expecially for People with Chinese Relatives

I am very happy to meet you.

见到你我很高兴。

Could you join me for a meal?

你能和我一起吃饭吗？

For tea? 你能和我一起喝茶吗？

In the hotel? 我们在旅馆里吃好吗？

Then follow me. 那么，咱们去吧！

In a nearby restaurant? 到附近的饭馆去吃好吗？

Do you know of a good place? 你知道有什么好饭馆吗？

Please lead the way, but you are my
guest. 请你带我去，不过让我请客。

Could you please order? 你点菜好吗？

Anything you like. 随便什么你喜欢吃的菜都行。

I don't know how to do it in
Chinese. 我不知道怎样用中国话说。

Not too much. I don't like to waste
food. 不要点太多菜。我不愿意浪费。

Did you know my father? 你认识我的父亲吗？

Did you know my grandfather? 你认识我的祖父吗？

Have you visited my ancestral
village lately? 你最近去过我的家乡吗？

How is it? 那儿怎么样？

Poor? 挺穷吗？

Prosperous? 富裕吗？

Far away? 很远吗？

Just getting along? 还过得去吗？

Can you take me there for a short
visit? 你能带我去看一看吗？

One of your children? 你的孩子？

Can you help me make
arrangements? 你能帮我安排吗？

As soon as possible. 愈快愈好。

When I get back from my tour. 我参观回来的时候。

Should I make the application now? 我要不要现在就申请？

293

Tomorrow?　明天？

I am sorry I know so little about
you.　我很遗憾对你不够熟悉。

What do you do for entertainment? 你参加什么娱乐活动？

sports?	运动？	movies?	看电影？
parks?	去公园？	visiting friends?	看朋友？
no time?	没有空？	television?	看电视？

How many ration coupons do you
get a month for ———?　你一个月有多少_____？

肉票	meat	公斤	kg.
粮票	grain	斤	catties
布票	cotton cloth	米	meters
油票	cooking oil	两	ounces
肥皂	soap	块	bars

Is it sufficient for your needs?　它够不够？

Do you have ———?　你有_____吗？

a bicycle	一辆自行车
a sewing machine	一架缝纫机
a television set	一个电视机
a fan	一个风扇
a radio	一个无线电
your own kitchen	一个自己的厨房
a refrigerator	一个冰箱
a gas stove	一个煤气炉

Where is the closest school to your
house?　离你家最近的学校在哪里？

primary	小学
middle	中学

Do your children walk to school?
你的孩子是不是步行去学校？

Do your children take a public bus?
你的孩子是乘公共汽车去吗？

How much does it cost for ———? _____是多少钱？

tuition	学费
room and board	膳宿费
university	大学

How many people are there in your household who make money?
你们家里有几人赚钱？

How much money did you all make last year?
去年你们全家的收入是多少？

Do you have any savings?

你们有储蓄吗？

How much did you spend for ———?

你（你们）_____化多少钱？

clothing	穿
food	吃
rent	房租
entertainment	娱乐
transportation	交通
medical expenses	医药
per month? 一个月？	per year? 一年？

May I see your house?

我能看看你的房子吗？

How many people sleep here?

多少人睡在这里？

Where do they all sleep?

他们都睡在哪里？

Who does the cooking?

哪一位烧饭？

Who takes care of the children while you are working?

你上班的时候，谁照顾孩子？

Do you have a clinic with a full-time doctor nearby?

你们附近有没有一个长驻大夫的诊所？

How much does it cost for a visit if you are sick?

每看一次病要付多少钱？

Do you get your salary if you are sick and cannot work?

如果你病了不能上班，工资是不是照发？

How much does it cost per day in the hospital?

住院一天要多少钱？

How many days maternity leave does a woman get with pay?

有工资的产假是多少天？

If she is nursing her baby, how many hours with pay does she get a day to feed it? 如果自己照顾婴儿，不扣工资的喂奶时间一天有几小时？

How many years of school have you had? 你上过几年学？

primary	小学
middle	中学
university	大学
technical school	技术学校
on-the-job training	在职训练

295

Please forgive me if I am asking too personal questions,

如果我的问题太冒昧，希望能得到你的谅解。

but I am very curious about the way of life in China.

但是我很想知道中国的生活情况。

Are you happy here?

你在这里幸福吗？

Do you like the government?

你喜欢这个政府吗？

Do you want your children to study abroad?

你想让你的孩子到国外去读书吗？

I think I can help you.

我想我可以帮你的忙。

I am sorry I cannot help you.

很抱歉，我不能帮你的忙。

It is very expensive to travel abroad.

出国路费很贵。

It is very expensive to go to school abroad.

到国外读书要化很多钱。

I am not wealthy.

我不是一个富裕的人。

Especially for Communes

What is the name of this ———? 这个_____叫什么？

How many people are there in this ———? 这个_____有多少人？

commune	公社？
production brigade	生产大队？
production team	生产队？
live here	在这里生活。
work here	在这里工作。

How many work points did the average commune worker make last year?

去年公社社员的平均工分是多少？

How many work points would you make per day if you spent the day weeding?

如果是除草，你一天能赚多少工分？

How much money does that mean for last year?

去年那样算有多少钱？

How much money did you make last year?

你去年的收入是多少？

Can a woman make the same amount as a man if she does the same job—like drive a truck?

男女是否同工同酬？例如驾驶卡车。

How big is your private vegetable plot?

你的蔬菜自留地有多大？

(1 hectare = 15 mou; 1 mou = 10 fen)

Do you raise for your own use ———?

你饲养的＿＿＿是给自已吃的吗？

    pigs   猪

    poultry   鸡

Did you raise enough meat to sell some on the free market?

你饲养的家畜和家禽除自已食用，还有没有多余的拿到自由市场去卖？

Did you sell vegetables on the free market?

你在自由市场卖过蔬菜吗？

If so, how much money did you make selling your surplus?

你卖了多少钱？

Your household?

这是你的家吗？

How many earners are there in your household?

你家里有几个人赚钱？

How many people are there in your household?

你家里有几口人？

Is there a barefoot doctor in this production brigade?

这个生产大队有赤脚医生吗？

Are there any urban-educated youth living and working here?

有没有城里的知识青年在这里住和工作？

Is there anyone here who speaks English?

这里有人会说英语吗？

Can I meet them?

我能见见他们吗？

Are your grown-up children living in this village?

你的成年子女住不住在这个村里？

If you are sick and unable to work, does the commune take care of you?

如果你病了不能工作，公社照顾你吗？

Your family?　你家里的人？

What if you have no family?　如果你没有亲属怎么办？

Is there a pension when you get too old to work?

你们有养老金吗？

Do you still have ———? 你们还有_____吗？
    ancestral tablets   祖宗牌位
    ancestral temple   祖庙
    ancestral family book   家谱

Do you decorate the graves during the Ching Ming still?
你们清明还去上坟吗？

Is this pond for fish? 这是养鱼池吗？
               ducks? 这是养鸭池吗？

May I see your ———? 我能看看你们的_____吗？
    composting techniques   堆肥技术
    irrigation system   灌溉系统
    old watchtower   老的守望塔
    retail store   零售店
    tractor   拖拉机
    school   学校
    house   房子
    private plot   自留地
    pigs   猪
    source of drinking water   饮水源
    latrine   厕所
    clinic—for family planning   诊所——负责节育的
    motorized water pumps   机器水泵

Who takes care of the children while you work?
你工作的时候谁照顾孩子？

What is the name of that ———? _____叫什么？
    tree   那棵树
    vegetable   那种菜
    building   那幢房子

Please write down the name here in Chinese so I can have it translated later.
请用中文把名字写在这儿，以后我再让人翻译。

Especially for Factories

How many people work here?
有多少人在这儿工作？

Salary range a month, i.e., lowest–highest?
最高和最低的月工资是多少？

How much do most workers make?
大多数工人的收入是多少？

What is the age range?
最年轻和最老的工人的年纪有多大？

298

How long does it take to make one
of those?

做一个那样的东西需要多长时间？

days	天
months	月
weeks	星期

cooperative? 合作社？
state-owned? 国有的？

Where do you get your raw
materials? 你的原料是从那里来的？

Where do you sell most of your
products? 你的产品大多在那里出售？

Do you have a store where I could buy something like this?

你们有出售这样产品的商店吗？

How old are you?

你多大岁数啦？

How many years have you worked here?

你在这里工作几年啦？

How much money do you make a month?

你一个月赚多少钱？

How many hours do you work a week?

你一星期工作多少小时？

Do you live in factory-provided housing?

你住在厂里给的房子吗？

How much rent do you pay?

房租多少？

How many years of training have you had to do this?

你经过多少年的训练才能做这个工作？

It is interesting.	很有趣
beautiful.	漂亮
very difficult.	很难

SHOPPING

For Daily Necessities

What do you recommend for ———?

_____你说吃什么好？

motion sickness 晕船（晕车）

Do you have any ———? 你有_____吗？

aspirin 阿司匹灵
toothpaste 牙膏

toothbrush	牙刷
razor	剃刀
razor blades	剃刀刀片
toilet tissue	卫生纸
mild soap	咸性不大的肥皂
hand soap	肥皂
laundry detergent	洗衣粉
shampoo	洗头水
sanitary napkins	卫生巾
sanitary belt	卫生带
ball-point pen	圆珠笔
notebook	笔记本
letter-writing paper	信纸
airmail paper	航空信封
envelopes	信封
foreign film	外国胶卷

something to cover this 可以包扎这个＿＿＿＿的东西。

        cut 伤口

        blister 水疱

something to keep my shoe from hurting
有什么东西可以防止我的鞋子把这儿磨疼。

an antiseptic ointment or cream
消灾药膏或软膏

menstrual cramps
月经痛

Mending

Where can I get this mended?	这个在什么地方可以修理？
How soon will it be finished?	多快能修好？
Can it be done faster?	能够快一些吗？
I will have it done later.	我以后再修。
Please do it now.	请你现在就修。
How much will it be?	要多少钱？

You may not be here when I come to get it. Please write down here what I should ask for. 我来取的时侯你可能不在。请将我要取的
东西写在这儿。

Shopping in General

Please show me on the map where there is a ———.
请指给我看地图上哪里是＿＿＿＿＿＿。

Please take me to a ———.

请带我到一个＿＿＿＿＿去。

Please point the way to a ———.

请指给我看到＿＿＿＿＿怎么走。

How many blocks is it?

要过几条街？

left	左面
right	右面
department store	百货商店
foreign-language bookstore	外文书店
cloth store	布店
Arts and Crafts Store	手工艺品商店
Friendship Store	友谊商店
Chinese traditional medicine store	中国药店
antique store	古董铺
more expensive	更贵一些的
less expensive	便宜一些的
bigger	大一点的
smaller	小一点的

Do you have others the same as this?

你还有这样的东西吗？

Different color?

不同颜色的？

Different design?

不同图案的？

How old is this?

这个有多少年了？

Will I be able to take it out of China?

我能把它带出中国吗？

What dynasty?

什么朝代的？

Can you wrap it so it won't break when I mail it?

能不能把它包好免得会在邮寄时打破。

Where can I have this wrapped and shipped?

哪里可以包装及运出这个？

I'm sorry, I don't have ration coupons.

很抱歉我没有布票。（粮票、工业券）

I was told I didn't need ration coupons.

人家告诉我我不需要给布票。

Will you be getting more within the next three days?
三天之内你们会有更多的来货吗？

Can it be washed in soap and water without damage?
这能用肥皂和水洗吗？

Should it be dry-cleaned?
需要不需要干洗？

Arts and crafts—also for Sightseeing

What is it made of? 这是用什么东西做的？

bamboo	竹子	marble	大理石
bone	骨头	metal alloy	合金
brick	砖	mother-of-pearl	螺母
bronze	铜	palm straw	棕榈章
carved	雕刻的	(for baskets	（编篮子和
celadon	青瓷	and mats)	席子用）
ceramic	陶瓷	paper	纸
clay	泥	pearl	珍珠
cloisonné	景泰兰	plastic	胶料
coconut	椰子	rattan	藤
coral	珊瑚	rayon	人造纤维
cotton	棉花	rice husks	谷壳
dough (flour mixture)	揉面	rice paper	宣纸
eiderdown	绒毛	satin	缎子
enamel	搪瓷	silk	丝
filigree	金丝	silver	银
glass	玻璃	soapstone	皂石
glaze	釉料	stone	石头
iron	铁	turquoise	松石
ivory	象牙	wire	铁丝
gold	金	wood	木头
jade	翡翠	wool	羊毛
lacquer	漆器	animal	动物
lapis lazuli	青金石	vegetable	蔬菜
leather	皮子	mineral	矿石
malachite	孔雀石		
(Animate objects)			

What is it? 这是什么？
banyan tree 榕树
bird 鸟

English	汉
bodhisattva (Lohan)	罗佛
Buddha	佛
camel (two-humped)	骆驼（双峰）
cypress tree	柏树
dragon	龙
(five-toed imperial)	五爪龙
dromedary (one-humped)	单峰金骆驼
emperor	皇帝
empress	皇后
fairy	仙女
god	神
goddess	女神
goddess of mercy	观音
flames	火焰
horse	马
imperial family	皇室
lion	狮子
leaders	领袖
Mao Tse-tung	毛泽东
Chou En-lai	周恩来
lotus	莲花
Lu Hsun (author)	鲁迅（作家）
mandarin	橘子
monkey	猴子
mountains	山
mountains of Kweilin	桂林的山
mythical animal	神兽
peach	桃子
phoenix	凤凰
poet	诗人
revolutionary hero	革命英雄
Soldier Lei Feng	战士雷锋
Dr. Norman Bethune	白求恩大夫
revolutionary theme	革命题材
e.g., episodes on the Long March	如长征组歌
scales of the dragon	龙鳞
scholar	学者
temple guardian	庙祝
tiger	老虎
tortoise	龟

303

What language?	哪一国文字？		
ancient Chinese	中国古文	Mongolian	蒙文
Arabic	阿拉伯文	Sanscrit	梵文
Chinese	中文	Tibetan	藏文
Manchu	满族文		

(Inanimate objects)

What is it?	这是什么？
bell	钟、铃
Buddha's footprint	佛的脚印
chariot	战车
cooking utensil	炊具
cosmetic box	化妆品盒
costumes—theatrical	戏装
drum	鼓
fan	扇子
food-serving utensils	餐具
funeral objects (buried with deceased)	陪葬品
gong	锣
house	房子
incense burner	香炉
inkstand	墨水台
jar	坛子
jewelry	手饰
jug	盂
mask—theatrical	戏台用面具
mirror	镜子
moon	月亮
musical instrument	乐器
ornament	装饰品
paperweight	纸镇
pearl (flaming usually)	夜明珠
pillow	枕头
poem	诗
by Chairman Mao	毛主席的诗
snuff bottle	鼻烟壶
spirit screen	招魂幡
toilet box	梳妆盒

tool	工具
toy	玩具
vase	花瓶
water buffalo	水牛
weapon	军器
wheel of the law	法轮
wine goblet	酒杯
yin-yang symbol	太极图
calligraphy	书法
carving	雕刻
copy	抄本、摹本、复制品
drawing	画
embossing	浮雕
embroidery	刺绣
engraving	雕刻
etching	蚀刻
fresco	壁画
handmade	手工的
ink	墨水
machine-made	机制的
original	原本
print	印刷
rubbing	摹拓
scroll	卷轴
sculpture	雕塑品
sketch	速写
watercolor	水彩
woodcut	木刻
woven photograph	丝织像
hand loom	手织机、纺车

Paying

How much does that cost?
那个多少钱？

Please write down that price here.
请你将价钱写在这儿。

That's too expensive
太贵了。

How about half the price? Na ge do shao qian?
半价怎么样？

How much then?

那样是多少钱？

yuan/kwai/renminbi

元／块／人民币

mao (1/10 of a yuan)

毛（１／１０元）

fen (coin)

分（硬币）

Do you know how much that is in U.S. money?

你知道合成美金是多少？

Please bring my bill.

请把帐单给我。

Do I pay you or the cashier?

我把钱付给你还是付给出纳员。

I am leaving early tomorrow morning. Can I pay the bill tonight?

我明天一早就走。我可以不可以在今晚付帐？

May I have a receipt, please?

能给我一个收据吗？

Can I pay with ———?　我能用＿＿＿＿付款吗？

a Bank of China traveler's check	中国银行的旅行支票
a foreign traveler's check	外国旅行支票
a personal check	私人支票
a company check	公司的支票
a credit card	信用卡

BUILDINGS

What is the name of this place?

这个地方叫什么名字？

Please write it in Chinese.

请把它用中文写下来。

What was it before Liberation?

解放前这个地方是做什么用的？

What dynasty was it built in?

它是那个朝代建造的？

What date?

什么年代？

How high is it? 它有多高？

stories? 多少层？

meters? 多少公尺？

Can I get a closer look?	我能走近一些看看吗？
Can I go inside?	我能进去吗？
What direction is it?	这是什么方向？

| north | 北 | bei | south | 南 | nan |
| east | 东 | dong | west | 西 | xi |

ancient?	古代的？
minorities?	少数民族的？
imperial?	宫殿式的？
modern?	现代的？
post-Liberation?	解放后的？
revolutionary?	革命的？
for children?	为孩子的？
for workers?	为工人的？
Is it religious?	是不是宗教性的？
ancestral	祖先的
atheistic	无神论的
Buddhist	佛教的
Christian	基督教的
Confucian	孔教的
Lamaist/Tibetan	喇嘛的／西藏人的
Moslem	伊斯兰教的
Taoist	道教的
Is it any of these?	它是这其中的一种吗？
air-raid shelter	防空洞
apartment building	公寓
aqueduct	沟渠
aquarium	水族馆
archaeological site	考古现场
bridge	桥
cemetery	公墓
church	教堂
cinema	电影院
dagoba (Indian stupa)	舍利子塔（印度神龛）
democracy wall	民主墙
drum or bell tower	鼓或钟楼
exhibition hall	展览馆
fort	堡垒
factory	工厂
garden	花园
gate	大门

hotel	旅馆
house	房子
kiln	窑
library	图书馆
military camp	军营城
moat	护城河
monastery	寺
monument—commemorative	纪念碑
mosque	清真寺
museum	博物馆
observatory	天文台
office building	办公大楼
pagoda	塔
palace	皇宫
park	公园
pavilion	馆、楼阁
playground	操场
restaurant	饭馆
resort	胜地
school	学校
primary	小学
middle	中学
university	大学
shipyard	船坞
shrine	神龛
sports stadium	运动场
stele	石碑
grave	墓
historical event	历史性的
poem	诗
subway	地下铁道
temple	庙院
theater	戏院
tomb	墓
train station	火车站
wall	墙
watchtower	瞭望台
water tower	水塔
zoo	动物园

PHOTOGRAPHY

May I take a photo of you?
　我能给你拍张照片吗？

Please smile.
　请微笑。

Can I have a photo of you and me together?
　我能和你合拍一张照片吗？

I would like to show my friends what nice people there are in China.
　我想让我的朋友看看在中国有多么友好的人。

I would like to show my friends who cannot visit China what things look like here. 我想让我那些不能来访问中国的朋友看看中国是什么样子。

Could you please take my photo in front of this place with my camera?
　请用我的照像机给我在这里拍一张照。

It is all set. Just press here. 都对好了，你只要在这里按一下。

Closer 靠近一些。　　　　　　Back up. 退后一些。

I'm sorry, I don't have any more film.
　对不起我没有胶卷了。

I'm sorry, I didn't know I couldn't take photographs here.
　对不起，我不知道不许在这儿拍照。

May I have my camera back?
　能将我的照像机还给我吗？

Where can I get film developed?
　哪里可以冲洗胶卷？

Black and white?
　黑白的。

Color slides?
　彩色幻灯片？

Color prints?
　彩色照片？

Do you cut the film and mount the slides?
　你们切装幻灯片吗？

How much for each print?
　印一张多少钱？

How long will it take?
　要多长时间？

What size film do you have?
　你们有几号胶卷？

Do you have any foreign film?

你们有外国胶卷吗？

ENTERTAINMENT

Is there a good cultural presentation on now in this city?

现在这里有没有一个好的文艺节目在上演？

movie	电影	ballet	芭蕾舞
acrobats	杂技	traditional opera	京戏
play	话剧	martial arts	武术
puppet	木偶戏	concert	音乐会
Chinese	中国的	foreign	外国的
English subtitles	英文字幕	sports competition	运动比赛

Where can I buy tickets? 在哪里买票？

What is the address?

什么地方？

I would like tickets ———. 我要_____票。

for today 今天的。
for tomorrow 明天的。
for the day after tomorrow 后天的。

What are the times? 有那些时间的？

How much do the best seats cost? 最好的座位多少钱一张？

Do you have seats close to the stage so I can take photographs?

有没有靠近舞台可以让我拍照的位子？

How about an aisle seat?

侧厢的座位怎么样？

Is the theater air-conditioned?

戏院有冷气吗？

Is the theater heated?

戏院有暖气吗？

What time is the performance over?

演出什么时候完？

Will you be my guest?

我请你看好吗？

Can you buy the tickets for me?

你能代我买票吗？

Where will I meet you?

我们在哪里碰头？

What time?

什么时候？

I have to cancel my tickets.

我得退票。

Can I have my money back?

能把钱退给我吗？

Would you like to use my tickets instead?

你愿意要我的票吗？

Can we go backstage to meet the performers?

我们能去后台看看演员吗？

I must tell you how very much I enjoyed the performance.

我一定要告诉你我是多么欣赏你的演出。

I hope someday you can come to perform in my country.

我希望有一天你能来我的国家演出。

May I touch your costumes?

我能摸摸你的戏装吗？

May I touch your musical instruments?

我能摸一摸你的乐器吗？

May I take a photograph with you?

我能和你合拍一张照片吗？

Can you show me how this works?

你能告诉我这个怎么用？

How much training have you had?

你受过多久的训练？

At what age did you start?

几岁开始的？

Will you be giving another performance here?

你在这里还将再演出一次吗？

When?

什么时候？

Will it be the same?

还是这个节目吗？

Where is there a dance party in this city?

这个城市里什么地方有午会？

When? What day and time?

什么时候？那一天？几点钟？

How much does it cost?

多少钱？

MISCELLANEOUS

Colors

red	红色	hong se	blue	蓝色	lang se
orange	橙色	cheng se	purple	紫色	zi se
yellow	黄色	huang se	black	黑色	hei se

| green | 绿色 | li se | brown | 褐色 | he se |

Directions

near	近		far	远	
up	上		down	下	
above	上面		below	下面	
inside	里面		outside	外面	
right	右		left	左	
center	中间				

Months of the Year

January	一月	July	七月
February	二月	August	八月
March	三月	September	九月
April	四月	October	十月
May	五月	November	十一月
June	六月	December	十二月

Days of the Week

Sunday	星期天	Thursday	星期四
Monday	星期一	Friday	星期五
Tuesday	星期二	Saturday	星期六
Wednesday	星期三		

Today, Yesterday, and Tomorrow

today	今天	jin tian
yesterday	昨天	zo tian
tomorrow	明天	ming tian

Seasons

| spring | 春 | cheung | summer | 夏 | xia |
| autumn | 秋 | qiu | winter | 冬 | dong |

Terms and Names

attendant (term used for room boy, waitress)

　　　　fu wu yuan　　　　服务员

interpreter (term used for guide)　　翻译

cadre (also leading member)　　干部

revolutionary committee　　革命委员会

management committee　　管理委员会

party member　　党员

Communist Party of China　　中国共产党

312

Politburo	政治局	
State Council	国务院	
peasant	农民	
worker	工人	
People's Liberation Army	中国解放军	
Four Modernizations	四个现代化	
agriculture	农业	
national defense	国防	
technology	技术	
science	科学	
Is there a campaign on now?	现在有运动吗？	
Chairman Mao	毛主席	
Vice-Premier Teng	邓付主席	
socialism	社会主义	
dictatorship of the proletariat	无产阶级专政	
democratic centralism	民主集中制	
Gang of Four	四人帮	

Numbers

one	一	yi	twelve	十二	shi er
two	二	er	twenty	二十	er shi
three	三	san	twenty-one	二十一	er shi yi
four	四	si	thirty	三十	san shi
five	五	wu	forty	四十	si shi
six	六	liu	fifty	五十	wu shi
seven	七	qi	hundred	百	bai
eight	八	ba	thousand	千	qian
nine	九	jiu	ten thousand	万	wan
ten	十	shi			
eleven	十一	shi yi			

15

MILESTONES IN CHINESE HISTORY

The Chinese interpret history in Marxist terms, pointing out that dynasties fell primarily because of peasant unrest and uprisings. Roughly, this is how they see history:

c. 1,000,000–4000 years ago—primitive society.

c. 21st century–476 B.C.—slave society. Slave holders owned all the means of production including slaves captured in wartime. Slaves were killed and buried with their deceased owners supposedly to continue their work of servitude in the afterworld.

475 B.C.–A.D. 1840—feudal society. While slaves were kept after the end of the 5th century, slave holders ceased to own all the means of production. A new class of landowners found that giving slaves some freedom resulted in better production. Land was contracted to them as serfs in return for a large part of the harvest. If the serf did not produce, the fields were contracted to someone else. The transition to feudal society took place in the Warring States period, and after 476 B.C. slaves were no longer sacrificed.

1840–1919—semi-colonial and semi-feudal society. Pure feudalism ended with the Opium Wars and the advent of foreign domination. In 1919 the May 4th Movement marshaled anti-imperialist and nationalistic sentiments.

The Chinese also call *1912-1927* the period of the First Revolutionary War, which failed when Chiang Kai-shek betrayed the revolution and massacred the Communists. They also consider this war a failure because of the divisions within the Communist Party itself.

August 1927–July 1937 was the Second Revolutionary War, a period of armed struggle against the Nationalists and the warlords from the first armed Communist uprising to the beginning of the Japanese war.

In July 1937 the Japanese invaded China and there was some attempt at cooperation between the Communists and Nationalists again. After the

Japanese surrender in 1945, the civil war resumed. That war and the semi-colonial and semi-feudal society ended with Liberation in 1949. Now is the socialist society.

With earlier dates approximations, the milestones are:

c. 8,000,000 years ago—Ramapithecus (Lufeng, Yunnan).

c. 1,000,000 years ago—Yuanmou Man.

c. 600,000–700,000 years ago—Lantian Man.

c. 400,000–500,000 years ago—Peking Man. (See Zhoukoudian under "Beijing.")

c. 20,000–30,000 years ago—Liuchiang Man (Guangxi), Hotao Man (Inner Mongolia), and Upper Cave Man (Zhoukoudian).

c. 5,000–7,000 years ago—Lungshan Culture (Shandong) and Yangshao Culture (Henan). (See "Xi'an"—Banpo Museum.)

Dynastic dates overlap because different dynasties controlled different parts of China at the same time. Eastern and Western usually refer to periods of the same dynasty with different capitals, e.g., Changan or Luoyang. Northern and Southern Sung refer to the Kaifeng and Hangzhou capitals.

c. 21st–16th centuries B.C.—HSIA: beginning of the slave system; irrigation and flood control work; rudimentary calendar; the earliest form of writing.

c. 16th–11th centuries B.C.—SHANG: earliest glazes, wine, and silk; highly developed bronze casting primarily of ritual vessels; jade handles on swords and spears; ivory cup inlaid with jade; iron; cowry shells used for money; trade outside of China; development of writing; ancestor worship; divination by tortoise shells; beginning of cities (Zhengzhou and Anyang).

c. 11th century—771 B.C.—WESTERN CHOU and 770–249 B.C.—EASTERN CHOU: welded bronze; flat building tiles; first lacquer; copper coins; crossbows; walled cities; elaborate rituals and music using jade as well as bronze vessels.

770–476 B.C.—SPRING AND AUTUMN PERIOD: warring states fighting for power; Confucius preached a return to the Chou rituals and tried to stabilize society by insisting on obedience to the emperor, father, husbands, older brothers, etc. Beginnings of feudalism; cylindrical tile sewer pipes; iron implements and oxen for plowing; steel; metal spade-shaped coins; knowledge of multiplication tables, mathematics, astronomy; medicine.

475–221 B.C.—WARRING STATES: transitional period to feudalism; *Master Sun's Art of War* written; Taoism, Mohism, and Mencius; first large scale irrigation and dams including erosion control; iron farm tools widely used; mining; use of arch in tomb and bridge building; discovery of magnets; carpenter's saw, plane, and square; manure for fertilizer; salt production; medical diagnosis through feeling the pulse; the first books on astronomy.

221–206 B.C.—CHIN: unification of China for the first time; building of Great Wall; standardization of weights and measures; strict legal code; unification of currency; standardization of writing; first clay burial figures; the burning of all historical records except those dealing with the Chin, medicine, and agriculture; the execution of some scholars.

206 B.C.–A.D. 220—EASTERN AND WESTERN HAN: water wheel, windmill, the first plant-fiber paper, seismograph, water-powered bellows for smelting; first important Chinese medical text; the first armillary sphere; the discovery that moonlight comes from the sun; the use of general anaesthesia in surgical operations, and acupuncture and moxibustion; jade burial suits and gold-coated bronze; Szuma Chien, China's first historian.

2nd century B.C.–14th century A.D.—The Silk Road: The Chinese exchanged silk, tea, iron and steel, knowledge of deep-well digging, paper making, peach and pear trees. They received grapes, pomegranate and walnut trees, sesame, coriander, spinach, the Fergana horse, alfalfa, Buddhism, Nestorianism, and Islam. Trade was with India, West Asia, and even Rome, and the main stops in China west from Xi'an were Lanzhou, Wuwei, Dunhuang, north through Turpan or south through Ruoqiang. Arab and Persian traders settled in Xi'an and Yangzhou (Yangchow).

*A.D. 68—*First Buddhist temple built by Emperor Han Ming-ti in Luoyang.

220–265—THREE KINGDOMS (Wei, Shu, and Wu): development of a water pump, celadon, and ships big enough to carry 3,000 men.

265–420—WESTERN AND EASTERN TSIN and 420–589—SOUTHERN (Sung, Chi, Liang, Chen) and NORTHERN (Wei, Chi, Chou) DYNASTIES: first arched stone bridge, widespread use of celadon, two crops a year. Northern Wei dynasty started Buddhist statues at Luoyang and Datong.

581–618—SUI: built the Grand Canal (2,000 km. long), ships up to 70 meters long, and an arched stone bridge still in use today (Zhaoxian county, Hebei).

618–907—TANG: one of China's most prosperous and culturally developed dynasties; three-color glazes, snow-white fine porcelains, inlaid mother-of-pearl, gold and silver, wood-block printing, fine silks, the weaving of feathers; water wheel and adjustable curved-shaft plow; attempt at land reform; the most prosperous period of the Silk Road and the opening of a special office for foreign trade in Guangzhou, a city where a mosque was built by Arab traders; cultural expansion—Tang princess took Buddhism to Tibet; Chinese monks took Buddhism to Japan and Korea (Kyoto is modeled on Xi'an); Chinese monk Hsuan Tsang went to India 629–645 to obtain Buddhist sutras. Chinese travelers also went to Persia, Arabia, and Byzantium; Tang poets still the most famous. Look for fat faces in paintings and sculptures—they are most likely Tang.

907–960—FIVE DYNASTIES (Liang, Later Tang, Later Tsin, Later Han, Later Chou): a transitional warring period.

916–1125—LIAO: controlled Inner Mongolia and part of southern Manchuria; invaded China and occupied Beijing; built extant 66.6-meter wooden pagoda, Ying Xian, Shaanxi.

960–1279—NORTHERN AND SOUTHERN SUNG: another of the most prosperous and culturally developed dynasties; first paper money, moveable type, compass, gunpowder, rocket-propelled spears; fine porcelains; red lacquer; the development of acupuncture and moxibustion; progress in mining and metallurgy; Hangzhou, then known as Qinsai, was the largest, richest city in the world.

1038–1227—WESTERN HSIA: controlled today's Gansu and western Inner Mongolia.
1245—Franciscan friars arrived at Inner Mongolia.

1115–1234—KIN (a.k.a. CHIN): captured Beijing and controlled Kaifeng, the Wei River valley, Inner Mongolia, and northwestern China.

1271–1368—YUAN (a.k.a. Mongol): water clock; improved cotton spinning and weaving; developed blue-and-white and underglaze red porcelain; cloisonné; controlled all of today's China and areas north and east including Moscow, Kiev, Damascus, Bagdad, and Afghanistan.
1275–92—Marco Polo visited China, serving in court of Kublai Khan.

1368–1644—MING: imported corn, potato, tobacco, peanut, sunflower, tomato (seeds that is) from America; refined blue-and-white porcelain; polychrome porcelain; sea links with Malacca, Java, Ceylon, East Africa; opium first introduced as a narcotic.
1513—First European to south China—Jorge Alvares of Portugal.
1557—Macao "lent" to the Portuguese.
1582—First Christian missionary, Matteo Ricci, S.J., to Macao and then in *1601* to Beijing.
1623—Dutch colony in "Formosa," a.k.a. Taiwan—until 1662.

1644–1911—CHING (a.k.a. Manchu): made some of the best porcelains in early part of dynasty; had to cope most with foreign powers; Cheng Chengkung, a.k.a. Koxinga, drove out Dutch from Taiwan; expanded into Russia, Korea, Vietnam, Burma, Sikkim at first, but later lost a great deal of territory.
1683—Taiwan became part of China.
1757—All foreign trade in south confined to Chinese trading associations (Co-hongs) in Guangzhou (Canton). Families of foreign traders live in Macao.
1784—First U.S. trading ship, *Empress of China*—Guangzhou.
1793—First British mission—Lord Macartney.
1807—First Protestant missionary, Robert Morrison of Britain.
1830—First U.S. missionaries.

1839—Chinese attempted to stop opium trade. Burned 20,000 chests near Guangzhou, more than half one year's trade.

1840–42—Opium War, mainly over freedom to trade with China and of course British objection to the government's opium policy. Britain needed to sell China opium to balance trade. British forces with French help seized a few cities along the coast and threatened Nanjing. The Chinese gave in, ceding Hong Kong to Britain and opening to foreign trade Guangzhou (Canton), Xiamen (Amoy), Fuzhou (Foochow), Ningbo (Ningpo), and Shanghai. This was the beginning of the foreign exploitation of a militarily weak and badly led China until 1949. Also involved were Germany, Italy, Japan, Belgium, Russia and the U.S.

1841—Uprising of people of Sanyuanli, Guangzhou, against the foreign imperialists.

1844—Treaty of Wang-hsia. First U.S. treaty with China.

1844—Emperor agreed to tolerate Christian churches.

1848–50—Chinese emigration to America and Australia started.

1851–64—Taiping Heavenly Kingdom, a rebellion against the Manchus led by a Christianity-inspired Cantonese who believed himself the younger brother of Jesus Christ. Starting in January 1851 in Jin Ting Village, Guangxi. This was the largest peasant movement in Chinese history. At one time or another it occupied most of China, including Zhejiang (but not Shanghai), Guilin, Suzhou, and almost Chongqing. It established a capital at Nanjing for eleven years, where there is now a Taiping museum. It was defeated in part by a foreign mercenary army led by a British officer Charles Gordon, known as Chinese Gordon, who was later killed in the Sudan. "Taiping" means "great peace."

1856–60—Second Anglo-Chinese War, a.k.a. Arrow War, and more unequal treaties. British took Kowloon.

1860—British and French sacked Beijing, burned down Summer Palace.

1870—China started to send thirty students a year to U.S. to study. Students also to Britain and France.

1870—Tientsin Massacre of French missionaries (see "Tianjin").

1885—French took Vietnam (then a tributary state of China) and turned over Taiwan and Pescadores to China.

1886—British took Burma.

1895—Sino-Japanese War. Japan took Taiwan, the Pescadores, and the Liaoning peninsula from China.

1898—Britain leased area north of Kowloon and about 235 islands around Hong Kong for 99 years.

1898–1908—The Kuang Hsu Emperor kept under house arrest by Empress Dowager Tzu Hsi for defying her and passing reforms that attempted to modernize China.

1899—"Open Door" notes on China, whereby the U.S. unilaterally declared that foreign powers should not cut up China into colonies, that all nations should be free to trade with China. Only Britain bothered to reply, but because of these notes, China looked for a while to the U.S. as its only foreign friend.

1900—Boxer Rebellion, a.k.a. the Rebellion of the Society of the Righteous and Harmonious Fists, a reaction, at times encouraged by the Manchu Empress Dowager, against the increasing foreign domination of China. Attacks on foreigners and Chinese Christians. (See "Beijing.") Foreign powers, including the Americans, responded by capturing Beijing, sacking it, and forcing another humiliating treaty on China.

1904—Russian-Japanese War fought on Chinese soil. A year later southern Manchuria taken by Japanese.

1908—Death of Empress Dowager. Succeeded by two-year-old Pu-yi.

April 1911—Most important of several small abortive attempts by Dr. Sun Yat-sen against the Qing. Huanghuagang Insurrection, Guangzhou.

October 10, 1911—First victory of Sun Yat-sen's republican revolutionists following an accidental explosion in one of their bomb factories. Hankou.

January 1, 1912—Dr. Sun Yat-sen declared provisional president of the Chinese Republic, with its capital at Nanjing.

1912—Outer Mongolia with Russian help declared independence from China.

1913—Yuan Shih-kai elected president of the new republic.

August 27, 1914—Japan declared war on Germany. Under guise of attacking German concession at Kiaochow Japanese troops gained foothold in China, also taking over naval base at Qingdao (Tsingtao).

1915—Yuan agreed to many of Japan's Twenty-one Demands. Much protest. More protest after Yuan proclaimed himself emperor.

June 11, 1916—Death of Yuan in Beijing of heart attack. Warlords controlled country.

1917—China sent coolies to France to dig trenches along Western Front.

1919—Versailles Treaty concluding World War I. Japanese kept gains in China. Western powers retained their pre-war concessions.

May 4, 1919—Student demonstrations against the Versailles Treaty mark the beginning of the nationalistic and cultural upsurge known as the *May Fourth Movement,* the training ground for many Communist revolutionaries.

July 1, 1921—Founding of the Chinese Communist Party in Shanghai with Russian Communist help, although the Soviets, for tactical reasons, preferred to support Sun Yat-sen.

1923—Sun Yat-sen agreed to cooperate with Russian and Chinese Communists. Chiang Kai-shek sent to Moscow for military training. Mikhail Borodin and General Vassily Blucher arrived as advisers. Communists were allowed to join the Nationalist Party as individuals. Sun Yat-sen could not be sure of help from Britain and America.

1924—Chiang Kai-shek established Whampoa Military Academy, Guangzhou, with Chou En-lai in charge of political indoctrination. The Soviet Union voluntarily gave up privileges and concessions in China and recognized Outer Mongolia as part of China.

March 12, 1925—Dr. Sun died of cancer in Beijing.

May 30, 1925—Demonstrations in the International Settlement in Shanghai.

1926—Northern Expedition started out led by Generalissimo Chiang Kai-shek and Whampoa-trained officers with Communist cooperation and Soviet supplies. It attempted to unify China, wrest control from the warlords, and fight the unequal treaties. The Nationalists aimed for support from merchants, landlords, and warlords; the Communists concentrated on the peasants and urban proletariat.

March 1927—The Northern Expedition took Nanjing.

April 12, 1927—Chiang purged Communists in Shanghai. Chou En-lai escaped. Chiang later killed Communists in other cities.

August 1, 1927—Nanchang Uprising. Founding date of the Chinese Red Army. (See "Nanchang.")

April 18, 1927—Chiang declared Nanjing his capital.

September 8, 1927—Autumn Harvest Uprising led by Mao. Miners from Anyuan, some students, peasant cadres, and a peasant militia set out to take Changsha. Ill-prepared, they withdrew to Jinggang Shan (Chingkang Mountains), Jiangxi (Kiangsi), where they met up with the army from the Nanchang Uprising and established the first Chinese soviet, distributing land to the peasants in the area.

June 4, 1928—Nationalists took Beijing, renaming it Peiping (Northern Peace).

1930—Communists unsuccessfully attacked Nanchang and Changsha. Chiang retaliated with three "extermination" campaigns which almost succeeded against Jinggang Shan.

September 18, 1931—Japanese invaded Manchuria and set up puppet government under Pu-yi. Chiang returned to Nanjing to head the defense. With no international help available, Chiang accepted a humiliating truce in 1933.

1933—Chiang renewed attack on Communists on Jinggang Shan with a "scorched earth" policy.

October 16, 1934—The Communists, aware they could no longer hold their base on Jinggang Shan, started out with 80,000 troops on what is now known as the *Long March*. It was not until they arrived three months later in Xunyi (Tsunyi), Guizhou (Kweichow), that they decided on northern Shaanxi as their goal, since that was the only Communist base big enough. In addition, there was the added incentive of being able to fight the Japanese invaders in that area. At that meeting also, Mao Tse-tung took over as leader of the March.

From Xunyi, the march continued in spite of Nationalist bombs and persistent Nationalist pursuers. The major battles were fought at Loushan Pass (February 1935) and Luting suspension bridge over the Tatu River, which forward units had to cross on its three chains under fire, the enemy having ripped up most of the wooden floor boards. There were uninhabited grasslands, snow-capped 16,000-foot mountains, and hostile tribesmen. Edgar Snow gives a good account of the march in *Red Star Over China*. Some of the important battles have been immortalized in ivory or porcelain.

During the Long March, the original Central Army was joined by other Communist armies. It officially ended in Wuqi in northern Shaanxi on October 20, 1935. For the original marchers now reduced to 8,000, including thirty women, it had been a journey of 12,500 kilometers.

From Wu Qi, the Communists eventually moved to Bao An where Edgar Snow visited them and researched his classic book. The move to Yan'an was made in January, 1937 (see "Yan'an").

1934—Chinese Communists declared war on Japan but Chiang concentrated on eliminating the Communists.

1936—Xi'an Incident. Chiang kidnapped by one of his own officers at Huaching Hot Spring and forced into a wartime coalition with the Communists against the Japanese.

July 7, 1937—Marco Polo Bridge Incident. Killing of Japanese soldiers near Beijing set off *1937–45* war between Japan and China. Japan occupied most urban areas. Chiang moved capital to Hankou and finally to Chongqing (Chungking). Western powers remained neutral. Many warlords with their private armies rallied in fight against Japanese. Badly armed, the warlords were destroyed.

Although Nationalists blocked supply routes, Communist Eighth Route Army and New Fourth Army waged guerrilla warfare against Japanese, engaged in political and economic work among peasants, and developed strategy, discipline, and plans for takeover of rest of China. (See "Yan'an.")

1938—Canadian surgeon Dr. Norman Bethune joined Eighth Route Army and died the following year of blood poisoning while operating without antiseptics. Because of his skills at improvisation and selfless devotion to duty, Bethune later became a Chinese national hero. (See "Shijiazhuang.")

December 7, 1941—The U.S. declared war after Japan's attack on Pearl Harbor. It increased aid to Chiang via the Burma Road until 1942, and then via transport planes over the Himalayan "hump" to Chongqing and Kunming. U.S. tried to reconcile Mao and Chiang against the Japanese.

1943—Treaties with U.S. and Britain abolishing concessions and extraterritorial rights. At the Cairo Conference, Chiang promised to make more effort to fight Japan; Roosevelt and Churchill promised more military aid and China's repossession of Manchuria, Taiwan and the Pescadores after Japan's defeat.

February 1945—Yalta Conference declared Outer Mongolia to be independent, Manchuria to be under Russian sphere of influence.

August 6 & 9, 1945—U.S. dropped atomic bombs on Hiroshima and Nagasaki, Japan. Russia invaded Manchuria.

August 14, 1945—Japanese surrender. Lin Piao, leading Communist Army, advanced into Manchuria to receive Japanese surrender. U.S. transported Nationalist army north also to receive Japanese surrender. Chou En-lai and Mao Tse-tung met with Chiang in Chongqing.

October 1945—Nationalists and Communists clashed in Manchuria.

November 1945—Chongqing talks broke off. U.S. President Truman ordered end of all aid to Nationalists, because the U.S. would otherwise be involved in a civil war. Civil war continued. Communists advanced because of severe inflation, Nationalist government corruption, breakdown of law and order, mass Nationalist troop defections, and the Communists' exemplary work in winning the hearts and minds of the peasants.

October 1, 1949—Known as *Liberation*. Chairman Mao proclaimed the birth of the People's Republic of China from the Gate of Heavenly Peace in Beijing. Later Chiang and troops and officials loyal to him fled to Taiwan. Refugees flooded Hong Kong. Communists tried but failed to take offshore islands of Matsu and Quemoy across from Taiwan.

December 1949—Mao visited Moscow.

February 1950—Sino-Soviet Treaty of Friendship and Alliance.

1950—Trials started against landlords. Two million people believed executed. Social reforms instigated. Remolding of intellectuals.

January 5, 1950—Britain resumed diplomatic relations.

1950–1953—Land reform. .15–.45 acres per peasant.

1950–51—Campaign to assert control over Tibet opposed by Khamba tribesmen. People's Liberation Army (PLA) took Tibet, September 1951.

1950—North Korea invaded south. In October, Chinese forces joined North Koreans after United Nations and South Koreans counterattacked north of 38th parallel border and threatened China.

In China, many foreign missionaries, teachers, and scholars jailed and then expelled as imperialist spies. China accused U.S. of poison gas and germ warfare and circulated maps showing American bases surrounding China. U.S. and Canada decided against resuming diplomatic relations.

1951—Americans began an embargo which wasn't lifted until the 1970s.

1953—China started to use Hong Kong and Macao as trading centers and sources of foreign exchange.

1954—Chiang signed mutual defense treaty with U.S.; French defeat and beginning of U.S. involvement in Indochina.

1954–55—Countryside reorganized into cooperatives with pooling of labor and land.

1955—Bandung Conference of nonaligned nations of Asia and Africa to continue "struggle against imperialism and colonialism" and to assert idea of peaceful coexistence. Attended by Chou En-lai.

1955—Khamba rebellion in Tibet. Dalai Lama fled to India.

1956–57—Hundred Flowers Movement. Free expression of opinion temporarily encouraged.

1957—Anti-Rightist Campaign. Public criticism and jailing of "Rightists," many of whom were not released until 1978.

1958–60—Great Leap Forward. Mobilization of masses to increase production; communes established; backyard furnaces smelted scrap metals. Mao resigned presidency to concentrate on this campaign, which apologists claim succeeded because it mobilized the masses. In 1979 the Chinese leadership admitted it was an economic disaster.

August 1958—Chinese attempted to capture Quemoy. Russia refused to give help, except to threaten retaliation if the Americans intervened. Nationalist air force outfought the Communists.

1959—Mao accused Russians of being revisionists, or giving in to capitalism and to nuclear blackmail. Chinese rejected Russia's offer of nuclear weapons in exchange for bases in China.

June 1960—Bucharest Conference. Rift between Russia and China became extremely bitter.

1959–62—Period of extreme economic difficulties due to "natural calamities." Some scholars also blame bad planning. Government insisted on repaying Russians for military aid immediately.

August 1960—Khrushchev ordered end of all Soviet aid to China. Advisers left many unfinished projects and took the plans back to Russia.

1962—Liu Shao-chi became president. Mao chairman of the Communist Party.

October 1962—India asserted control of disputed border territory. China sent punitive invasion force into India. It defeated the Indians and then unilaterally announced ceasefire in November and withdrew.

1963—China started to supply Hong Kong with fresh water.

October 1964—First atomic bomb exploded at Lop Nor testing grounds in Xinjiang (Sinkiang).

1964—Chiang Ching, wife of Mao Tse-tung, started campaign to make culture serve the revolution. Traditional Peking opera abolished. From this time until her downfall, only eight revolutionary operas allowed, all written by committees.

1965—PLA under Lin Piao abolished all outward display of rank.

November 1965—Publication of article instigated by Mao in a Shanghai daily *Wen Hui Pao* brought the Cultural Revolution into the public eye for the first time.

May 25, 1966—First important "Big Character Poster" put up at Beijing University.

July 29, 1966—Chairman Mao swam the Yangtze River at Wuhan (9 miles) to show he was still powerful.

August 18, 1966—First of many Red Guard rallies in Tian Anmen Square, Beijing, in support of Chairman Mao with PLA Commander Lin Piao at his side. Schools closed so that students could travel and learn how to make revolution. From this time until the end of the Cultural Revolution, much violence took place; the British embassy was sacked (August 22, 1967) by a group of extremists called the May 16th Detachment, which also took over the Foreign Ministry and the media at the same time.

The *Great Proletarian Cultural Revolution* was started by Chairman Mao to regain lost power, an attempt to return to his ideals of the Chinese Communist revolution. Supporters of "revisionism" as propagated by President Liu Shao-chi had been promoting, among other things, an intellectual elite and an urban base. One big quarrel was over which incentives to use to increase production: bonuses versus pure political idealism. Liu wanted bonuses. (He was to succeed in 1978.)

Chairman Mao had always taught that the workers and the peasants, not the intellectuals, are the basis of the Chinese revolution. So as Mao regained his power with Red Guard and army help, many party cadres were sent to May Seventh Cadre Schools to be reeducated in the "correct" political thinking by learning to respect and love physical labor. Police chiefs pounded beats; doctors swept floors to help them identify with the masses and understand their problems. Officials who took privileges like personal use of office cars and the acceptance of "gifts" were violently attacked.

Red Guards, riding free on the trains and sleeping in school dormitories while fed by the municipalities, traveled around the country taking part in revolutionary movements such as the "Four Olds." In this, they physically destroyed many religious statues, buildings, ancestral tablets, and opposed many of the old virtues like long life, happiness, and personal wealth. They changed the names of streets and parks from old dynastic names to "The East Is Red" and "Liberation," stripped some women of their tight trousers (it was the style then), and cut off long "bourgeois" hair. They sought to eliminate "old ideas, old culture, old customs, and old habits." They also attacked elements of foreign influence. They believed all these were obstacles to completing the course of the revolution. Teng Hsiao-ping was denounced. Liu was deposed in 1968 and has since died. He was officially rehabilitated in 1979.

1967—Communist-inspired riots in Macao and Hong Kong.

1969—Border clashes with Soviet Union. Schools reopened with emphasis on "more red than expert." Students were chosen for university, after they completed at least two years of manual labor, by fellow peasants and workers according to level of political consciousness—how well they knew Maoist theory and how enthusiastic and selfless they were in serving the people.

1970—First Chinese satellite launched.

1971—U.S. Secretary of State Dr. Henry Kissinger and U.S. table tennis team visited China. Lin Piao accused of plotting to overthrow Mao, killed in plane crash while fleeing to Soviet Union. Death announced in 1973. China took United Nations seat from Taiwan. Canada resumed diplomatic relations.

1972—President Richard Nixon's historic visit.

1973—Campaign criticizing Lin Piao and Confucius. Teng Hsiao-ping rehabilitated and became Vice-Premier in charge of planning.

1974—Chinese aided Frelimo guerrillas in Mozambique and Angolan guerrillas against Portuguese. Asserted control in Paracel Islands. Seized stray Russian helicopter. One million Soviet troops along border. Russian tanks within 600 miles of Beijing. Teng Hsiao-ping announced Three Worlds policy in speech to United Nations.

1975—Death of Chiang Kai-shek in Taiwan.

January 1976—Death of Premier Chou En-lai. Succeeded by Teng Hsiao-ping (Deng Xiao-Ping) as acting premier.

April 1976—Tian Anmen incident (see "Beijing"). Supporters of Chou put wreaths on monument honoring former premier. Chiang Ching, Mao's wife, ordered removal. Clash ensued. Teng blamed.

July 1976—Tangshan earthquake. China refused all outside help.

September 9, 1976—Death of Mao Tse-tung. Hua Kuo-feng succeeded.

October 6, 1976—Gang of Four arrested. *The Gang of Four,* along with Lin Piao, are blamed for many of the country's ills. They are Chiang Ching, widow of Chairman Mao, and three leaders from Shanghai who rose to prominence during the cultural revolution.

1977—Split with Albania, for many years China's only ideological friend.

August 1977—Teng completely rehabilitated. Resumed previous posts.

January 1, 1979—The U.S. and China resumed full diplomatic relations.

February 1979—Vice-Premier Teng visited U.S.

February 17–March 16, 1979—Because of continued Vietnamese "armed incursions" Chinese forces invaded Vietnam. Border clashes since then.

March 1979—Government bans wall posters critical of Communists. See chapter 8 and INTRODUCTION.

January 1, 1980—First of series of new laws on crime and judicial procedures officially came into effect.

1980–81—Multicandidate county-level elections.

1980—Zhao Ziyang succeeded Hua Guo-feng as premier. Leaders tried to improve living standards and eliminate "left deviation, i.e. over-rigid and excess control of economic system, the rejection of commodity production, and the mistaken attempt to transfer prematurely the ownership of all enterprises to the state." Admitted financial deficit. Began economic reassessment and retrenchment. Banned all Democracy Walls.

December 1980—Pan-Am flew first direct U.S.-China flight in 30 years. China protested Netherland's plan to sell two submarines to Taiwan.

February 1981—Chiang Ching (Jiang Qing) and one other member of the Gang of Four given suspended death sentences following November trials. Other members given long prison sentences.

June 1981—Hu Yaobang replaced Hua as Chairman of the Communist Party.

Also see INTRODUCTION

ᘑ16ᘒ

IMPORTANT ADDRESSES AND INFORMATION

SOME CHINESE MISSIONS ABROAD

Telephone

Embassy of the People's Republic of China
2300 Connecticut Avenue, N.W.
Washington, DC 20008, U.S.A.

202-797-8909 (visa)
202-797-9000 (chancery)

Consulate General of the People's Republic of China
3417 Montrose Boulevard
Houston, TX 77066, U.S.A.

Permanent Mission of the People's Republic of China to the United Nations
520 12th Avenue
New York, NY 10036, U.S.A.

Consulate General of the People's Republic of China
1450 Laguna Street
San Francisco, CA 94115, U.S.A.

Embassy of the People's Republic of China
415 St. Andrew Street
Ottawa, Ontario, Canada K1N 5H3

(613) 234-2706
234-2682
234-2718

Consulate General of the People's Republic of China
3380 Granville Street
Vancouver, B.C. V6H 3K3, Canada

Embassy of the People's Republic of China
31 Portland Place
London W1, England

(01) 636-5726

Embassy of the People's Republic of China
11, Avenue Georges V
75008 Paris, France

256.04.24
256.20.30
256.04.25

Embassy of the People's Republic of China
Inkognitogt. 11
Oslo 2, Norway

44 96 74
(Oslo) 44 74 91

Embassy of the People's Republic of China
Kalcheggweg 10
Bern, Switzerland

(31) 447333

	Telephone
Embassy of the People's Republic of China Konrad Adenauer Allee 104 5307 Wachtberg-Niederbachem, West Germany	02221 (Bonn)/345051
Embassy of the People's Republic of China 247 Federal Highway Watson, Canberra, A.C.T. 2602, Australia	412447 412446
Embassy of the People's Republic of China 22/6 Glenmore St. Wellington, New Zealand	721382 721383
Embassy of the People's Republic of China 2038 Roxas Boulevard (Consulate), Metro Manila, or 4896 Pasay Road, Dasmarinas, Metro Manila Philippines	57.25.85 86.77.15
Embassy of the People's Republic of China 5-30 Minami Azabu, 4-chome Minato-ku, Tokyo, Japan	446-6781

SOME FOREIGN MISSIONS IN CHINA
See chapter 18, DIRECTORY, "Beijing."

SOME FOREIGN ORGANIZATIONS IN CHINA
Canada-China Trade Council, Beijing Hotel Room 1109, Beijing
National Council for U.S.-China Trade, Beijing Hotel, Suite 1136, Beijing
Foreign Affairs Department, Academy of Sciences, Wen Ching Chieh No. 3, Beijing
Foreign Affairs Department, Scientific and Technical Association, Beijing
Chinese Medical Association, c/o Academy of Sciences, Wen Ching Chieh No. 3, Beijing
All-China Sports Federation, Beijing
Information Department, Ministry of Foreign Affairs, Beijing
Committee for Cultural Relations with Foreign Countries, Beijing
Chinese People's Association for Friendship with Foreign Countries, Beijing
Chinese People's Institute for Foreign Affairs, Beijing
Chinese Mountaineering Association, Beijing

Airlines. (See Beijing and Shanghai.)

Bank Representatives. These can usually only give advice. Most are not branches and therefore cannot handle daily banking business.

Bank of America
23 Qian Men Dong Dajie

Beijing   552685

Banca Commerciale Italiana
Suite 5022, Beijing Hotel
Beijing   552231, ext. 5022, 5137, or 5138

Barclays International
Exhibition Center Hotel
South Building, Block 1
Xi Zhi Men Wai St.
Beijing   890541, ext. 466/7

The Chartered Bank
4th floor, 185 Yuan Ming Yuan Lu
Shanghai   214245 or 218858

The Chartered Bank
Room 560, Dongfang Hotel
Guangzhou   69900

Chase Manhattan
Beijing Hotel, Suite 1509 or 1522
Beijing   552231

The First National Bank of Chicago
Beijing Hotel 7022
Beijing   558331

The Hongkong and Shanghai Banking Corporation
Room 8024
Beijing   556257

The Hongkong and Shanghai Banking Corporation
Room 660, Dongfang Hotel
Guangzhou

The Hongkong and Shanghai Banking Corporation
185, Renmin Ren Lu
Shanghai   218383

Midland Bank Group
Room 4088, West Wing, Beijing Hotel
Beijing   552231, ext. 4088

Royal Bank of Canada
Beijing Hotel
Beijing   552231, ext. 5088

CHINA INTERNATIONAL TRAVEL SERVICE

Head Office: 6 Chang'an Dong Ave., Beijing.   551031 or 557217.
Cable: LUXINGSHE BEIJING   Telex: 22350 CITSH CN.

Branches and Sub-Branches: (Some C.I.T.S., C.T.S., and Provincial Travel Offices are in the
same building)
NOTE: It is always best to have someone call for you in Chinese.

Anshan	Anshan Hotel	4403
Baotou		
Beidaihe	Beidaihe Travel Co.	2748
Beijing	2, Qianmen Dong Ave.	757181 or 755374
Changchun	2, Stalin Ave.	38459
Changsha	130, Sanxin St.	22250, 24855, or 27356 (English)
Chengdu	Jinjiang Hotel, Room 129	28226 or 24481, ext. 129
Chongqing	People's Hall, Renmin Rd.	51449
Dalian	56, Fenglin St.	35795

		Telephone
Datong	1st floor, Revolutionary Committee	2704
Fuzhou	May 4th St.	33962
Guangzhou	179, Huanshi Rd.	32648 or 33454
Guilin	14, Ronhu Bei Rd.	3870 or 3628
Hangzhou	10, Baochu Rd.	22487
Harbin	124, Dazhi St., Nangang District	33001 or 31495
Hefei	Jianghuai Hotel, Changjiang Rd.	2221 or 2227
Huangshan	Tuhua Guest House	43 or 44
Huhhot	Guest House	4494
Jilin	661, Songjiang Rd.	27141 or 27142
Jinan	240, Jingsan Rd.	35351
Jiujiang	Nanhu Guest House, 7 Nanxi Rd.	4015 or 3390
Kaifeng	No. 102, Ziyou Rd.	3737
Kunming	Huashan Xi Rd. 145, Tung Feng Ave.	2192, ext. 362 39621
Lanzhou	Friendship Hotel, 14 Xijin Rd.	49621
Liuzhou	Liuzhou Hotel	3379
Luoyang	c/o Friendship Hotel	2139
Lushan	443 Hedong Rd.	2497
Nanchang	Jiangxi Hotel, Ba Yi Ave.	62571
Nanjing	313 Zhongshan Bei Rd.	85921, ext. 115
Nanning	Xinmin Rd.	2042 or 4793
Ningbo	Overseas Chinese Hotel	3175
Qingdao	9, Qingdao Nan Rd.	28877

		Telephone
Shanghai	59 Xianggang Rd.	217200
	66, Nanjing Dong Rd.	214960
	Peace Hotel	217117
	Tourism Corp.	
	14 Zhongshan Rd.	219341 or 219305
Shenyang	2, Sec. 6, Huanghe St.	24653 or 34653
Shenzhen	Luohu	2241 or 2243
Shijiazhuang	Weiming Rd.	8962
Suzhou	115, Youyi Rd.	4646, ext. 375
		4646, ext. 97
Taiyuan	Ying Ze St.	29155
Tianjin	55, Chongqing Rd.	32107 or 34831
Wuhan	1395, Zhongshan Ave.	25018
Wuxi	7, Xinshen Rd.	25416
Xi'an	Renmin Hotel	21191 or 25111
Xiamen	444, Zhongshan Rd.	4286 or 2729
Xilinhot	Simeng Hotel	
Yangzhou	Xi Yian Hotel	22805
Yan'an	c/o Yan'an Guest House	2363, 2767, or 2252
Yixing	Yixing Hotel	
Zhengzhou	No. 8, Jinshuihe Rd.	5578
Zhenjiang	407, Zhongshan Rd.	23281 or 24663
Zibo	Zibo Guest House	22038

CHINA TRAVEL SERVICE, Guangdong Province

Guangzhou	4, Qiaoguang Rd.	61112
Shenzhen	Heping Rd.	2243
Shantou	Shan Zhang Rd.	2149
Foshan		86292

331

Foshan District	61, Weiguo Rd. Foshan	87209
Conghua Hot Spring		County Switchboard
Jiangmen	Gangkou Rd.	33137
Xinhui	Zhongxin Rd.	62419
Chaozhou	Hetou Xihao Rd.	391
Hainan Administrative Area Branch	Fangxiu Rd., Haikou City, Hainan Island	Switchboard
Zhaoqing District Branch	Star Lake	
Zhaoqing	16, Jiangbin Rd.	4126

HOTELS IN SOME TOURIST CITIES

NOTE: The spelling of hotel names is not always consistent. The words "hotel" and "guest house" here are interchangeable, with no regard for size or quality. In Chinese, *binguan* usually means the best and biggest, *fandian* means restaurant or hotel, *luguan* or *ludian* means a small hotel or hostel. For hotels in Beidaihe, Beijing, Guangzhou, Guilin, Luoyang, Lushan, Nanchang, Nanjing, Shanghai, Suzhou, Tianjin, Xi'an, Yan'an, and Zhenjiang, see DIRECTORY.

It is always best to have someone call for you in Chinese.

City	Hotel	Telephone
Anshan	Anshan Hotel	4403
	Shinglee (Victory) Hotel	
Baotou	Kunqu Hotel, Kun Du Luen District	
Changchun	Baishan Guest House, Xinmin Square	53693
	Nanhu Guest House, Nanhu Ave.	53571
Changsha	Hunan Hotel, Yingbin Rd.	26331
	Xiangjiang Hotel, Zhongshan Rd.	26261
Chengdu	Jingjiang Hotel, Renmin Nan Rd.	24481
Chongqing	Renmin Hotel, Renmin Rd.	53421
	Chongqing Hotel, Minsheng Rd.	53158
Dalian	Nanshan Hotel, 56, Fenglin St.	25103
	Bangchuidao Hotel,	25131

City	Hotel	Telephone
	Bangchuidao Dalian Guest House, 3, Zhongshan Rd.	23111
	Dalian Hotel, 6, Shanghai Rd.	23171
Datong	Yungang Hotel	
Fuzhou	Minjiang River Guest House, May 4th St.	
Hangzhou	Hangzhou Hotel, Huanhubei Rd.	22921
	Xiling Guest House, Huanhubei Rd.	22921
	Huagang Hotel, Huanhuxi Rd.	24001
	Hua Jia Shan Guest House, Huanhuxi Rd.	26450
	Zhejiang Guest House, Huanhuxi Rd.	24483
	O.C. Hotel, Hubin Rd.	23401
Harbin	Guoji Hotel, 124 Dazhi St.	31431
Hefei	Jianghuai Hotel, Changjiang Rd.	2221 or 2227
Huhhot	Huhhot Guest House	
Jilin	Dongguan Guest House, 223 Songjiang Ave.	23555 or 23556
	Xiguan Guest House, 661 Songjiang Ave.	27141 or 27142
Jinan	Jinan Hotel, 240, Jingsan Rd.	35351
	Nanjiao Hotel, 2, Maanshan Rd.	23931
	Qilu Hotel (1983), Qianfoshan Rd.	43423
Jiujiang	Nanhu Hotel, 7, Nan Xi Rd.	4015
Kunming	Kunming Hotel, 122, Dongfeng Dong Rd.	2240
	Xiyuan Hotel, Xiyuan	9969
	Qihu Hotel, Qihu Park	3514
Lanzhou	Youyi (Friendship) Hotel, 14 Xijin Rd.	49621
Liuzhou	Liuzhou Hotel	2900

City	Hotel	Telephone
Luoyang	Youyi Hotel	2157 or 6006
Lushan	Lushan Hotel, Hexi Rd.	2932
	Lu Lin Hotel, Hexi Rd.	2424
	Yun Zhong Hotel, Henan Rd. and Hsiang Shan Rd.	2547
Nanchang	Jiangxi Hotel, Ba Yi Ave.	
Nanning	Min Yuan Hotel, Xing Ming Rd.	2986
	Yong Zhou Hotel, Xing Ming Rd.	3120
	Yong River Hotel	3951
	Xi Yuan Hotel	3921
Ningbo	Overseas Chinese Hotel, 100 Liuting St.	3175
Qingdao	Qinqiao Hotel, 31 Qingdao Taiping Rd.	27402
	Huiquan Hotel, 9, Nanhai Rd.	25216
	Badaguang Hotel, Shanhaiguang Rd.	26800
	Overseas Chinese Hotel, Hunan Rd.	27738
	Friendship Hotel, Xinyang Rd.	27779
Shenyang	Huaqiao (Overseas Chinese) Hotel, 3, Sec. 1, Zhongshan Rd.	34214
	Liaoning Hotel, 27, Sec. 2, Zhongshan Rd.	32641
	Liaoning Mansion, 1, Sec. 6, Huanghe St.	62546
	Youyi (Friendship) Hotel, 1, Sec. 7, Huanghe St.	62822 or 61666
Taishan	Stone Flower Mountain Inn	2834
Taiyuan	Yingze Hotel, Yingze St.	23211
	Jinci Hotel, Jinci Nan St.	29941
	Bingzhou Hotel, Yingze St.	25924
	Sanjin Hotel, Yingze St.	23489
	Yu Shan Hotel, Yingze St.	23452
	Tangming Hotel, Yingze St.	25775
Wuhan	Xuangong Hotel, 45 Jianghanyi Rd., Hankou	24404
	Jianghan Hotel, 211 Shengli St., Hankou	21253
	Shengli Hotel, Shengli St., Hankou	22531

334

City	Hotel	Telephone
Wuxi	Taihu Hotel, Huanhu Rd.	23001
	Hubin Hotel, Liyuan	26712
	Shuixiu Hotel, Liyuan	26591 or 23519
Xiamen	Overseas Chinese Hotel, 444 Zhongshan Rd.	2729
Xilinhot	Simeng Hotel	
Xishuang Banna	Xishuang Banna Guest House	
Yangzhou	Xiyuan Hotel, 1, Fung Le Shang Jie	24202 or 24388 22296 or 22298
Yueyang	Jaodaso Hotel	2064
Zhangzhou	Overseas Chinese Hotel	
Zhengzhou	Zhengzhou Hotel, Jinshuihe Rd.	4255 or 4938
Zibo	Zibo Guest House	22138

ADVANCE BOOKINGS OF CHINESE HOTELS

Some agencies in Hong Kong are booking Chinese hotels in advance, an advantage for those who have to know what hotel they will be staying in. The booking fee is included in the price of the room which must be paid in advance. You can save money if you are staying a long time by booking only the first few days. The danger, however, is having to give up your room for someone else if you do this, if the hotel has been completely booked. Agencies like CTS in Hong Kong will make a reservation for a fee, and after that you pay the hotel directly at the lower per diem rate, but they cannot guarantee the hotel of your choice.

As we went to press, some of these agencies said that the Beijing hotels rarely had an opening, but for other hotels, they could book about a week in advance. Some of these agencies reserve a block of rooms, which may have to be booked months in advance. The situation may change in 1982 because of the recentralization of tourism.

Beijing	Yanjing Hotel	Silkways, Pacific World
	Peace Hotel	Good Land Tour, Silkways, Arlymear
	Fragrant Hill Hotel	Pacific World
Guangzhou	Nanhu Hotel	HK and Yaumati Ferry Co.
	Many Guangzhou hotels including Nanhu, Dongfang, Baiyun, Liuhua, Overseas Chinese Mansion, Guangzhou	HK Student Travel Bureau, Vista Travel, Silkways
Guilin	Dangui (Osmanthus) Hotel	Vintex Travel, Silkways
Hangzhou	Hangzhou Hotel, Zhejiang Hotel	Silkways

	XiHu Guest House	Good Land Tour, Arlymear
	Overseas Chinese Hotel	Arlymear
Shanghai	Jing Jiang, Peace, Park, Shanghai Mansions, Jing'an, and Overseas Chinese hotels	Silkways
	Jing Jiang and Shuijin (Water Gold) hotels	Hong Kong Student
	Jing Jiang and Peace hotels	Good Land Tour
	Shanghai Mansions,	Arlymear
	Park Peace, and Jing Jiang hotels	Arlymear
Suzhou	Suzhou Hotel and Nam Lam Hotel	Silkways
Wuxi	Shuixiu Hotel	Silkways
	Hubin Hotel	Arlymear

MAIN CAAC BOOKING OFFICES

		Telephone
Beijing	117, Dongsi Xi Ave.	Int. 556720, Dom. 592361
Changchun	2, Liaoning Rd.	39772 or 39662
Changsha	5, Wuyi Dong Rd.	23820
Chengdu	31, Beixin St.	3038 or 3087
Chongqing	190, Zhongshan San Rd.	52643, 52970, or 52813
Dalian	20, Changtong St.	35884
Fuzhou	Nanmendou	31188
Guangzhou	181, Huanshi Rd.	Int. 34079, Dom. 31460
Guilin	144, Zhongshan Zhong Rd.	3063
Haikou	50, Jiefang Rd.	515
Hangzhou	304, Tiyuchang Rd.	24259
Harbin	85, Zhongshan Rd.	52334
Hefei	73, Changjiang Rd.	3798
Kunming	146, Dongfeng Dong Rd.	4270
Lanzhou	46, Dong-gang Xi Rd.	23432 or 23421
Nanchang	26, Zhanqian Rd.	62368
Nanjing	76, Zhongshan Dong Rd.	43378

Nanning	64, Chaoyang Rd.	3333 or 4272
Qingdao	29, Zhongshan Rd.	26047
Shanghai	789, Yanan Zhong Rd.	Int. 532255, Dom. 535953
Shantou	26, Shanzhang Rd.	2355
Shenyang	31, Dongfeng Ave., Sanduan	33705 or 34944
Tianjin	290, Heping Rd.	24045
Urumqi	Fanxiu Rd.	2536 or 2351
Wuhan	209, Hankou Liji Bei Rd.	51248 or 52371
Xi'an	296, Xishaomen	42264
Yan'an	Dong-guan Airport	2485

CHINA TRADE DIRECTORY

Business people should write directly to any of the following trading corporations relevant to the products they want to buy or sell. People interested in handicrafts can use this list to locate the factories for visits or sales.

CHINA COUNCIL FOR THE PROMOTION OF INTERNATIONAL TRADE
Fuxingmenwai St., Beijing
CHINA NATIONAL CEREALS, OILS AND FOODSTUFFS IMPORT & EXPORT CORP.
82 Donganmen St., Beijing. Branches in Beijing, Shanghai, Guangzhou, Qingdao, Tianjin, Dalian, Fuzhou, Hankou, Changsha, Nanning, Kunming, Zhengzhou, Nanjing, Nanchang, Shijiazhuang, Hangzhou, Chengdu, Changchun, Taiyuan, Xi'an, Harbin, Hefei, Guiyang, Urumqi, Huhhot.
CHINA NATIONAL NATIVE PRODUCE AND ANIMAL BY-PRODUCTS
IMPORT & EXPORT CORP.
82 Donganmen St., Beijing. Branches in Beijing, Shanghai, Tianjin, Dalian, Qingdao, Fuzhou, Guangzhou, Nanning, Hankou, Changsha, Kunming, Nanjing, Shijiazhuang, Taiyuan, Zhengzhou, Chengdu, Harbin, Xi'an, Changchun, Guiyang, Hangzhou, Nanchang, Hefei, Xining, Lanzhou, Urumqi, Yinchuan, Huhhot.
CHINA NATIONAL TEXTILES IMPORT & EXPORT CORPORATION
82 Donganmen St., Beijing. Branches in Shanghai, Beijing, Tianjin, Nanjing, Qingdao, Guangzhou, Dalian, Shijiazhuang, Fuzhou, Zhengzhou, Wuhan.
CHINA NATIONAL LIGHT INDUSTRIAL PRODUCTS IMPORT & EXPORT CORP.
82 Donganmen St., Beijing. Branches in Beijing, Shanghai, Tianjin, Shijiazhuang, Guangzhou, Dalian, Qingdao, Fuzhou, Nanjing, Zhengzhou, Hankou, Changsha, Hangzhou, Chengdu, Xi'an, Changchun, Harbin, Hefei, Nanning, Huhhot, Urumqi.
CHINA NATIONAL ARTS AND CRAFTS IMPORT & EXPORT CORPORATION
82 Donganmen St., Beijing. Branches in Beijing, Shanghai, Tianjin, Guangzhou, Qingdao, Fuzhou, Dalian, Nanning, Changsha, Hankou, Nanjing, Shijiazhuang, Nanchang, Jingdezhen, Zhengzhou, Changchun, Harbin, Hangzhou, Hefei, Kunming, Huhhot.
CHINA NATIONAL CHEMICALS IMPORT & EXPORT CORPORATION
Erligou, Xijiao, Beijing. Branches in Guangzhou, Shanghai, Qingdao, Tianjin, Beijing, Dalian, Nanjing, Fuzhou, Shijiazhuang, Hangzhou.

337

CHINA NATIONAL MACHINERY AND EQUIPMENT IMPORT &
EXPORT CORPORATION
12 Fuxingmen Wai St., Beijing. Branches in Beijing, Shanghai, Tianjin, Dalian, Nanjing,
Qingdao, Shijiazhuang, Nanning, Hangzhou, Guangzhou, Fuzhou.
CHINA NATIONAL METALS AND MINERALS IMPORT & EXPORT CORPORATION
Erligou, Xijiao, Beijing. Branches in Shanghai, Beijing, Tianjin, Guangzhou, Qingdao, Dalian,
Nanning, Kunming, Nanjing, Fuzhou, Shijiazhuang, Hangzhou, Changsha.
CHINA NATIONAL MACHINERY IMPORT & EXPORT CORP.
Erligou, Xijiao, Beijing. Branches in Shanghai, Tianjin, Guangzhou, Qingdao, Dalian, Beijing,
Nanjing, Fuzhou, Shijiazhuang, Hankou, Hangzhou.
CHINA NATIONAL TECHNICAL IMPORT CORPORATION
Erligou, Xijiao, Beijing.
CHINA NATIONAL INSTRUMENTS IMPORT & EXPORT CORPORATION
Erligou, Xijiao, Beijing.
CHINA NATIONAL FOREIGN TRADE TRANSPORTATION CORPORATION
Erligou, Xijiao, Beijing.
CHINA NATIONAL CHARTERING CORPORATION
Erligou, Xijiao, Beijing.
CHINA FOREIGN TRADE CONSULTATION AND TECHNICAL SERVICE CORP.
2 Changan St. E., Beijing. Other foreign trade corporations in Shanghai, Tianjin, Beijing,
Guangzhou, Fuzhou, Dalian.
CHINA GUOZI SHUDIAN (for Chinese publications, paper cut-outs, records, language tapes,
etc.) P.O. Box 399, 21, Chegongzhuang Rd. W., Beijing.
CHINA STAMP CO.
28, Donganmen St., Beijing (for first day covers, souvenir sheets, etc.).
CHINA NATIONAL PUBLICATIONS IMPORT & EXPORT CORPORATION
P.O. Box 88, Beijing (for books, newspapers, periodicals, documents, etc.).
CHINA FILM EXPORT AND IMPORT CORPORATION
25, Xin Wai St., Beijing (sole exporter of Chinese films and importer of foreign films).
BANK OF CHINA
17, Xijiaominxiang, Beijing. Branches in every major city in China; also in Luxembourg, Hong
Kong, London, Singapore, and New York.
CHINA INTERNATIONAL TRUST & INVESTMENT CORPORATION
2 Qianmen Dongdajie, 14/F, Beijing (for joint ventures).

SOME PRIVATE TRAVEL COMPANIES

	Telephone
Arrow Travel Agency Ltd.	5-247788
Room 2101, Alexandra House	5-230790
Hong Kong	
Arlymear Travel Co. Ltd.	3-690011
Suite 614A, Ocean Center	
Tsim Sha Tsui, Kowloon	
China International Convention Service Ltd.	3-7217898-9
Suite 821, Peninsula Center, Ching Yee Rd.	3-7217689-1
Tsim Sha Tsui, Kowloon	
China Youth Travel, All-China Youth Federation	
Room 904, Man Yang Commercial Bank Bldg.	
151 Des Voeux Rd., C.	
Hong Kong	
Compass Travel Ltd.	5-250206
406 Shell House	
Hong Kong	
Crosspoint Tours	Ms. Sero Leung
Room 801, Hung On Mansion	5-8910191
177 Jaffe Rd.	
Wan Chai, Hong Kong	

Good Land Tour and Travel Room 110, Federal Bldg. 369 Lockhart Rd. Hong Kong	5-727670 5-727871
Hang Wai Shipping Co., Ltd. 3/F Chinese General Chamber of Commerce Bldg. 24-25 Connaught Rd., C. Hong Kong	5-501384
Hong Kong Student Travel Bureau Room 1024, Star House Tsim Sha Tsui, Kowloon	3-694847
Hong Kong and Yaumati Ferry Co. Trade Dept., Central Harbor Services Pier 1/F, Pier Rd., C. Hong Kong	5-214428
International Tourism Burfield Bldg. 2/F, 143 Connaught Rd., C. Hong Kong	5-412011 5-449364
Linblad Travel, Inc. 2010 Swire House, 20/F Hong Kong	5-263356
Pacific Delight Tours 4, Carnarvon Rd. 3/F, Lee Kar Bldg. Tsim Sha Tsui, Kowloon	3-692288
Pacific World Ltd. Suite 1630, Hyatt Regency Hotel Kowloon	3-678133
Silkway Travel Ltd. Room 1408, Sincere Bldg. 173 Des Voeux Rd., C. Hong Kong	5-410078
Travel Advisers Ltd. Peninsula Hotel Tsim Sha Tsui, Kowloon	3-698321
United (Tai Shan) Travel 43D, Dundas St. 1/F, Flat B Mongkok, Kowloon	3-320019 3-320010
Vintex Travel Ltd. 48-62 Hennessy Rd. Wah Kwong Bldg., Room 1302 Hong Kong	5-278361 5-279013
Vista Travel Service Room 1109, Lane Crawford House Queen's Rd., C. Hong Kong	5-211251

Voyages Jules Verne	5-7953181
Travel Promotions (H.K.) Ltd.	5-767211, ext. 2210
Office 214, 2/F Arcade	
Lee Gardens Hotel, Hysan Ave.	
Hong Kong	

Welcome Travel & Trading Co. — 3-313422
Room 703, 7/C Kwangtung Provincial Bank Bldg. — 3-309862
589 Nathian Rd.
Mongkok, Kowloon

Westminster Travel — 3-695051
Room 1129, Star House
Tsim Tsa Tsui, Hong Kong

HONG KONG ADDRESSES

China Travel Service (H.K.)
77, Queen's Road, Central, Hong Kong — 5-259121
Cable: TRAVELBANK

Branches:

27-33, Nathan Road, 1st floor — 3-667201
(entrance on Peking Road), Kowloon
(Usually open afternoons on holidays and Sundays)

24-34 Hennessy Road, Hong Kong — 5-280102
Hung Hom Railway Station, Kowloon — 3-330660
Tai Kok Tsui HK/Kwangchow Pier — 3-929403

China National Aviation Corp. (CAAC)
G/F Gloucester Tower, Pedder St. — 5-211314
Hong Kong — 5-211315

Bank of China
2A Des Voeux Road, Central, Hong Kong — 5-234191

American Chamber of Commerce
1030 Swire House, Hong Kong — 5-260165

U.S. Consulate
26 Garden Road, Hong Kong — 5-239011

Office of the Commission for Canada — 5-282222
14/15 floor, Asian House
1 Hennessy Road, Hong Kong

Luxingshe (International) Hongkong Ltd., (C.I.T.S.)
2025, East Wing, Hotel Miramar, 134, Nathan Rd., Kowloon — 3-7215317, 3-681111

Visa Office, Ministry of Foreign Affairs, People's Republic of China
387, Queen's Rd. E., Hong Kong — 5-744163

China Resources Co.
Causeway Center, Gloucester Rd., Hong Kong — 5-7569111

Some Chinese Government Stores, Hong Kong
Chinese Arts and Crafts (H.K.) Ltd.
    Star House (at Star Ferry Terminal), Kowloon

233 Nathan Road, Kowloon
Shell House, Queen's Road Central, Hong Kong

Yue Hwa—Chinese Products Emporium Ltd.
301-309 Nathan Road, Kowloon, tel. 3-840084
54-64 Nathan Road, Tsim Sha Tsui, tel. 3-689165

Some Companies Offering Residential or Commercial Property in China
Busch Worldwide Property Brokerage Ltd.
3701 Windsor House
311 Gloucester Rd., Hong Kong (Shanghai)

Sun Luen Group of Companies
Av. Almeida Ribeiro No. 26-28
6 Andar, Macau (Zhuhai)

Hua Jay Joint Venture Co., Ltd.
98 Wheelock House, 20 Pedder St., Hong Kong (Shenzhen)

Chung-Fat Tai-Tung Property Co.
Flat A 19/F, Wah Kit Commercial Center
300-302, Des Voeux Rd., C., Hong Kong (Shenzhen, Swatow Xiamen, and Guangzhou)

For Background on China
China Liaison Office, World Division
Board of Global Ministries, The United Methodist Church
2 Man Wan Rd., C-17, Kowloon, tel. 3-7135271

The Edgar Snow Society, Sunlight Garden
2 Man Wan Rd., C-17, Kowloon, tel. 3-7135271

Tao Fong Shan Ecumenical Center
P.O. Box 33, Shatin, N.T., Hong Kong, tel. 12-611450

Holy Spirit Study Center
6 Welfare Rd., Aberdeen, Hong Kong, tel. 5-530141

MACAO ADDRESSES

China Travel Service, 33 rua Vis. Paco de Arcos, tel. 3770
International Tourism, 10B rua da Praia Grande, tel. 86522 or 86298
Sintra Tours, Avenida da Amizade, tel. 86394

AUSTRALIA ADDRESSES

Wim J. Bannink, 11 Hamilton Place, Mt. Waverley, Victoria
Marco Polo Travel, 45 Dixon St., Sydney 2000
Minghua Friendship Cruises, Five Shipping & Agency Co. Pty., 7 Bridge St., Sydney 2000
Travman Tours, Hothlyn House, 7th Floor, 233 Collins St., Melbourne, 3000

CANADA ADDRESSES

Canada-China Trade Council, Suite 900, 199 Bay St., Toronto M5J 1L4, Ont. tel. (416)
364-8321
Blyth & Co., 93 Bloor St. W., Toronto, Ont. M5S 1M1, tel. (416) 964-2569
Canadian Friendship Tours, Box 431, Station "K", Toronto, Ont. M4S 1Z7

USA ADDRESSES

Bank of China, 415 Madison Ave., New York, NY 10017
CAAC, 477 Madison Ave., Suite 707, New York, NY 10022, tel. (212) 371-9898

4230E Pan Am Terminal Bldg., J.F. Kennedy International Airport, NY, tel. (212) 656-4722 or (212) 656-4723

1450 Laguna St., San Francisco, CA 94115, tel. (415) 563-4858

National Council for US-China Trade, Suite 350, 1050 Seventeenth St., NW, Washington, DC 20036

National Committee on U.S.-China Relations, 777 United Nations Plaza, New York, NY 10017

Yangtze River Patrol Association, Art S. Boylesen, Sec.-Treas., 417 Chicago, Hastings, NE 68901

China Program Administrative Committee, National Council of Churches, 475 Riverside Dr., 6/F, New York, NY 10115 (for Catholics and Protestants)

Some Travel Companies

Arrow Tours USA, 300 Wilshire Blvd., Los Angeles, CA 90017

American Youth Hostels, 132 Spring St., New York, NY 10012

China Connection, World Trade Center, Ferry Bldg., Room 250 "S", San Francisco, CA 94111

Chinamerican Corp., 471 Fifth St. W, Suite 14, Sonoma, CA 95476

Club Universe, 1671 Wilshire Blvd., Los Angeles, CA 90017

Inter Pacific Travel-in-China, 417 Fifth Ave., New York, NY 10016

Kuo Feng Corporation, 2 East Broadway, New York, NY 10038

Kuoni Travel, Inc., 10880 Wilshire Blvd., Los Angeles, CA 90024 or 770 Lexington Ave., New York, NY 10021

Lindblad Travel, Inc., 8 Wright St., Westport, CT 06880

Mountain Travel, 1398 Solano Ave., Albany, CA 94706

OC Tours, 800 Airport Blvd., Burlingame, CA 94010 tel. (213) 687-6645 or outside CA (800) 227-5083

Orient Paradise Tours, Inc., 31 Pell St., New York, NY 10013

Pacific Delight Tours, 132 Madison Ave., New York, NY 10016 (Offices also in L.A., S.F., Minneapolis, and Seattle)

Pan Asian Travel Headquarters, 652 Kearny St., San Francisco, CA 94108

Silkway Travel & Trading Ltd., 927 Kearny St., San Francisco, CA 94133

Society Expeditions, 723 Broadway East, Seattle, WA 98102

Special Tours for Special People, Inc., 250 West 57th St., New York, NY 10019

Travis Pacific Inc., 210 Post St., Suite 718, San Francisco, CA 94108

Voyages Jules Verne (see Hong Kong), 516 Fifth Ave., Suite 1005, New York, NY 10036

FOR SCHOLARS, STUDENTS, AND FOREIGN EXPERTS

Office of Chinese Affairs, Department of State, Washington, D.C. 20520

Association of Universities and Colleges of Canada, 151 Slater St., Ottawa, Ont. K1P 5N1

Committee on Scholarly Communication with the People's Republic of China, National Academy of Sciences, 2101 Constitution Ave., Washington, D.C. 20418

Social Sciences and Humanities Research Council, 255 Albert St., Ottawa, Ont.

Employment Office, Foreign Experts Bureau, Box 300, Beijing, China. tel. 890621, ext. 2491, or 892845

US-China Education Clearing House, 1860 19th St. NW, Washington, D.C. 20009 (sister-universities program)

China Affairs Office, East Asia and Pacific Affairs Office, International Communication Agency, 1750 Pennsylvania Ave. NW, Washington, D.C. 20547

University Service Center, 155 Argyle St., Kowloon, Hong Kong. tel. 3-7110263

PERIODICALS

Asia Mail
P.O. Box 1044
Alexandria, VA 22313, U.S.A.

Asia Travel Trade
Interasia Publications, Ltd.
200 Lockhart Road, 13th floor, Hong Kong

Asian Wall Street Journal G.P.O. Box 9825, Hong Kong

Asian Wall Street Journal Weekly
Dow Jones and Company, Inc.
22 Cortlandt St.
New York, NY 10007, U.S.A.

Business China
Business International Asia/Pacific Ltd.
Asian House, One Hennessy Rd., Hong Kong

The China Phone Book Company
G.P.O. Box 11581, Hong Kong

China Sights and Insights
China Travel and Tourism Press
Room 1201 Western Center
48 Des Voeux Rd. W., Hong Kong

China Trader (magazine and weekly bulletin)
711 Third Avenue
New York, NY 10017, U.S.A.
Also: Sino Communication Co., Ltd.
1303 Easey Commercial Bldg.,
253 Hennessy Road, Hong Kong

China Tourism Pictorial
Hong Kong China Tourism Press
28 Wellington St., 5/F, Hong Kong

Economic Reporter, English Supplement
342 Hennessy Road, 11th floor, Hong Kong

Far Eastern Economic Reviews
G.P.O. Box 160, Hong Kong

New Horizon (CAAC)
Kingsway International Publications Ltd.
20/F, Ritz Bldg.
625 Nathan Road, Kowloon, Hong Kong

Pearl (dist. on ships to China and by the Hong Kong Tourist Assoc. overseas),
World-Wide Commercial Bldg., 7/F, 34 Wyndham St., Hong Kong

South China Morning Post
Morning Post Building
Tong Chong St.
Quarry Bay, Hong Kong

Shanghai Hotels and Tourism
South China Morning Post
Tong Chong St.
Quarry Bay, Hong Kong

Ta Kung Pao—Weekly supplement,
342 Hennessy Road, 7th floor, Hong Kong

Distributors

China Books and Periodicals,
2929 Twenty-fourth St.,
San Francisco, CA 94110;
174 W. Randolph St., Chicago, IL 60601;
125 Fifth Ave., New York, NY 10003

Peace Book Co.,
9 Queen Victoria St., 7/F, Hong Kong

Joint Publishing Co., Readers' Service Center,
9 Queen Victoria St., Hong Kong

BANKS
If your bank cannot handle China transactions or give you information on China trade, try:

Bank of America, Asia Representative Office
Gloucester Tower, 12/F, Hong Kong

The National Bank of Australia
3610 Connaught Centre
Connaught Road Central, Hong Kong

Chase Manhattan Bank, N.A.
Alexandra House
7 Des Voeux Road, Central, Hong Kong

The First National Bank of Chicago
Connaught Centre, 13th floor, Hong Kong

People's Republic of China Co-ordinator,
Citibank, N.A., Citibank Tower,
G.P.O. Box 14, Hong Kong

Hang Seng Bank Ltd.
77 Des Voeux Road, Central, Hong Kong

Area Manager China
The Hong Kong and Shanghai Banking Corp., 23F Admiralty Center Tower 1
Harcourt Rd., Hong Kong

Lloyds Bank International
40/66 Queen Victoria Street
London EC4P 4EL, England

Manufacturers' Hanover
Alexandra House, 27th floor, Hong Kong

The Bank of Nova Scotia
4004 Connaught Centre, Hong Kong

Banque Nationale de Paris
Central Building, Queen's Road Central, Hong Kong

Banks whose traveler's checks and international bank drafts are accepted by China. Mentioned here are banks in Australia, England, Hong Kong, U.S., and Canada, only.

The National Bank of Australia	National Westminster Bank
Bank of New South Wales	Thomas Cook & Son Ltd.
Rural & Industries Bank of Western Australia	Hongkong & Shanghai Banking Corp.
Australia & New Zealand Banking Group	Citicorp
Commonwealth Trading Bank of Australia	Bank of America
Barclays Bank International	Manufacturers Hanover Trust
Lloyds Bank Limited	Chase Manhattan
Standard Chartered Bank	American Express Co.
Royal Bank of Scotland	First National Bank of Chicago
Grindlays Bank	Republic National Bank of Dallas
Midland Bank	The Royal Bank of Canada

CREDIT CARDS

China is not only limited to a cash economy, it charges a 4% surcharge if you use your credit card to obtain cash. The exception is the American Express credit card with which you can cash personal checks at a branch of the Bank of China without extra charge, in Beijing, Guangzhou, Shanghai, Xiamen, Nanning, Guilin, Quanzhou, Fuzhou, Qingdao, Hangzhou and Tianjin.

Visa, Diners Club, Federal, and MasterCard can be used at a variety of Friendship Stores, Trade Centers, Banks of China, etc. especially in Shanghai, Guangzhou, and Beijing to obtain cash.

Since the situation is improving in favor of card holders, check with your bank before you go.

⚛ 17 ⚛

BIBLIOGRAPHY

Barber, Noel. *The Fall of Shanghai.* New York: Coward-McCann and Geoghegan, Inc., 1979.
Barr, Pat. *To China With Love—The Lives and Times of Protestant Missionaries in China, 1860–1900.* New York: Doubleday & Co., Inc., 1973.
Bonavia, David. *The Chinese.* New York: Lippincott and Crowell, 1980.
Bonavia, David, and Bartlett, Magnus. *Tibet.* Shangri-la Press. China Guides Series. Hong Kong. 1981.
Catchpole, Brian. *A Map History of Modern China.* London: Heinemann Educational Books Ltd., 1977.
Chen, Jack. *A Year in Upper Felicity.* New York: Macmillan, 1973.
Chen, Jerome. *Mao and the Chinese Revolution.* Oxford, 1976.
Chen, Yuan-Tsung. *The Dragon's Village.* New York: Pantheon, 1980.
Chi Hsin. *Teng Hsiao-ping—A Political Biography.* Hong Kong: Cosmos Books, 1978.
Daubier, Jean. *A History of the Chinese Cultural Revolution.* New York, Toronto: Vintage Books, 1974.
Dawson, Raymond. *Imperial China.* New York: Pelican Books, 1976.
Fairbanks, John, et al. *East Asia, the Great Tradition* and *East Asia, the Modern Transformation.* George Allen and Unwin, Ltd.
Fairbanks, John. *The United States and China.* Cambridge: Harvard University Press.
Fitzgerald, C.P. *The Tower of Five Glories—a Study of the Minchia of Dali, Yunnan.* West Point, CT: Hyperion Press, 1973.
Fraser, John. *The Chinese, Portrait of a People.* Toronto, London: Collins, 1980. New York: Summit Books, 1980.
Gao Min. *Beijing Address and Telephone Handbook.* Hong Kong: Hai Feng Publishing Co., 1981.
Gernet, Jacques. *Daily Life in China on the Eve of the Mongol Invasion, 1250–1276.* Stanford, Ca.: Stanford University Press, 1973.
Gottschang, Karen Turner. *China Bound: a Handbook for American Students, Researchers and Teachers.* Committee on Scholarly Communication with the People's Republic of China. Washington.
Haldane, Charlotte. *The Last Great Empress of China.* New York: Bobbs-Merrill, 1965.
Han Suyin. *Birdless Summer.* New York: Putnam, 1968.
———. *The Crippled Tree.* New York: Bantam, 1972.
Hsu Kai-yu, ed. *Literature of the People's Republic of China.* Bloomington: Indiana University Press.
Latsch, Marie-Liuse. *Peking Opera as a European Sees It.* Beijing: New World Press, 1980.
Ling, Ken. *The Revenge of Heaven.* New York: G.P. Putnam's Sons, 1972; Toronto: Collier-Macmillan, Ltd., 1973.
Lo Kuan-chung. *Three Kingdoms.* Robert Moss, trans. & ed. New York: Pantheon, 1976.
Malloy, Ruth Lor. *Beyond the Heights.* Heinemann Educational Books Ltd. (Asia), 1980.
Malraux, André. *Man's Fate.* New York: Random House, 1969. (Reprint of 1933 novel.)
McCullough, Colin. *Stranger in China.* New York: William Morrow, 1973.

McKenna, Richard. *The Sand Pebbles*. Greenwich, Conn.: Fawcett, 1962.

Medley, Margaret. *A Handbook of Chinese Art*. New York: Icon Ed., 1974.

Mooneyham, W. Stanley. *China: A New Day*. Plainfield, N.J.: Logos International, 1979.

Qi Wen. *China: A General Survey*. Beijing: Foreign Languages Press, 1979.

Rolnick, Harry. *Eating Out in China*. Hong Kong: South China Morning Post, Publications Division, 1979.

Schell, Orville. *Watch Out for the Foreign Guest: China Encounters the West*. New York: Pantheon, 1980.

Schram, Stuart. *Mao Tse-tung*. New York: Penguin, 1967.

Sewell, William. I *Stayed in China*. Cranbury, N.J.: A.S. Barnes & Co., Inc., and London: George Allen & Unwin, Ltd., 1966.

Snow Edgar. *Red Star Over China*. New York: Penguin, 1977.

Spence, Jonathan. *To Change China: Western Advisers in China, 1620–1960*. Boston, Toronto: Little, Brown, 1969.

Sullivan, Michael. *The Arts of China*. Los Angeles, Berkeley, London: University of California Press, 1977.

The Tibet Guidebook. New York: Eurasia Press, 1979.

Tolley, Kemp. *Yangtze Patrol: The U.S. Navy in China*. Annapolis, Md.: Naval Institute Press, 1971.

Tung Chi-ming. *An Outline History of China*. Hong Kong: Joint Publishing Co., 1979.

U.S. Government. Post Report on China. S/N 044–000–01844–6. Government Printing Office, Washington, D.C.

Warner, Marina. *The Dragon Empress: The Life and Times of Tz'u-Hsi, Empress Dowager of China, 1835–1908*. New York: Macmillan, 1972.

White, Theodore. *In Search of History*. New York: Warner, 1978.

Williams, C.A.S. *Outlines of Chinese Symbolism & Art Motives*. New York: Dover Publications, 1976.

Witke, Roxanne. *Comrade Chiang-Ching*. Waltham, Ma.: Little, Brown, 1977.

Woodcock, George. *The British in the Far East*. New York: Atheneum, 1969.

Wu Zuguang. *Peking Opera and Mei Lanfang*. Beijing: New World Press, 1981.

———. *The China Phone Book*. GPO Box 11581, Hong Kong. Issued annually in October. (Lists diplomats by name, foreign businesses and news bureaus, as well.)

———. *China Telephone Directory*, Beijing: Ministry of Post and Telecommunication of the People's Republic of China. 1981.

———. *15 Cities in China*. Beijing: "China Reconstructs" Magazine, 1980.

———. *60 Scenic Wonders in China*. Beijing: New World Press, 1980.

———. *Doing Business in Today's China*. The American Chamber of Commerce in Hong Kong. 1980.

347

18

DIRECTORY

This directory of fourteen important destinations is designed primarily to help you get around on your own. If you are lost, or if you want to go to any of these tourist attractions, just point to the Chinese. For C.I.T.S. telephone numbers see Chapter 16. Store hours are approximate. Summer hours are longer than winter hours.

BEIDAIHE DIRECTORY

Beidaihe	北戴河
Pigeon's Nest	鹰角亭
Tiger Stone	老虎石
Qinhuangdao	秦皇岛
Shanhaiguan Pass	山海关
Old Dragon Head	老龙头
(where the Great Wall meets the sea)	
Yansai Lake	燕塞湖
Kuanyin Temple	观音祠
Meng Chiang Nu Temple	孟姜女庙
China International Travel tel. 2748	中国国际旅行社
Zhonghai Tan Hotel tel. 2398	中海滩宾馆
Xishan (West Hill) Hotel tel. 2678	西山宾馆
Service Bureau	服务部
Hebei Arts and Crafts	河北工艺美术
Xiaobaohe Zhai Production Brigade	小薄河寨大队
Beidaihe Beach Club	北戴河海滨俱乐部

BEIJING DIRECTORY

Tian Anmen Square	天安门广场
Tian Anmen Gate	天安门
Gu Gong—Imperial Palace	故宫

348

Meridian Gate	午门
North Gate	北门
Coal Hill	景山公园
Great Hall of the People	人民大会堂
Museum of the Chinese Revolution	中国革命历史博物馆
Museum of Chinese History	中国历史博物馆
Monument to the People's Heroes	人民英雄纪念碑
Chairman Mao Memorial Hall	毛主席纪念堂
Temple of Heaven	天坛
Summer Palace	颐和园
Great Wall at Badaling	八达岭
Ming Tombs	十三陵
Beihai Park	北海公园
Zhongnanhai	中南海
Temple of the Azure Clouds	碧云寺
Temple of the Sleeping Buddha	卧佛寺
Fragrant Hill	香山
Marco Polo Bridge	卢沟桥
Ching Tombs	东陵
Chengdeh	承德
Choukouden	周口店
Xi Dan Da Zi Bao (Democracy Wall)	西单民主墙
Beijing Library	北京图书馆
Beijing Zoo	北京动物园

Shopping (for hours, see "Shopping" in Beijing)

Friendship Store (on same street to east of Beijing Hotel), tel. 593531	友谊商店
Wang Fu Jing Street (beside Beijing Hotel)	王府井大街
Dungfeng Bazaar	东风市场
Liu Li Chang Street (antiques)	琉璃厂大街（古玩商店）
Foreign Languages Bookstore	外文书店
Arts & Crafts Peking Trust Co. 12 Chong Wen Men, tel. 554666	北京工艺品信托商店（崇文门大街十二号）
Peasant's Market	农民市场

Services

International Club (on same street to east of Beijing Hotel), tel. 521007, 522144	国际俱乐部
Bank of China (head office)	中国银行总行

Capital Hospital, tel. 553731　　　　　　首都医院

Ambulance, tel. 555678

Police or Fire, tel. 550720, 552725, 553772

Overseas telephone operator, tel. 337431

Domestic long-distance operator, tel. 330100, 331230.

Transportation

Subway　　　　　　　　　　　　　　地下铁道

Taxi, call nearest hotel or tel. 557461　　出租车

Railway station　　　　　　　　　　　北京火车站

　　Train inquiries, tel. 554866, 755272　火车询问处

Airport　　　　　　　　　　　　　　机场

　　Plane inquiries, tel. 552515, 555531 ext. 382　机场询问处

Aeroflot, tel 522181　　　　　　　　　苏航

Air France, tel. 523487, 556531　　　　法航

CAAC (Information), tel 558861, 557591　中国民航局

　　International bookings, tel. 557878　国际售票处

　　Domestic bookings, tel. 553245　　国内售票处

Airport, tel. 558341, ext. 2917

Ethiopian, tel. 523285　　　　　　　　埃航

Iranair, tel. 523249, 523843　　　　　伊航

JAL, tel. 523457　　　　　　　　　　日航

Lufthansa, tel. 522626

PAL, try embassy, tel. 522794　　　　　菲航

Pan Am, tel. 521756, 522590 or airport 522931, ext. 5466

PIA, tel. 523274, 523989　　　　　　　巴航

Swissair, tel. 523284　　　　　　　　瑞航

Religious Services

Roman Catholic 9:30–10　　　　　　　宣武门天主教堂

Sunday mornings

Protestant 9:30–10　　　　　　　　　米市大街基督教堂

Sunday mornings

Moslem 1:30–2　　　　　　　　　　东回清真寺

Friday afternoons

Miscellaneous

Foreign Ministry (switchboard) 553831　外交部

　　　　　　　information 555505

　　　　　　　protocol 552642

Ministry of Foreign Trade 553031 外贸部

Embassies

Australia: 15 Tung Chih Men Wai, San Li Tun, tel. 522331

Britain: 11 Kuang Hua Lu, Jian Guo Men Wai, tel. 521961

Canada: 10 San Li Tun Road, Chao Yang District, tel. 521475, 521571, 521724

France: 3 San Li Tun Road, Chao Yang District, tel. 521331, 521332

Japan: 7 Ri Tan Road, Jian Guo Men Wai, tel. 522361

New Zealand: 1 Ri Tan Donger Jie, Chaoyang District, tel. 522731

Philippines: 23 Hsiu Shui Pie Jieh, Jian Guo Men Wai, tel. 522794

Switzerland: 3 Dong Wujie, tel. 522831

U.S.A.: 17 Guanghua Road, tel. 522033

Office hours: 8–12, 1:30–5:30 winter; 8–12, 2 or 2:30–6 or 6:30 summer

Rush hour: 8–9, 5–7

Most embassies: 8:30 or 9–12 or 12:30, 1:30 or 2 or 2:30–5 or 6, Monday–Friday; Saturday mornings also. Summer hours, even more complicated: some open only 7–12 noon.

Most embassies are north of the Friendship Store and International Club.

Hotels

Beijing Hotel, tel. 558331, 556531, 552231

Xin Qiao Hotel, tel. 557731

Qianmen Hotel, tel. 338731

Minzu Hotel, tel. 668541

Friendship Hotel, tel. 890621

Yanjing Hotel, tel. 868721

Xiangyang Hotel, tel. 757181

Airport Hotel, tel. 522931

Diauyutai Guest House, tel. 868831

Peace Hotel, tel. 558841

Overseas Chinese Hotels, tel. 558851

GUANGZHOU DIRECTORY

National Peasant Movement Institute 广州农民运动讲习所

Memorial Gardens to the Martyrs of the 1927 Guangzhou Uprising 广州起义烈士陵园

Mausoleum of the Seventy-two Martyrs at Huanghuagang 黄花岗七十二烈士墓

Zoo 广州动物园

Zhenhai Tower 镇海楼

351

Sun Yat-sen Memorial Hall	中山纪念堂
Temple of the Six Banyan Trees	六榕寺
Guangzhou Cultural Park	广州文化公园
Guangzhou Foreign Trade Center (Trade Fair) tel. 30849	中国出口商品交易会
Orchid Garden	兰圃
South China Botanical Garden, tel. 76604	华南植物园
Shamian Island	沙面
Zhen Family Hall	陈家祠
Huai Sheng Mosque, tel. 31878, 35803	怀圣寺
White Cloud Mountain	白云山

Shopping (9 a.m.–9 p.m.)

Main areas: Fifth Section, Zhongshan Road, North Renmin Road,	中山五路 人民北路
South Renmin Road,	人民南路
Beijing Road	北京路
Nanfang Department Store, tel. 86022	南方大厦
Friendship Store (next to Baiyun Hotel) 9 a.m.–8 p.m. daily), tel. 77230	友谊商店

Services

Railway station, tel. 33333	火车站
Customs, tel. 32778	
C.I.T.S. (next to main railway station; tel. 33454)	中国国际旅行社广州分社
CAAC (next to main railway station), tel. 31271	中国民航
Airport Service Desk, Dep. Lounge, tel. 32878	
Baiyun Airport, tel. 31934	
Domestic, tel. 31600	
International, tel. 34079, 33684	
Thai International, tel. 33684	
Foreign Affairs Section, Public Security Bureau, (863 Jiefang Bei Rd.), tel. 31060	公安局
China Travel Service—C.T.S. (next to Overseas Chinese Mansion; tel. 61112)	中国旅行社
U.S. Consulate, Dongfang Hotel, tel. 69900	美国驻广州领事馆
Foreign bank representatives, see page 326	

Hotels

Dongfang Guest House, tel. 69900;
   taxi tel. 32227　　　　　　　东方宾馆

Guangzhou Hotel, tel. 61556
   taxi tel. 61556, ext. 32277　　　广州宾馆

Overseas Chinese Mansion, tel. 61112
   taxi tel. 61112　　　　　　　华侨大厦

Renmin (People's) Hotel, tel. 61445
   taxi tel. 82599　　　　　　　人民大厦

Liuhua Hotel, tel. 68800
   taxi tel. 68800, ext. 61251　　　流花宾馆

Kuangchuan (Spa Villa) Hotel　　广州矿泉别墅
Baiyun (White Cloud) Hotel, tel. 67700
   taxi tel. 67700　　　　　　　白云宾馆

Nanhu Hotel, tel. 78052
   taxi tel. 78052　　　　　　　南湖宾馆

Shengli Hotel, tel. 61223

Other taxis:

North Railway Station Square, tel. 34390

Kwangchow Taxi, tel. 88133

Guangdong Prov. Tourism (for buses or taxis)
tel. 34888 or 67700, ext. 2972 or 2971

Restaurants

Pan Xi (Pan Hsi) Restaurant, tel. 85655　　　泮溪酒家
Moslem Restaurant, tel. 84664　　　　　　　回民饭店
Bei Yuan (Pei Yuan) Restaurant, tel. 33365　北园酒家
Nan Yuan Restaurant, tel. 50532　　　　　　南园酒家
Snake Restaurant, tel. 82517　　　　　　　蛇餐馆
Datong (Ta Tung) Restaurant, tel. 86396　　大同酒家
Beixiu (Peihsiu) Restaurant　　　　　　　　北秀饭店

GUILIN DIRECTORY

Reed Flute Cave　　　　芦笛岩
Seven Star Cave　　　　七星岩
Dragon-Hiding Cave　　龙隐岩
Camel Hill　　　　　　骆驼山
Zoo　　　　　　　　　动物园
Du Xiu Park　　　　　独秀峰

Die Cai Hill 叠采山

Fubo Hill 伏波山

Elephant Trunk Hill 象鼻山

Western Hill 西山

Hidden Hill 隐山

Li River Hotel, tel. 2881 漓江饭店

Ronghu (Yunghu, Banyan) Hotel, tel. 3881, 3150

Jiashan Hotel, tel. 2986, 2240

Dangui (Osmanthus) Hotel, Zhong Shan Nan Rd.

Public Security Bureau, tel. 3202

Railway station 火车站

Airport 机场

CAAC, tel. 3063

Li River 漓江

Peach Blossom River 桃花江

LUOYANG DIRECTORY

Luoyang 洛阳

White Horse Temple 白马市

Luoyang Municipal Museum 洛阳市博物馆

Wang Cheng Park, a.k.a. Working People's 王城公园
   Park

Longmen Grottoes 龙门石窟

Old City 老城

Tomb of Guan Yu 关帝塚

Tomb of Liu Xiu 刘秀坟

Mang Shan Hill 邙山

Arts and Crafts Store 工艺服务部

Friendship Store 友谊商店

Guangzhou Market 广州市场

Guangzhou Market Restaurant 广州市场饭店

Shanghai Market 上海市场

State Secondhand Store 国营寄卖商店

Railway station 洛阳火车站

Airport 洛阳机场

Friendship Hotel, Wei No. 4, tel. 2157 友谊宾馆

LUSHAN DIRECTORY

Lushan 庐山

China International Travel Service, tel. 2497 中国国际旅行社

China Travel Service, tel. 2497	中国旅行社
Lu Hotel, tel. 2932	庐山宾馆
Lu Lin Hotel, tel. 2424	庐林宾馆
Yuen Zong Hotel, tel. 2547	云中宾馆
Gulin	牯岭
Flower Path Park	花径公园
Grotto of Taoist Immortal	仙人洞
Big Heavenly Pond	大天池
Han Po Kou	含鄱口
Botanical Garden	植物园
Three Treasure Trees	三宝树
Museum	博物馆
Da Han Yang Peak	大汉阳峰
Pavilion for viewing Yangtze	望江亭
Jiujiang	龙江
Jinggang Shan	井冈山

NANCHANG DIRECTORY

August 1st Uprising Headquarters	"八一"起义指挥部
Residence of Chou En-lai and others during August 1st Uprising	周恩来同志等在"八一"起义时的旧居
Site of Officers' Training Corps founded by Chu Teh	朱德同志创办的军官教育团旧址
Site of the Eleventh Army Headquarters in the August 1st Uprising	"八一"起义时第十一军指挥部旧址
Exhibition Hall of Jiangxi Revolutionary History	江西省革命历史展览馆
Jiangxi Revolutionary Martyrs Memorial Hall	江西省革命烈士纪念堂
Jiangxi Communist Labor University	江西共产主义劳动大学
Jiangxi Guesthouse (tel. 64861)	江西宾馆
Jiangxi Provincial Museum	江西省博物馆
Jiangxi Stadium	江西体育馆
Nanchang Emporium	南昌百货商场
People's Park	人民公园
Green Mountain Lake Hotel	青山湖宾馆
C.I.T.S. (tel. 62571)	中国国际旅行社
CAAC (tel. 62571)	中国民航
Plum Hill—temples	梅岭
Hundred Flower Islet	百花洲
Ba Da Shan Ren Museum	八大山人博物馆

Nanchang Restaurants

The East Is Red—Dong Fang Hong	东方红餐厅
Shixianlou	时鲜楼
Xing Yia	新雅餐厅
Hsin Guei Yuan	新桂园餐厅
Fu Wu Da Lou	服务大楼餐厅
Yie Wei Chan Ting—wild game restaurant	野味餐厅
winter: wild duck, goose;	
summer: snake	

NANJING DIRECTORY

Nanjing Yangtze River Bridge	南京长江大桥
Sun Yat-sen Mausoleum	中山陵
Lin Gu Park and Pagoda	灵谷公园和灵谷塔
Jiangsu Provincial Museum	南京博物院
Purple Gold Mountain Observatory	紫金山天文台
Ming Tomb	明孝陵
Liang Tombs	六朝石刻
Xuanwu Lake	玄武湖
Mochou Lake	莫愁湖
Yuhuatai Park	雨花台
King of Borneo Tomb	印尼波伦王墓
Drum Tower	鼓楼
Shanxilu Square	山西路广场
Taiping Museum	太平天国历史博物馆
Botanical Garden	植物园
Zhan Yuan Garden	瞻园
City of Metallurgy	冶城（朝天官）
Stone City of Wu Dynasty	石头城
Zhonghua Gate	中华门
Thousand Buddha Grottoes	千佛岩
Site of Former Ming Palace	明宫遗址
Tang Dynasty Tombs	南唐二陵
Six Dynasties Tombs	六朝墓
No. 30 Meiyuan Xincun (former residence of Chou En-lai)	梅园新村三十号
Wutai Hill Stadium	五台山体育馆
Nanjing University	南京大学
Bell Pavilion	大钟亭

Jiu Hua Hill (Monk Tang Pagoda)　九华山三藏塔

Nanjing Hotel, 259 Zhongshan Bei Rd., tel. 34121　南京饭店（中山北路）

Dingshan Hotel, 90, Cha Ha Er Rd., tel. 85931　丁山饭店

Victory Hotel, 75, Zhong Shan Rd., tel. 42217　胜利饭店

Shuangmenlou Guesthouse, 38, Zhong Shan Rd.,
　Shuangmenlou, tel. 85931　双门楼宾馆

Jinling Hotel, Xin Jie Kou

CAAC, tel. 41114, ext. 364 or 365

Store hours: 7 or 7:30 a.m.–7:30 or 8 p.m.; some
　open 24 hours

SHANGHAI DIRECTORY

Site of the First National Congress of the Communist Party of China	中国共产党第一次代表大会会址
Museum and Tomb of Lu Hsun (Lu Xun), Hung Kou Park	鲁迅博物馆和鲁迅墓虹口公园
Lu Hsun's Former Residence	鲁迅故居
Former Residence of Dr. Sun Yat-sen	中山故居
Shanghai Municipal Museum	上海博物馆
Shanghai Industrial Exhibition Hall	上海工业展览会
Shanghai Culture Square Theater	上海文化宫
Shanghai Indoor Stadium	上海体育馆
Shanghai Municipal Children's Palace	上海市少年宫
International Seamen's Club 33 Zhongshan Dong Ye Road, tel. 216149	海员俱乐部
People's Square	人民广场
People's Park (formerly a racecourse)	人民公园
Jade Buddha Temple	玉佛寺
Shanghai Art & Handicraft Research Studio	上海工艺美术研究室
Yu Yuan Garden	豫园
Lung Hua Pagoda and Temple	龙华庙
Zoo	动物园

Shopping See also pg. 210

Friendship Store 33 Zhongshan Dong Yi, tel. 210183	友谊商店
No. 1 Department Store 830 Nanjing Dong Rd. at Xizang Rd., tel. 223344	上海第一百货商店
Herbal Medicine Shop, 433 Guangdong Rd.	中药商店(广东路４３３号)

Western Medicine Shop, 1919 Huang Shan Rd.　西药商店(华山药1919号)

Arts and Crafts Store, 190 Nanjing Xi Rd., tel.　美术工艺品商店（南京西
538206, 537684　　　　　　　　　　　　　　　路190号）

Chuan Xin Secondhand Store　创新旧货店（淮海中路
1297 Huai Hai Road　　　　　1297号）

Shanxi Secondhand Store　陕西旧货店（延安中路
557 Yan'an Road　　　　　　557号）

Services

CAAC　　　　　　　　　　　　　　中国民航（延安中路
789 Yan'an Road Central, tel. 532255　789号）
Cathay Pacific
Room 123 North Wing, Jing Jiang Hotel, tel.
 377899 or 534242, ext. 123

Japan Air Lines
1202 Huaihai Zong Rd., tel. 378467, 532255

Pan American World Airways, Inc.
Jing'an Guest House, tel. 530210 or 563050, ext.
 701

C.I.T.S.　　　　　　　　　　　中国国际旅行社上海分社
　59 Xiang Gang Road, tel. 214960　（香港路59号）

　Peace Hotel branch, tel. 217117

C.T.S.　　　　　　　　　　　中国旅行社（南京西路
104 W. Nanjing Road, tel. 226606　104号）

Railway station　上海火车站

Hong Qiao Airport　虹桥机场

Wai Hong Qiao Wharf (for passenger ships)　外虹桥码头（外轮停泊处）

U.S. Consulate
　1469 Huaihai Zhong Rd., tel. 379880, 378511,
　378680

Consulate-General of France
　1431 Huaihai Zhong Rd., tel. 377414

Consulate-General of Japan
　1517 Huaihai Zhong Rd., tel. 372073

Quay for Riverboat Trip (near Peace Hotel)　游江船停靠处
　　　　　　　　　　　　　　　　　（离和平饭店不远）

Hospital for foreigners:

Huang Dong Xi Yuen　华东医院
　257 Yan'an Xi Lu, 7th floor, tel. 530631

International Club,　国际俱乐部
　56 Yan'an Xi Lu, tel. 538455

Jing Jiang Club, tel. 370115

Churches

Protestant
Roman Catholic

国际礼拜堂（衡山路）
徐家汇天主教堂（松江、
　青浦长途汽车站后面）

Restaurants

Xin Ya Restaurant (Cantonese)
719 Nanjing Dong Lu, tel. 222246

新雅饭店

Szechuan (Sichuan) Restaurant
475 Nanjing Dong Lu, tel. 221965

四川饭店

Yangzhou Restaurant (Yangzhou)
308 Nanjing Dong Lu, tel. 222779

杨州饭店

Hong Fang Zi (Red House) (Western)
37 Sanxi Nan Lu, tel. 565220, 565748

红房子

Shanghai Old Town Restaurant (Shanghai)
(Yu Yuan Market), tel. 282782

上海老饭店
　（豫园商场）

Mei Xin Restaurant (Cantonese)
314 Shanxi Nan Rd., tel. 373991

美心酒店

Chengdu Restaurant (Sichuan)
795 Huaihai Zhong Rd., 376412

Jade Buddha Temple Vegetarian Restaurant
170 Anyuan Rd., tel. 535745

Yanyunlou Restaurant (Beijing)
755 Nanjing Dong Rd., tel. 226174

Hotels

Chin Chiang (Jin Jiang) Hotel
59 Mao Ming Nan Rd., tel. 534242

锦江酒店

Guo Ji (International) Hotel
170 W. Nanjing Road, tel. 225225

国际饭店

Heng Shan Hotel
534 Heng Shan Road, tel. 377050

衡山饭店

Hua Chiao (Overseas Chinese) Hotel
104 Nanjing Xi Road, 20 Nanjing Dong Rd. at
　waterfront

华侨饭店

He Ping (Peace) Hotel
Nanjing Road at waterfront, tel. 211244

和平饭店

Shanghai Da Sha (Shanghai Mansions)
20 Suzhou Bei Road, tel. 246260

上海大厦

Da Hua Guesthouse
914 Yan'an Xi Rd., tel. 523079

达华宾馆

Jing'an Guest House

370 Huashan Rd., tel. 563050

Shanghai Guest House

460 Huashan Rd.

Shenjiang Hotel

740 Hankou Rd., tel. 225115

Airport Hotel

Hong Qiao Airport, tel. 536530

Taxis

Friendship Taxi Service, tel. 536363 and Shanghai
Taxi Service, tel. 564444. For airconditioned taxis,
Shanghai Touring Car Service, tel. 216564 and
Touring Car Dept., China Travel Service, tel.
225796.

SUZHOU DIRECTORY

Shizilin (Lion Forest) Garden	狮子林
Chang Lang (Gentle Wave Pavilion)	沧浪亭
Yi (Joyous) Garden	怡园
Liu (Lingering) Garden	留园
Wangshih Garden (of the Master of Nets)	网狮园
Zhuozheng (Humble Administrator's) Garden	拙政园
Hu Qiu (Tiger Hill)	虎丘
North Temple Pagoda	北寺塔
Han Shan Temple	寒山寺
Xiyuan (Western Garden) Temple	西园
Purple Gold Nunnery	东山紫金庵
Sky High Hill	天平山
Divine Cliff Hill	灵岩石
Precious Belt Bridge	宝带桥
Friendship Store, Youyi Rd.	友谊商店
Suzhou Hotel, Youyi Rd., tel. 4641	苏州饭店
Nanlin Hotel, tel. 4641	南林饭店
Gusu (Ancient Suzhou) Hotel, 115 Shiqian St., tel. 5127	古苏饭店

TIANJIN DIRECTORY

Overseas Chinese Hotel, 198 Jie Fang Rd., tel.
35087, 34996

Friendship Hotel, Shengli Rd., tel. 35663 　友谊宾馆

Tianjin Hotel, 219 Jiefang Rd., tel. 31114, 34325 天津饭店

Tianjin Grand Hotel, Youyi Rd., tel. 39613, 39288	天津宾馆
The Water Park	水上公园
Mt. Panshan	盘山
Dule Temple (Solitary Joy)	独乐寺
Zhou Enlai (Chou En-lai) Museum	周恩来纪念馆
Port area (passenger-ship quay)	新港
Railway station	火车站
Airport	飞机场
CAAC office, 290, Heping Lu, tel. 24045	中国民航售票处
Public Security Office	公安局外事科
Art Gallery	艺术博物馆
Dagong Oil Field	大港油田
Friendship Store, open 9–7:30, tel. 33183	友谊商店
Heping Lu	和平路
Museum of Natural Science (may not be open to foreigners yet)	自然博物馆
Museum of Tianjin History (may not be open to foreigners yet)	天津历史博物馆
Catholic church (may not be open to foreigners yet)	天主教教堂
Friendship Club	友谊俱乐部
Kissling Restaurant (European food; near Friendship Hotel)	起士林餐厅
Deng Ying Lou Restaurant (Shandong food; near Friendship Hotel)	登瀛楼饭庄
Tianjin Baozi Restaurant (famous dumpling; near Friendship Hotel)	天津包子铺
Tianjin Roast Duck Restaurant (like Beijing duck)	金聚德烤鸭店
Hongqiao Restaurant (Tianjin food)	红桥饭庄
No. 1 Hostel	第一招待所

XI'AN DIRECTORY

Xi'an	西安
Shaanxi Provincial Historical Museum	陕西省历史博物馆
Big Wild Goose (Dayan) Pagoda	大雁塔
Little Wild Goose (Xiaoyan) Pagoda	小雁塔
Banpo Museum	半坡博物馆
Bell Tower	钟楼
Drum Tower	鼓楼
West City Gate	西城门

Great Mosque	大清真寺
Xingqing Park	兴庆公园
Museum of the Eighth Route Army Xi'an Office	八路军西安办事处博物馆
Horse and Chariot Pit	车马坑
People's (Ren Min) Hotel, tel. 25111	人民大厦
Shaanxi Guesthouse	陕西宾馆
Lintong Hot Spring Hotel	临潼温泉旅馆
Huaqing Hot Springs	华清池
Qin (Chin) Army Vault Museum	秦俑坑博物馆
Tomb of Qin Shi Huang Di (Chin Shih Huang-ti)	秦陵
Qian (Chien) Ling Tomb	乾陵
Zhaoling Tomb	昭陵
Maoling Tomb	茂陵
Huxian County	户县
Chao Tang Temple	草堂室
Huashan	华山
Yang Kuei-fei's Tomb	杨贵妃墓
Big Stone Buddha Temple—Binxian (county)	大佛寺——彬县
Friendship Store	友谊商店
Railway Station, tel. 25075	火车站
Airport, tel. 21855	飞机场
CAAC, tel. 42761	

Recommended Restaurants

Xi'an Restaurant	西安饭店
Dongya (Eastern Asia) Restaurant	东亚饭店
Wuyi (May 1) Restaurant	五一饭店

YAN'AN DIRECTORY

Yan'an Guesthouse, tel. 2767, 2252	延安宾馆
Yan'an Revolutionary Memorial Hall (also known as Museum of Chairman Mao's Leadership of the Chinese Revolution from Yan'an)	延安革命纪念馆
Residences of Chairman Mao:	毛主席旧居
1. Foot of Fenghuang (Phoenix Hill)	凤凰山麓
2. Yangjialing	杨家岭
3. Zaoyuan (Date Orchard)	枣园
4. Wangjiaping	王家坪
Baota (Precious Pagoda), also known as Yan'an Pagoda	宝塔（延安宝塔）

362

Wanfo Dong (Cave of the 10,000 Buddhas)	万佛洞
Nanniwan	南泥湾
Huangling (on road to Xi'an)	黄陵

Recommended Restaurants

Yan'an Guesthouse	延安宾馆
Yan'an Hotel	延安饭店
Yanhe Hotel	延河饭店
Reception House No. 1	第一招待所
Yan'an Pagoda Reception House	延安宝塔招待所
Yan'an Bridge Restaurant	延安大桥食堂
Youth Restaurant	青年食堂
Mutton Restaurant	羊肉馆

Store hours:

Usually 9 a.m.–8 p.m., some closed for lunch.

ZHENJIANG DIRECTORY

Zhenjiang	镇江
Jingko Guesthouse, 407, Zhongshan Rd., tel. 23561	京口饭店
Jin Shan Hotel, 1, Jinshan Xi Rd., Zhenjiang, tel. 24962	金山饭店
Dashikou	大市口
Railway station	火车站
Bus station	汽车站
Jin Shan	金山
Bei Gu Hill	北固山
Jiao Hill	焦山
Museum	镇江博物馆
Gymnasium	体育馆
Grand Canal	大运河
Handicraft Workshop	手工艺商店
Shang Juan Dong Cave	善卷洞
Zhong Gong Cave	张公洞
Yixing Porcelain Factory	宜兴陶器厂

❊❊ 19 ❊❊

QUICK REFERENCE

Official Chinese Holidays

January 1	New Year's Day
January or February	Spring Festival or New Year depending on lunar calendar (three days)
May 1	Labor Day
October 1 and 2	National Days celebrating the founding of the People's Republic of China in 1949

In addition the following are celebrated with special programs but offices and schools are open.

March 8	International Working Women's Day
May 4	Youth Day (May 4th Movement)
June 1	Children's Day
July 1	Founding Day of the Communist Party of China
August 1	Founding Day of the People's Liberation Army

PINYIN AND OLD SPELLING—PLACE NAMES

	Old Spelling	*Pinyin*	*Province in Pinyin*
厦门	AMOY	Xiamen	Fujian
鞍山	ANSHAN	Anshan	Liaoning
安阳	ANYANG	Anyang	Henan
常州	CHANGCHOW	Changzhou	Jiangsu
长春	CHANGCHUN	Changchun	Jilin
长沙	CHANGSHA	Changsha	Hunan
肇庆	CHAOCHING	Zhaoqing	Guangdong
漳州	CHENGCHOW	Zhangzhou	Fujian
郑州	CHENGCHOW	Zhengzhou	Henan
承德	CHENGTEH	Chengde	Hebei
成都	CHENGTU	Chengdu	Sichuan
嘉峪关	CHIAYUKUAN	Jiayuguan	Gansu
景洪 (西双版纳)	CHINGHUNG, HSISHUANG PANNA	Jinghong, Xishuangbanna	Yunnan
井冈山	CHINGKANG MOUNTAINS	Jinggang Shan	Jianxi

景德镇	CHINGTECHEN	Jingdezhen	Jianxi
镇江	CHINGKIANG (also Chenkiang)	Zhenjiang	Jiangsu
秦皇岛	CHINWANGTAO	Qinhuangdao	Hebei
酒泉	CHIUCHUAN	Jiuquan	Gansu
九华山	CHIUHUA MOUNTAINS	Jiuhua Shan	Anhui
曲阜	CHUFU	Qufu	Shandong
重庆	CHUNGKING	Chongqing	Sichuan
福州	FOOCHOW	Fuzhou	Fujian
佛山	FASHAN (also Fatshan)	Foshan	Guangdong
抚顺	FUSHUN	Fushun	Liaoning
海口	HAIKOW	Haikou	Guangdong
杭州	HANGCHOW	Hangzhou	Zhejiang
邯郸	HANTAN	Handan	Hebei
哈尔滨	HARBIN	Harbin	Heilongjiang
衡阳	HENGYANG	Hengyang	Hunan
合肥	HOFEI	Hefei	Anhui
襄樊	HSIANGFAN	Xiangfan	Hubei
湘潭	HSIANGTAN	Xiangtan	Henan
新会	HSINHUI (also Sunwai)	Xinhui	Guangdong
咸宁	HSIENNING	Xianning	Hubei
锡林浩特	HSILINHOT	Xilinhot	Nei Monggol
新乡	HSINHSIANG	Xinxiang	Henan
西柏坡	HSIPAIPO	Xibaipo	Hebei
徐州	HSUCHOW	Xuzhou	Jiangsu
黄山	HUANG MOUNTAINS	Huang Shan	Anhui
呼和浩特	HUHEHOT	Hohhot	Nei Monggol
辉县	HUIHSIEN	Hui Xian	Henan
宜兴	IHSING (also Yising)	Yixing	Jiangsu
开封	KAIFENG	Kaifeng	Henan
江门	KIANGMEN (also Kongmoon)	Jiangmen	Guangdong
吉林	KIRIN	Jilin	Jilin
九江	KIUKIANG	Jiujiang	Jiangxi
巩县	KUNGHSIEN	Gongxian	Henan
昆明	KUNMING	Kunming	Yunnan
广州	KWANGCHOW (also Canton)	Guangzhou	Guangdong
桂林	KWEILIN	Guilin	Guangxi
桂平	KWEIPING	Guiping	Guangxi

拉萨	LHASA	Lhasa	Xizang (Tibet)
兰州	LANCHOW	Lanzhou	Gansu
连云港	LIENYUNKANG	Lianyungang	Jiangsu
林县	LINHSIEN	Linxian	Henan
柳州	LIUCHOW	Liuzhou	Guangxi
乐山	LOSHAN	Leshan	Sichuan
洛阳	LOYANG	Luoyang	Henan
路南—石林	LUNAN—STONE FOREST	Lunan—Stone Forest	Yunnan
马鞍山	MAANSHAN	Ma'anshan	Anhui
莫干山	MOKAN MOUNTAINS	Mogan Shan	Zhejiang
紫金山	MT. CHIKING	Zijin Shan	Jiangsu
庐山	MT. LUSHAN	Lushan	Jiangxi
峨嵋山	MT. OMEI	Emei Shan	Sichuan
南昌	NANCHANG	Nanchang	Jiangxi
南京	NANKING	Nanjing	Jiangsu
南宁	NANNING	Nanning	Guangxi
宁波	NINGPO	Ningbo	Zhejiang
北雁荡山	NORTH YENTANG MOUNTAINS	Bei Yandang Shan	Zhejiang
包头	PAOTOW	Baotou	Nei Monggol
北戴河	PEHTAIHO (also Peitaihe)	Beidaihe	Hebei
北京	PEKING	Beijing	
宾阳	PINYANG	Binyang	Guangxi
三门峡	SANMEN GORGE	Sanmenxia	Henan
上海	SHANGHAI	Shanghai	
绍兴	SHAOHSING	Shaoxing	Zhejiang
韶山	SHAOSHAN	Shaoshan	Hunan
沙市	SHASHIH	Shashi	Hebei
沙石峪	SHASHIHYU	Shashiyu	Hebei
胜利油田	SHENGLI OIL FIELD	Shengli Oil Field	Shandong
沈阳	SHENYANG	Shenyang	Liaoning
石家庄	SHIHCHIACHUANG (also Shihkiachwang)	Shijiazhuang	Hebei
石河子	SHIHHOTZU	Shihezi	Xinjiang
西安	SIAN	Xi'an	Shaanxi
苏州	SOOCHOW	Suzhou	Jiangsu
汕头	SWATOW	Shantou	Guangdong
大寨	TACHAI	Dazhai	Shanxi

大庆油田 TACHING OIL FIELD	Daqing Oil Field	Heilongjiang
泰安(泰山) TAIAN (Mt. Tai)	Tai'an (Mt. Tai)	Shandong
太原 TAIYUAN	Taiyuan	Shanxi
大港油田 TAKANG OIL FIELD	Dagang Oil Field	Tianjin
大连 TALIEN	Dalian (also Luda)	Liaoning
唐山 TANGSHAN	Tangshan	Hebei
丹江 TANKIANG	Danjiang	Hubei
大同 TATUNG	Datong	Shanxi
天津 TIENTSIN	Tianjin	
济南 TSINAN	Jinan	Shandong
青岛 TSINGTAO	Qingdao	Shandong
从化 TSUNGHUA	Conghua	Guangdong
遵化 TSUNHUA	Zunhua	Hebei
敦煌 TUNHUANG	Dunhuang	Gansu
吐鲁番 TURFAN	Turpan	Xinjiang
淄博 TZUPO	Zibo	Shandong
新疆 URUMCHI	Urumqi	Xinjiang
万县 WANHSIEN	Wan Xian	Sichuan
潍坊 WEIFANG	Weifang	Shandong
温州 WENCHOW	Wenzhou	Zhejiang
武汉 WUHAN	Wuhan	Hubei
芜湖 WUHU	Wuhu	Anhui
武鸣 WUMING	Wuming	Guangxi
无锡 WUSIH	Wuxi	Jiangsu
扬州 YANGCHOW	Yangzhou	Jiangsu
阳泉 YANGCHUAN	Yangquan	Shanxi
阳朔 YANGSHUO	Yangshuo	Guangxi
延安 YENAN	Yan'an	Shanxi
烟台 YENTAI	Yantai	Shandong
岳阳 YOYANG	Yueyang	Hunan
禹县 YUHSIEN	Yuxian	Henan

DYNASTIES-pinyin (old spelling)

夏	Xia (Hsia)	c. 21st–16th century B.C.
商	Shang (Shang)	c. 16th–11th century B.C.
西周	Western Zhou (Chou)	c. 11th century–771 B.C.
春秋	Spring and Autumn Period	770–476 B.C.
战国	Warring States Period	475–221 B.C.
秦	Qin (Chin)	221–206 B.C.
西汉	Western Han (Han)	206 B.C.–A.D. 24

Distances Between Main Tourist Cities

(Shortest distance between cities by rail in kilometres)

	Beijing	Shanghai	Tianjin	Guangzhou	Nanning	Changsha	Shaoshan	Wuchang	Nanjing	Wuxi	Suzhou	Hangzhou	Jinan	Qingdao	Xi'an	Kunming	Chengdu	Chongqing	Zhengzhou	Shijiazhuang	Dalian	Shenyang	Changchun	Harbin
Beijing	Beijing																							
Shanghai	1462	Shanghai																						
Tianjin	137	1325	Tianjin																					
Guangzhou	2313	1811	2450	Guangzhou																				
Nanning	2565	2063	2702	1334	Nanning																			
Changsha	1587	1187	1724	726	978	Changsha																		
Shaoshan	1718	1216	1855	755	1007	131	Shaoshan																	
Wuchang	1229	1534	1366	1084	1336	358	489	Wuchang																
Nanjing	1157	305	1020	2116	2368	1492	1521	219	Nanjing															
Wuxi	1334	128	1197	2191	2982	1315	1344	317	177	Wuxi														
Suzhou	1376	86	1239	2149	2805	1383	1425	275	219	42	Suzhou													
Hangzhou	1651	189	1514	1897	2488	998	1027	1448	663	494	275	Hangzhou												
Jinan	494	968	357	2284	2536	1558	1689	1200	663	840	882	1157	Jinan											
Qingdao	887	1361	750	2677	2929	1951	2082	1593	1056	1233	1275	1550	393	Qingdao										
Xi'an	1165	1511	1302	2129	2381	1403	1534	1045	1206	1383	1425	1700	1177	1570	Xi'an									
Kunming	3179	2677	3316	1501	1592	1503	1950	1045	2982	2805	2763	2488	2019	3512	1942	Kunming								
Chengdu	2048	2353	2185	2544	1829	1920	1831	1503	2048	2225	2267	2542	2019	2412	842	1100	Chengdu							
Chongqing	2552	2501	2689	2040	1325	1416	1327	1774	2552	2729	2771	2312	2523	2916	1346	1102	504	Chongqing						
Zhengzhou	695	1000	832	1618	1870	892	1023	534	695	872	914	1189	298	666	511	2865	1765	1857	Zhengzhou					
Shijiazhuang	283	1266	420	2030	2282	1435	1304	946	961	1138	1180	1455	298	691	923	2311	1353	2269	412	Shijiazhuang				
Dalian	1238	2426	1101	3551	3803	2956	2298	2121	2340	2615	2403	1851	1458	923	2865	1765	3393	1933	1521	1124	Dalian			
Shenyang	841	2029	704	3154	3406	2559	2070	1724	1901	2218	2006	1454	1061	1851	2006	2889	3790	1536	1933	1429	397	Shenyang		
Changchun	1146	2334	1009	3459	3711	2864	2375	2029	2206	2523	2218	1366	1759	1454	2311	3393	3698	1841	1841	1671	702	305	Changchun	
Harbin	1388	2576	1251	3701	3953	3106	2617	2271	2448	2490	2763	1608	2001	2553	4567	3436	3940	2083	1671	2083	944	547	242	Harbin

东汉	Eastern Han (Han)	25–220
三国	The Three Kingdoms	220–265
魏	Wei (Wei)	220–265
蜀	Shu (Shu)	221–263
吴	Wu (Wu)	222–280
西晋	Western Jin (Tsin)	265–316
东晋	Eastern Jin (Tsin)	317–420
南北朝	Southern and Northern Dynasties	420–589
南朝	Southern Dynasties	420–589
宋	Song (Sung)	420–479
齐	Qi (Chi)	479–502
梁	Liang (Liang)	502–557
陈	Chen (Chen)	557–589
北朝	Northern Dynasties	386–581
北魏	Northern Wei (Wei)	386–534
东魏	Eastern Wei	534–550
西魏	Western Wei	535–556
北齐	Northern Qi (Chi)	550–577
北周	Northern Zhou (Chou)	557–581
隋	Sui (Sui)	581–618
唐	Tang (Tang)	618–907
五代	Five Dynasties	907–960
辽	Liao (Liao)	916–1125
宋	Song (Sung)	960–1279
北宋	Northern Song (Sung)	960–1127
南宋	Southern Song (Sung)	1127–1279
西夏	Western Xia (Hsia)	1038–1227
金	Jin (Kin)	1115–1234
元	Yuan (Yuan)	1271–1368
明	Ming (Ming)	1368–1644
	Hongwu (Hung Wu)	1368–1399
	Jianwen (Chien Wen)	1399–1403
	Yongle (Yung Lo)	1403–1425
	Hongxi (Hung Hsi)	1425–1426
	Xuande (Hsuan Teh)	1426–1436
	Zhengtong (Cheng Tung)	1436–1450
	Jingtai (Ching Tai)	1450–1457
	Tianshun (Tien Shun)	1457–1465
	Cheng Hua (Cheng Hua)	1465–1488

	Hongzhi (Hung Chih)	1488–1506
	Zhengde (Cheng Teh)	1506–1522
	Jiajing (Chia Ching)	1522–1567
	Longqing (Lung Ching)	1567–1573
	Wanli (Wan Li)	1573–1620
	Taichang (Tai Chang)	1620–1621
	Tianqi (Tien Chi)	1621–1628
	Chongzhen (Chung Cheng)	1628–1644
清	Qing (Ching)	1644–1911
	Shunzhi (Shun Chih)	1644–1662
	Kangxi (Kang Hsi)	1662–1723
	Yongzheng (Yung Cheng)	1723–1736
	Qianlong (Chien Lung)	1736–1796
	Jiaqing (Chia Ching)	1796–1821
	Daoguang (Tao Kuang)	1821–1851
	Xianfeng (Hsien Feng)	1851–1862
	Tongzhi (Tung Chih)	1862–1875
	Guangxu (Kuang Hsu)	1875–1908
	Xuantong (Hsuan Tung)	1908–1911

HOW TO PRONOUNCE CHINESE LETTERS

Following is a table of the Chinese phonetic alphabet showing pronunciation with approximate English equivalents. Letters in the Wade-Giles system are in parentheses.

"**a**" (a), a vowel, as in far;

"**b**" (p), a consonant, as in be;

"**c**" (ts), a consonant, as in "ts" in its; and

"**ch**" (ch), a consonant, as in "ch" in church, strongly aspirated;

"**d**" (t), a consonant, as in do;

"**e**" (e), a vowel, as "er" in her, the "r" being silent; but "**ie**," a diphthong, as in yes and "**ei**," a diphthong, as in way;

"**f**" (f), a consonant, as in foot;

"**g**" (k), a consonant, as in go;

"**h**" (h), a consonant, as in her, strongly aspirated;

"**i**" (i), a vowel, two pronunciations:
    1) as in eat
    2) as in sir in syllables beginning with the consonants c, ch, r, s, sh, z and zh;

"**j**" (ch), a consonant, as in jeep;

"**k**" (k), a consonant, as in kind, strongly aspirated;

"**l**" (l), a consonant, as in land;

"**m**" (m), a consonant, as in me;

"**n**" (n), a consonant, as in no;

"**o**" (o), a vowel, as in "aw" in law;

"**p**" (p), a consonant, as in par, strongly aspirated;

"**q**" (ch), a consonant, as "ch" in cheek;

"**r**" (j), a consonant pronounced as "r" but not rolled, or like "z" in azure;

"**s**" (s, ss, sz), a consonant, as in sister; and "**sh**" (sh), a consonant, as "sh" in shore;

"**t**" (t), a consonant, as in top, strongly aspirated;

"**u**" (u), a vowel, as in too, also as in the French "u" in "tu" or the German umlauted "u" in "Muenchen;"

"v" (v), is used only to produce foreign and national minority words, and local dialects;
"w" (w), used as a semi-vowel in syllables beginning with "u" when not preceded by consonants, pronounced as in want;
"x" (hs), a consonant, as "sh" in she;
"y," used as a semi-vowel in syllables beginning with "i" or "u" when not preceded by consonants, pronounced as in yet;
"z" (ts, tz), a consonant, as in zero; and "zh" (ch), a consonant, as "j" in jump."

—from *China Reconstructs,* March 1979

CURRENCY

Chinese money is called Renminbi (RMB). The Chinese dollar, known as Yuan (or Kuai), equals 10 Jiao or 100 Fen. Yuan notes are in denominations of 10, 5, and 2. The smaller Jiao notes are 5, 2, and 1. The coins are 5, 2, and 1 Fen.

Foreign exchange rates fluctuate. There is a slight variation for cash or traveler's checks. Please consult your bank, Bank of China, or the *China Daily.*

The following tables are based on varying exchange rates. Find the column with the exchange rate in effect when you go.

DOLLAR TO YUAN CONVERSION TABLE
(Prepared by Martin and Terry Malloy)

Dollar	Yuan	Yuan	Yuan	Yuan	Yuan	Yuan	Yuan	Yuan
1	1.75	1.70	1.65	1.60	1.55	1.50	1.45	1.40
2	3.50	3.40	3.30	3.20	3.10	3.00	2.90	2.80
3	5.25	5.10	4.95	4.80	4.65	4.50	4.35	4.20
4	7.00	6.80	6.60	6.40	6.20	6.00	5.80	5.60
5	8.75	8.50	8.25	8.00	7.75	7.50	7.25	7.00
6	10.50	10.20	9.90	9.60	9.30	9.00	8.70	8.40
7	12.25	11.90	11.55	11.20	10.85	10.50	10.15	9.80
8	14.00	13.60	13.20	12.80	12.40	12.00	11.60	11.20
9	15.75	15.30	14.85	14.40	13.95	13.50	13.05	12.60
10	17.50	17.00	16.50	16.00	15.50	15.00	14.50	14.00
20	35.00	34.00	33.00	32.00	31.00	30.00	29.00	28.00
30	52.50	51.00	49.50	48.00	46.50	45.00	43.50	42.00
40	70.00	68.00	66.00	64.00	62.00	60.00	58.00	56.00
50	87.50	85.00	82.50	80.00	77.50	75.00	72.50	70.00
60	105.00	102.00	99.00	96.00	93.00	90.00	87.00	84.00
70	122.50	119.00	115.50	112.00	108.50	105.00	101.50	98.00
80	140.00	136.00	132.00	128.00	124.00	120.00	116.00	112.00
90	157.50	153.00	148.50	144.00	139.50	135.00	130.50	126.00
100	175.00	170.00	165.00	160.00	155.00	150.00	145.00	140.00
200	350.00	340.00	330.00	320.00	310.00	300.00	290.00	280.00
300	525.00	510.00	495.00	480.00	465.00	450.00	435.00	420.00
400	700.00	680.00	660.00	640.00	620.00	600.00	580.00	560.00
500	875.00	850.00	825.00	800.00	775.00	750.00	725.00	700.00
600	1050.00	1020.00	990.00	960.00	930.00	900.00	870.00	840.00
700	1225.00	1190.00	1155.00	1120.00	1085.00	1050.00	1015.00	980.00
800	1400.00	1360.00	1320.00	1280.00	1240.00	1200.00	1160.00	1120.00
900	1575.00	1530.00	1485.00	1440.00	1395.00	1350.00	1305.00	1260.00
1000	1750.00	1700.00	1650.00	1600.00	1550.00	1500.00	1450.00	1400.00

YUAN TO DOLLAR CONVERSION TABLE
(Prepared by Linda and Martin Malloy)

			If your dollar is worth					
Yuan	**y1.75**	**y1.70**	**y1.65**	**y1.60**	**y1.55**	**y1.50**	**y1.45**	**y1.40**
1	$ .57	$ .59	$ .61	$ .63	$ .64	$ .67	$ .69	$ .71
2	1.14	1.18	1.21	1.25	1.29	1.33	1.38	1.43
3	1.71	1.76	1.82	1.88	1.94	2.00	2.07	2.14
4	2.29	2.35	2.42	2.50	2.58	2.67	2.76	2.86
5	2.86	2.94	3.03	3.13	3.23	3.33	3.45	3.57
6	3.43	3.53	3.64	3.75	3.87	4.00	4.14	4.29
7	4.00	4.12	4.24	4.38	4.52	4.67	4.83	5.00
8	4.57	4.71	4.85	5.00	5.16	5.33	5.52	5.71
9	5.14	5.29	5.45	5.63	5.81	6.00	6.21	6.43
10	5.71	5.88	6.06	6.25	6.45	6.67	6.90	7.14
20	11.43	11.76	12.12	12.50	12.90	13.33	13.80	14.29
30	17.14	17.64	18.18	18.75	19.35	20.00	20.69	21.43
40	22.86	23.52	24.24	25.00	25.81	26.67	27.59	28.57
50	28.57	29.41	30.30	31.25	32.26	33.33	34.48	35.71
60	34.29	35.29	36.36	37.50	38.71	40.00	41.38	42.86
70	40.00	41.18	42.42	43.75	45.16	46.67	48.28	50.00
80	45.71	47.06	48.48	50.00	51.61	53.33	55.17	57.15
90	51.43	52.94	54.55	56.25	58.06	60.00	62.07	64.29
100	57.14	58.82	60.61	62.50	64.52	66.67	68.97	71.43
200	114.29	117.65	121.21	125.00	129.03	133.33	137.93	142.86
300	171.43	176.47	181.82	187.50	193.55	200.00	206.90	214.29
400	228.57	235.29	242.42	250.00	258.06	266.67	275.86	285.71
500	285.71	294.12	303.03	312.50	322.58	333.33	344.83	357.14
600	342.86	352.94	363.64	375.00	387.10	400.00	413.79	428.57
700	400.00	411.76	424.24	437.50	451.61	466.67	482.76	500.00
800	457.14	470.59	484.85	500.00	516.13	533.33	551.72	571.43
900	514.29	529.41	545.45	562.50	580.65	600.00	620.69	642.86
1000	571.43	588.24	606.06	625.00	645.16	666.67	689.66	714.29

CELSIUS-FAHRENHEIT CONVERSION TABLE

Centigrade (Celsius)		Fahrenheit
−40°		−40°
−20°		− 4°
0°	Freezing Point	32°
10°		50°
20°		68°
30°		86°
40°		104°
50°		122°
60°		140°
70°		158°
80°		176°
90°		194°
100°	Boiling Point	212°

To convert Fahrenheit to Celsius subtract 32, multiply by 5, and divide by 9. To covert Celsius to Fahrenheit multiply by 9, divide by 5, and add 32.

MILE-KILOMETER CONVERSION TABLES

Miles	Kilometers	Kilometers	Miles
1	1.6093	1	.621
2	3.2186	2	1.242
3	4.8279	3	1.863
4	6.4372	4	2.484
5	8.0465	5	3.105
6	9.6558	6	3.726
7	11.2651	7	4.347
8	12.8744	8	4.968
9	14.4837	9	5.589
10	16.093	10	6.21
20	32.186	20	12.42
30	48.279	30	18.63
40	64.372	40	24.84
50	80.465	50	31.05
60	96.558	60	37.26
70	112.651	70	43.47
80	128.744	80	49.68
90	144.837	90	55.89
100	160.93	100	62.1
200	321.86	200	124.2
300	482.79	300	186.3
400	643.72	400	248.4
500	804.65	500	310.5
600	965.58	600	372.6
700	1126.51	700	434.7
800	1287.44	800	496.8
900	1448.37	900	558.9
1000	1609.3	1000	621

(Prepared by Linda Malloy)

WEIGHTS AND MEASURES

China uses both the metric system and the Chinese system.

1 gong-jin (kilogram)	= 2.2 pounds
1 jin or gun (catty)	= 1.33 pounds = .604 kg.
1 dan (picul) = 100 catties	= 133 pounds or 60.47 kg.

(Prepared by Martin and Terry Malloy)

1 mi (meter)	= 39.37 inches
1 gong li (kilometer)	= .6 mile = 1 km.
1 li (Chinese mile)	= .3106 mile = ½ km.
1 mu	= .1647 acres
1 hectare	= 2.471 acres = 10,000 sq. meters
100 hectares	= 247.1 acre = 1 sq. km.
259 hectares	= 1 sq. mile

GLOSSARY

CAAC—China's national airline
cadre (kanpu)—In Chinese the term literally means "core element," and is used to describe any person who plays a full- or part-time leadership role.
C.I.T.S.—China International Travel Service (for Foreign Friends and Overseas Chinese)

QUICK REFERENCE TO WORLD TIME ZONES

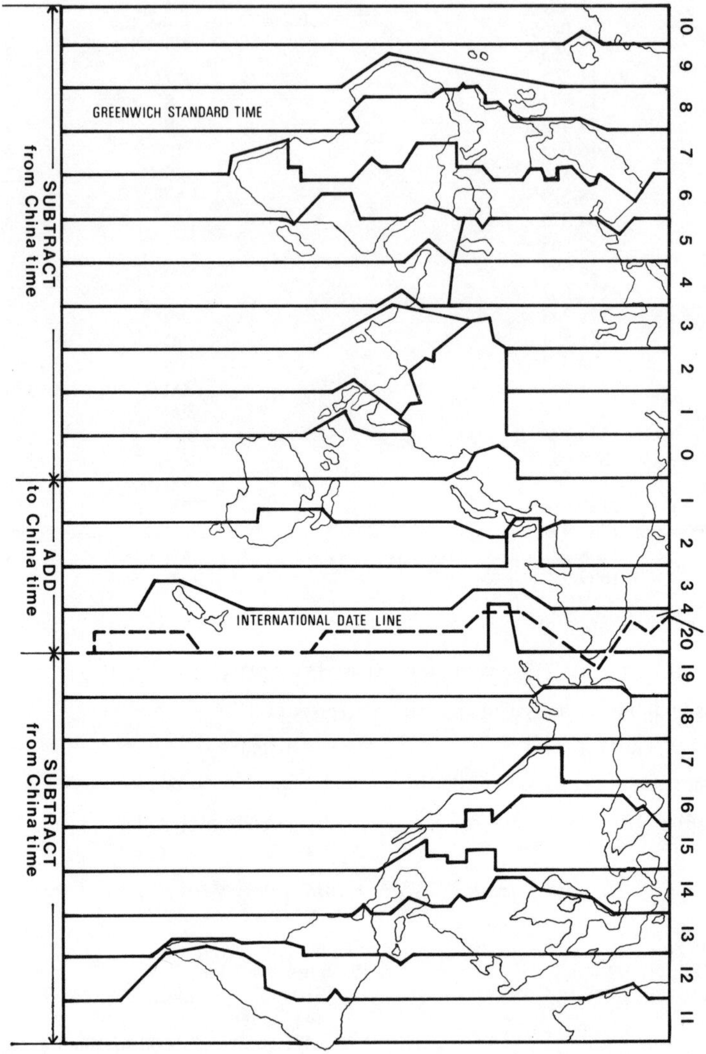

GREENWICH STANDARD TIME
INTERNATIONAL DATE LINE
SUBTRACT from China time
ADD to China time
SUBTRACT from China time
10 9 8 7 6 5 4 3 2 1 0 1 2 3 4 20 19 18 17 16 15 14 13 12 11

All of China is in one time zone. At 8 a.m. in China the time is 1 a.m. in West Germany or 7 a.m. in Singapore. The time in China is 13 hours later than in the eastern United States. For example, 8 a.m. in China is 7 p.m. Eastern Standard Time, or 6 p.m. Daylight Savings Time, the *previous* day in New York City.

C.T.S.—China Travel Service (for Overseas Chinese and Compatriots)
dagoba—similar to an Indian stupa, a bell-shaped tower under which is buried a Buddhist relic. It is the forerunner of the Chinese pagoda.
F.F.—Foreign Friends
FXC—Foreign Exchange Certificate
H.K.—Hong Kong
Luxingshe—another name for China International Travel Service
Manchu—a group of people from north China who ruled China under the name Qing dynasty
Mongol—a group of people from north China who ruled China under the name Yuan dynasty
PLA—People's Liberation Army
pinyin—the new system of romanizing the Chinese language now adopted as official
RMB—ren mi bi—people's money, one of the terms used to refer to Chinese currency
stele—a large stone table used to commemorate an event, a life, or an important piece of writing
Wade-Giles—one of the old systems of romanizing the Chinese language
wok—a large rounded pan fitted into a stone for cooking
work unit—every Chinese is responsible to the group with which he works
Y—yuan, the basic unit in Chinese currency

Some names in pinyin-Wade Giles

Deng Xiaoping	Teng Hsiao-ping
Zhou Enlai	Chou En-lai
Mao Zedong	Mao Tse-tung
Jiang Qing	Chiang Ching
Guo Moruo	Kuo Mo Ruo
Zhongshan	Chungshan (the honorific name of Dr. Sun Yat-sen)
Sun Yi-xian	Sun Yat-sen

See MILESTONES IN CHINESE HISTORY for *Long March* (October 16, 1934); *Liberation* (October 1, 1949), *Cultural Revolution* (1966), *Red Guards* (under Cultural Revolution), *Gang of Four* (1976).

LIST OF HISTORICAL SITES UNDER CHINA'S STATE COUNCIL PROTECTION OPEN TO FOREIGN VISITORS

In 1961 the State Council announced a list of several historical sites that it considered important enough to be maintained by the national government. In a country of many historical sites, these are the top. Do not miss them if you are in the province:

Henan Province

Longmen Buddhist Caves
You Guo Si Pagoda (Iron Pagoda)
White Horse Temple
Remains of a Shang Dynasty city wall at Zhengzhou
Yin ruins

Shaanzi Province

Yenan revolutionary remains
Dayan (Big Wild Goose) Pagoda
Xiaoyan (Little Wild Goose) Pagoda
Xingjiaosi Pagoda
The City Wall of Xi'an
Forest of steles
Banpo Site Museum
Qin Shi Huang Mausoleum
Maoling Mausoleum
Huo Qu-bing tomb

Zhaoling Mausoleum
Qianling Mausoleum

Gansu Province

Mo Gao Grotto
Binglingsi Thousand Buddhist Caves
The Great Wall—Jiayuguan Pass

Zhejiang Province

Liuhe (Six Harmonies) Pagoda
Yue Fei's Temple

Shanghai

Former residence of the late Dr. Sun Yat-sen
Site of the First National Congress of the
    Communist Party of China
Tomb of Lu Xun

Liaoning Province

Former Imperial Palace in Shenyang

Guangdong Province

Huanghuagang Mausoleum of the Seventy-
    Two Martyrs
Former Peasant Movement Cadres' Institute

Beijing

Lugouqiao (Marco Polo Bridge)
Tian Anmen
Monument to the People's Heroes
Cloud Terrace at Juyongguan Pass
The Imperial Palace (Forbidden City)
The Great Wall—Ba Da Ling
Bei Hai Park and Round City
Yi He Yuan (The Summer Palace)
Peking Man Site
Thirteen Tombs of Ming Dynasty (Ming
    Tombs)

Jiangsu Province

Sun Yat-sen Mausoleum—Nanjing
Zhuo Zheng Yuan (Humble Administrator's
    Garden)—Suzhou
Liu Yuan (Tarrying Garden)—Suzhou
Ming Xiao Ling Tombs

Hunan Province

Shaoshan, Mao Tse-tung's old home

Shanxi Province

Yungang Caves
Jin Temple
Huayan Monastery

Jiangxi Province

Former site of the headquarters of the
    Nanchang Rising
Jinggang Shan revolutionary remains

Hebei Province

Long Xing Si
The Great Wall—Shanhaiguan Pass
Pu Ning Temple
Du Le Temple
Pu To Sect Temple
Hau Mi Fu Shou Temple
Imperial Mountain Resort—Cheng de
Eastern Qing (Ching) Tombs

Shandong Province

Simen (Four-gate) Pagoda
Qufu Temple of Confucious (Kong Miao)
Residence of the Descendants of Confucius (Kong Fu)
Woods of Confucius (Kong Lin)

Sichuan Province

Former Site of Eighth Route Army Office in Zhongqing
Wu Hou Ci (temple in memory of Zhu Ge-liang)
Du Fu Cottage
Bronze Buddhist image on an iron elephant in Shenshou Wannian Temple at Omei Mountain

Xinjiang Uygur Autonomous Region

Kizil Thousand Buddhas Caves
Ancient City Gaochang

THE CHINESE CALENDAR

The Chinese calendar, based on the moon, is consulted for the weather as well as for agriculture. It does not coincide with the Western calendar every year. The following is for 1980, but it will give you an idea of what to expect for other years. It would be interesting to see if indeed it starts getting cold on November 7, for example.

THE TWENTY-FOUR SOLAR TERMS

Date				
1982	**1983**	**1984**	**Chinese Name**	**Solar Term**
Jan. 6	Jan. 6	Jan. 6	Xiao Han	Moderate cold
Jan. 20	Jan. 21	Jan. 21	Da Han	Severe cold
Feb. 4	Feb. 4	Feb. 4	Li Chun	Spring begins*
Feb. 19	Feb. 19	Feb. 20	Yu Shui	Spring showers
Mar. 6	Mar. 6	Mar. 5	Jing Zhe	Insects waken
Mar. 21	Mar. 21	Mar. 20	Chun Fen	Spring equinox
Apr. 5	Apr. 5	Apr. 4	Qing Ming	Clear and bright
Apr. 20	Apr. 20	Apr. 20	Gu Yu	Grain rain
May 5	May 6	May 5	Li Xia	Summer begins*
May 21	May 21	May 21	Xiao Man	Grain forms
June 6	June 6	June 5	Mang Zhong	Grain in ear
June 22	June 22	June 21	Xia Zhi	Summer solstice
July 7	July 8	July 7	Xiao Shu	Moderate heat
July 23	July 23	July 23	Da Shu	Great heat
Aug. 8	Aug. 8	Aug. 7	Li Qiu	Autumn begins*
Aug. 23	Aug. 24	Aug. 23	Chu Shu	Heat recedes
Sept. 8	Sept. 8	Sept. 7	Bai Lu	White dew
Sept. 23	Sept. 23	Sept. 23	Qiu Fen	Autumnal equinox
Oct. 9	Oct. 9	Oct. 8	Han Lu	Cold dew
Oct. 24	Oct. 24	Oct. 23	Shuang Jiang	Frost descends
Nov. 8	Nov. 8	Nov. 7	Li Dong	Winter begins*
Nov. 23	Nov. 23	Nov. 22	Xiao Xue	Light snow
Dec. 7	Dec. 8	Dec. 7	Da Xue	Heavy snow
Dec. 22	Dec. 22	Dec. 22	Dong Zhi	Winter solstice
Jan. 25	Feb. 13	Feb. 2		Lunar New Year

*The beginnings of the four seasons, as here listed, are by the traditional Chinese usage—connected with agricultural practice.

NAMES OF CHINESE ADMINISTRATIVE REGIONS

Pinyin   *Old Spelling*

Municipalities (Shi)

Pinyin	Old Spelling
Beijing	Peking
Tianjin	Tientsin
Shanghai	Shanghai

Provinces (Sheng)

Pinyin	Old Spelling
Hebei	Hopei
Jilin	Kirin
Jiangsu	Kiangsu
Jiangxi	Kiangsi
Hubei	Hupeh
Shaanxi	Shensi
Sichuan	Szechwan
Shanxi	Shansi
Heilongjiang	Heilungkiang
Anhui	Anhwei
Fujian	Fukien
Hunan	Hunan
Gansu	Kansu
Guizhou	Kweichow
Taiwan	Taiwan
Liaoning	Liaoning
Shandong	Shantung
Zheijiang	Chekiang
Henan	Honan
Guangdong	Kwangtung
Qinghai	Chinghai
Yunnan	Yunnan

Autonomous Regions (Zizhiqu)

Pinyin	Old Spelling
Nei Monggol autonomous region	Inner Mongolia autonomous region
Guangzi Zhuang autonomous region	Kwangsi Chuang autonomous region
Ningxia Hui autonomous region	Ningsia Hui autonomous region
Xinjiang Uygur autonomous region	Sinkiang Uighur autonomous region
Xizang autonomous region	Tibet autonomous region